Interwoven Conversations

LEARNING
AND TEACHING
THROUGH
CRITICAL REFLECTION

Judith M. Newman

OISE Press Toronto, Canada • Heinemann Portsmouth, NH

The Ontario Institute for Studies in Education has three prime functions: to conduct programs of graduate study in education, to undertake research in education, and to assist in the implementation of the findings of educational studies. The Institute is a college chartered by an Act of the Ontario Legislature in 1965. It is affiliated with the University of Toronto for graduate studies purposes.

The publications program of the Institute has been established to make available information and materials arising from studies in education, to foster the spirit of critical inquiry, and to provide a forum for the exchange of ideas about education. The opinions expressed should be viewed as those of the contributors.

Canadian Cataloguing in Publication Data

Newman, Judith Marta, 1943-
Interwoven conversations

Includes bibliographical references and index.
ISBN 0-7744-0374-8

1. Teaching. 2. Learning. 3. Reflection
(Philosophy). 4. Mount Saint Vincent University.
Summer Institute (1989). I. Title.

LB1025.3.N48   1991   370'.71   C91-095271-X

Library of Congress Cataloging-in-Publication Data

Newman, Judith, 1943-
Interwoven conversations : learning and teaching through critical
reflection / Judith M. Newman.
     p.   cm
Includes bibliographical references (p.   ) and index.
ISBN 0-435-08712-6
1. Language arts—United States. 2. Reading—United States—
Language experience approach. 3. Language experience approach in
education—United States. 4. Teaching. 5. Newman, Judith, 1943-
. I. Title
LB1575.8.N42   1992
428'.007—dc20   91-31091
                                        CIP

Cover design: HELMUT WEYERSTRAHS

ISBN 0-7744-0374-8   Printed in Canada
1   2   3   4   5   AP   59   49   39   29   19

Contents ❖

Foreword

Since teaching is something we always do with other people, we don't often think of how isolated and lonely a profession it is. But anyone who has tried to explain to someone else a particular teaching situation, to make clear and understandable some specific incident, has encountered the radical isolation of the teacher. The words we use to describe the acts of teaching are all understood in different ways according to our own backgrounds.

When I use the word "teach" to one of my colleagues a few doors away, for example, I know very well that the image in her mind is one of me standing at the front of a class, probably behind a lectern, possibly reading from notes, but certainly producing oral language addressed to a group of perhaps twenty or thirty listeners. If I go a few doors down the hall in the other direction, the image would be of me seated on a desk conducting a discussion, acknowledging students with a nod or a gesture, and trying to get students to address each others' concerns rather than directing each contribution to me.

I would have to go all the way down the hall to find someone whose image was a little closer to my reality—which might involve my leaving the room to go to the photocopier while the students, in groups, argued out, in written conversations, strategies for library research. And even he understands only a small portion of the specific circumstances of any teaching situation.

To some extent, this isolation is true of everything we do, of course; it's not just a problem for teachers. But it's particularly important to remember it when we're thinking about teaching, because we spend so much time talking across this isolation, pretending it doesn't exist, assuming that a "common curriculum," for example, means that in some fundamental way what happens in different classrooms is similar because we use the same words to describe it.

This is one of the fundamental dilemmas of all writing about teaching and of all research into teaching. It is also a central factor in the tension in educational research between the empiricists on the one hand, interested in statistical generalizations, replicable situations, and testable results, and, on the other hand, the naturalists, interested in the uniqueness of particular situations, the concrete, specific story of one person's learning, one class's achievement, one teacher's brilliant capitalizing on one unique teachable moment.

Every teacher knows the feeling of reading a traditional research report, based on the conventional psychological methods of statistical generalization, and realizing that it seems to be talking about a world she doesn't even recognize. Or reporting as a triumphant "discovery" an observation phrased in such general terms that she and all her colleagues since the dawn of time have known it.

Why does this happen? In every teaching situation there are so many unique, imponderable, and imperceptible variables that traditional research strategies are only of limited use. The process of learning from teaching experience, like that of learning from most experience, is one which often involves learning from contingencies, accidents, peculiarities, and entails learning things we can't quite state, or can only state partially and inadequately. That's why apprenticeship is so important in learning to teach; it's why reflection on our practice is so important.

To say that reflecting on practice is a powerful learning tool is to say that we learn from experience, to say that some things are almost impossible to learn any other way. But, of course, this is not to say that such things can only be learned by experience, that there's no way to learn from the experience of others. We can learn from each other. We learn, for example, from the experiences of fiction; we learn from the kind of reportage which gives us the tools to construct our own experiences of other places, other people, other situations. In such cases, we experience not only the convenient and the congenial, the predictable and the generalizable, but we also encounter noise, contingency, and chaos; the resilience of reality, the continual surprise that dealing with the wealth of the world affords.

What Judith Newman does in this book represents, in my view, a courageous move into a territory which those of us interested in teaching and how teaching happens have not dealt with very much, or very well. Many teachers and teacher educators concerned with meaning-centred education—with the set of understandings and assumptions which we've been calling "whole language," with moving toward making learning more a matter of transactions and less a matter of transmission—have written very well about learning. There are many valuable, energizing descriptions and theories of learning available. But I do not know of many similarly powerful theories of teaching. Most really good teachers seem to attend primarily (as, perhaps, as teachers, they ought) to what their students are doing and to what kinds of learning are occurring; and not so much or so attentively to what they themselves are doing (and, equally important, to why they're doing it).

This is probably because so many of the traditional teacher-centred theories of education, against which current writers are often reacting, have tended to ignore or marginalize the learner, treating instead "content" and strategies, tips, and lesson plans. As a consequence of attempting to avoid those emphases, we concentrate on the learner.

Often, in fact, we phrase this contrast as an opposition between "student-centred" learning and more traditional "subject-centred" or "teacher-centred" modes. This has the frequent consequence for descriptions of "student-centred" approaches that it seems as if there's no real role for the teacher: if the teacher simply gets back out of the way, learning will occur. Students want to write, we're told; they want to learn; learning is what human beings are about, so all we have to do is stop doing the bad or dysfunctional things we're doing now and everything will get better.

Of course, it turns out not to be so easy. I have known teachers inspired by whole-language or other meaning-centred approaches to be disillusioned by this discovery, and to go back to more traditional methods.

What this book offers, it seems to me, is a model of what a teacher might do and think that doesn't entail that too-easy opposition. In order to give us this model, Newman has to pay a great deal of attention to herself. Indeed, the "conversations" of the title are as much within herself as with others (Vygotsky would suggest it's pretty difficult to make a clear distinction, in any case). Thus the "others" in the book (whether the participants in the workshop she describes, or the other voices which appear in the margins), though they seem in some ways to be introduced as fictional characters might be, remain quite deliberately very much shadow figures. They're out there, all right, but what we're attending to in this book are the shadows they cast in the teacher's mind, as she struggles with her own role in this complex situation. It may seem from time to time that the book is self-absorbed, but it seems to me to be so in the sense that a writer like Annie Dillard or Henry Thoreau is "self-absorbed": the idea is that by coming to understand how this particular person sees the world, we learn something about the possibilities of seeing.

This book, then, seems to me an attempt to enact, as a teacher, the kind of reflection on practice that Donald Schön has recommended. Here it is the author's own teaching practice which comes under scrutiny (as we might expect at a time when in our culture generally we are tending to focus rather on the nature of the observer's gaze than on what is being observed).

One of the things which becomes clearest through the author's practice as presented and reflected upon in this book is what it entails to be theory-driven as a teacher. Perhaps most clearly the book dramatizes that the good teacher is an improviser: that overall goals are stated (if at all) only in the most general terms—in terms of growth, awareness, and reflection, of commitment and engagement. More specific plans are tentative at best, subject to revision and negotiation and recasting on the fly, in the light of general goals and fundamental theoretical conceptions (often tacit) about how learning occurs.

An instance of this is the way the book treats "teachable moments." Such moments, Newman shows us, are always unplanned, improvisatory. The problem with planful teaching-by-telling is that the listeners don't automatically have the proper schemata activated to build the incoming ideas and connection into when they come in. What activates those schemata are questions (actually, the question is a signal that the schemata are active) or a skilled ability to assume a questioning posture. But most listeners or students aren't so skilled; we don't have easy control over such mechanisms. That's why it's important that, in Newman's words, "a teachable moment lesson is volunteered in response to students' questions." The teacher's job is to see what questions are really being asked, and find ways, on the fly, to help students get answers.

This is why Newman insists, and our instincts agree, that "information may come from sources other than the teacher or the textbook." Steering the student toward a source of information rather than offering the answer or handing her a textbook ensures (or at least makes more probable) that the question was authentic, and that answers thus will encounter an active reception: will BE answers. If the student puts forth effort to find the answer, either she does so because it was a real question, or it becomes a real question as she invests the effort in answering it. But of course the creation of situations in which this occurs are not plannable, not easily constructed, never sure-fire.

This kind of teaching is, in other words, not a neat process. Another element of the teaching situation which Newman foregrounds is the sheer mess involved. Often our best teachers, writing about teaching, create the impression that things usually go in orderly and neat ways toward foreseeable goals, that learners learn pretty much what we expect them to learn, and that they do so fairly continuously and willingly. Teachers who want to change their own practice are often disillusioned at how unpredictable, sporadic, and chaotic learning seems to be. One power of this book is that it gives the teacher who expects to re-examine or change his practice a clear sense of the different kind of order (coherence) he's going to have to be prepared to see, and how much of his traditional notions of order (neatness) in education will have to be jettisoned. Good teaching is not, in other words, done by superhumanly organized planners: it's more likely to occur as the result of inspired and thoroughly theory-driven and reflective improvisations.

And many of them won't work, as the book makes clear. Newman prepares the reader for the discovery that education is not only not neat, it's not efficient. Much of what any teacher does doesn't work. Like communication generally, it's an im-precise, organic, chaotic process, full of noise and interference and misunderstandings.

Perhaps the most important thing this book achieves is the production of a language for talking about teaching which is not reductive. Avoiding the kinds of generalizations we all use in talking about teaching, Newman offers us not conclusions, not statistical averages, not even abstract statements of her princi-ples: rather, she invites us into the mess, the contingencies, the rich chaos of a complex teaching and learning experience. The summer institute she presents here—or, rather, which she presents her experience of—can become a learning experience for us as well, precisely because she does include so much of the texture of this teaching situation—the second thoughts, the missed opportunities, the irrelevant considerations which some-how have relevance, the difficult holding back while learning happens (or doesn't), the planning of the unplannable, the risk taking. And as she reflects on her practice herself, asking the wonderful question, "What's been going on here?", we're invited to reflect too, to do the kinds of learning that we might have done on the basis of our own experience.

It's no accident that this language is achieved through so adventurous a use of dialogic devices, either. (Many readers, I suspect, will find the book's multi-voicedness its central achievement.) That the truth of any situation—teaching, perhaps, especially—is to be found through the interweaving of many voices and many perspectives, that it is socially con-structed, is a view which is at the leading edge of theoretical reflection at this moment. I would call the book overtly Bakhtinian and dialogical, except that I think the author has arrived at the position not so much through theoretical reflection about the nature of language and epistemology as through practi-cal reflection on the concrete situation at hand.

What can we learn from this book? I can't say, of course, exactly. As you might expect, much of what I learn is the kind of understanding that doesn't easily translate into general propositions about the world. But I know I'm a different teacher for having read it. And I know that one way I'm different is that I have more confidence that the mess, chaos, and risk involved in my own teaching is okay, that it's shared, that it's known—and that it's part of what I do, and ought to do.

Russell A. Hunt
Saint Thomas University

Preface   ❖

...the printed page let him read himself.
Spencer, 1987, p. 6

This is not the book I thought I was going to write. I had intended writing a more academic and theoretical piece on reflective practice, on control in the classroom, on transmission vs transactional views of teaching—issues on which much current educational debate focuses. But when I sat at the computer the writing took a direction of its own; I had no choice but to follow its lead. For the first time I experienced what I suspect many fiction writers experience—a book writing itself.

I began with two general purposes in mind: to convey something of what I have come to understand about what John Mayher (1990) calls "uncommon sense" learning and teaching, and to examine reflective practice. To my surprise I discovered I was writing directly about my own experience of teaching, struggling with what it means to be a teacher. As the writing unfolded I found myself focusing on a Summer Institute, held in 1989 at Mount Saint Vincent University, during which twenty teachers and I engaged in an exploration of writing and reading.

I am a classroom teacher. In my graduate classes I grapple with many of the same problems any grade 2 teacher does. Like other classroom teachers I operate within many institutional constraints. I am required to submit grades, plan curriculum, engage reluctant and resistant students, calm antagonistic colleagues, respond to administrative dicta, and cope with external trivia that continually interfere with the learning and teaching in my classroom. Like other classroom teachers, I struggle to make sense of my own teaching, to deal with the complexity of my classroom life, and to learn with and from my students. As I was writing this story, I found that among other things I was trying to show how classroom teaching is classroom teaching regardless of how old the students are.

Many people want to distinguish between teaching second graders and graduate students, and aren't eager to apply the label "classroom teacher" to someone who deals primarily with graduate students or adults. But I believe there are more similarities than differences. Learning is learning; it doesn't matter whether the learner is five or forty-five years old. The conditions which foster engagement aren't dependent on a learner's age. Distinguishing between public school and university teaching, in fact, creates unnecessary barriers to communication; it leads to a breakdown of collaboration among people engaged in the same enterprise.

While writing this book I requested feedback from many classroom teachers. I needed their input because I believed I was writing about their experience, too. These teachers entered the reflective conversation using it to help them see their teaching differently; their participation in the process helped me see my own teaching in new ways. In fact, their responses and questions were so helpful I decided to incorporate them into the text. The teachers' commentaries are a powerful example of how a text can let us read ourselves.

In other words, this book tells a personal story. As such, it ought to be read, not as a text book but in the way we read stories: aesthetically—living the experience—and fast. You need to read aesthetically so you can make connections to your own life, and fast so that the narrative elements can connect for you. I have included an index to help you return to parts of the story you might wish to revisit, but let me suggest that on your first reading, you read this book like a novel.

A danger with this story is that you may infer the teacher I try to be is what I think a transactional, whole language teacher should be. Let me make a disclaimer—although I began this journey more than twenty years ago I am a long way from reaching any destination. Given the nature of our evolving theoretical understanding, none of us can ever arrive. The journey is unending. There will always be new theoretical arguments to contemplate, new research findings to consider. The best I can do is just try, knowing there will always be contradictions between my beliefs and my classroom practice.

In fact, as outsiders to the situation I'm describing, I imagine you will see many more contradictions between my beliefs about teaching and what actually happens in my classroom than I can. I am not dismayed by that possibility. On the contrary, I have written to invite you to examine what I was attempting as a teacher and to use it to reflect on your own teaching, to consider the issues the teachers and I explore, and their relevance in your own classroom. I hope that in this way you'll be able to join our conversation.

The Summer Institute as I've presented it here is a story developed from transcriptions of small and large group discussions and from both the teachers' and my own writing. Initially I used the teachers' real names. That turned out to be problematic. My presentation could have been construed as attacking particular individuals. To be able to retain the undercurrent of conflict which was occasionally present between me and certain teachers I have therefore chosen to use pseudonyms for everyone attending the Institute and for any other teacher who features in the critical incidents I relate.

All this is perhaps a way to make it clear that I have not written a "how-to" book. This story is not about a particular instructional methodology. It is not filled with implementation tips (although you may find in these conversations ideas you'd like to try yourself). Instead, this story is an inquiry into my own teaching. I have written primarily to uncover what I could of my own pedagogical assumptions and to explore contradictions in my own practice. This book, therefore, is about practice, about theory, and about the transaction between them. In it, I have attempted to share the ongoing reflection without which a collaborative learning classroom cannot exist— my reflection and the students' reflection, too.

Among the many metaphors for teaching discussed during the Summer Institute the notion of learning/teaching being created from a fabric of interwoven conversations struck a powerful chord. The metaphor highlights the social character of learning and teaching and the fundamental role of language— spoken and written—in the classroom. Much of this story is told through the conversations between the teachers and me, through my reflective conversations with myself, and through our conversations with the writing of many educational, literary and children's authors as well as a few film-makers. Through these many conversations I try to deal with different aspects of what has become for me the basis of reflective practice—a critical examination of my own teaching.

Acknowledgements

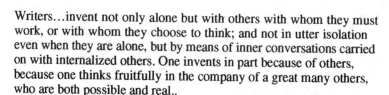

> Writers...invent not only alone but with others with whom they must work, or with whom they choose to think; and not in utter isolation even when they are alone, but by means of inner conversations carried on with internalized others. One invents in part because of others, because one thinks fruitfully in the company of a great many others, who are both possible and real..
>
> LeFevre, 1987, p.93

No writer works in a vacuum. Although my name appears as author, writing this book has been an act of social invention. The ideas have often originated elsewhere and have evolved through intensive and ongoing conversations with many people. I apologize, in advance, to anyone who might recognize his or her ideas which I have presented as my own. I have tried to acknowledge as many sources as I can; however, given the nature of conversational exchanges, it is often hard to recall the precise moment when a particular idea has connected and to attribute a source to it.

My ideas have been influenced by many researchers—Maria Montessori, John Dewey, Frank Smith, Louise Rosenblatt, Margaret Donaldson, James Britton, Janet Emig, Donald Graves, Lucy Calkins, Nancie Atwell, Tom Romano, Donald Schön, Garth Boomer, John Mayher, Jerry Harste, Carolyn Burke, Ken and Yetta Goodman, Lev Vygotsky, Harold Rosen, Elizabeth Jones, Gordon Wells, Glenda Bissex, Tom Newkirk, Jane Hansen, Toby Fulwiler, James Moffett, Margaret Spencer, James Burke, James Gleick, Henry Giroux, David Dillon, and Russ Hunt. My many conversations with the writing of these and many other academic colleagues have had an enormous influence on my present teaching perspective.

I couldn't have written this story without the wonderful conversations I had with the teachers in the first MSVU Summer Institute. My thanks to Rhonda Balzer, Larry Bent, Linda Bergevin, Mary Jane Cadegan, Susan Church, Linda Cook, Marlene Dalrymple, Lynn Hubley, Nancy Julian, Florence Kanary, Marjory Kenny, Beth Lloyd, Agnes MacCormack, Vaughan Marriott, Marilyn Milner, Linda Pike, Gladys Robertson, Chris Scott, Susan Spence-Campbell and Garland Standing for their dedicated effort as learners and teachers.

My conversations with the study-group teachers during the writing and revising of this story provided many new critical incidents and insights into the political issues of power and control in the classroom. My thanks to Marion Anderson, Nancy Anthony, Reta Boyd, Mary Jane Cadegan, Linda Cook, Michael Coughlan, Susan Church, Maureen Gow, Heather Hemphill, Roberta Jones, Florence Kanary, Judy Mossip, Martha Norris, Kathlene Rosborough, Lynn Sawyer, Susan Settle, Linda Swinwood, Margaret Swain, Sumitra Unia, Karen Webber, Cherry Whitaker, and Murray Wickwire for their willingness to discuss this unfolding story and to argue with me about it.

Thanks also to the teachers in my Spring/90 writing class who read and responded as I revised. Katherine Bishop, Glenda Burrows, Avard Daley, Sandy Gow, Deborah Howe, Emily Levi-Purdy, Lynn Moody, Darnell Paynter, Cathy Pieroway, Karen Powell, Gladys Robertson, Penny Roche, Rosemary Savory, Heather Sherry, and Judy Snow provided a sounding board which helped me bring clarity to the writing.

There are many friends and colleagues whose conversations have been, and continue to be, invaluable. Marlene Davis, Ann Vibert, Mary Schoeneberger, Andy Manning, Alan Neilsen, Lorri Neilsen, John Portelli, Russ Hunt, John Mayher, Wayne Serebrin, Jerry Harste, Diane Stephens, Frank Smith, and Susan Church. My ideas about teaching are forever being refined through contact with their experiences and their questions about issues which concern us.

I want to express my gratitude to the teachers who gave permission to include excerpts from their stories and journal reflections: Glenda Burrows, Larry Bent, Mary Jane Cadegan, Linda Cook, Marlene Dalrymple, Beth Lloyd, Lynn Sawyer, Chris Scott, Judy Snow, Susan Spence-Campbell, Garland Standing, Linda Swinwood, and Fred Williams. I learned a great deal from their writing journeys.

Particular thanks are due the teachers who took time to read and respond with marginal commentaries to various drafts of the manuscript: Susan Church, Linda Cook, Ron Hodder, Marilyn Hourihan, Russ Hunt, Lynn Moody, Lynn Sawyer, Diane Stephens, Linda Swinwood, Sumitra Unia, Ann Vibert, and Patricia Whidden. Their reactions and suggestions helped me shape this final text.

I must thank John McConnell for his editorial acumen. And finally, my heartfelt thanks to Ann Nicholson at OISE Press. Her willingness to risk publishing a book as unconventional as this one gave me the energy to revise the manuscript once again. Without her encouragement *Interwoven Conversations* might have remained buried on my shelf.

J.M.N.
Halifax, N.S.

t
b
w

Taking Off   1 ❖

The intercom buzzed. "Please answer that Anita," I asked.

Anita rose from her seat, skipped across the room and stretched to reach the answer button with her fingertips.

"Hello," she said.

"Is Miss Newman there?"

"Yes."

"Can she come to the intercom?"

"No she can't. She's sitting on Gerry," Anita replied.

A pause.

"Well, will you tell her to be sure to bring her register to the office as soon as possible. It's late."

"I'll tell her," she said. She turned to see if I had heard. I nodded and without saying anything, Anita marched back to her seat and resumed whatever it was she had been doing.

Sitting on Gerry.

I seemed to be doing that more and more these days. Gerry was behaving with less control than ever—or maybe it was simply that I had less resilience for handling his unruly behavior. I was swamped by the work involved in keeping this special ed class afloat. Weak learners all of them, the children were very dependent on my support and direction. They were reluctant to attempt much of anything on their own. I needed to offer individual input and encouragement repeatedly during the day.

To create that time I had set up an instructional agenda for each child. The preparation was a nightmare. I would spend the entire weekend working up a collection of individual lessons for each of the twelve children for that week. In addition, I had to gather or prepare materials for any group activities I wanted to try. There was no time left over for any relaxation.

Then there was the matter of their behavior. The children actively avoided engaging in learning activities. They were forever out of their seats, bothering one another. It took an enormous amount of energy to persuade them to just try. Because they were forever fighting with the other children the administration had decided they should be isolated from the rest of the school. That meant spending recess and lunch in the classroom. So, from eight in the morning, when I arrived ahead of the bus, until four in the afternoon, when the last child was picked up, I had no opportunity to be alone. Just getting to the bathroom was a major undertaking since the children couldn't be left unattended.

It didn't take long to realize I had really been hired to baby-sit these nine to twelve year olds. No one expected me to teach them much of anything. The message was quite clear: just keep them quiet and under control. That was why the class was located where it was, a safe distance away from the other classrooms. We couldn't disrupt anyone else at the back of the school next to the janitors.

What was the problem with Gerry? It wasn't that his behavior was so dreadful. He wasn't overtly malicious towards the other children. He didn't attack them physically, although he hit out at me fairly often.

No, it had more to do with how I was struggling to deal with his inability to sustain himself at any task for more than a couple of minutes. I understood that he needed more room. But I was trapped. While I wanted to extend him more freedom, if I let him wander, Anita, David, and Sharon promptly followed suit and instead of having one unmanageable child in the class, I had four. Four unengaged children were more than I could handle alone.

So there I was sitting on Gerry again.

What had he done this time? He'd ensconced himself beneath the corner painting table with his old dinky truck and I knew he hadn't even looked at the reading assignment I'd asked him to try.

Exasperated, I watched him for a moment. There he sat cross legged, another rip in the left knee of his jeans, probably from a recent fight, running the toy truck across the floor in front of him. "Vroom, vroom," again and again, oblivious to the goings on elsewhere in the room. Or maybe not. As I observed, I caught him glance at me and away again. He was aware I was watching, perhaps challenging me to make him return to his seat.

As I approached the table, I glanced around the room. Half of the children were productively engaged. The rest were watching me, curious, I suspected, about how I'd handle this situation.

I reached Gerry and knelt down. I touched his arm to stop the play, then held out my hand, palm upward—a request for the toy. Gerry hesitated. He positioned the truck in front of his feet, then he snatched it from the floor and hurled it at me. Not hard, but it grazed my leg and flew across the room.

I grabbed his shoulder and pulled him to his feet in front of me. "I'd like you to pick it up," I told him firmly. He stood there, his fists clenched, chin thrust forward, his angry gaze direct.

Here we were again. Being drawn into the now familiar battle of wills. I wanted him to extend some small effort on his school work, to try to engage. He consistently balked, challenging me to take charge which provoked further resistance from him. I would insist; he'd hit out, then I would be pushed to contain him.

That's why I was now sitting on the floor holding an immobilized, yet struggling, child in the middle of the classroom.

How had we reached this impasse?

I recalled the day Gerry joined the class.

I had been reading to the children when I caught movement out of the corner of my eye. When I turned, there he was framed in the doorway.

A smallish boy. Blond, somewhat tousled hair, clear blue eyes. He was just standing there, a battered lunch box in one hand by his side. The scruffy sneakers, his well worn jeans, baggy green cardigan—he reminded me of a Rockwell painting. It was his guarded expression which caught my attention, though.

"Can I help you?" I asked.

"I'm here for school," he said.

"Which room are you looking for?"

"Four."

"Well, you've come to the right place. C'mon in," I invited him.

Slowly dragging his feet, he entered.

I approached him with my hand extended—he didn't accept my gesture of welcome. "I'm Miss Newman," I told him, "Who are you?"

"Gerry."

"Do you have a last name?" I asked.

"Rogers."

"Welcome, Gerry Rogers," I said as I steered him toward the coat rack at the side of the room and pointed to the other lunch boxes on the shelf above it. Gerry added his battered box to the collection then I drew him towards the group of children crowded around a table.

There had been eleven girls and boys in the class. Gerry now made it twelve.

I offered him a chair. He slumped into the seat, his feet extended under the table, his hands clasped tightly in his lap. Although he didn't look around, I was aware of him sizing us up.

I introduced him to the others and then explained that we were reading a story together. I gave him my copy of the book. He took it, placing it on the table in front of him. He folded his arms across his body, as if to ward off the book. Without raising his head he mumbled, "Can't read."

"Everyone's following along as I read," I said to him. "Here, I'll help you."

I placed my chair beside his, positioned the book between us and began pointing to the words as I continued reading where I'd left off. Voices chimed in as I read what had become a now familiar story to the other children.

As I finished the chapter, I glanced at Gerry. He was still firmly slumped in his chair, arms tightly folded across his body, eyes downcast. I suspected we were in for a difficult time.

During the following weeks my fears were realized. Gerry engaged me in a standoff. No matter what invitation I offered, he refused to engage. Any reading activity was out of the question. There was no point in asking him to write anything. His math proficiency was minimal. There wasn't a great deal he could or would attempt on his own. That pushed my ingenuity to the limit. Whatever I offered him had to have the semblance of school work or I'd face rebellion from the others. So playing with plasticine or building with Lego was out of the question. Each weekend I'd create a battery of things for Gerry to do, wondering if anything would catch his interest. First thing Monday morning I'd find my work in vain.

In late September and early October when half of the class was absent for the Jewish holidays Gerry was a different child. With only four others vying for my attention I was able to spend more time by his side. As long as I stayed beside him he remained involved. And in the smaller group his wandering was less disruptive. I could keep the others busy while ignoring what Gerry was doing. But with a full house life was hectic.

Gerry would be one of the first to arrive in the morning. He'd shuffle his way into the room, drop his lunch box in the vicinity of the coat rack, and begin wandering aimlessly. As I watched him, I could feel my tension build. I often wondered if I would make it through the day.

Then came the day when I pushed Gerry too far. I could tell from the moment he entered the room something was wrong. I tried to settle him down with some work but he was restless. He reluctantly picked up his pencil, quickly tossed it aside and turned away from the notebook. He reached into his pocket, pulled out a small toy truck, and began playing with it.

We had one class rule: no toys. I had banned toys because at the first indication of frustration the children would haul out a toy as a way of avoiding the school work. Whether they wanted to or not, I was determined they would engage with learning activities. So no toys.

But here was Gerry blatantly flaunting the rule. I watched for a moment then went over to him. I asked him to put the truck in his lunch box. He ignored me and continued wheeling the toy across the table top. I knelt beside him and asked him to put the toy away. No response. I made a move to take the truck from him. An outburst. Wildly flailing, Gerry hit at me shouting obscenities. I grabbed his wrists in my hands, swung him around so his arms were immobilized across his body and sat us both on the floor.

Holding him tightly, I tried calming him down.

"You can't hit people," I said to him. "I'll let go as soon as you're quiet. We can talk about why you're so angry."

At that moment I noticed the scars on the back of both his hands.

Gerry wasn't my only problem. The other children were incredibly demanding and the more my conflict with Gerry escalated, the more demanding they became. Exhaustion set in. I needed some relief.

I tried obtaining a little free time for myself each day. I approached the principal with an idea. Would it be possible for someone to stay with the children during lunch? There were no funds in the budget to cover such exigencies, I was told. The children would have to be supervised and I would have to do it.

I tried another idea. Couldn't we team up these children with others who lived in the neighborhood and have them go home for lunch? Well, the behavior of these children was unpredictable. It wasn't a good idea to inflict them on the community. No, I would simply have to stay with them.

Could I, then, contact the Home and School to see if any parents would help out? It wasn't the parents' responsibility to teach my children. After all I only had twelve of them to work with. Surely I could manage the class.

I was no longer so sure I could.

Early in October I had thought the children would enjoy an outing. A trip to the airport seemed like it might be fun so I contacted the schoolboard's transportation department to schedule a school bus. A week later, however, I received a call informing me that the buses were engaged for the particular day I'd requested—the trip was off and I thought no more about it. I was more than a little surprised, therefore, when on November 21st there was a knock on the classroom door and the bus driver announced: "Ready to take you to the airport."

I considered for a moment and made a rash decision. I would take the class, including Gerry, on the airport trip. I notified the office about our improvised excursion then directed the children to prepare. We grabbed our coats and lunch boxes. We marched in some vague semblance of a line out the nearest exit beside the janitors' room and boarded the waiting bus.

The trip to the airport foreshadowed what was to come. The children were rowdy, bouncing around in their seats, pushing one another, yelling at the top of their voices. It seemed as if, once released from the constraints of the classroom, all self-control evaporated. By the time we reached the airport I knew I'd made a dreadful mistake but it was too late to do anything about it.

When the bus arrangements had fallen through I'd dropped all plans for the trip. There would be no guided tour of the facilities, no other adult on hand to help keep the lid on this rambunctious group. What if one of them became separated in the crowd, how would I locate a missing child and still keep track of the others? And the bathroom. I dreaded to think of Gerry loose on his own in the men's room without an adult to supervise.

No sooner had the bus dropped us at the departure level than we were caught up in the bustle of the terminal building. I paraded the children past the ticket counters toward the gate area. Windows lined the large outer circular corridor and planes parked at the various ramps were readily visible. We gathered to look at one large jet. Passengers were boarding from the adjacent lounge and the cockpit crew could be seen making preparations for their upcoming flight.

The children had loads of questions.

"Where is this plane going?"

"Where's it come from?"

"Which one is the pilot?"

"How many people can it take?"

"How does the food get on?"

"Where does the luggage go?"

I was busy with explanations, not watching the children very closely. Their interest and excitement kept me occupied so it was several moments before I realized, with a sudden sinking feeling, Gerry was nowhere in sight.

It took a while to gain the children's attention. Had anyone seen Gerry? Had he told anyone where he was going?

"No, Miss Newman," came their unanimous reply.

What to do? I knew I couldn't go off to search for Gerry on my own, nor could I disperse the children to look for him for fear I'd lose someone else. I decided the safest course would be to locate the airport police and enlist their aid.

Finding the police was easier said than done, however. I spent a good ten minutes, with the entire troupe in tow, weaving my way through the crowded terminal, trying not to lose anyone else. When we still hadn't found a policeman, I dragged the children to one of the less busy ticket counters to ask for help.

"Please, I need the police," I said to the ticket agent. "I've lost a child. He's wandered away from the group and I have no idea where he is."

The agent contacted the police who immediately appeared. I described Gerry and said I thought it quite likely they might find him in one of the many washrooms. It was not inconceivable that he might even have drifted into one of the women's toilets, I told them.

With the police now tracking him down, I stationed the children in a row of seats to wait and worry. In fifteen minutes Gerry was back. He'd become bored with the plane and had decided to explore on his own. He'd found the escalators in the middle of the terminal and had been riding them between the arrival and departure levels. That's where an officer had found him.

Taking Gerry firmly by the hand, I decided I needed to get the children away from the crowd as quickly as possible. Since none of them had ever flown, I thought they would enjoy watching the planes take off and land. The best vantage point for such viewing was from the top floor of the parking garage. The open west side of the building faced the runway and there was a clear view of the steady incoming and outgoing air traffic. Besides, I could more easily keep an eye on everyone there.

So I marched the children, lunch boxes in hand, through the crowd to the elevators. I bundled them aboard the first one to arrive, pushed P10 and breathed a sigh of relief. As the elevator rose, I explained to the children where we were headed and how I expected them to behave.

"We're going to the roof of the building," I said. "You'll need to be careful near the wall. If you lean too far, you might fall over and it's a long way down. Be careful!" I shouted as the elevator doors opened and they tore out. I followed behind past the few cars parked on that level toward the outside wall of the garage to watch the planes.

Although mid-morning wasn't a terribly busy time at Pearson Airport, there was some traffic. We could see a DC-9 readying for take off at the far end of the runway. The children stretched to pull themselves up onto the parapet so they could see more clearly. Bunched together at one location they jostled for position.

"You can spread out," I told them. "There's no need to push." I moved behind them trying to help them settle down.

The plane revved its engines and began to taxi down the runway. We watched it slowly gain speed. As it came abreast of us the nose lifted and the plane began its steep ascent. Gerry stepped onto his lunch box, balanced on the tip of his toes with his torso leaning on the narrow parapet.

With the roar of the engines at full throttle I felt Gerry strain to pull himself further onto the ledge to watch the take off.

I reached to restrain him—

and see myself catching one of his legs in my hand,

lifting it sharply, unbalancing him

arms fly out   feet rise

the soles of his sneakers pass in front of my face

a sky diver, his body hangs suspended

arms wide

legs spread behind him   wind flaps at the falling body

silent screams masked by the engines' roar

plane lifting—

hung in the overwhelming middle of things

amazement at the nightmare unfolding

heat shimmering from the runway

plane banking left into wisps of low level cloud

a flock of small birds swooping over the grassy verge

miniature cars along the 401

lunch box skidding

THUMP!

Gerry lay in a heap on the floor beside me, his whimpering drowned by the roar of the still climbing jet.

"I warned you to be careful, didn't I?" I said shaken. He wiped his chin, drawing away a bloody hand. I just stood there, watching, making no move to help him. Wiping the blood on his jeans he looked up at me. His clear blue gaze guarded. For a moment he stared, then he quickly scrambled to retrieve his lunch box from beneath a nearby car.

I hastily gathered the other children into a group and oblivious to their protests and complaints I hurried them across the garage and aboard a waiting elevator. When we reached the departure level I herded them toward the car park and onto the waiting bus.

Once back at school I settled them for lunch and headed for the office.

"I've had it," I said. "Someone will have to replace me." Then I turned and took off.

That afternoon, November 21, 1971, I walked away from the school and didn't return. It would have been the end of my teaching career except that Martin Fischer, a friend and therapist, believed I was meant to be a teacher. Like Alf Johnson, the swim instructor I'd had as a child who helped me climb back on the three-meter diving board immediately after an initial, unnerving bellyflop, Fischer promptly lured me back to teaching. He had a number of school-phobic adolescent patients who were terrified to so much as enter a school building. They might, however, be able to learn at home, he thought. So he made arrangements for me to instruct two of them. Freed from the constraints of a school setting I found myself being drawn into teaching again.

Why teaching? I had never imagined myself a teacher. I had excelled in math and science in high school and there had been an unspoken expectation in my family that I would become a doctor. To that end I did an undergraduate degree in honors biology, with courses in chemistry, physics, and mathematics. I had taken the minimum of humanities courses. English, in fact, had been my nemesis; I'd only managed to scrape through the two required undergraduate English courses with the help of my closest friend, Marlene, who prompted and prodded me through the weekly 'themes,' tests and final exams.

Upon the completion of my undergraduate program in 1963, I went to study zoology at the University of Toronto. I took graduate courses in biochemical genetics and taught under-graduate biology labs. Although I found the courses humdrum, I thoroughly enjoyed teaching the labs.

I was, at that same time, also playing and studying classical guitar. My interest in music soon overtook my interest in biochemical genetics. Midway through the second year of graduate study I became a graduate school drop-out. I devoted the next several months to working on the guitar, preparing an audition for the undergraduate performance program in the Music Department. Accepted into the program, I practised guitar five to six hours each day, attended classes on the history of music, harmony, and so on, as well as continuing to teach undergraduate biology labs.

By the end of the second year of the music program, however, I had little sense of myself as a concert performer and I couldn't see becoming a music teacher. If I was going to teach, I realized, it would have to be math and science. So once again, I became a drop-out. This time I registered for the summer program in education. The shortage of teachers, although less severe than a few years earlier, remained acute enough that people with my sort of background were still required. That fall of 1967, I found a position teaching science in a newly opened suburban high school without any difficulty.

The classroom presented me with many serious problems. My beliefs about learning and instruction had yet to be articulated let alone examined. My teaching was exactly like the teaching I'd experienced myself. Like most people, I taught as I had been taught.

As a high school science teacher I believed, as did most fellow teachers, that my students knew very little and my responsibility was to dispense the facts, to assign exercises and drills for them to practise the stuff, and to correct and grade their assignments. My assumptions were what John Mayher (1990) refers to as 'commonsense beliefs.' I believed that knowledge was an objective commodity, independent from the knower. I believed in the fundamental tenet of commonsense teaching: that students learn what teachers teach. Like many other teachers, I was reasonably comfortable with what Douglas Barnes (1976) refers to as transmission teaching. The only problem with teaching this way was that while some of the students learned, at least to the extent that they could regurgitate what I'd told them on a test or exam, a large number of them did not.

I remember how, frustrated by my students' disinterest, I tried to change the instruction in my classroom. I'd recalled that the most engaging experiences of my own schooling had been those occasions when I'd had a chance for hands-on learning. Since I was the only teacher responsible for teaching science to the four grade 9 general track classes, I decided to set up a lab-like classroom. I planned a series of experiences, collected materials, and prepared guide sheets for the students who rotated through the activities in pairs. The activities had some tenuous connection with the textbook curriculum but on the whole, they involved isolated observations and experiments. The students were offered little opportunity to build a coherent sense of some aspect of science and I had to contend with their inexperience at working on their own. Nevertheless, they found the activities more interesting than listening to me talk and I did have less trouble with them in class because they were enjoying themselves more.

It didn't take me long to recognize teaching was a complex undertaking and that I needed to learn a great deal more. So I began reading about education. At that time, my guitar teacher's youngest daughter was attending the Toronto Montessori school. I became intrigued with what went on there and decided to learn more about Montessori's ideas. I made a couple of visits to the Toronto Montessori school; I read some of Montessori's books. The more I delved, the more intrigued I became by Montessori's ideas. So in the fall of 1968 I travelled to Italy to study at the International Centre for Montessori Studies.

Bergamo, a medium-sized town in northern Italy, was just far enough off the beaten path that few tourists stopped there. English was not widely spoken and I arrived with virtually no Italian. However, by the end of the year I had learned to speak Italian reasonably fluently. My experiences as a foreign student also made me much more sensitive to cultural differences. And the Montessori program set me on a path toward what Mayher (1990) calls 'uncommon sense' teaching. I began to think about the learning environment in new and open ways, to think about the learner at the centre of the learning situation and to think about 'error', not as something to be eradicated, but as a fruitful part of learning.

Upon my return to Canada, I took a teaching job in a treatment centre for disturbed adolescents. I had a hard time with these students. Most had severe emotional problems; some were delinquent. The majority couldn't handle being in a regular school classroom. I would often awaken dreading the day. I'd lie in bed, wishing the alarm hadn't gone off, wondering whether it would be a one or a two valium morning. I'd test the tension in my body by slipping my right foot over the side of the bed, slowly pulling myself upright, and swinging my left foot to the floor. My body would feel leaden, a heavy fatigue holding me on the edge of the bed, and I would sense anxiety begin to gnaw in the pit of my stomach.

I was upset by the kids' violent outbursts, their flat refusals to try anything, the excessive profanity. Working with five students, an hour at a time, was taxing. After a while I did learn to read the kids better, but the tension while I was at school never quite dissipated. I was, for example, always watchful of Keith—careful not to push him too far. You could never trust him not to hit out with his large fists. Or Christopher. The day he directed a large gob of spit at me, and purposefully missed, I learned to teach from behind. I was always fearful of an outburst: a pencil unexpectedly jabbed through a hand, an angry kick in the shin, a fistful of hair grabbed. Sometimes there'd be some warning. Often, it would all have happened so fast I'd wonder where it had come from.

There was the day Jennifer attacked me. I'd seen that outburst coming for nearly three weeks, but her hands went around my throat so quickly I barely had time to drop my chin to protect myself a little. I knew I wasn't in mortal danger (the child care workers were close by and moved in to handle her quickly), I was, however, still unnerved. So, often it was a two valium morning.

I survived the year and, although at the end I knew I wouldn't return, I realized I'd learned a great deal from the experience. I'd had to confront most of my intellectual, white, middle-class, Jewish values—they didn't fly with those kids who had been physically and sexually abused, abandoned, stressed out in ways I could only imagine. I had been forced to examine some of my instructional assumptions as I struggled day after day to teach those very unhappy, disturbed, difficult, acting out young people.

The next year, 1971, I took a special education position in what was then called a 'junior opportunity' class consisting of a dozen 9- to 12-year-old children. Today they would be labelled 'learning disabled.' Gerry was a member of that class and I've already shared something of that teaching experience.

To this point, then, many of my teaching experiences had been harrowing. Why did I continue? The truth is I came very close to leaving the profession. What kept me a teacher was the opportunity to tutor the school phobic students sent my way by Martin Fischer. Working outside the classroom allowed me to glimpse a different side of teaching. I was able to establish some trust with those students and they, in turn, engaged me in some rather complex problem solving which I found very satisfying. I had also begun a graduate education program. Between tutoring and studying I found new connections with teaching. I completed a master's degree in education theory, then undertook doctoral study. After completing the doctorate, I took a teaching appointment in a university department of education.

While I had learned a great deal about learning and teaching as a graduate student my teaching was slow to change. I can still remember lecturing undergraduate elementary education students on 'the reading process' and for a number of years I presumed to tell both prospective and practising teachers how to teach in a more student-centred way. Nevertheless, for a long time I remained a transmission teacher myself.

I can actually recall the incident which made me aware of this glaring inconsistency in my own teaching. I was attending a Miscue Workshop. Carolyn Burke, one of the workshop leaders, had presented us with a book written in an invented alphabet and we were using whatever cues we could to make sense of the text. We were discussing the purpose of the activity and had numerous questions about various improvisations. Carolyn's responses were interesting. "I can't answer you," she kept responding, "without first considering whether that change violates my model, or not." She was demonstrating that we teachers needed to consider whether our activities reflected our beliefs and were consistent with what we wanted our students to experience.

> I have been slowly letting go—although I still exercise a fair amount of control over learning outcomes. I have tried to give my grade 8s increasing freedom to explore the *how* of what we're doing and more and more I understand the importance of personal experience, of using the students' insights and experiences to add relevance to the curriculum, to provide a springboard.
>
> Ron Hodder

I remember my discomfort at that moment. I was suddenly very conscious of the many contradictions between my own espoused theory and my instructional practices. I realized I was violating what I said I believed about creating learning contexts for kids with everything I was doing with my adult students.

After the workshop I found myself with a dilemma—to carry on as I had been: a transmission teacher—or to take a big leap and try something quite different. I leapt. I set up a collection of reading and writing activities and turned the class loose on them. At that time, however, I didn't have any clear sense of how to orchestrate the entire event so students (about half undergraduate education students and half experienced classroom teachers) could see the point I was wanting them to see: that people become literate by engaging in purposeful reading and writing that matters to them.

Part of the problem, I now understand, was that while my activities were reasonably engaging, they didn't connect with any larger design; each activity stood alone. More important, the students still had a predominantly passive role in the classroom—I had designed the activities, established the rules, and graded the outcomes. In other words, the students were yet to be engaged in literacy experiences in which they had any serious personal investment. Yes, I was moving away from teaching by telling, as Don Murray (1982) calls it, but I still had a long way to go.

For the last dozen years I have been consciously struggling to change how I teach. I have moved from teacher-controlled teaching, through student-centred learning, to learning-focused education—I have shifted from a transmission view of teaching to a transactional perspective (Dewey, 1963; Rosenblatt, 1978), an 'uncommon sense' conception (Mayher, 1990) of learning.

My journey has been anything but smooth. The learning has often been unpredictable, situation specific, and painful. There have been awkward steps forward accompanied by many slips backward, gains on one front cancelled out by regression on another. When I think I've finally made some headway, I find many of the issues I thought I'd resolved need to be reconsidered again.

At this point I can articulate some of the theoretical assumptions which inform my teaching. First, and foremost, I have come to believe that learning and teaching are distinct ventures (Lindfors, 1984). Learning is constructing out of our individual experiences some sense of how the world works. Teaching involves intentionally helping to extend another's knowledge or skill. Sometimes these two activities connect; frequently, however, they don't. It is certainly true that while teaching can facilitate learning, lots of learning happens without any teaching at all or in spite of the teaching that's going on. Although students can learn from teachers, they may not be learning what we think we're teaching; they may be learning that they're stupid, or that learning is boring and pointless.

I now recognize that collaboration is at the heart of learning. Learning is social. People don't learn in isolation; we learn as members of learning communities. While we each construct an individual interpretation of a particular event or situation, our understanding is shaped by contact with other people's perceptions of what is taking, or has taken, place. Our particular interpretations stand until a discrepancy of some sort catches our attention and causes us to re-examine and to reinterpret the situation.

I understand that the motivation for learning must come from the learner. That means creating open instructional situations which allow students to establish connections that matter to them. I have had to learn to abandon specific tasks I've initiated in favor of something students prefer to explore; to use their interests to achieve my instructional ends.

I am convinced that learning, in school and out, involves the same fundamental processes. I can no longer assume learners have no strategies for dealing with new situations, that I have to teach them everything they need to know. Instead, I have had to learn to create opportunities which allow students to use learning strategies they already possess. That hasn't meant I can't suggest alternate ways of trying something, only that my suggestions must build on what students have already sorted out for themselves.

I believe much of the knowledge and many of the skills we develop are acquired incidentally on the way to doing something else. People (children as well as adults) learn constantly out of school, in their work and play, so inconspicuously that most of the time we're unaware that any learning is actually going on. The research literature (see Halliday, 1975; Harste, Woodward & Burke, 1984; Wells, 1986) is replete with studies demonstrating how children don't learn to talk, or to read and write either, as ends in themselves but because they are trying to make sense of everything people are doing in the world around them (Hunt, 1989).

Coming to understand that learning is collaborative, universal, and incidental has meant learning to think about instruction, and my role in the classroom, in a radically different way. Frank Smith (1988) describes learning situations based on these beliefs as **enterprises.**

> Enterprises are group undertakings whose purpose is self-evident. No one who participates in an enterprise ever has to ask, "Why am I doing this? " (p.70)

There are unlimited possibilities for classroom enterprises: conducting a census, investigating family history or doing surveys on anything that catches students' interest, engaging in hands on science (not following textbook recipes or memorizing facts), creating and performing plays, exploring other performing arts, making videos and movies, writing letters (poems, stories, notices, cartoons, job applications, complaints...), a weekly publication, building boats and kites, a whole range of community projects.

There are considerable differences, Smith believes, between enterprises and regular school activities. In fact, he identifies four stringent criteria that must be met before he'd consider any activity an enterprise.

> Ah! Enterprises! Twenty-one grade 9s pulling together, giving up every noon hour for two weeks to plan, practise, and present a workshop for teachers. Now that's an enterprise! It leaves me with a nagging question, though: Why is there more learning occurring during noon hours than in my classes? Motivation, commitment, and choice must be the answer. My class is missing Smith's criteria. The workshop leaders are freed from the usual classroom constraints. Immediate feedback, not grades from the workshop participants, determines whether they were effective or not. I can see I need to think about the relevance of enterprises for the classroom.
>
> Pat Kidd

No grades. In everyday life, Smith contends, nobody gets 'marked' for engaging in any aspect of an endeavor. No one is tested. Enterprises are judged, but only in the ways in which all real life, out-of-school enterprises are judged—by how well they succeed in satisfying their intentions.

No restrictions. Enterprises aren't defined in advance by the teacher or restricted to what the teacher 'wants.' They aren't constrained by school timetables or confined to school buildings. Real learning ventures are bound neither by clocks nor by venue; learning occurs at unexpected moments, in unlikely locations: in bed, on the bus, in the shower. Enterprises result in interesting and often unpredictable 'products.' They are collaborative ventures; seeking and receiving help is legitimate and expected.

No coercion. No learner, Smith believes, should be forced to partake in any learning enterprise although learners may be encouraged to have a go. No one is excluded because of insufficient talent or experience.

> The role of the teacher is not to force children, which can never result in useful learning, nor to demand that they be interested and attentive when they are obviously bored or bewildered, but to ensure that sufficiently interesting and open enterprises exist to appeal to every child (p. 72).

No status.

> The distinction between 'teachers' and 'learners' must be erased. There will always be some members of clubs and participants in enterprises who are more experienced than others, and there may even be management and supervisory functions, but these roles need not be filled by the the teacher (and never **because** the person is the teacher) (p.72).

In other words, in an enterprise everyone is a learner; everyone is a teacher.

Enterprises work, Smith believes, when learning is at the heart of what's going on. However,

> If the teacher is automatically the person in charge, even in pulling strings from offstage, then the activity may again become another school project, engaged in to satisfy or placate authority rather than for intrinsic satisfaction (p. 72).

Learning how to lead without being in charge has been difficult. I don't do it as well as I would like to. There are still times when I overstep someone's boundaries and interfere with their learning, or worse, stop it altogether. However, with each new teaching situation I learn more about how to create learning-focused enterprises. I am slowly getting better at engaging and sustaining people's learning and at learning along with them.

Today I can envision a very different junior opportunity class than the one I attempted to create nearly twenty years ago. Enterprises would have helped Gerry and the others engage as learners far more readily than those endless structured individualized lessons which brought compliance from some but offered no real learning for any of those children.

What follows is the story of one recent learning/teaching venture. I have chosen to write about the 1989 Mount Saint Vincent University Summer Institute because that situation has come closest to what I'm attempting to learn how to do: teach a group of teachers in exactly the same way as I'd teach five year olds—in a collaborative learning classroom, where the motivation for learning comes from the learners, where students take risks and are able to build on their existing strategies, where learning is largely incidental (the result of doing something that really interests the students); in a situation where there is no fear of being graded, constrained by the minimum of restrictions, where no one is coerced into complying with teacher demands but encouraged to find her own way, where everyone is a learner and everyone is a teacher.

Preparing the Environment

Learning enterprises. What's involved in creating open-ended learning experiences? How do you initiate and sustain a learning-focused endeavor? What is the teacher's role in a collaborative learning effort?

In an enterprise-based curriculum the teacher's role is a complex one and very different from the transmission role we're used to. Some of these differences are evident in John Picone's description of his first lesson on landing a small aircraft (Picone, 1990).

"Do you think we're too high, or too low?" [Angus, his flight instructor, asked John.] My immediate response was what in the name of Wilbur Wright are you asking me for? I'm not sure whether it was the question itself, or the casual posture of the young fellow sitting beside me that was the more unsettling. Immediately in front of me was a meaningless cluster of dials and needles; about two miles beyond that was the fast approaching pavement of Runway 14 which looked even shorter and narrower than I had imagined! Beside me was Angus McTavish, my flight instructor: seat pushed all the way back; feet comfortably crossed in front of the rudder pedals; arms, likewise, back of the control column. Here I was, white-knuckled, at the controls of a Cessna 152 for the first time in my life, on final approach to land a heavier-than-air-craft, and Angus was asking **ME** what I thought about our altitude! Putting absolute faith in the wisdom of his question, I steadied what I knew would be a quiver in my voice and answered, "I think we're too high." Of course, I imagined this to be some kind of a little quiz, and Angus would then say something like, "That's right, or that's wrong." But not **THIS** flight instructor, no way! Instead: "Well, what are you going to do about that?" I couldn't believe it! "Let me not be mad!" I thought. I tried to recall everything that we had been practising for the past hour in this first lesson to familiarize me with the aircraft. "Raise the nose a little and ease back on the throttle?" I asked. You can probably guess Angus' response to that: "Maybe. Why don't you try it?" Eight feet (or was it 8 inches?) above the pavement, Angus took control and safely brought us back to terra firma. It was the last time he ever did. And less than 15 hours of air time later, I was making a final approach to the same runway—and the seat beside me was empty. My first solo flight. Angus' style of instructing never changed. He was always asking me questions, helping me articulate the nature of the problem or situation, and letting me make decisions in response. He encouraged me to try things, experiment with the plane's controls, observe its response, draw my own conclusions—really learn how to fly (p.1)!

Not how most of us would expect a flight instructor to teach. After all, flying a plane is serious business—not much room for error. Yet Angus's instruction embodies the essential aspect of Mayher's **uncommon sense teaching**: letting learners engage in the actual experience, allowing them to encounter actual problems, to make mistakes, so they learn from what happens (Mayher, 1990).

Picone, himself an English teacher, was interested in Angus's reasons for teaching the way he does. He continues:

> There was a certain affinity I had with this young man that I couldn't identify right away. It wasn't until we stopped for coffee in Hamilton one day after an hour of "circuits" that it became clear. I recalled to him that first landing and shared my puzzled response at the time. Why didn't you just tell me how to land the plane, I asked. "I don't think it's possible to teach someone how to land an aircraft," he said. "Not really. You set up the situation, ask the right questions, show a lot of encouragement and patience, and sooner or later a pilot just learns it. Landing a plane is a lot more than just knowledge about what the plane can do, or even the skill in doing it. It's judgement. No two landings are ever the same. A good pilot exercises good judgement; you can't teach that. You have to give the student lots of opportunities to develop it. And that's going to mean some rough landings!" (p.1)

Exercising good judgement—that's at the heart of any learning enterprise. Whatever the situation, learning involves a lot more than acquiring some specific knowledge and a few learning strategies. My dilemma as a teacher is that I can't teach good judgement; I can only create circumstances which make it possible for learners to experience the consequences of their own decisions. Whether it's helping someone learn to fly a plane, use a computer, become a more fluent reader and writer, or a more proficient teacher my role is to structure conditions so that learners are willing to risk engaging in the experience and exploring the unfamiliar. And when students run into difficulty, when they don't understand what's happening, when they encounter something they aren't sure how to handle, I need to be on hand to ask questions, to offer suggestions, or just to provide moral support.

❖

As I contemplate the upcoming two-week Summer Institute, I think about the learning enterprise I want to initiate. What sort of learning conditions do I want to create? What beliefs about learning do I want to convey and how might I implement them?

Gordon Wells (1990) has outlined five beliefs which currently shape his teaching. He contends

- what we learn at school should be seen as meaningfully related to the questions and predicaments we meet both inside the classroom and out;
- all knowledge is tentative and provisional, open to revision in light of further evidence and experience;
- on many issues there are many possible interpretations of any evidence since interpretations depend upon the values and assumptions of the interpreters as well as on the evidence itself;
- each individual has a dual responsibility to be open-minded to different views but at the same time not accept unquestioningly assertions made by 'experts';
- students should have opportunities to discover the procedures and modes of discourse that have evolved within various disciplines and test them in a collaborative manner.

These are my beliefs, too. Together these beliefs frame what I want to call a **transactional** view of learning. The term transactional comes from Bentley & Dewey (1949). It calls attention to the belief that learners are themselves an integral part of any learning situation. Learners shape situations by engaging in conversation with them; both the situation and the learners change as a result of the transaction. Unlike a traditional transmission classroom, a transactional learning context is open-ended. Students are engaged in experiences that connect directly with what's going on in the world outside of school. They are invited to experiment, to make mistakes and to change what they're doing based on the outcome of their experiments. They are encouraged to examine and question their own strategies and assumptions as well as the strategies and assumptions of people around them. By working together they are able to discover the various ways in which things in the world are done.

But setting up such a learning context is complicated. I need to think about creating a milieu that enables a social, collaborative venture. I need to consider the physical aspects of the situation, the materials we might want to use, and activities that encourage and support engagement and make it necessary for people to work together. All of this constitutes **preparing the environment**.

I encountered the notion of a prepared environment during the year I spent at the International Centre for Montessori Studies. Montessori believed that the physical layout of the classroom and the materials which are present are crucial for establishing an engaging learning context. She describes particular learning materials and how to use them (Montessori, 1964, 1965), but she offers little insight into how the teacher improvises based on feedback from the children. There is no indication that the teacher is learning along with and from the students and how that affects the structuring and restructuring of the learning situation.

I'm interested in the relations between **prepared** environments and **real** environments. I think we need to think hard about what people learn about the real environment from a prepared one—what I'd like to think is that they learn to **treat** the world the way they treat a really rich prepared environment. Lots of people are very reluctant to respond to even extremely rich environments by trying to take control of them and learn in them; I think they've learned one way or another that the real environment (and thus anything they run into in a class) is going to be unmanageable and dangerous and unrewarding, and thus they'd better just hunker down and take it. How do we get them out of that posture? How do we convince them not only that they can take charge of their own learning in the prepared environment we create but also that they can take charge of it when no one's facilitating? I try as much as possible to work with an environment that's outside my control. That's why I don't use texts or reading lists and why I send the students to the library so much? I want them to be learning about the eighteenth century as closely as possible to the way they'd do it if I or some other facilitator weren't involved at all.

Russ Hunt

My concept of a prepared environment is a much broader, dynamic view than Montessori's. Indeed, I no longer talk of "the prepared environment" (a static notion) but of preparing the environment. My recent teaching experiences have made me think about the learning context as very fluid. While I am responsible for initiating experiences, the environment is sustained in collaboration with my students. I begin by establishing a physical setting with materials I think might be engaging. I prepare an opening invitation but then I'm no longer on my own. The students have a central role to play in how the experience will unfold.

There are several interconnected aspects to preparing a learning-focused, enterprise-based classroom environment. There's thinking about global intentions and underlying beliefs. There's planning, initiating, and sustaining activities, digging up resources, choosing materials, arranging the physical setting. There's also watching what's happening as students are working, reacting to the ongoing situation, and responding to the moment.

There is no linear sequence implied here. While I am forced to write about these aspects of planning as though they were discrete and in some logical order, the planning usually takes place constantly and occurs in anything but a tidy way. I write notes to myself and stick them on the wall, on my computer, in file folders. I am forever making piles of stuff on my study floor, in the upstairs hall, and beside my bed. I jot reminders and ideas to think about in my planning notebook, but a lot of preparing goes on in my head and never manages to be recorded anywhere.

Preparing is an ongoing and vital aspect of teaching. The thinking about global intentions and underlying beliefs, for example, is never complete but brought to the fore continually in response to what's happening. So, while I am responsible for setting things in motion, the moment students arrive on the scene whatever follows will need to be negotiated.

I begin preparing for the Institute months in advance. I start by listing some assumptions:

Learning
> is collaborative;
> requires risk-taking and experimentation;
> involves constructing meaning and making
> > connections between new information
> > and old;
> occurs when learners are actively
> > involved, when they have real purposes,
> > when they make choices and share in
> > decision-making.

This current list of assumptions/beliefs emerged when my friend Susan Church, a curriculum supervisor with one of the local district school boards, and I collaborated on an article— "Myths of Whole Language" (Newman & Church, 1990). While writing, we had a number of conversations about various beliefs underpinning a whole language theoretical perspective. I put this version of the list in my Institute folder to have on hand as I was beginning to think through the up-coming two-week experience.

With some of my assumptions explicit, I think about ways of implementing them. I ask myself some questions:

What's one thing I would like people to understand?
Why do I think it's important?
How might I help them experience it?

These questions have an interesting history. Several years ago I was asked to write a computer column, ONLINE, for **Language Arts**. I was thinking about the first article for the column while attending an NCTE conference and had an opportunity to engage in a conversation with Don Graves about it. He asked me two questions: What was the one thing I wanted my readers to understand? I thought for a moment, then answered him. How was I going to show, not tell, them about that? Later, when I sat down to write, Graves's questions helped me focus and that opening article (Newman, 1984) flowed surprisingly easily. After that, I found myself remembering Graves's questions whenever I sat down to write something new. What was the one thing I wanted my readers to understand? How was I going to show, not tell, them?

Graves's questions also influenced my teaching although I wasn't immediately aware of it. I found myself thinking less in terms of having to cover a particular curriculum and more about an over-arching focus for my courses. I was becoming less concerned about transmitting everything I knew and believed to teachers and was shifting, instead, to helping people examine a few critical issues.

My question changed after reading Don Murray's "Writing as Process: How Writing Finds Its Own Meaning" in which he contends

> We do not teach our students rules demonstrated by static models; we teach our students to write by allowing them to experience the process of writing (Murray, 1980, p. 20).

It was no longer "How am I going to show that?" but "How am I going to help them **experience** that?"

This new question shifted the focus from me as a transmitting teacher to the learning situation. In fact, it may well have been this question that pushed me to reconnect with my Montessori past and I began consciously thinking about preparing an open learning environment. I started exploring how to set up situations that made it possible for people, children as well as adults, to assume much greater responsibility for their own learning.

Nevertheless, I still didn't realize the extent to which my teaching was being directed by these questions until two teachers, students in one of my winter graduate classes, asked me to help them plan a workshop. Faye, Arlene, and I sat down together and my first question to them was "What's the one thing you want the teachers to understand?" They had some difficulty answering. It meant laying out some of their assumptions about learning and teaching in order to decide just what they might focus on in their workshop.

My next question: "How are you going to help them experience that?" was no easier for them to answer. Their concept of a workshop was to tell what they'd done in their own classes. That they might want to create a tightly focused activity which would let teachers question some personal assumptions was a new idea. With some help, Faye and Arlene were able to use some data from their students as the basis for an activity which let workshop participants not only see junior high students taking risks but also let them become risk-takers themselves. This conversation made me see important parallels between writing and teaching.

"Why do I think that's important?" was an adaptation of two questions Harste, Woodward and Burke (1984) raise in connection with curriculum development:

> What do we know about language, language learning, successful
>   language users, and the evolution of literacy?
> What do I know about my students' language use?

These questions, I realized, serve as the link between practice and theory. It isn't enough to know what I'd like people to understand, I also need to be able to explain why I think it's important.

In connection with the Summer Institute, the first question "What's the one thing I'd like people to understand?" lurks in my head unanswered for months. Other than a vague sense of wanting to set up some kind of reading/writing experience I have no specific focus in mind. That changes abruptly at the end of January with a visit to Beth Hendry's third grade class.

For some time, Beth has wanted me to come and be part of a classroom publishing party. There have been a number of reasons why I haven't been able to make it, but finally it's Friday, end of January, and I've arrived to help the children with their writing.

I'm a little surprised by the situation. I had assumed publishing party meant adults were there simply to help with typing, putting covers on books, sewing, etc. That doesn't seem to be the case. Several of the children have writing underway, but a number are still in initial drafting stages.

Beth directs me to a pair of boys who have just begun a new adventure very like a dungeons and dragons scenario. So far, Josh and Noah have selected a setting (some ancient Egyptian tombs) and have identified a central character (an archaeologist in search of treasure) but what they've written doesn't hang together as a story—at least for me it doesn't. I listen to what they've produced, and ask them what ideas they have for proceeding. They aren't sure. They discuss fantastic monsters in the cave. From their conversation I can't tell whether their central character is intended to be hero or villain. I ask them about it.

"Hero," they reply.

"How can you tell someone's a hero," I ask. They look at me with incomprehension.

"Well, think about a story you've read recently. How did you know who were the good guys and who were the bad?" No answer.

"What books have you been reading," I persist. Both Noah and Josh are vague.

"What has Miss Hendry been reading to you in class?"

"Well, she hasn't been reading anything lately."

*So much for making a reading/writing connection here. I try having them recall a familiar fairy tale. They don't know any. I notice some artifacts in the room that suggest the children have discussed **Jack and the Beanstalk** recently.*

"What about Jack in **Jack and the Beanstalk**," I ask them. "Is there a hero? A villain? How do you know?" They consider my questions. Jack's the hero, Noah decides because he gets into dangerous situations and he manages to figure his way out of things.

"What about the Giant?"

"Villain."

"Why?"

"Well, he stole stuff from Jack's family."

I'm trying to help the boys connect with their experience of stories but I can tell neither is very interested in what they consider to be a diversion. They want to get on with their story. They're not really interested in exploring ideas of plot or characterization with me.

"Any idea how to show your archaeologist is the hero?"

The boys shrug so I suggest they work on their story some more and I'll get back to them later.

As I move away to sit on an upturned milk crate nearby one of the girls grabs me. Here is another child who has barely begun a story. She reads me what she's written—a couple of sentences about one of her stuffed animals—and I ask her what her story will be about. She doesn't know.

"What are some things that could happen to Hoppy," I ask her. She shrugs. Again, I try making contact with stories she's read.

"What kinds of things happen to animals in stories?" Crystal just looks at me. "What are some animal stories you like?" Another shrug.

I can see I'm not going to get very far here, either. I'm not sure how to proceed. I suspect she would like me to tell her what to write but I won't be drawn in.

I suggest Crystal tell me three things that could happen to Hoppy. She chews the end of her pencil in silence.

"Try making a list of some things that could happen," I offer, "then we can talk some more, later."

What strikes me about this situation is that while there's lots of writing going on here, and many of the children have done a great deal of writing over the past few months, there seems to be little contact being made with books and stories. Beth has been excited about the children's writing but an important ingredient is missing for me: the children aren't being helped to connect with reading. The necessary interplay between reading and writing isn't being overtly developed here. This concerns me, because last year Beth was one of my strongest graduate students and if she's missed the importance of the reading/writing connection I can see I have to rethink my own teaching.

My visit to Beth's classroom was productive. Not for the children—my wanting to connect writing with reading missed the mark with them—but it raised some questions about my own teaching I think are important.

> How can I help build a stronger relationship between reading and writing?
> What are some invitations I might extend that would let teachers experience the close interplay between writing and reading so necessary for writing to evolve?

I was attempting to connect reading and writing but Beth's students offered me little to draw on. I can see how, if I were their teacher, I would want to read to them a lot. But more than that. I'd want to engage the children in discussing questions like: How can you tell who the heroine is? How does the author make the story funny? How does the author let you know what's likely to come next? I'd want to ask similar types of question about non-fiction texts. And I'd want to help the children discuss their own writing in this same analytic way.

As I think about building closer reading/writing connections for the children I consider the Summer Institute. I clearly need to help teachers explore how to wed writing and reading much more closely. Could I build closer writing/ reading connections with a group of teachers? Could I help them find solutions to their writing dilemmas through reading?

❖

Up to this point, I haven't known how to shape the Summer Institute. I realize on my way home from Beth's class that it is time to explore writing/reading relationships overtly with a group of teachers.

Now that I have a curricular focus for the Institute—helping people understand the intricate relationship between reading, writing, learning and talking—I begin to think about ways of structuring the experience.

> *What could we read to start us off as a group and how*
> *will we share our interpretations?*
> *What sorts of writing would be helpful and how can*
> *we work collaboratively on that writing?*
> *How might I promote the interplay of writing and*
> *reading and of reading and writing?*

Over a period of weeks I reread books and articles trying to choose a few items that might raise questions about how writing and reading are learned and how we might teach them. In the end, I choose five[1]:

"Reading Like a Writer" by Frank Smith (1983). Smith's discussion of the incidental influences of reading on writing has had an important impact on how I think about reading/writing connections. This article made me question the kinds of reading I offered students and how I can help people make connections with their current as well as past reading of books, stories, poetry, and professional articles. This article, I hope, will raise some useful questions about how reading and writing are related.

"A Writer and an Author Collaborate" by Wayne Serebrin (1986). Serebrin relates a brief incident with a seven-year-old student having difficulty writing. His simple question to Kristin had a powerful impact on how I saw myself as teacher bringing students' experiences with reading to bear on their writing. This article might let the teachers think about different ways of connecting writing and reading.

---

[1] Because these five articles feature prominently in the conversations that follow I have included them in an Appendix.

"'Could you put in lots of holes?' Modes of Response to Writing" by Russ Hunt (1987). Hunt's distinction between 'mockingbird' and 'chipmunk' responses to writing is a powerful metaphor which helped me watch my own questioning during conversations about writing. I'm including this article to raise issues about responding to students' writing.

"Teacher as Partner in the Writing Process" by Nina Mikkelsen (1984). Mikkelsen's article is a funny account of her personal struggle to "find" her own story. While I no longer have a dreadful time choosing topics for myself I suspect the teachers attending the Institute will experience some fear at having to find something of their own to write about. This article should offer them moral support.

I had trouble choosing between this article and Mimi Schwartz's "Wearing the Shoe on the Other Foot: Teacher as Student Writer" (1989). The Institute teachers would find Schwartz's struggles with learning to write narrative interesting. I think I'll make her article available but not send it in advance.

"The Risks of Whole Language Literacy: Alienation and Connection" by Susan Harman and Carole Edelsky (1989). This Harman/Edelsky article had a powerful impact on me as a teacher. It made me consider the political consequences of my pedagogy. Not only can instruction based on a whole language philosophy create alienation for students by separating them from their cultural community, I know, if I'm successful, the teachers I teach may find themselves cut off from fellow teachers.

I also decide to send **Experience and Education** by John Dewey (1938) for everyone to read. Although Dewey doesn't use the term **transaction** in this slim book, his description of **experience** raised some provocative questions for me about the learning/teaching situations I try to create. I think the teachers will find it interesting to see that current ideas have a distinguished heritage.

❖

I'd like to send two other articles in advance but I'm faced with an interesting problem. The five readings I've selected all appear in periodicals which allow me to make copies for educational purposes. The two others I'd like to include are book chapters and, as often happens, it's too late to write for permission to reproduce them. I have some choices. I could duplicate the chapters anyway. I could make a single copy and have everyone copy it themselves; or I could offer the books to someone when the opportunity presents itself and mention them to the class as something useful to read. I decide on the latter strategy. The chapters may not get read by everyone but the ideas I'd like to introduce should make it into the conversation.

This matter of copyright in Canada has become a serious problem for me as a teacher. In order to build shared experience and to establish a sense of collective purpose it's important to have people read some of the same material. I can manage common readings if I choose articles from professional journals which allow reproduction (those published, for example, by the National Council of Teachers of English and the International Reading Association do). However, lots of material the teachers might find useful appear in sources which don't waive copyright so I can't take a book that's just arrived and share a chapter. The problem causes me endless frustration particularly because I would like our discussion to be as current as it can be.

This copyright issue, on the other hand, has been useful in that it has compelled me to consider the role of reading in my classroom. I've been forced to think about the kinds of reading people might do, whether it needs to be common, whether I want to retain sole responsibility for selecting material, and so on. Russ Hunt (1989) has written about an alternative he uses with his undergraduate English classes. He sends his students to the library to scout out books and articles for the class to read. In groups they present written recommendations about original source material, literary histories, textbook anthologies, critical and historical writing about the period and about authors and their work. Certain works are agreed on as needing to be read by everyone. Other works will be reported on by groups and individuals.

I've been moving toward such collaborative investigation for a while but my problem has been that my students are all working teachers barely able to attend class. In order to facilitate our exploration of writing, I've generally selected most of the reading material myself. During the Institute, however, with the teachers able to devote their full attention to the enterprise, I will have an opportunity to open things up.

I write a letter to accompany the readings. In it I share my sense of what the Institute experience might involve.

June 7

Dear Theresa, Bruce, Barb, Norma, Hanna, Debra, Lorna, Cathy, Maggie, Janice, Connie, Shelagh, Michael, Diane, Helen, Leslie, Carmina, Penny, Earl, and Susan

I am writing to welcome you to the MSVU Summer Institute and to say I am looking forward to having you in the Writing/Reading Relationships Workshop.

I know you are probably coming to the Institute expecting to learn how to teach writing and reading. However, while I expect you'll have a better idea about literacy development and writing and reading instruction by the end of our experience, the point of this workshop is to help you learn about writing and reading first hand. Your learning about how to teach writing and reading will come from three sorts of experiences:

1) from trying to make sense of the issues and disagreements in the research literature by writing about whatever seems to strike you as interesting or controversial;

2) by engaging in written conversations with each other about what you are experiencing through the reading and writing you are doing; and

3) from being writers as well as readers of one another's writing.

> This letter made me think about something that has recently started to bother me about my own teaching: there are few turnabouts implied in what I write to my classes. I'm not inviting people to respond to me: it's pretty monological discourse. You clearly do a lot more of that than I do. I get preoccupied with getting them to respond to each other, but it's not really occurred to me before that I might be able to get written dialogue going more powerfully by initiating it with me— maybe I'm scared of the amount of writing I'd wind up having to do.
>
> Russ Hunt

As you become familiar with the debates in the research literature and how they relate to your own writing, as you become more relaxed about writing, and as you reflect on your pedagogical assumptions you will see things you might try with your students. But first and foremost you will be learning about writing and reading by writing yourself and by reacting to one another's writing. So, be prepared for a lot of writing. We will be freewriting. We will write about and share our responses to readings as well as our in-class experiences with one another. We will work on some writing for an audience beyond our workshop group.

In preparation for the first day, I would like you to read the five articles and John Dewey's **Education and Experience** I've sent you. After you've finished reading the stuff, write a response reflecting on the issues they raise for you. Try a freewrite in which you **explore connections among the readings and to your own experience as writer, reader, learner, and teacher**. Bring **two** copies of your response: one for me to read, one for someone else in the group. Thereafter, there will be time each day for reflecting in writing on this learning experience and for sharing and responding to one another's reflections. This sharing of one another's ideas in writing will be an important part of the collaborative learning context we'll be attempting to build.

Now comes the tough part. Grading. The workshop will take considerable engagement. You will be doing a lot of reading, writing, and reflecting. I will be responding to you in a variety of ways but I won't be grading anything. That doesn't mean I won't be evaluating your efforts—I couldn't function as a teacher if I weren't making judgements about how I think you're doing. I will be evaluating, but only in so far as that evaluation allows me to support your writing/ reading efforts. Because I want to encourage you to explore your vulnerabilities what I've decided to do is give you an "A" at the outset and say as Donald Murray does "Now earn it." Should I sense you aren't giving the Institute your best shot, I'll tell you clearly and directly and we will discuss the matter of a grade should it become necessary (I don't anticipate it will).

This Institute workshop is really about learning and teaching. It's about becoming aware of our learning and considering what implications this has for us as teachers. What I'm asking you to do is become aware of the learning context I'm trying to create for you and its effect on you as a learner. I realize I'm asking you to take some risks in ways you might not have tried before, so let me assure you that this will be a **just try** experience.

Welcome aboard. I look forward to having you in the group.

Judith

❖

There are a variety of other preparations to make. I want an in-class library. I assemble some books from my personal collection, books that have helped me reflect on my own teaching. As I think of issues I select new titles and add them to the growing pile on the floor of my study. I end up with over a hundred recently published books. I also have an evolving collection of articles that people have brought in to share for other courses. I screen the articles, removing duplicates and any that have no source citation. I make arrangements with the University library to borrow all the issues of **Language Arts** for the past ten years. I want the journal to be in our classroom so people have immediate access to it. Although the library doesn't usually circulate periodicals, the chief librarian is willing to lend the issues for a two-week period provided I guard them with my life.

I'm aware that I've done a lot of the preliminary selection here, but I've made a point of including materials that represent divergent points of view. I don't have to agree with everything an article or book espouses in order to include it in the library collection; in fact, I include quite a lot of material I disagree with. I try to juxtapose arguments so people are encouraged to examine their own beliefs.

I want to make available a reasonably rich in-class library of books, articles, and periodicals. I have a number of reasons for doing that. First, and most important, I'm trying to create a situation analogous to the kind of small group and independent activity setup that teachers could contemplate for their own classrooms. Second, we have a limited amount of time to explore writing/reading relationships. Having many materials close at hand should encourage a more open, in-depth exploration. So while I've preselected a lot of reading material, I'm really only looking for a way of initiating conversation—I will invite the teachers to contribute material as soon as we're underway.

Because this is a writing/reading experience I also look for some possible novels, short stories, critical incidents, poetry, children's books, magazines, newspaper editorials, and factual pieces; anything I think might be engaging. I collect a variety of children's books from my own library and from our Curriculum Resources Centre. For several weeks I browse through bookstores looking for short stories. Less familiar with poetry, I borrow some anthologies from friends who are English teachers. I'm trying to build up a wide variety of resources in case we might want them.

During last winter's class I discovered just how far afield we might want to go. As one of our collaborative projects, we'd written and published a collection of short stories. In response to the collection, Joanne, one of the teachers, had suggested we write reviews of one another's stories. The following week we each arrived with a couple of book reviews from magazines and newspapers to discuss. We wrote our reviews based on what we'd discovered from reading reviews. This summer, we could well find ourselves in a similar situation and I feel I should be prepared for that and other possibilities.

Thinking about reading is only a part of my initial preparation. I consider my assumptions and how we might implement them in a writing context. I start by listing some potential writing invitations:

a reading/writing log in which to track what happens
    as we read and write,
some freewriting,
some short narrative pieces,
reflective writing in the form of correspondence,
notes and memos—me to them, them to me, and to
    one another.

All of us will use some of these forms of writing. I intend asking everyone to try freewriting, to keep a journal/log, to dialogue with me and at least one other person through writing. Other kinds of writing will be up to them. I also want to invite everyone to tackle an unfamiliar genre: poetry, a short story, an editorial, a journalistic piece, perhaps a children's book, a professional article—something they've not tried to write before. The point of our enterprise will be to use our writing/reading experiences to help us think about learning and teaching.

In addition to planning reading and writing experiences, I spend a lot of time considering the physical setup of the class:

will the room layout permit a variety of ways of
    working?
are there places where individuals can work alone?
are there locations for small working groups?
will it be possible for me to bring the entire class
    together to discuss what's been going on, to talk
    about what we've been learning?

where should I put books and other reading
materials?
what about the reference materials?
how shall we organize the collection of children's
and young adult literature as well as professional
books and articles as it grows?
are there plenty of different kinds of writing
materials (pens, different kinds of paper, etc.)
and can we get our hands on them easily?
are the computers readily accessible?
can we move freely between the computers and our
other working locations?

I can't anticipate the kind of working arrangements that will feel comfortable for everyone—we'll want to rearrange furniture and materials to make them more convenient and accessible as we go along.

Finding appropriate classroom space is a big hassle. Most of the classrooms at the University are set up with rows of individual desks facing the front of the room. I need tables and chairs which can be arranged and rearranged as discussion requirements dictate. During the academic year, I do most of my teaching in the Curriculum Resources Centre. The ambiance there is inviting—the shelves filled with books and other resources, the round tables which seat four or five comfortably, the six computers on long tables at the side of the room, the wall of windows that open, all make the Resources Centre a reasonably integrated working space, congenial for conversation. The children's books, the professional journals, the reference curriculum materials are right there so when a question arises it's easy for us to use the resources.

However a colleague will be teaching a computer class while the Institute is in session and needs to use the Resources Centre, so I've had to scout out another location.

Moveable tables are an absolute necessity. I can cope with other limitations: no shelf space, no windows, inadequate electrical outlets, computers elsewhere— but without tables I'm sunk.

A few days before the Institute begins, I arrange the classroom. Room 431, used primarily by the Business Administration Department, has thirty long narrow rectangular tables, in six rows, all facing a blackboard. It's intended to house fifty to sixty students for lecture classes. My first job is to get rid of half of the furniture. I remove fifteen tables, with accompanying chairs, to the hallway. I place them strategically under overhead lights to create some out-of-classroom working space. People will be able to use this furniture, along with the sofas that are already there, when they want a quiet location to work. In the middle of the classroom I create five square tables and place five chairs around each one. I put the remaining tables along the back wall next to the main door for storage space.

I'm trying to set the classroom up in exactly the same way as I would for a group of elementary age students—with working groups and centres for different materials and activities. I know this is unusual—we expect adults not to need a supported learning situation. We systematically strip the environment, forcing older students to track down limited resources and to work on their own. My belief is that if a rich, collaborative environment helps five-year-olds learn, it's also going to help high school and adult students, too. So I go out of my way to make the classroom inviting and supportive. I provide as rich an array of materials as I possibly can. I arrange the furniture so people can work together easily.

I need to think about how this all connects to the six year olds I'll have next year. Seems to me I need to think about setting up a classroom which reflects my beliefs about learning. Some of these 'ways' will be similar to ways I've proceeded in the past—lots of learning centres, lots of talk and sharing, an expectation that they can and will write from day one. However, my new questions for this class include: How do I provide more opportunity for reading-writing connections to happen? How do I set it up for the kids to handle responsibility for classroom goings-on? How can I work in more sharing of myself as a writer and learner? How can I help kids have conversations about their learning and writing?

Lynn Moody

While I'm setting up, I accidentally discover there's an evening class scheduled for this room during our occupancy. That's a problem. I'm intending to take over the space, to make it our home for two weeks. We need to be able to leave the furniture the way we want it, leave materials, books and articles, periodicals, and our personal belongings overnight without having to worry about theft. So I spend some time making alternate arrangements for the intruding class. As an afterthought I acquire a key for the room so we can secure our materials and belongings when we're not there. Finally, I bring the books, articles, and other materials from home.

I spend quite a bit of time thinking about where to locate materials. I want to entice people into the books. I decide to put them on the tables along the wall at the back of the room; people will have to walk past the display every time they enter or leave the

*class. I also want the paper, markers, tape, scissors,
stapler, and three-hole punch (all important writing
tools) to be easily accessible. People should have no
difficulty finding them if they are at the back alongside
the books.*

I've thought about two other resources as well: the
photocopier and the bookstore. The photocopier has become a
necessary tool for me as a teacher. It allows me to make multiple
copies of the reflective letters I share with the class.
Furthermore, I can no longer read without dialoguing with the
author. That means I often need to copy articles and chapters so
I can highlight portions of the text and write in the margins. I
want to engage the teachers in the same kind of reading. So I've
made sure they will be able to purchase cards for the
photocopiers in the building. I suspect the teachers might also
like to own some of the books they'll read. I've placed an order
with the bookstore so they will be able to buy some of the more
popular titles.

I've mentioned computers in passing. They're actually going
to play a substantial role in this Institute. I expect (based on
what occurs in my winter classes) that most of the teachers won't
have much prior computer experi-

> I was struck by the way you said that
> you wanted people to do written dia-
> logue on computers so you could run off
> copies. You can as easily do that with
> typed or handwritten copies, of course,
> if you have easy access to a
> photocopier. I've been thinking for a
> long time that we tend to mix our
> technologies, that Xerox is at least as
> revolutionary a pedagogical technology
> as the computer, but most people
> haven't noticed it. We tend to think of
> the computer as doing things that it
> would be a lot cheaper and simpler to do
> with a photocopier (or fax).
>
> Russ Hunt

ence. So I have to think about the
initial engagement as well as subsequent use. I think about how I
use my computer myself. It isn't
necessarily useful for everything I
do. I find, for example, keeping a
reading/writing log on computer
inhibits my exploration; I prefer
a small hard-covered notebook
which I can carry around with me
and I usually write with a pencil
(maybe some of the teachers
would prefer to think about what's happening as they read and
write directly on computer—I'll suggest they try it and find
out what feels comfortable). I also freewrite more easily with
pencil and paper, perhaps the teachers will too. I'll invite them to
explore. But I will definitely request that we do our written
dialogue journals on computer—that way we can run off
multiple copies and respond to one another's responses easily.
Same with the short narratives, or poetry, or whatever genres
each of them chooses to try. There's no point in composing
something and then recopying it.

> I used computers for the first time last year with my grade 12 general classes. Usually a hard group to motivate, these students took to the computer right away. They learned what they needed to know about computers as they needed to know it, and many of them experienced a degree of fluency in their writing that could not have been achieved with a pen. Knowing that they didn't have to rewrite that final copy made revising and editing much more attractive to them.
>
> Patricia Whidden

We are going to want to write during class time so I book the microcomputer lab on the third floor directly below our classroom. I will want the teachers to start using the computers right away. The Zeniths are equipped with **WordPerfect**. Because I'm not very familiar with that particular word processing software myself, I spend a couple of days preparing a cribsheet for the Institute group. The cribsheet has only a few commands—nothing elaborate, just enough so the teachers can access the word processor, create a document, edit, save, and print it. I also sidestep a number of technical details. I format data disks in advance so people don't have to worry about doing it themselves. We'll get into that kind of computer stuff later once everyone is over their initial fear and feeling more comfortable about using the machine.

Why do I bother bringing computers into our writing/reading/learning enterprise? I can create the learning context I want without using computers. I have often done so when computers haven't been available. However, the technology facilitates the sharing that I want to make an explicit element of the learning situation. It enriches the learning environment by making it easy to use writing for sorting out ideas, for trying out solutions to writing problems, and for sharing our thinking with others. Computers make learning a collaborative venture—one where ideas are communally owned. They also make it easy to take risks, to experiment, to explore ideas in novel ways. Having computers on hand makes it much easier to establish an active community of learners.

The advance preparing is done. Some materials have been selected and are on display. The computers are reserved, disks formatted, and the crib sheets duplicated. The room has been set up. We're ready to begin.

Opening Moves

3 ❖

Well, we're almost ready.

Three weeks before the Institute starts, I get nervous. I've written the participants a letter and sent them five articles and a book to read and respond to. I know we'll be fine once we have some writing and reading in progress but I'm not sure how to start off the first morning.

I discuss the problem with a number of colleagues. I mention my dilemma to Jerry Harste in an electronic mail message. He writes back:

> Try Family Stories. Read **The Relatives Come** (Rylant, 1985). Put on the overhead "What makes this good literature?" Let them discuss. Talk about the simplicity of the story and how Rylant has managed to capture her culture. Invite them to write a Family Story that captures their culture. Break up and explore topics. Draft a family story next day. (I usually take these through revising and editing and publish them as a course publication.) It's a great assignment—students get to know each other and make connections at a level different from any other activity. Sometimes I also use multiple copies of **Sarah, Plain and Tall** (MacLaughlan, 1985) and have them pair up and do a shared reading, a 'say something' kind of activity at the end of each chapter. This is another type of Family Story. Then I invite them to write one or the other. Another way. Read **Nightmare in My Closet** (Mayer, 1968) and then invite them to write about their curricular nightmares—what they are scared of. What is the worst things they can see happening if they tried something new (Sharon Andrews found that teachers in her study had many concerns and that the concerns they had continued to reflect their initial nightmares). Hope this helps.

Harste's ideas are interesting. They'd be great for focusing a day long workshop/inservice session but they don't feel quite right for the extended collaborative experience I want to establish with the Institute group.

I discuss the problem with my friend Sumitra Unia on one of our regular evening walks. Sumitra, a grade 5 teacher, often has interesting insight into my teaching dilemmas.

"Why don't you just start by having them discuss the readings you sent? You don't need an activity to start them off. You've already created your initiating experience haven't you? Why not use it?" she asks.

Sumitra's right. I don't think I realized the full potential of what I was doing when I sent out the articles. I knew I wanted people to have a common basis for opening a discussion. I also wanted the readings to raise some of the problems and issues of creating a reading/ writing learning context. But I didn't appreciate that sending out the articles could, in fact, be my initiating experience. I need to think about that further. What question could I ask to open discussion?

I drop in on Susan Church. "What do I do on Monday morning?" I wail.

"Couldn't you list a number of writing genres and have them decide what kind of writing they'd like to try?"

That won't work. It puts me squarely in front as teacher. I'm laying out my expectations without any negotiation at all. Doing it that way, it's my agenda, not theirs.

On Saturday before the Institute begins I mention my fears in an electronic mail message to Wayne Serebrin:

The Institute starts Monday. Life is going to be hectic. I still don't have an initiating experience—one which will let us take off in different directions, so we can explore a variety of genres as a group. Harste suggested some teacher-directed reading/writing activities, but they're too text-dependent for what I'm wanting to do—they are based on particular texts which would lead to the same kind of writing for the whole group; while I'm wanting some people to have a chance to explore poetry, others short stories, children's books, political cartoons, editorials, professional articles, or whatever they want to try. We've only two weeks to write something and I'm pretty sure, given the rest of the agenda, we'll only manage a single piece of writing through to some kind of completion. I know how to handle the open structure once I get things underway, but I just don't know how to start them off. An idea floating around in my head is based on the readings I sent the teachers six weeks ago—on writing/reading connections. I'm thinking I want them to discuss in small groups what problems as readers and writers these arguments raise for them individually and then to have them consider how they might read/write to see how these problems get dealt with. That would leave the door open for some of them to start by writing, others to start with reading, still others to begin by talking. And the genre stuff is wide open. The more I write about it, the more I think that might actually work.

As I'm writing Wayne, a new mail message arrives from Harste:

> Well, I can't believe it. My best ideas rejected. How's this: have them write about their Best Teaching Moment—any genre. Then have them go see the film **Dead Poets Society** and write on "What is Education?" "What is Curriculum?" "What is teaching?" Need not be finished. (I'm using this in my summer course.)

> ***Dead Poets Society** is playing in town right now and I know I want to incorporate it into the experience but using it to respond to my questions doesn't feel right. I think I have to wait until someone raises an issue that makes my suggesting we all see the film a more natural outcome of our learning enterprise.*

Sunday evening I quickly reread the articles and write a personal response which I will duplicate in the morning and distribute to everyone in the class sometime during the day:

> A fast reaction to the readings. I'm not sure how I respond. Part of the problem is that I've read these articles many times and I have to think about what new insights they hold for me. Perhaps I should just think about why I chose these pieces in the first place.
>
> Smith's 'reading like a writer' notion is a powerful metaphor for thinking about the role reading plays in writing. The temptation for me as a teacher is to force the relationship—I suppose that's been a large part of what English literature courses have actually been about. But the first time I read the article I was struck by Smith's contention that reading like a writer is largely unconscious. I know that's true for me both as reader and writer. What I find interesting is how some aspect of what I'm currently reading pops out at me because I happen to be working on a particular piece of writing. For instance, I noticed this week that the dialogue in the novel I'm reading is enclosed in single, not double, quotes. I've actually read that novel (a six-volume saga) four times over the last decade and never noticed it before. Why did it catch my attention this time? Probably because the writing I'm doing at the moment involves dialogue, which I'm not very experienced at handling, and I've been thinking about how to deal with it. That

kind of thing happens often—I notice something a writer does, I think, specifically because I'm engaged in writing myself.

Is it possible to bring reading into play so that kind of incidental noticing can occur? Serebrin shows me an interesting way to make that reading/writing connection in the classroom. "How does a writer you know do what you're trying to do?" he asks Kristin. His question makes the reading-like-a-writer intentional but that's not a problem, I don't think, because I'm now reading to solve a specific writing problem of my own. I've actually used that strategy a lot myself without realizing that's what I was doing. When I'm stuck, I often look to see how various authors have done something. But I didn't think of asking that question until I had read Serebrin's piece. What's interesting is that this reading like a writer, initially, is propelled by the writing, but what has happened to me is that I have noticed all kinds of other things while I'm reading, things I was struggling with myself on other occasions or which one of the other writers around me is working on.

Learning to respond to other people's writing is another important aspect of a reading/writing classroom. The trouble is, as a teacher, I have to fight the tendency to read as a copy editor; that is, while I read the writing of published writers for meaning I am used to reading students' writing looking for errors. Hunt has made me very aware of the difference between these two kinds of responses. The point of talking through a piece of writing is to help the writer make decisions. Hunt's distinction between 'mockingbird' and 'chipmunk' responses made me realize I have to focus on responding to the intentions, the meaning, of a student's writing and not just surface features.

I've learned most about how to respond to other writers' work by having other people respond to what I've written. Mikkelson's contention is that to be an effective teacher of writing I have to be a writer, too. I have learned about writing by being a writer and by talking about my writing with other writers. I've discovered what sorts of feedback are useful and what kinds of reactions aren't.

And the Harman/Edelsky article raises some interesting questions about my own teaching for me. If I am successful in engaging teachers in my instructional experiences I risk setting them up for alienation. As one teacher wrote me recently: "At our school, there's a standing joke about teachers who go away on sabbatical and come back speaking a new language. I am going to have to watch what I say and avoid the appearance of putting on airs, yet at the same time try to implement what I now believe." Such comments have made me very aware that I have some responsibility for raising this alienation issue.

These, then, are my reactions to the readings. What questions do my musings raise for you?

This isn't quite a freewrite; I've worked at this response a bit, knowing it will serve as a demonstration of what a reflective reaction can be like. Often in my reflective letters to a class I attempt to draw people into conversation about the issues we're exploring. Here I'm more concerned with reflecting on what these articles have had to say to me and what implications I think they have for my teaching. I don't want to lay out rules for doing reflective writing; instead, I prefer helping people read like writers.

Monday morning arrives. I watch how people situate themselves around the room. Friends with friends, acquaintances with acquaintances, a few new people by themselves.

People have filled up the tables at the back of the room, leaving a couple of individuals on their own near the front. Since I want the teachers to work in groups of four or five, I consolidate the groups (partly to fill up space and partly to put people in contact with new people) then I ask for help to move the extra furniture to the side of the room out of our way. Although I had planned on having five groups of four, we're now in four groups of five.

Sometimes I ask people to discuss why I've arranged the groups and the working space as I have—I want them to begin thinking about preparing the environment—but I don't remember to do it this time. It's probably just as well. We'll get to that kind of discussion before long and besides I want to connect with the readings as soon as possible.

I welcome everyone to the Institute and ask them to introduce themselves to one another. As the introductions proceed around the room I sense a very mixed group.

Bruce Hussey is an experienced high school English teacher from Bridgewater.

Bruce's wife, a student in a couple of my classes, completed her M.Ed.degree two years ago. I've talked with Bruce before today but this is the first time he and I will be working together.

Theresa Madden, a second grade teacher, has been a participant in a special off-campus M.Ed. program.

These teachers live some distance from the city and MSVU faculty have been commuting to meet with them on a regular basis for two years now. I haven't taught the group myself. I'm looking forward to working with some of them here in the Institute.

Barb Dunn, also in the off-campus group, teaches grade 4.

From what I've heard I think I can expect these teachers to engage reasonably easily.

Norma Thompson is an elementary reading resource teacher.

Norma and I have worked together for a number of years. Norma's taken courses with me and she's been a member of one of the writing groups I initiated a while back so she and I have been in contact with one another frequently. Two winters ago Norma and I both taught sections of an inservice course for teachers. We collaborated closely on the course. We shared resources and met regularly to discuss what was happening with our students. She's moving to a new resource position this coming fall—to work with high school students. She hopes the Institute will help her think through what she might try with those students.

Hanna Whitman teaches grade 5.

Two years ago Hanna used her sabbatical leave to study full-time at MSVU. She was in a couple of my classes. Last year she returned to the classroom and joined a study group which met weekly at my home. She's been struggling all year with a very difficult class. She's attending the Institute "to regain some sense of the possible," she tells us.

Debra Sloven teaches first grade. This is her first course in the M.Ed. program. She's anxious about the whole undertaking. She's at the Institute because a friend of hers, another teacher in her school, has reassured her she'll enjoy the experience. She hopes so.

I note Debra's anxiety. I'll have to be careful not to confront her too quickly. I'll need to let her feel her way and to offer help often.

Lorna MacLean is another new M.Ed. student. She's from the Eastern Shore. A second grade teacher, she's been teaching for a couple of years. She's begun questioning what she's doing in her classroom. She thought taking the Institute would be a good way to begin graduate study.

I take note of Lorna as well. I have a tendency to assume people have been thinking about critical issues in education when they haven't. I'll have to keep an eye on Lorna to make sure I don't push too hard too soon.

Cathy Roche is an elementary school principal.

I had Cathy in a course four years ago. At that time she was struggling to accept a more open view of teaching. Since then she's taken a sabbatical year during which she took a language arts course and a course on hands-on science. I have heard from a teacher on her staff that Cathy's been supportive of his efforts to teach in a more learning-focused way.

Shelagh Bennett is a junior high English teacher.

Shelagh took a couple of my classes two years ago while studying full time in the MSVU graduate education program. Both of us had a rough time. She participated, she read and wrote, but I just wasn't able to help her look at herself more reflectively. I had the feeling our discussion raised no personal questions for her. I pushed her on a couple of occasions which upset her. We talked about what I was trying to help her explore. I suggested she read the reflections of some of the teachers who were looking at themselves with new eyes. But I was never really able to help her examine contradictions between her own belief and practice. I find it interesting that she's here. I wonder what she expects from this two-week experience.

Maggie Harris is a close friend of Shelagh's. They've been teaching in the same junior high school for a number of years. Maggie also teaches English.

Maggie was in one of my classes last winter. I enjoyed her participation a great deal. Our written conversations were full of surprises for both of us. Without any nudging from me, Maggie engaged in some wonderful analysis of her teaching. She was able to use a reflective mirror to great advantage. Each week she wrote about how some small insight affected the way her students were learning. I'm glad she's here. Perhaps her critical reflection will help Shelagh become more open to examining assumptions.

Janice Cody teaches grade 4.

I know nothing about her. She's taken some courses in the graduate program. She seems reasonably comfortable.

Connie Carpenter. Another teacher in the off-campus M.Ed. group.

Connie looks like a quiet one.

Michael Jordan teaches fifth grade in the Valley.

Michael's sitting with his arms folded carefully across his body. This one might not be so easy to engage.

Diane Wilkes is a third grade teacher from the Northumberland Shore.

Diane has taken other graduate courses at MSVU so she shouldn't be too apprehensive.

Leslie Merchant, also a third grade teacher, took an under-graduate language arts course last winter; this is her first graduate course.

I can hear the nervousness in her voice. I'll have to keep an eye on her.

Helen Sullivan, from Newfoundland, is a reading resource teacher. This is her first course in the graduate education program.

There's a good deal of Newfoundland in her speech and she has a wonderful smile. I think I'm going to enjoy her.

Carmina Cluett is a first year, first grade teacher.

*This one reminds me of Tigger from **Winnie the Pooh**—bouncy. Wonder how much reflection we'll get here?*

Penny Slaunwhite, from Truro, also teaches first grade. She's been participating in the science education project in her school. She's seen close connections between what they've been learning about science teaching and language arts. Time to explore writing, she feels.

It should be interesting to draw out parallels between hands-on science and the reading/writing we'll be doing. It might help the others make some useful connections about learning in general.

Earl Quinlan, a teaching principal, works with grade 5 students. He has taken graduate courses at MSVU for the past two summers.

His Cape Breton accent is noticeable. A small wiry man, he emanates a sense of mischief. Earl should be fun.

Susan Church is also present. I have invited her to participate with us for as much of the two weeks as she can manage.

Susan and I have been friends and colleagues for more than ten years. She was a junior high reading resource teacher when I first met her. In addition to working with students having difficulty reading and writing, Susan helped fellow teachers think about literacy instruction in more transactional ways. Five years ago she became a curriculum supervisor. She's worked hard at developing support resources for elementary as well as junior and senior high school teachers in her sub-system. I'm looking forward to having her with us; I can count on her to ask probing questions.

That's the entire group. I know a number of people from previous courses, some of the teachers have completed their M.Ed. degree and have returned to keep abreast of the research literature, others are members of the off-campus program. A quarter of the participants are taking their first graduate course— they have no idea what to expect.

I often wonder whether it's useful to have people introduce themselves, but this time, because I have made notes as I listened, I've learned some useful things about the teachers. This introduction time has given me a place to start. I now have a sense of where to look for openings to push and where to tread more cautiously.

Introductions over, I hand out a small collection of short stories and poems, as well as a couple of additional articles I think might be useful for us to read. I also hand out cribsheets for the word processor along with the floppy disk I formatted in advance. I suggest the teachers put the computer stuff aside for the time being.

A typical teaching blunder—handing things out at the wrong moment. I should have waited until after lunch just before we used the computers.

I check whether they have a written response to the readings. I don't collect their responses at that moment, but I ask them to leave them with me by the end of the day so I can read them.

"I will leave anything I have for you on the table by the door so you can pick it up as you come in. It's a good idea to check that location in the morning and again after lunch," I tell them. "In fact, I'll leave my response to the readings there for you this afternoon. I'd like you to react and return it to me tomorrow."

I'm actually asking people to write back to me directly on my response. I've left a wide right margin so there's room to write. By writing about what I'm reading myself, and by having the teachers respond to my writing, I'm trying to become a legitimate member of the writing community I'm working to build. I have a secondary purpose for responding and sharing my writing. When my ideas, questions, and concerns enter the conversation via this informal route they carry less authority.

"Oh, by the way, about copying materials. There are a number of photocopying machines in this building—one around the corner on this floor and two downstairs. You'll need a credit card to operate them; you can buy one at the secretarial office. Also visit the bookstore at lunch time. I've ordered some books you might want to look at."

These opening activities have taken more time than I thought they would; they always do. I keep thinking of them as preliminaries; but they're not. Introducing ourselves and dealing with procedural matters sets the tone for everything that follows. If I rush through this stuff I leave everyone feeling overwhelmed and I don't want that.

Now to discussion. I invite people, in their small groups, to talk about some of the issues raised by the readings. I purposely busy myself straightening up the piles of handouts, unpacking my belongings for the day, etc. I want to give people time to talk to one another before I enter the conversation. I eavesdrop, however, while I'm going about my business trying to hear what's being said at each table as I pass by.

I used to feel very uncomfortable staying out of the discussion but I've seen that if I enter it too quickly I shut down the conversation. So I've learned to occupy myself—sometimes even leaving the room to pick up my mail, just so I'm not hanging around.

I organize things for perhaps ten minutes before I join one of the conversations. With my notebook in hand, I kneel beside the table and listen for a while. I jot a few phrases. This group is talking about the issue of alienation raised by Harman and Edelsky. They're exploring what it means to have "a democratic relationship both between the student and the teacher, and between the student and the material" (p. 397). I listen briefly, then move on.

> *I'm just trying to get a feel for where people are so I listen only long enough to get a sense of the discussion.*

At the second table the teachers are talking about conferencing. Someone has voiced frustration at not knowing how to respond to kids' writing. "Talk to me about how you got here," I ask.

Leslie offers a synopsis. The Hunt article made her question the way she's been responding to her students' writing.

"Definitely as a mockingbird," she says.

"That's right," pipes in Norma, "I'm good at telling the kids what's wrong with their writing. I just don't know what else to say."

"What did you get from Hunt's chipmunk responses?" I ask. "Can you describe how they're different from the mocking-bird's?"

I listen as they articulate some differences.

"Well, the chipmunk tells the bat just how scared the poem makes him feel. He's letting the bat know what effect his poem has," Barb says.

"The mockingbird gives him technical information. I suppose he's trying to teach him about rhyme schemes and metre," Theresa adds.

"Which would be more helpful for you as a writer?"

"Wouldn't the mockingbird's comments help the bat understand how poems are constructed better?" Michael asks me.

"I don't think so," Barb answers him. "I think I might find it more useful to know that the part I tried to make scary worked.

"How does the bat feel about the mockingbird's response?" I wonder.

"It didn't help him. Even though the mockingbird said he liked the poem, the bat felt terrible. 'Why do I care how many feet it has?' the bat says to himself. He really wants some kind of gut reaction to his poem."

"How does Hunt's distinction between chipmunk and mockingbird responses help you think about your own responding to children's writing?"

> *I'm not expecting the teachers to be able to answer my question—they won't fully appreciate the distinction between mockingbird and chipmunk kinds of*

responses until they begin responding to one another's writing, but I'm asking it right now to raise questions about their own teaching.

I join each of the other groups for a few moments. My sense is people are trying to figure out what it is I want them to discuss. Although they don't ask me what I want directly, I can tell, by the way they address their questions and comments to me, they'd like more specific direction. However, I refrain from telling them what to do. Instead, I listen and ask questions to help people probe the issues in more depth.

I actually have no carefully itemized lesson plan for the day. All I've written in my notebook is
> develop a focus

My intention is to encourage each teacher to find his or her own direction. The articles raise important issues for me but I need to find out what issues they raise for the teachers. That's why I haven't distributed my written response yet. It's their articulation of issues that will serve as our point of departure. So I have to let them talk, and listen to what they are saying.

On my second round, each visit is brief. I ask directly "What is one major concern these articles raise for each of you?"

Although I'm trying to help the teachers find a personal focus, my question adds to the confusion somewhat. What do I mean by a major concern? Are they supposed to agree on a concern as a group?

"Since this two-week learning experience will be so condensed," I explain, "you will only be able to explore one major idea or issue in that time. I'm trying to help each of you find an issue or concern to focus your reading and writing during the coming two weeks."

I want to help each person zero in on a question of their own to pursue during the Institute. My reason for having a wide range of books, articles, periodicals, children's and young adult books, short stories and poetry on hand is to support their many different investigations.

As I move from group to group I am trying both to sustain the conversation and to shape it a little at the same time. I have one eye on the clock. I would like to reach a tentative closure point by lunch time, in a little less than an hour. By then, I'd like each teacher to have identified an area of concern she or he wants to explore in some fashion.

I know my expectation is unreasonable. It generally takes several classes for students to establish an individual focus. I'm not really expecting these Institute people to commit themselves to a particular issue yet. I'm really only trying to help them articulate a general direction.

❖

I step back for a few moments, watching to see how people are working. Is anyone not engaged? Are people keeping track of the discussion by taking notes? I haven't asked that they record the conversation. I want to find out if that's something people will do on their own.

The conversation is animated in all four groups but I don't observe much spontaneous writing occurring. I write in my notebook:

Tuesday:
—mention reading / writing / thinking with a pencil in hand

That will give me an opportunity to raise note-making and collaborative versus co-operative learning.

I wait a few minutes more then address the whole group. "Have you decided what you'd like to focus on?"

Nods of assent seem to indicate we're further than I thought we might be.

I make notes as people respond around the room.

Earl:	comprehension
Diane:	getting ideas on paper
Helen:	responding to writing
Leslie:	(not sure yet)
Lorna:	responding to writing
Norma:	how to create a social context for reading/writing
Shelagh:	evaluation
Cathy:	students experiences as writers
Penny:	dealing with writing anxiety
Maggie:	writing anxiety
Hanna:	how to hold conversations about children's books
Debra:	what's involved in seeing self as a writer
Bruce:	influence of reading on writing
Janice:	responding to writing
Connie:	(no question yet)
Michael:	wants to find out more about reading like a writer

Barb:	writing anxiety
Theresa:	seeing self as a writer
Carmina:	role of grammar
Susan:	orchestrating the teaching event

I read the list back to them identifying common interests:

> responding to writing
> dealing with writing anxiety, both our own and students'
> the role of grammar and conventions in writing/reading
> creating the social context for learning
> role of reading, using children's books, for developing writing.

'Pressure to keep moving.' This, I think, is the origin of my 'orthodoxies. I experience one successful approach and since I have learned through it, the process is shoved onto other classes. The kids aren't stupid; they fall into line and give me what they think I want and I mistake it for learning. What was in the first instance a genuine exploration becomes ritual because I didn't feel I had the time to begin from scratch with the other classes. Time: the enemy of real learning.

Pat Kidd

I should have recorded their interests on the blackboard as they were offering them and then asked the groups to identify half-a-dozen common interests. The categories would have been their own and not mine. But I was feeling some pressure to keep moving.

My next question to the teachers is "How do you see yourself pursuing these various interests?" I invite them to discuss in their groups how they might individually proceed.

This is the point at which my major intention comes into play. In my opening letter I made several references to them being writers and readers: "...you will be learning about writing by writing yourself and by reacting to one another's writing." I could have simply directed them to select a writing genre and begin writing. I choose not to do that because I would like our multiple agendas to connect more naturally. I would like the teachers to realize they discover a great deal about writing and reading by investigating themselves in the process of writing and reading. Most of these teachers still believe the answers to their questions about teaching, to the kinds of concerns they've articulated, are to be found in the writing of experts; someone else will tell them the 'right' thing to do. While the experts do have interesting and important things to say about how language is learned, about successful language use, and the evolution of literacy, I'm convinced teachers need to see their own experiences—as teachers, and as writers and readers—as valid and important for understanding literacy development and literacy instruction.

The teachers, in their groups, discuss ways of dealing with their questions. I listen briefly at one table. I move on to a second. Hanna mentions various authors she's read and what they have had to say about helping kids develop their writing. Her concern is that she's never written a children's story herself.

"I really feel uncomfortable trying to help my kids write. I'm never sure what strategies to suggest."

"Do you write along with them?"

"Oh, I could never do that," she replies.

"Why not?"

"I don't have anything to write about," she tells me.

"I actually don't believe that. I have no doubt that you've had all kinds of experiences that would make interesting children's stories."

"I wouldn't know where to begin," she says.

"You might want to try writing a children's story here, then, to see what you can learn."

"Oh, gracious. How would I start?" Hanna asks.

"How about reading some children's books? There's a pile on the table at the back and there are more in the Resources Centre. It wouldn't take you long to generate several plausible ideas."

"But I've never done anything like that. It terrifies me."

"I can understand that. I imagine, though, you'd find you'd have a much better sense of how to help your students when they're writing if you tackled a project like this."

"You're right. I guess I'll try."

I make note of the trepidation on Hanna's face.

"What about the rest of you?" I ask.

This conversation is repeated, with variations, at each table in turn. I check the clock—fifteen minutes till lunch. Time to do a fast class check.

I know most people haven't decided what to work on, however it's nearly lunch time and I'd like us to break with a sense of how far we've come and where we're going. A quick class check lets people hear one another. It validates what's been going on and provides a bit of structure. Hearing other people's ideas usually helps the uncommitted to make a decision.

"Let's hear what you've decided to try."

Bruce: a short story.

Norma: me, too.

Janice: I'm terrified of poetry; I'm going to try writing a poem.

Cathy: I'll join Janice.

Barb: I want to try a professional article.

Hanna: a children's book.

Theresa: yes, I think I'll try a children's book as well.

Several of the teachers haven't made up their minds. That's OK. I'm asking them to jump into deep water and many aren't sure they can swim.

"What I need is a lifeguard," says Earl.

"I'm watching out for you," I tell him.

"But will you be able to get to me in time if I'm drowning?"

"I'm keeping a close look-out. I've been lifeguarding a long time and have a pretty good idea where the undertow is." Earl laughs.

"I don't want to pressure you, but we can't really engage in meaningful conversation, I can't help you out, until you have something going. I'm dependent on you taking the lead. We have to get some writing and reading underway as quickly as possible so we can see what kinds of problems arise. Think about it and see what you come up with."

As the group leaves for lunch I reflect a moment.

*I was able to get us started but I forgot to ask a crucial question, "What's been going on here?" An important aspect of helping teachers become reflective, I've discovered recently, is asking them to think about **our** particular teaching/learning situation. I have to help them get inside both **their** learning and **my** teaching. When we're successful their learning strategies, their decisions about proceeding as well as my planning, my intentions, the structure of the class, the situational support are all transparent. I have to put that stuff on the table and help the teachers examine it.*

In large letters I write in my notebook

What's going on here?

We won't get to that question this afternoon; dealing with the computers will be more than enough. But I must find a way of working it in tomorrow.

Reflection, I've learned, is at the heart of teaching. According to Donald Schön (1987):

> We may reflect **on** action, thinking back on what we have done in order to discover how our knowing-in-action may have contributed to an unexpected outcome. We may do so after the fact...or we may pause in the midst of action to..."stop and think." In either case, our reflection has no direct connection to present action. Alternatively, we may reflect in the midst of action without interrupting it. In an **action-present**— a period of time, variable with the context, during which we can still make a difference to the situation at hand—our thinking serves to reshape what we are doing while we are doing it. I shall say, in cases like this, that we reflect-**in**-action (p.26).

I am attempting a difficult move here—not only to reflect-in-action myself, but to draw the teachers into reflecting. This reflection-in-action, I'm learning, involves not only noticing critical moments when they occur, but thinking about them subsequently in ways which permit me to adjust the on-going learning situation. This reflection-in-action serves an important function: it forces me to examine my assumptions, my intentions, and my instructional invitations critically. I have to think about where we are at the moment, what problems have arisen or what unexpected opportunities have just presented themselves. I may, as I reflect, restructure my strategies for action, or my understanding of what's going on, or I may reframe the situation. At this moment, as I bring the morning to a close, I note that I haven't made an opening for the teachers to reflect. I restructure my strategies for action by reminding myself to ask "What's going on here?" later.

In fact, after lunch, I ask the teachers to reflect briefly in writing. I ask them to think about one thing that surprised them this morning and why they think it surprised them. I write, too.

> This morning has been interesting. People began in a safe place with the issues raised by the readings—by creating a distance from themselves—"if **one** wants to..." as opposed to "if **I** want to..."—with judicious input from me, we've moved to a more personal focus— "**I** think..."—and some sense of being willing to tackle a piece of writing of some sort.
>
> We've accomplished two things this morning: people have identified a tentative focus for themselves and they've begun to think about ways of exploring writing. Both of these foci will allow us to regroup. I can see potential for genre-based groups and for issue-based groups. Tomorrow, I think I'll suggest a genre-based emphasis. That way they'll be able to support one another as they begin working on some writing.

Now I'm feeling a stronger sense of direction. Time is really a factor here. I needed to get us off the ground, but not too fast and not by forcing my agenda on them. I think we've managed to get where we can now work on this global agenda and people still feel commitment to their own questions.

Susan Church shares her reflection on the morning's experience with me:

It's been interesting eavesdropping on this session. I enjoyed watching Judith's orchestration. She had a very clearly defined agenda yet she let the underlying structure rather than her overt direction carry that agenda. She actively intervened in the process when learners seemed to be experiencing frustration; she stood back and let the process evolve when the struggle seemed to be productive. Judith is getting better and better at living with the learners' initial confusion and lack of direction—that's the toughest part of all this—the overwhelming desire is to jump in and "fix" things by taking control.

> Standing back is the hardest thing to do. But now I question whether there is a point that is too far back, that appears to the learner to be abdication. Among my junior high students there are many 'Earl's who are insecure. I realize if I jump in I rob them of an opportunity to find out for themselves; but it seems to me they need some assistance to start them off. I suppose deciding when to stand back or intervene depends on knowing the learners.
>
> Pat Kidd

❖

The issues of power/control and intervention are central to this Institute enterprise. I am forever struggling with them. Susan's comments evoke a memorable incident. A couple of years ago, while I was waiting in the Toronto airport between flights, I became aware of a twenty-month-old girl and her mother near me. The child was the wandering sort; she ventured a good distance from Mum without regard for where or how far she was going. Mother would let her travel a short distance; then she would call the child to return. When the child disregarded her, Mum would dash after her, pick her up, and bring her back to where their belongings were stashed, the child struggling and now screaming loudly.

This performance was repeated at least a dozen times in the hour or so before we boarded the plane. Each time she took off,

I noticed the child glance at Mum with a look that said, "This game is fun!" As I watched, I thought to myself, "Mum should really let this child get lost." By that I mean, Mum should have appeared to pay little attention to her daughter's wanderings, and when the child had wandered far enough away, followed at a safe distance, careful not to be seen so the child would have the experience of actually realizing herself to be on her own with no Mum in sight. It would have been quite safe to have let the child wander; early afternoon, mid-week, the airport was relatively deserted. What was clear to me was how Mum, by being so careful not to let her daughter wander too far, was actually teaching her how **not** to be responsible for herself.

The incident made me think about teaching. How often do we let students actually get lost? It seems to me as teachers we spend much of our time creating safe situations in which learners are prevented from making mistakes rather than letting mistakes happen so strategies for dealing with problems can be raised and discussed. I recall vividly an undergraduate language arts class I taught a couple of years ago. We were investigating mealworms. I kept trying to encourage the students to watch and handle the creatures to see what they could find out but the majority of the class persisted in avoiding the animals and simply read about insects in books—neither doing Science nor using language for learning in any significant way.

I attempted repeatedly to redirect the students' efforts before deciding they needed to make the mistake so they could understand the difference between doing dummy run science and really engaging in a scientific investigation and using language for learning. Because we were still in the middle of term and had several weeks yet in which to work things out, I decided to let the groups complete their "projects," do their presentations, then

---

I love the notion of getting lost. The woman at the airport is a really powerful example in lots of ways—she comes back to the notion of a prepared environment, for example. The airport's not 'prepared,' obviously, but you can take advantage of it as though it were. What you do is make sure the kid doesn't really get lost, but in another sense really is lost. And that's more likely to happen in a real environment. I think it's true that teaching is dangerous, that you really have to run the the risk that sometimes someone might actually get lost. An interesting parallel. I had some students in my eighteenth-century literature class a few years ago who selected Samuel Butler as the writer they were going to explore. When they came to report, it was obvious they'd picked the wrong Samuel Butler. It was only after they'd had the rest of the class read what they'd written that they realized what they'd done. Powerful lesson, that. But it wouldn't have been so powerful if I'd said before I distributed the report that they had the wrong man. Was I being dishonest by simply copying their report (in fact I did read it and I had noticed)?

Russ Hunt

I pointed out some problems with what they'd done. "Where's the beef?" I asked them.

Had this been the end of term I would have let well enough alone. The reason I pushed the issue was that we still had ample time to explore language for learning in greater depth.

The students were very angry. In their view I'd led them down a garden path—I'd wasted their time. But, in fact, their time hadn't been wasted at all; at least I didn't think it had been. The students now had an opportunity to examine what they had done and to think about the many roles of language for learning. We immediately engaged in a number of new investigative projects and this time people really did investigate. By the end of term the students had come to understand that science and language arts aren't separate subjects; they began to appreciate that language is a tool for learning about the world and they experienced first hand what this meant in the classroom.

Although I've often discussed with teachers the positive value of mistakes, I hadn't fully appreciated their importance both for helping learners assume responsibility for learning and for assisting them to develop productive problem-solving strategies. The airport incident in conjunction with this retrospective look at a classroom experience of my own have helped me see more clearly why getting lost is a necessary part of learning.

I didn't actually let the Institute teachers get lost this morning; I did, however, let them cope with their confusion and frustration until, with assistance they were able to sort out some directions for themselves. If I'm going to help people assume responsibility for their own learning, I do have to stay out of their way for a while. I think Earl's 'lifeguard' metaphor is apt. The lifeguard is nearby watching to make sure no one drowns. And yet there are limitations to teaching as lifeguarding. A teacher, I think, must also be swim coach—supporting, encouraging, and challenging the swimmers to stretch themselves. A teacher must be a pool architect, too.

My colleague Allan Neilsen (1989) discusses the control/intervention issue in an interesting way. He points out

One of the most disturbing interpretations of learner-centered education is the one which sees any action on the part of the teacher as interference with the student's right to be independent and to determine her own destiny. When accepted uncritically, this notion can cause teachers to feel sufficiently guilty or at least sufficiently uncertain about their role to become paralyzed into inaction. They not only 'back off' for fear of being interventionist, but in effect, often back right out of the classroom.

Independence is learned; it doesn't just 'happen' by leaving students on their own. During [any new] exploration..., it is likely that the teacher will need to be quite actively involved in helping learners identify consequential issues, problems, and tasks and in helping develop effective strategies for examining the issues, solving the problems, and completing the tasks (p. 21).

I've thought about my teaching role a great deal lately. I'm beginning to understand how extending invitations or preparing the environment is only a start. I also have to think about how to sustain engagement, how to support students' struggles, how to celebrate their accomplishments, as well as help them examine their strategies more closely.

This morning I attempted to initiate a new experience for all of us. Despite prior planning, my teaching efforts were mainly directed at responding to the teachers' interests, concerns, and anxieties. While it might have appeared to be a rather loose learning situation to some of the teachers, I was heavily involved in sustaining the discussion, helping people find a focus, constantly evaluating what they were doing and saying. I had to resist taking control, but I also had to avoid backing out of the room.

During the afternoon, we spend a good part of our time at the computers. Susan Church, Norma, Hanna, Shelagh, Michael and Penny are competent computer users; the other teachers have little or no hands-on experience. Although these days more people are familiar with computers these teachers are predominantly novices and they're scared. That means I have to make them feel comfortable quickly by letting them know they have more resources than they realize.

I begin by asking the teachers to read the cribsheet. I explain that if they follow the directions (which I've simplified to just a few essential commands), they should be able to create, save, print, and retrieve a file quite easily. I invite them to experiment.

WORDPERFECT

WORD PROCESSOR COMMANDS

Using the Computer

To Start:

1. Turn the computer on using the switch on the right side at the back.
2. Turn on the monitor (switch at front right) and printer (switch at top left).
3. When computer prompt appears   **c:**
   insert WordPerfect disk and type **WP** (can be in lower case) <CR> to start WordPerfect. (**<CR> means press the RETURN key**)
4. When WordPerfect is ready, you will find the cursor at the top left of the screen. At the bottom of the screen you will find:
   > your document number
   >
   > your page number
   >
   > your line on that page
   >
   > your character position on that line.

   In order to do the most basic work on a word processor you need to know how to do **FIVE** things:
   > **INPUT** a document
   >
   > **SAVE** the document
   >
   > **RETRIEVE** and **EDIT** the document
   >
   > **PRINT** the document
   >
   > **EXIT** WordPerfect

Once everyone has successfully loaded WordPerfect, I suggest they just start writing.

"How do I get rid of these typing mistakes?" Hanna wants to know.

I show her, then refer to 'Inputting Text' on page 2 on the cribsheet. "There's also more information on page 5: Deleting text."

"Capital letters?" asks Bruce.

"Inputting text, page 2," I point out to him.

We spend about twenty minutes writing. Predictable problems arise: people want to know how to move the cursor, how to delete words, how to insert text, how to centre and underline. I show them, then indicate where to find the specific information they're looking for on the cribsheet. I also suggest they ask a neighbor.

I notice Norma has written a couple of paragraphs.

"This might be a good time to save what you've done," I suggest.

"How do I save with this word processor?" she asks. I show her the information on the cribsheet.

Rather than take everyone through a lengthy explanation about how to do everything they need to know, I have learned to let people's questions arise spontaneously. The answers are available on the cribsheet or from a neighbor and I want people to discover as soon as possible that using the computer is easy; that a little playing around and a question or two will overcome most difficulties they might encounter. (I realize it's not always as easy as that—I've spent days, myself, learning some new applications on my own, but learning enough to output a bit of text is not difficult and with support we'll have documents saved and hardcopy printed out within the hour.)

I move about the computer lab asking questions and encouraging people to help one another out. As soon as someone learns how to do something I identify him or her as a resource to the next person. In this fashion, information diffuses throughout the group as people either need or want to know how to execute various operations. At the end of an hour and a half everyone has learned how to save their text, they have learned to retrieve it, and they have learned how to obtain a printout.

I suggest they write their reflective journal for tomorrow on the computer. I make it clear that I know they are feeling overwhelmed and reassure them I'm not expecting fluent writing or a beautifully formatted product; I am only asking them to try.

When we return to the classroom, I am tempted to launch into another structured activity but I manage to refrain. What people need now is time—so for this last hour I back away from the front of the room. I invite people to relax with a professional book or article or some literature they would like to read, to reflect on some surprises that have occurred during the day, to play on the computer if they want to, or chat with someone else about education issues which concern them.

I pick up my copy of Schön's **Educating the Reflective Practitioner** (1987) and make myself comfortable on one of the sofas in the corridor. Schön's argument is compelling. Students cannot be **taught** what they need to know, but they can be **coached**, he contends.

[They have] to **see** on [their] own behalf and in [their] own way the relations between means and methods employed and results achieved. Nobody else can see for [them], and [they] can't see just by being 'told,' although the right kind of telling may guide [their] seeing and thus help [them] see what [they] need to see (Dewey, 1974, p.151, cited in Schön, p.17).

I highlight the quote because I recognize in Dewey's words a statement of my own belief. I'm trying to create an experience which will allow these Institute participants to see for themselves. I'm trying to initiate a number of enterprises which permit the kinds of problems inherent in our activities to surface naturally so the teachers and I can discuss strategies and outcomes.

Dewey's phrase 'the right kind of telling' makes me uncomfortable. What is the right kind of telling? The word 'telling' evokes transmission—something I've been struggling to distance myself from. Yet I have no problem providing information or suggesting strategies when students ask for help. Asking a question can be the right kind of telling. So can a lecture if it engages the listeners, raising questions, fostering connections in response to the audience's tacit questions. Perhaps I'm reacting to the predominant 'teaching by telling' I see in classrooms everywhere to the exclusion of any other kind of learning engagement.

I continue reading:

...reflection-in-action is a process we can deliver without being able to say what we are doing. Skillful improvisers often become tongue-tied or give obviously inadequate accounts when asked to say what they do. Clearly, it is one thing to be able to reflect-in-action and quite another to be able to reflect **on** our reflection-in-action so as to produce a good verbal description of it; and it is still another thing to be able to reflect on the resulting description (p.31).

An important caution for me to remember. I may be able to reflect on what I'm doing but I can't expect the teachers to reflect as readily, nor should I expect they'll be able to describe what they're experiencing with any ease.

I read for a little while longer before touching base with the teachers. I chat briefly with Cathy and Barb who are discussing some reading they've done. I have a word with Earl. I check with Maggie and Shelagh. During the next fifteen minutes or so I track down each of the teachers to see how things are going.

We reconvene for a few moments before going home. I have a reading strategy I want to suggest: an adaptation of Peter Elbow's freewriting. In his description of freewriting Elbow (1973) talks about writing something four times, not once, to let an idea evolve. I have found the strategy works just as well for reading—particularly for professional material I have difficulty understanding. I explain it.

"Take the time you have available, divide by four. Skim everything quickly, marking whatever catches your attention with a highlighting pen. Then jot down your impressions, or any questions you have. Read again, with your highlighter, react briefly once more—confirming previous impressions, changing your interpretation, whatever. Read a third time, this time attend to what you've highlighted. Now write your reactions to some of the highlighted portions. Finally, quickly read a last time from beginning to end and sum up your reactions. You might actually find the fourth reading isn't necessary."

The point is to help readers avoid becoming bogged down in terminology or caught up in difficult explanations until they have the drift of the argument as a whole.

"Mark any words/phrases you might want to deal with later, but keep on reading; the information you need isn't where you're having difficulty, it's somewhere later on in the text. The more difficult the passage, the faster you should read. Experiment and see what happens."

This is a judgement call. I'm offering this 'read fast' strategy before anyone has an explicit problem. Given my espoused beliefs—that I shouldn't intervene before there is a need—I should be holding back. But two factors are influencing my decision here: the Institute is short and many of the teachers I've worked with in the past have tended to read slowly and carefully which has prevented them from covering a lot of ground quickly. What 'read fast' has done in the past is permit people to get through a lot of reading in a short period of time and to see connections because they are taking in a lot at once. So I've decided to throw this one out. I'll soon see if it helps or hinders.

Later this evening, after reading the teachers' initial journals and responding to them, I write my reflection/letter for the next day.

A brief reaction to your responses. Something that struck me was how many of you chose to write about "teachers" instead of "I"—distancing yourself from the issues and avoiding looking at what questions the articles raise about your own teaching. I know being critically reflective is uncomfortable and difficult, but it is an important vehicle for learning about teaching. As Dewey (1939) comments:

Any theory and set of practices is dogmatic which is not based upon critical examination of its own underlying principles (p.22).

We all need to become reflective by making the questions which various authors help us ask overt so we can use them to look at our **own** teaching beliefs and practices. I'm pushing this point a bit sooner than I would during a regular course because I think we need to speed up the critical reflective process if we can.

Another thing which struck me this evening has to do with your perception of the "journal writing" task. As readers you can't help engaging transactionally. As Dewey describes it

every experience enacted and undergone modifies the one who acts and undergoes, while this modification affects, whether we wish it or not, the quality of subsequent experiences (pg.35).

In other words, the reading you did, the order in which you did it must have affected what you saw in the various arguments. Nevertheless, most of you chose to write about each article as if it had nothing to do with any of the others. An important skill we need to develop as readers (teachers and students alike) is to explore connections among many different articles and between the articles and our own experiences. Again, I'm pushing this point sooner than I might with a winter course where we have time to allow this idea to evolve. But we have relatively little time together, so I'd like to encourage you to think about what you are reading in a more global, yet connected, way.

I'll quit for now. More later.

The first day has drawn to a close.
In my notebook I highlight
What's gone on here?

and

reading/writing/ thinking with a pencil in hand
and I scrawl:

freewrite

—reminders about issues I want to raise and experiences I want to initiate tomorrow.

Things Take Time 4 ❖

Put up in a place
Where it's easy to see
The cryptic admonishment
T. T. T.
When you feel
How depressingly slowly you climb
It's well to remember that
Things Take Time

Piet Hein (1969)

I have a copy of Hein's poem prominently displayed on my study wall. It's especially relevant this second day of the Summer Institute because today I have to be careful not to rush matters. Instead, I want to leave the agenda fairly loose so people can start feeling their way.

Yesterday was hectic. The problem with an enterprise-based curriculum is that I have to initiate a number of activities very quickly so people can make some decisions about what they'd like to focus on and how they might pursue those interests. Although I was attempting to pace things yesterday so the teachers wouldn't feel too deluged, most people, I'm sure felt overwhelmed. Today, I want to go much more slowly.

The first thing I do when I arrive in the morning is put copies of my reflection/ journal on the table by the door ready to be picked up as people enter. Last evening, I also prepared a class list with everyone's name and phone number. I put the list beside the reflection/letter. I'm hinting that it's legitimate for people to work together.

My agenda for the day is straightforward. I have three notes to myself:

Introduce freewriting.
Remember to ask **"What's happening here?"**
Raise the issue of thinking, talking, and reading with a
    pencil in hand.

I've chosen to introduce freewriting immediately because this strategy has had such a profound influence on my own writing. Learning to freewrite was the turning point for me as a writer. It allowed me to stand back and let the writing find its centre of gravity, its direction and focus, its voice. With this strategy in my repertoire I have been able to write much more easily.

Peter Elbow's metaphor explains why freewriting is helpful:

> Producing writing is not so much like filling a basin or pool once, but rather getting water to keep flowing **through** till finally it runs clear (Elbow, 1973, p. 28).

The hardest thing for me is to get the writing flowing, to keep words appearing on the page, without worrying whether they're good or not. If I stop to correct and edit, I care too much about what I have and can't give it up even though I know I should.

As a writer, I had to learn to trust that I could always produce more. Not necessarily on the particular piece I'm trying to work on. Sometimes I have found myself in the midst of something totally different as I struggle with a particular bit of writing. Through freewriting I have learned to shift gears and write what wants to come rather than continue slogging away at what doesn't seem ready to grow.

Frank Smith explains the purpose behind freewriting quite well, I think:

> Our words...reflect underlying purposes and intentions. These intentions are not themselves directly observable; we cannot be aware of our intentions unless we manifest them in some way. Nevertheless, we can control them to some extent and thereby indirectly control the words that they produce. Paradoxically, the way we can do this is by putting our intentions into words. By doing so, we can reflect upon which intentions should receive our attention; we can select the intentions that will determine the language produced (Smith, 1982, p. 109).

Smith is describing what James Britton (1978) refers to as "shaping at the point of utterance." It took me a long time as a writer to accept that the only way I could find out what I knew or wanted to say was by writing—by putting my ideas into words; the longer I put it off, feeling I had nothing to say, the less I was able to write. It is mainly through writing that I am able to discover what I am thinking.

Most of the teachers who attend my classes, however, believe in the commonsense, conventional view of writing as a two-step process: first you figure out what you want to say, then you put it into language. But as Elbow contends

This idea of writing is backwards. That's why it causes so much trouble. (p.15)

I want the teachers to discover writing is a way of creating meaning and freewriting should help them out. It should help them overcome misplaced concerns for clarity and correctness and let them develop some fluency.

❖

The teachers seem energetic this morning. I chat with people as they arrive. Lorna mentions how overwhelmed she was feeling yesterday afternoon. Janice pipes in, "Me, too."

I make a mental note to raise the issue. I'm so accustomed to an initial period of confusion that I didn't think to say anything as we were drawing to a close yesterday afternoon. We should have discussed how confusion is a natural and expected part of any new learning situation. During the last several years I've learned it takes anywhere from a third to a half of the duration of any course for people to feel comfortable taking control of their own learning. That seems to be the case whether we're involved in a year-long enterprise or a three-day workshop. I'll have to remember to give people an opportunity to talk about their expectations and anxieties right at the start another time.

I glance at the clock. It's ten past nine—time to bring the class together.

"I'd like to start off with a freewrite. Lorna was just talking to me about yesterday and how she felt confused. I thought it would be a good idea for us to take a couple of minutes and reflect on what happened yesterday.

"How many of you are not familiar with freewriting?"

About half the hands go up.

"Well, let me show you how a freewrite goes." To demonstrate, I freewrite on an overhead transparency:

You just start in. You don't bother to think about what it is you're going to write first, you just write and write, to see what comes out. If you run out of things to say, you can write "I don't know what to write" or you can repeat the last word you've written,…written,…written, but the point of freewriting is to keep your pencil going, to keep ideas flowing. NO STOPPING AND THINKING ALLOWED.

"Does that give you an idea of what a freewrite is?"

They laugh.

"OK, I'd like you to freewrite about something that surprised you yesterday. Let's freewrite for about five minutes or so, then we'll talk."

I freewrite myself. If I want to be seen as a member of the group, I have to participate in most, if not all, the activities I ask people to try. There's a good deal of rhetoric about teachers needing to be writers. Much of it contends we need to write in order to present good models for our students. That's not why I write in class. I write because I experience the same writing difficulties my students do. I want to be able to discuss the problems I encounter with them. I need to ask for their help. By making my writing public I become a valid member of the writing community.

My freewrite:

> "I write because I experience the same writing difficulties my students do. I want to be able to discuss...." A crucial point. What we must teach from is not out there in books or manuals or curricular programs or methodologies but in our own and our students' experience of what we're teaching and learning.
>
> Ann Vibert

Those opening moments yesterday were scary—would I be able to get this off the ground without being too directive? Would I be able to listen carefully enough so that I could respond and shape /negotiate the experience. I was wanting to help people clarify an issue that interests them, to have some frame for focusing the experience for themselves so that they could begin engaging as writers/readers. I think they have some questions operating now. I also needed to hear their questions so I could learn a bit about people's beliefs, their concerns, their anxieties. Their questions also were important for helping me think about grouping and about issues we will need to put on the table.

I stop writing. It's taken me a little less than five minutes to scrawl this page in my notebook.

As I reread what I've written I can see I haven't dealt with any surprises. Freewriting is like that; I never know what's going to appear. Were there any surprises for me yesterday? Actually, yes. Not a new surprise but a confirmation of something I've noticed before—just how much difficulty teachers have sustaining a focused discussion. That shouldn't surprise me; but for some reason I keep expecting teachers will know how to choose a question or a concern and stay with it. The skill does come with time, and as we develop some common experience, but I'll have to think about ways of working explicitly on discussion as we go along.

"Finish the sentence you're on," I say to the group. I wait a few moments till everyone is done.

Now, here would be a good opportunity to offer another strategy—one Russ Hunt and his colleagues call **inkshedding** (Parkhill, 1988). Inkshedding builds on freewriting. By sharing the freewrites and responding to what other people have written, the exploration is extended in interesting and unexpected ways.

Here's one way it can go in small groups. Each person takes his or her freewrite and passes it to another person in the group. People read the freewrite they now have and react to it. They can react in different ways. They might choose simply to put a mark in the margin next to something they agree or disagree with. They might want to include graffiti (marginal notes, in other words) beside something that catches their attention. The idea is to dialogue with that other person's ideas and to do it quickly. We're not looking for definitive responses but spontaneous reactions. When they've finished, they pass that one on and read and react to another. The idea is to read and respond to most of the others in the group.

With large groups I sometimes collect the freewrites, redistribute them randomly, ask people to react, then I collect them back and redistribute them again until everyone has read and responded to what three or four other people have written. I sometimes then take the freewrites and responses, type them up, and duplicate them for everyone in the class to read. *This morning, because I didn't indicate that we might want to share the freewrites, people may have written something they would be uncomfortable sharing. So I decide not to inkshed on this occasion; I ask people to discuss what they wrote about instead. I want to hear, and I would like everyone else to hear, what people*

What I want to know is how you seem to know which invitations to send out? Is it really as simple as responding to our needs in the class? My problem is making my invitations fit with the needs of my grade 5 students. I always worry about whether the invitation will be accepted. One thing I've seen is that an invitation can appear meaningless at first but become authentic once I engage in the task. The same must be true for others, including my students. I guess if I'm really observing my students I will be able to tell what they need and issue invitations that may at first seem pointless to them but become meaningful once they get going.

Marilyn Hourihan

found surprising. Surprise, says Schön (1987), is at the heart of reflection-in-action.

> Surprise leads to reflection within an action-present. Reflection is at least in some measure conscious, although it need not occur in the medium of words. We consider both the unexpected event and the knowing-in-action that led up to it, asking ourselves, as it were, "What is this?" and, at the same time, "How have I been thinking about it?" Our thought turns back on the surprising phenomenon and, at the same time, back on itself (p. 28).

I'm trying, at the moment, to engender reflection on learning. I want to bring out surprises about learning and the learning situation the teachers experienced yesterday.
"Let's talk about what you've written."
Norma reads her freewrite:

I was astonished at how quickly the day passed. I found myself engaged the entire time. How did Judith construct the situation so that I always had something I wanted to be doing? I need to think about that in connection with my new resource job—I'm terrified of those high school students. Will they be willing to 'just try' as I am? Or will they sit there, arms folded and refuse to do anything?

"What are you really concerned about?" I ask her.
"I guess I have to watch how you're structuring this experience for us. In other courses I've taken with you, I was very involved with writing and learning but I didn't watch the teaching very closely. I think I'm ready to learn about the teaching, this time. In the spring, I felt that some of the learning moved from here (she puts both hands on her head) to here (moves her hands to her abdomen). I felt I had a better understanding of the theory and could use it more effectively."
Norma has been ready for some time to examine her instructional assumptions. I'll have to remember to ask questions which will help her look at both her teaching and mine; but it's too soon right now to raise the issue of structure. The others aren't ready for that conversation.
"Anyone else?"
Diane volunteers.
"It wasn't something that happened yesterday, but I reread the Harman/Edelsky article last night. I thought about my last

year's students and how they'll cope with this year's teacher. He's very traditional. He doesn't let them talk. Marks everything with a red pen. Last year those kids became accustomed to making decisions for themselves. I wonder if I did them a disservice. Perhaps I shouldn't be giving so much freedom."

"Yes, that's an important question."

Interesting that Diane has connected with the alienation argument raised by Harman/Edelsky. Her concern is a sophisticated one and has important political implications. Do we accept the prevailing ideology or challenge it? If we challenge, how do we deal with the potential alienation which our students then face? Again, I think it's too soon to make these political issues an overt aspect of our agenda. Next week, when we've built some trust, more people will be able to engage in that particular conversation.

"Did anyone write about feeling overwhelmed yesterday?"

"I did," says Janice. "I went home and thought a lot about whether I wanted to continue. I didn't know what I was doing. I felt totally out of it with the computer. I couldn't tell where the discussion was going. There just seemed to be so many things going on all at the same time."

"I realized," I respond, "when Lorna mentioned it this morning that we should have discussed how people were feeling before we ended yesterday. Feeling confused, feeling overwhelmed, is a natural part of learning. It's OK to not have everything under control. In a day or two you'll have established some directions for yourself. You'll have a better idea of what you want to read. You'll have some writing underway. The computer won't be so intimidating."

"Yes, but I'm used to the teacher handing out a course outline telling me what I have to do, how to do it, how I'm going to be graded, and what it's worth. I'm much more comfortable when I can lay out the work and do bits of it in some kind of order. Yesterday, I left feeling that I'd never sort out what you expect of me."

"What do you think I'm expecting of you?"

"I think," Diane responds, "you want us to make some decisions for ourselves. You've laid out the resources and have hinted at some possible directions but you're waiting for us to decide where we want to go."

"Yesterday," says Bruce, "you helped us formulate a question. You're expecting us to read to see what we can find out about that. You asked us to begin playing around with some writing as well. You also asked us to respond to some reading and to respond to your journal. You may not have given us a homework list but I knew what I needed to do last evening."

It's helpful for me to hear Diane's and Bruce's comments. I hope Janice and others who are feeling lost can hear what these two are saying. Perhaps after listening to Diane and Bruce they'll talk with them about their uncertainty and confusion.

"If any of you are still confused or anxious, talk to me. There's no need to continue feeling uncomfortable."

We share a few more freewrites then it's time to move on.

I want people to start writing this morning. I would also like to rearrange the groups so people can get to know one another better.

"Who has decided to try a children's book?" Several respond affirmatively.

"Short stories?" Bruce, Michael, Lorna, and Connie indicate their interest.

The rest sort themselves out.

"How about working together?" I suggest. "I think it would be helpful to talk about the genre and to spend some time reading it, as well."

Before we reshuffle, however, I want to share another strategy with everyone. Several people, I'm sure, have either heard of, or read about, reading/writing logs but I suspect few have had any experience actually keeping one.

I want to introduce reading/writing logs at this point. It will help the teachers keep track of what they're learning as they read, help them think about how authors solve various writing problems, help them think about connections to their own writing.

"Let me read you an excerpt from the reading/writing log I kept last winter," I begin. "I was reading **Kiss of the Spider Woman** by Manuel Puig (1980), a political novel recommended by a friend. It was a difficult but interesting book that really taxed my reading strategies. Here's my first log entry:

Jan. 11
I should have begun this log as soon as I started but I was so engaged in actually reading I couldn't stop. I'm now at the end of Chap. 2 and I'm sure I've forgotten many of the questions I had along the way. I'll try to recapture some of what went through my head. Although I'm at page 48 (the start of chapter 3) I haven't resolved

a lot yet. I know I have two men— actually I wasn't sure it was two men talking until page 7 or so—I didn't know what to make of the conversation—about this beautiful dark haired woman at the panther cage in the zoo and an architect. It was when one of the men says: "You saw the film," I realized what I thought was going to be the story wasn't. I didn't reread at that point—perhaps I should have—but I quickly had to re-adjust my sense of what was going on—now rather than trying to sort out the story of the woman and the architect which I know is a film—I began to watch the dialogue between the two men more closely....

"I continued writing at intervals as I read the novel. I found keeping the log interesting because it made me much more aware of various strategies I use when I'm reading. For example, in the part I just read you, I realized I am able to tolerate quite a lot of uncertainty and ambiguity as a reader—I quickly carry on past stuff that's not making sense until I get to something that does. I think you'll find if you keep track of what happens while you're reading, not only literary works but the professional material as well, you'll find out quite a lot about how you read.

"Here's also a snippet about some writing I was working on. One of the classes last winter decided to write personal narratives. I thought it was a good idea and had every intention of writing a piece myself but I had a hard time getting anything going. I started a narrative piece about my mother's recent heart attack which worked itself into a poem about my last visit with a dying aunt. Here's how it happened.

I'm caught up here in another freewrite. Suddenly I see a need to juxtapose several parallel moments: my mother on her bed at home, on the stretcher in the ambulance, in the emergency room, later in intensive care hooked up to all those machines...and through all of that I feel tension—a sense of her impending death and yet no fear—not even a sense of loss only a matter of factness—the naturalness of it all. What I'm wanting to explore is why I didn't feel panic through this episode, only a sense that there were things that needed to be done, people to be supported—not a denial, I don't think—but a getting on with things—hey, suddenly this feels like a poem.
Later:

I'm not getting anywhere with this poem—I have a page
of images which aren't coming together. As I read the
first few lines:
>She looked like death
>Lying there in bed
>Still
>Gasping for breath...

I'm suddenly aware of the contrast with Helen. My
feelings on that trip to the hospital were very different; I
knew she was dying. I wonder if I can capture some of
that experience....

"Does that give you an idea of what a reading/writing log can
be like?"

"You're writing stream of consciousness stuff, aren't you?"
asks Janice.

"Yes, although I try to keep in mind that I'm using this
writing to explore connections I'm making as a reader or
writer."

Maggie interjects, "I've tried introducing reading logs with
my junior high students but I didn't keep a log myself. I can see
now I should have because I was unhappy with the quality of
their reflection. If I had been keeping a log myself I would have
been able to share it with them."

"What this has let me see is just how informal a writing log
can be," says Diane. "I know I would have written a more
formal analytical response if you hadn't read that to us."

"You'll be doing a lot of reading and writing over the next
several days. I think you'll find it useful if you keep track of
some of your experiences in a log. It'll offer you a window into
your own learning that you're likely to lose otherwise."

Another strategy tossed out. It'll be interesting to see
who picks it up and who doesn't.

"Ok, let's work on writing." As people regroup, I leave to
attend to some Institute business. When I return I find everyone
engaged. Janice, Cathy, and Penny are discussing poetry at a
table in the hallway. I eavesdrop a moment on my way past.
They're doing fine without me. Bruce, Connie, Lorna, Michael,
and Earl are all comfortably settled on the sofas quietly reading.
I leave them alone.

I'm learning that I don't have to control everything
that happens in the classroom. I now trust that if
people are engaged some useful learning will result.

Two groups are still in the classroom. I join Hanna, Leslie, Theresa, Diane, Debra, and Helen—the children's book group. They're sitting at a table strewn with children's books.

"What are you finding out?" I ask.

"Well," begins Hanna. "They're mostly about everyday things. I mean here's one about a boy who's built a sand castle and then imagines himself defending it against invaders. Or there's this one about the kid who locks his mother out of the house by accident and she has to help him figure out how to open the door."

"I like John Burningham's books, the way he has two stories going at once like Shirley's parents sitting on the seashore while Shirley is having an imaginary adventure (Burningham, 1977). I couldn't do what Burningham has done because most of his second story is portrayed through the illustration more than the text, but it gives me an idea for a story that has two things going on at the same time," says Diane.

"What I never noticed before is how the fantasy is grounded in reality," says Debra.

"Explain what you see."

"Well, what surprises me is the way someone like Stephen Kellogg or Mercer Mayer are telling stories about real problems in kids' lives but they use some extension of reality to do it. Take Mercer Mayer's **There's a Nightmare in My Closet** (Mayer, 1968). I can empathize with that child. There he is in bed with the light out and he just knows there's a monster waiting for him in his closet. Everything in the story is real except the nightmare. Now the text doesn't tell you much about the nightmare but in the illustrations it's funny, not scary at all. So I can see how the story acknowledges we're all afraid of the dark to some extent but, in fact, it's poking fun at our fear."

"How do these books help you think about your own writing?"

*I ask this question to see what connections, if any, they're making between reading and writing. Margaret Meek (1988) talks about "how **texts** teach what **readers** learn." I want to extend that—how texts teach what **writers** learn.*

"What I've got to do now," says Hanna, "is make a list of things that have happened around home. Common, everyday things. I don't know just what they might be yet."

A nice connection—many good children's books are about the commonplace.

"Good strategy. I'm sure something will come from it," I encourage her. "How about the rest of you?"

"I haven't any ideas at the moment. I think I need to look at more children's books," says Helen. "I want to see if I can find any Robert Munsch."

"Why Munsch?"

"I really like his stories. I want to reread them."

I always find it helpful to reread a favorite author.

"Have a look in the Resources Centre. Some of his books might be in the children's collection there."

Leslie indicates she wants to try writing a children's factual book.

"Talk about your idea."

"Something I do with the kids in my class is make clear-toys at Christmas time—you know, those molded candy shapes made from boiled syrup. I think I'd like to try a story about how they're made."

"Sounds OK. Any idea how to proceed?"

"No, not really."

"Take a look in the Resources Centre. There are a lot of good factual books in the science education section. And are you familiar with Tomie de Paola's books about popcorn, clouds, and cats? There's also the one about wool, I think. They may be in the collection. If not, write me a note reminding me to bring my de Paola books tomorrow."

de Paola takes factual information and weaves a story out of it in a very skillful way. Leslie might find that an interesting possibility which is why I mention his books. I also ask her to write me a note, reminding me to look for my copies if she can't find them, because I'm trying to make many different kinds of writing functional in this learning context. Note writing, to me and anyone else, is important for sustaining our various enterprises.

That leaves Diane and Theresa.

Neither is quite sure how to begin.

"How about trying a freewrite? You could simply start by saying you don't know what to write and see what happens. I wouldn't be at all surprised if after ten minutes or so something will emerge."

"OK," they reply.

I start to leave, but turn back.

Here's an opportune moment to help the teachers begin reflecting on the learning/teaching situation.

"What has just gone on here?" I ask them.

The five of them look at me solemnly. Eyes aren't averted, but nobody ventures a response.

I wait a moment then ask, "What did I do? How did you respond?"

"You joined us and asked us about what we'd been doing," said Diane.

"Yes, what was I wanting to find out, what was I evaluating?"

"You wanted to find out what connections we were making from looking at the children's books," she continues.

"I was. What did I do?"

"You just asked us what had we found out."

"And what did you tell me?"

"One of us said something about the way children's authors use reality to ground the imaginary and how they are telling about real concerns in kids' lives," says Hanna.

"How did I respond?"

"You asked how that would help us with our own writing," says Debra.

"Then what?"

"We told you about some connections we could see."

"How does what has just happened here with us help you think about your own teaching?"

I'm trying to help the teachers become aware of the learning/teaching situation. People are generally so caught up in their own learning they don't stop and think about what I, as teacher, did and what effect it had on them. I want our interaction to be the focus of some discussion so the teachers can begin reflecting on their own teaching.

Silence.

"I'm not expecting you to answer right this moment but begin thinking about that. The reason we're doing what we're doing is so you can think about its impact on you as a learner and how it helps you think about teaching. I'll be asking 'What's going on here?' again and again."

Now I leave them to carry on.

I check the hallway to see if anyone wants help. As I pass people I mention it's nearly lunchtime. "Let's meet back here at one o'clock, OK? Then I head downstairs for the computer room.

Norma and Susan are there. We chat briefly.

"I've been wanting to try out WordPerfect for some time," Susan tells me, "but I've just been too busy lately."

"Are you trying to write anything?" I ask her.

"I'm just trying to get down some thoughts I had yesterday and this morning. I've been working with a couple of groups of teachers and what you did yesterday helped me think about about what we've been doing."

"Norma, how are you getting on?"

"I'm fine. I'm just playing around with a few ideas. I've been thinking about a short story. I had a long conversation with a man, in his early fifties, recently. He was telling me about his experiences which made him decide to become a school dropout. He wasn't dumb. It wasn't a question of not being able to do the work but of becoming so alienated that he couldn't stay. I thought about him again when I read the Harman/ Edelsky article. I think I could make his experience into a story."

"Sounds interesting. I'm going for lunch. See you upstairs about one o'clock."

After lunch we reconvene. I ask about people's plans for the afternoon. Some want to read, others are intending to write on the computers for while. A few want to work outdoors in the sunshine.

"If you want me or need me I'll be around here somewhere. Let's meet again at half-past three."

With that, we all disperse.

I did take time this morning to introduce two working strategies: freewriting and log-keeping, both of which may help people with what they're doing. However, I'm mainly trying to leave today as open as possible so people can begin some writing and reading. It always seems overloaded at the start of an enterprise-based curriculum; then there's a lull while people stumble around trying to find a direction for themselves. I have learned to stay on the periphery during that time, watchful and supportive, asking questions, but on the whole trying to keep out of people's way.

I want to chat with Lorna for a moment to see if she's feeling more comfortable. This is her first course in the M.Ed. program so I'm not surprised she found yesterday overwhelming. I locate her around the corner reading on her own. I join her on the sofa.

"How're things going now?"

"Much better," she says."

"Talk to me about it."

"Yesterday there were so many different things going on and you weren't telling us 'do this' or 'do this'. I wasn't sure what you wanted us to do or how you wanted us to do it. Last night I was in a panic. How did you want me to respond? What did you mean 'begin thinking about something to write about'? I expected you to give us topics to choose from."

"What helped you out?"

"Talking to the others last night and this morning. I was reassured when other people said they felt the same way I did. And now I understand what you want from us. You're wanting us to take the lead. I'm still not sure how to go about that exactly, but I'm not feeling so anxious."

"I realized this morning after we talked I should have said something yesterday before we left so you wouldn't have felt that way over night. Another time I must remember to do that. How about your piece of writing? Any ideas yet?"

"I've read three of the short stories you gave us. I found them interesting. While I was reading one of them I thought about my grandmother and how she's so cut off from her children. She's much closer with us, her grandchildren. I think I might try writing about that."

> I suppose this is what I'm aiming for when I encourage the kids to do their major writing pieces—selecting genres, starting the writing, letting them work together in genre groups, even across classroom lines. Somehow, though, I feel I'm falling short these last few years. Maybe I'm shortcutting the process by not allowing more time up front for the writing to develop and more coaching time to open up other alternatives for them. Perhaps passing on 'student made' criteria from previous classes is what is short circuiting the process for the kids. I can see as well there aren't enough 'How are you getting along?' sessions so the whole class can share across genres.
>
> Pat Kidd

"Good idea. Any sense of where you might start?"

"Not really."

"You might find it useful to brainstorm. Do you know how to do that?"

"I think so. I take a blank piece of paper and just write anything that comes to mind."

"It's just another kind of freewriting, but it doesn't have to be prose. You can make a list of your ideas, you can write anywhere on the paper. Try and see what happens. There'll be lots of unexpected connections, I'm sure. I'll check with you later to see how you're doing, OK? By the way, what's been happening here?"

Looks like Lorna is settling in. I must try to get back to her before the end of the afternoon to see how her writing's coming.

Right now we're in a working alone time. Some people are reading; others are writing (a few at the computer, the rest with pencil and paper). I tour the classroom, the hallway, the computer room just to make sure no one is stuck. If people are engrossed, I don't interrupt.

I decide to read for a while myself. I find a comfortable place to settle. I open Schön again.

> ...in order to participate in this [reflection-in-action] process, the student must already be able to get in touch with and describe her own intuitive understanding and enter into the studio master's, both in the domain of designing and in the domain of her interaction with the master. She must be able to put aside what she knows in order to enter in the as yet unknown world of someone else, to experience a zone of uncertainty where, having given up for the moment her usual ways of seeing, she is still unconnected to the other's ways of seeing. For this, she needs a capacity for cognitive risktaking (Schön 1987, p.139).

Schön's talking about the architectural design studio but the same is true of what I'm trying to do here in the Institute. The teachers must be able to look at their beliefs and instructional practices and at the same time look at their own engagement in our learning enterprises, juxtaposing the two so that questions and contradictions can surface. In order to use our learning situation as a mirror, people have to be willing to be vulnerable, to risk entering my 'just try' world.

For most students, the wish to avoid uncertainty, coupled either to a win/lose theory-in-use or to an unreflective deference to the instructor's authority, makes it impossible to participate in such a process. A demand that they do so would place them in a vicious learning circle— asking them to exhibit, in order to learn, that which they most need to learn (Schön 1987, p.139).

*Precisely what Gregory Bateson (1972) would describe as a **double bind**. So how do I extricate the teachers from this untenable position of being expected to exhibit what they haven't yet learned? Having made mistakes of that kind in the past, I think I've learned to avoid creating a double bind—first, by having people work together so no one person is on the spot; second, by openly reflecting myself on what I'm learning from our engagement; and third, by asking reflective questions, yet at the same time making it clear I'm not expecting immediate answers, I'm only asking people to begin thinking about these issues.*

Schön extends Smith's concept of enterprises with his elaboration of the coach's functions in a design studio context. He identifies three role functions:

- First, to ask what the student wants the project to be, thereby legitimating her own preferences and intentions—indeed, conveying the message that her personal preferences **ought** to be expressed and used to guide her design.
- Then, to encourage her to try to produce what she likes, demonstrating in quick sketches different ways she might do so, "opening up the possibilities." It is important here that [the teacher] suggest many ways—not one best way—to achieve the effects [the student] wants. [The teacher] does not instruct her [the student] in the best way to do it; he works with her to open up a range of possible means for her experimentation.
- Finally, to judge the results of her work in terms of her effectiveness in "realizing those qualities she defined" (Schön 1987, p. 152).

That's what I'm attempting here. I initiated a project by inviting everyone to explore writing. I suggested each person decide on a genre for the project and now I have to wait until the teachers begin producing something so I can 'open up possibilities.' One major difference between what I'm trying to implement in this reading/writing workshop and Schön's design studio example, however, is that I'm supporting a collaborative venture. That is, I'm not the only coach in this situation. Every person can, and likely will, function as coach for many others. I'll have to help people learn how to do that, though; it's not something most people know how to do intuitively.

I read for about an hour then touch base again with anyone I can find. At three thirty the class reassembles.

"How have you been getting on?" I ask.

I know everyone has been working; however, I find it helps people to hear what others have been doing and how they've been progressing.

"I've been looking at children's factual books in the Resources Centre," says Leslie. "There really are a number of ways of presenting information, aren't there?"

"What did you find?"

"Heaven's, there were some factual books done in poetry, others in a more conventional presentation, pop-up books, you name it. I was surprised by the wide variety."

"Did you come across anything by Tomie de Paola?"

"No, I didn't."

"Write me a note reminding me to bring you my de Paola books, otherwise I'm likely to forget them."

Leslie hasn't yet handed me a note. I'm no good at remembering these details without a written reminder.

"I've spent the afternoon reading Nancie Atwell's **In the Middle**," Bruce says. "It's the first thing I've read that deals with implementing a whole language-based writing curriculum with older students. I think I'm beginning to see what I could do with my high school kids. I haven't really known how to get beyond dividing the week into three periods for writing and four for reading. And I've had no idea how to go about responding to all that writing. Atwell has answered some of my questions."

I make a note to bring something else for Bruce to read.

"I've been at the computer," Norma reports. "I've been trying to start a short story about this man who was a school drop-out."

"How did it go?"

"Well, I started at a couple of different places. I tried a description of the class but I couldn't get very far with it. Then I wrote about Robert, the central character, but I don't have a feel for him so that didn't go very well either."

"How well do you know this person? Could you interview him?"

"I actually could," Norma replies.

"Try that. I think you'll find you now have some idea about the kind of background information you need. Talk to him and see if that helps."

"Good idea," she responds.

We teachers tend to forget a journalist's strategies are very helpful for writing, even fiction writing. I'm trying to let Norma see she doesn't have to invent this story entirely out of her head. If she can't write from her own experience, it's legitimate for her to interview someone to discover what she needs to know so she can write.

Earl reports next. "I picked up some stuff on comprehension. I'm still trying to sort out how to help my kids read better."

"What were you reading?"

"I spent quite a lot of time on an article by Harste & Burke (1980). It described different ways of seeing reading comprehension but I still don't know how to help the kids make sense when they read."

"Have you read Frank Smith's **Essays Into Literacy** (Smith, 1983)? I think you'd find his 'A Metaphor for Literacy' chapter raises interesting questions."

We continue around the room. It takes about fifteen minutes for everyone to report.

I have a second motive for doing this round-up: the teachers will be reading both professional and literary material and I want them to be aware of what other people are pursuing. I know they aren't used to reading with interests other than their own in mind but I'm trying to open that door a smidgen. I made notes as I listened to the teachers report; I will bring some books and articles for a couple of people, tomorrow.

Next, I lay out a possible agenda for Wednesday.

Although learning about writing (and reading/writing relationships) is our major focus, there are other education issues that need attention. I don't want to set up a fixed timetable, although I think it's now clear that we will have a variety of tasks to work on each day and that people are free to engage with them as they wish. I have initiated this multiple agenda because I want the teachers' experience to come as close as it can to what I think children could experience in school.

"Tomorrow, I'd like us to start sharing our writing. However, if we're going to do that we have to have something concrete to discuss. You don't need finished products, but you do need something on paper to make conversation possible. Try to have a bit of writing underway so we can talk about it.

"We also want to make time tomorrow to discuss the professional issues you're interested in—responding to writing, influences of reading on writing, and so on. While you're reading, keep other people's interests in mind. If you come across something you think someone else would like to read, note it, so you can share it with them.

"I would like to respond to some reflections a couple of times between now and Friday. I can see from what's happened today we aren't going to manage a written conversation every day, but if you and I could correspond twice in the next four days it should help us stay in touch. It will also help me if you respond to my reflection. That way I can see what questions you have about issues I'm raising.

During the winter classes I manage to correspond with students each session but not everyone was able to produce some reflective writing today. I want to let the teachers know I'm not pushing for something everyday, but we need to correspond a couple of times this week.

"Finally," (they laugh) "I'd like to start thinking about the relationship between reading and writing. If you would quickly reread Smith's 'Reading Like a Writer' we could initiate that conversation tomorrow.

I intend raising the issue of homework near the end of this week or early next week. I'm hoping, by then, people will be able to articulate what functions their out-of-class work is serving and to examine what questions about homework that raises for them.

"Does anyone have something you want to raise?" I ask.

"Last weekend I saw **Dead Poets Society**," says Hanna. "I enjoyed it a lot but I had questions about what the teacher was doing. Has anyone else seen it?"

"I've heard about it, but I haven't seen it yet," Bruce answers. "It's about a high school English teacher, right?"

"Yes, and he does some intriguing things with poetry," Hanna responds.

"I saw the film two weeks ago," I say. "It might be interesting if everyone went and we discussed it. There are some connections with what we're trying to do here in the Institute. Why don't we do that. Let's try to see the film sometime before next week, OK?"

"Anything else?" I ask.

"No. That's it, then, for the day."

As I gather up my belongings, I notice the highlighted memo in my notebook:

Raise the issue of thinking, talking, and reading with a pencil in hand.

Didn't get there today. It's an important issue, though; perhaps tomorrow. More important, however, I was able to initiate the writing and then step back and give people room to pursue it in their own way. 'Things take time.' Today needed time. Most people will have something on the go by tomorrow. I don't intend to panic about the writing until perhaps late Friday.

❖

Later in the evening, while I'm responding to the teachers' reflections and logs, I think to myself I've been very lucky here.

I don't seem to have a 'Berlin Wall' in this group. Nearly every class has its Berlin Wall, it seems—someone who has built solid defenses behind which to hide, or someone who insists on playing 'make me'. Although I learn more about teaching, and about myself as a teacher, as a result of the problems these people present, I live in dread of them. I know I'm going to have to spend a lot of time and energy thinking about dispelling hostility, creating subtle invitations, encouraging productive collaboration in an effort to help them become responsible, independent learners.

Before meeting each new group of graduate students I always feel a twinge of tension—will there be a Berlin Wall this time. I've come to expect at least one per class, occasionally I encounter more—Berlin Wall sometimes brings along a buddy. But these Institute participants are an enthusiastic, open group of people. I sensed that straight off and I am thankful. It means I won't have to summon the energy to deal with confrontation. I much prefer expending effort on productive involvement. With this Institute group I feel a wonderful sense of anticipation and adventure that I don't feel when I know I have to work at redirecting the 'make-me's.

My most memorable Berlin Wall was a forty-one-year-old junior high school vice-principal, Richard. I knew within the first half-hour we were not going to have a smooth ride. He was on the lookout for a confrontational issue. He found it easily.

Someone had made a comment about 'creative' writing. "As far as I can tell," I had replied, "all writing is creative."

The notion that some writing either can, or should be, placed in a special category designated 'creative' disenfranchises a good many people who are, in fact, creative writers.

"But there's something special about fiction writing," Richard challenged. "You have to be creative, after all, to write fiction."

"Take a look at some non-fiction writing—some essays, biography, or opinion pieces. See what you can find there. Some of my favorite writers, in fact, write non-fiction—Adele Wiseman's **Memoirs of a Book Molesting Childhood and Other Essays** is a fine collection of personal narrative; Jonathan Miller's **The Body in Questions** is a poetic history of medicine; Lewis Thomas's **The Lives of a Cell** are witty glimpses into many facets of both man and nature. The writing these writers do is certainly as creative as any fiction writing."

"I don't know any of those writers you named. And I still believe some writing is creative and other writing is not," he persisted.

"Would you consider billboards a form of creative writing? I've seen some very imaginative ones. One I remember, for example, had a picture of a juicy half orange with a second orange just behind it, revealing part of the brand name 'Sunkist'. The caption read 'The Top Banana.' I've noticed another billboard lately advertising motor oil—it has a picture of a Volkswagon Beetle with the word 'baby' above it, and beside it a can of motor oil captioned 'baby oil'. Aren't those both creative efforts?

This is a particular hobbyhorse of mine, I couldn't stop myself responding. It wasn't so much his comment, but the tone in which Richard made it that set me off. Unfortunately, I'd brought out a lead pipe. What I should have done was ask others in the group to respond to the issue.

"Billboards and grocery lists are not creative writing," Richard insisted.

I decided to try a different tack.

"Think of the consequences for your students of categorizing writing in this way. What effect does privileging some writing genres over others have on them?" I asked.

My question wasn't directed only at Richard. I wanted the others to think about the issue as well. Of course, this discussion was premature. None of the teachers would be ready to tackle an issue as complex as this for a while but this was where we were at the moment and I didn't want to let the issue pass without comment; it was too important.

"I'm not familiar with the word 'genre'," Richard said, before I could ask people to discuss the issue in their groups.

I explained the word ("genre means a distinctive type or category of writing like poetry, short story, or editorial") and then asked the teachers to consider some questions: What effect does valuing some writing genres over others have on people? What effect has it had on them personally?

That ended the conversation with Richard but I knew battle lines had been drawn.

During subsequent classes, we had many similar exchanges. One evening, after reading Richard's journal, I happened to catch a television program commemorating the 40th anniversary of the building of the Berlin Wall. It prompted me to write

Berlin Walls

Last night as I relaxed watching TV,
I saw some old film footage about the Berlin Wall.
    Huge, flat concrete blocks
    Cemented one atop another
    Crowned with barbed wire
    Patrolled by armed troops
To contain East Germans and keep foreign ideas out.

It brought to mind the image of a student's journal,
Stark in contrast to the others.
    Terse, angry words
    Compressed into tight sentences
    Reinforced with underlinings
    Garrisoned by quotes
To shield personal beliefs and keep foreign ideas out.

Walls as formidable as these
Aren't open to frontal assault.
They are, however, vulnerable to infiltration.
In the end such walls are breached from within.

We each have our Berlin walls
Keeping at bay attacks on our convictions.
But just as with that wall through Berlin,
Foreign ideas sometimes gain entry.

Richard's antagonism was unexpectedly intense. His taunts indicated a resistance which I didn't understand. He wasn't just throwing barbs; he was launching javelins. I could see them coming—he would turn one shoulder toward me and then lean away as if preparing to hurl his challenges. If I was reasonably energetic I could deflect them; I would wait for one of the others to make a response or I would come back with a question either to him or to the group. But if I was tired I couldn't always avoid a retaliatory attack.

Richard's resistance manifested itself in different ways. Because he was generally a non-productive group member, two of the groups shut him out. These people would arrive for class a bit early and make sure the seats at their tables were occupied so when Richard arrived there was no room for him to join them. He got the message. On occasion he sat by himself. More generally he joined the least assertive teachers, people who were struggling to understand the theoretical arguments, who were taking fewest risks as writers. I wanted him to be with teachers who could argue with him. I tried reshuffling groups: "Tonight, people with glasses, wearing running shoes, or with something red on, in different groups." That would move Richard around. But the next class, the others would close ranks again. I sympathized with them; I wouldn't have wanted to be in a group with him either.

I'd ask the class to freewrite. Richard would make a token effort. I'd ask them to discuss questions raised by the reading they'd done, Richard would take a children's book from a nearby shelf and sit, reading it. He was clearly playing 'make me.' After every class I'd call my friend Mary, describe the latest behavior, and wail: "What do I try next?"

At one point during the winter we were writing 'learning stories' and everyone was struggling to get a handle on revising. The other teachers were trying to capture some striking personal incident. Not Richard. He'd alluded to an interesting family experience in one of his recent journals but when I mentioned it to him he insisted he had no learning stories to tell. So I was surprised when, the following class, he actually added his name to the writing list.

Our conversation began with Richard thrusting his writing at me. I slid it back gently toward him, asking him what his story was about. From his recounting of the incident I could tell he'd done little with his story beyond the brief synopsis he'd written in his journal.

"What's one thing you want your readers to think about after they've read this?"

Richard didn't answer. I tried a different direction.

"How did you try crafting the writing? Did you try making the incident funny or did you want it to be serious?"

He shrugged.

"I didn't think about how I was writing it," he said.

"Well, perhaps, you might find it useful to think about the point of the story and how you're trying to tell it."

"I'm finished with it, though," he said.

"Doesn't feel like it," I commented. "I don't have any sense of how you felt about your daughter's comments, for example, or why you think the story's important."

"But I'm not going to work on it any more."

"That's your decision," I said, "but let me say something. The point of this course is to find out about writing by exploring writing yourself. I can understand if you don't feel committed to this particular story. Find something else you would like to write about. However, I expect you to engage in writing. What that writing might be is entirely up to you."

Richard departed leaving me flummoxed yet again.

My problem was I expected a teacher who enrolled in a graduate course on writing would be prepared to explore writing, to be a participant. I was constantly being thrown by Richard behaving like a reluctant ten or twelve year old, refusing every invitation. I couldn't understand why he stayed in the class, but stay he did. There were many times during the year when I had to fight the temptation to throttle him. Instead, I tried being supportive, encouraging, and helpful. **He** had to decide whether to engage or not to. He chose not to.

I ask myself if I could have done anything differently. Was there some way I could have drawn him in? I tried lots of different tactics—I shuffled groups. I tried to help him freewrite, to conference with other students, but his participation was always, at best, half-hearted. I wrote him notes in response to his journals inviting him to talk to me. I tried to arrange private conversations before or after class; he always arrived late and left promptly at 9:30.

At one point in February I was so exasperated I wrote him a scathing letter, intending to send copies to his faculty advisor, the department chair, and the dean. In it I threatened a failing grade if he didn't make a genuine attempt to engage in the writing experience. Before posting the letter, however, I discussed it with Mary who pointed out that by sending it I was buying into his 'make me' game. My letter might achieve compliance; it wouldn't engender engagement. I stashed the letter in my files unsent. By ignoring my requests to discuss the class and his participation in it, by distancing himself from the learning activities, Richard was making it clear to me just what his decision was. I realized I had no choice but to accept it.

> "This is another Gerry story, isn't it? I found myself thinking about what I'd do in such circumstances. There are a whole lot of Berlin Walls in high school classrooms, and the strategy I rely on is to ask the owner why the Wall is there. Most adolescents will actually tell you, which is one of the differences between teaching them and teaching adults. I'm thinking you missed the scars on Richard's wrists, too. I wonder if that happened because you saw this as a struggle between you?
>
> Ann Vibert

After the course was over, I talked with him.

"Why did you stay?" I asked him.

"I wanted to know how to **make** someone write," he told me.

"Looks like you found out," I said. "You can't. You can help someone learn, you can support their efforts, but you can't make them do it."

Richard, more than any student I've ever had, child or adult, forced me to appreciate that no matter how much I might want to teach, students control what they learn. Although I'm responsible for setting up inviting situations, in the end, they determine just what risks they're willing to take, how much effort they're willing to put forth. If they reject my invitations I have to dream up new ones. But ultimately the decision to learn is theirs, not mine. I had to accept that Richard had made his decision.

There are a couple of teachers in the Institute asking tough questions. Bruce, Shelagh, and Maggie, for example, are skeptical about implementing open-ended writing/reading enterprises in Junior and Senior High School. They challenge with 'Yes, but...'s. Their questions and comments aren't taunts, however; I sense them as invitations to explore and explain. Their willingness to 'just try' makes all the difference. They will find answers for themselves in their own writing and reading experiences. Richard was not prepared to do that.

Before quitting for the evening I compose a quick reflection/letter:

> Just a fast reaction to today's experiences. I found it interesting to watch how you all were able to assume control over the decisions about what you were going to write and how you might go about it. You'll be interested to know, though, that I had to work at not interfering—at staying out of your way once you got going. Touching base with you, trying to decide if it might be useful to offer a strategy or ask a focusing or sustaining question, were all conscious decisions I had to make. One thing I'm trying to do is to watch to make sure you don't overextend yourself and at the same time to give you free rein so you can find your own way. A difficult juggling act. I tried to keep out when I sensed engagement, but I may not have always have made the right judgement so you need to let me know if you want some assistance.
>
> I had conversations with most of you during the afternoon. Were you aware that my questions, touching base, offering suggestions were writing conferences? How long did most of these conversations take? How did they affect your writing? You might find it useful to think about those brief conversations and how they affected you. Something else I want to mention here is the danger of working everything out on your own, of completing a piece of writing without seeking feedback.

I know most people are uncomfortable showing their writing to anyone before it's completed, but the problem with working something through is that you're too committed to what you've written to change it easily at that point. The most useful feedback, I find, comes when I'm not sure where the writing wants to go, when I still have lots of problems unresolved. So not only is it OK to bring unpolished writing to a sharing session, it's actually desirable.

I also want you to know I am available for support and assistance. Don't hesitate to ask for my input. I realize that asking for my help is scary. After all, your experience for the most part with a teacher's input into your writing has been largely of the 'correcting' or 'grading' sort. Peer conversations are useful, and I'll be encouraging a lot of them, but you may find that I can be of help as well.

Another thing. Don't forget to keep a log-book on the go. As you're reading and writing, try and keep track of what's going on. What strategies do you use for reading professional articles? Are they different from how you read fictional material? What do you do when you run into difficulty? What role does writing play for you at that juncture? I think you'll find a lot of surprises lurking there for you.

I realize I've used this written conversation to offer mostly questions and hints. I've not done a great deal of reflecting about how I saw my role in today's experiences. I suspect that's in part because I'm tired. I'll try being more reflective tomorrow, OK?

Finally, I take a few moments to plan for the morning. I've asked people to reread the Smith "Reading Like a Writer" article. This article should raise interesting questions about their own reading/writing at a point where reading can influence the writing they're doing. I jot

Smith—discussion, freewrite

under **Wednesday** on a new page in my notebook.

Tomorrow I want to begin talking about writing. All of the teachers feel insecure and uncomfortable about writing conferences. With each of them starting a new piece of writing we can explore various kinds of conversations.

I consider a couple of ways to introduce conferencing, then I go to my book shelf and reach for Peter Elbow's **Writing Without Teachers.** Chapter 4 on the 'Teacherless Writing

Class' is just the thing to get us going. My copy of the chapter is highlighted in three colors—a record of previous readings. I reread it again, thinking about how to use it. I decide the best plan is to do a quick class lesson. I'll outline and talk about Elbow's ideas briefly, then put my copy of the book in the class library so people can photocopy the chapter for themselves if they wish to. Elbow's notion of 'giving movies of your mind' should provide a solid starting place.

Juggling   5 ❖

I start the day by handing back yesterday's journals. Then I pick up new correspondence, including responses to my reflection, from the table next to the door.

I suggest we start by discussing Smith's "Reading Like a Writer." Before we begin, though, I distribute the books and other reading material I've brought in for specific people.

I made a point last evening of picking out books and articles for various individuals in response to what they were doing yesterday. I could have disbursed this material before starting but I want people to see me handing it out. I'm not going to say anything about sharing. I'll wait to see whether my actions will open the door to a wider collaboration.

"Leslie, here are the de Paola books I brought from home. See what you think of them."

"Bruce, you mentioned Atwell's book yesterday. I thought you might find **Clearing the Way** by Tom Romano (1987) useful as well."

"Norma, you said you'd tried starting your story in a couple of different places. This is some writing by Alice Munro. Notice how she assembles her short stories by relating a lot of different, yet connected, vignettes."

"Here, Earl. I've brought you Chapter 24: "The Writing-Reading Workshop" from Lucy Calkins's **The Art of Teaching Writing** (1986). Have a look at how that teacher helps her students read analytically."

Your metaphor is somewhat misleading. A juggler exercises tight control and allows little, if any, leeway for unplanned moves. Your teaching-learning situation, on the other hand, is much more dynamic. You allow your students to negotiate the curriculum, without losing sight of your own agenda. You try to be flexible as you listen and respond to them.

Sumitra Unia

Teaching has a lot in common with juggling. Setting the first enterprise in motion isn't too terribly difficult. The second is a bit more tricky; timing now matters. Maintaining a third and a fourth activity requires the teacher's full attention. The first lesson jugglers learn is not to watch their hands but to keep their eye on the balls. I position my eye on the students. I have to watch closely to make sure the students are engaging

*in something that interests them and that each person
is making sense of what he or she is doing.*

Then I turn to the whole class.

"OK. Let's discuss reading like a writer. Talk about some connection that surprised you as you read Smith's article."

*I'm trying to help the teachers slip into critical
reflection. By suggesting they talk about surprises I
may be able to help them examine their own classroom
practices more closely.*

Conversation begins immediately. I listen on the edge of a group for a few moments.

"You know what surprised me? After reading Smith's article when I went on to some other stuff I found myself noticing how other authors had written," Hanna remarks.

"I found myself noticing their openings. I wonder if that's because I'm trying to start some writing myself? It's funny, isn't it, how with anything new you start seeing it everywhere, just like when you're buying a new car," adds Penny. "Every one of the other articles I read last evening began differently. Like this one:

> I confess, sometimes all I did was take it out to the car, leaving it on
> the back seat hoping it would disappear. I hated it, my kids hated it, my
> husband hated it, even my cat...

That opening grabbed me. The author's talking about her big bundle of marking. I never really noticed before how authors did something like that."

"I found myself seeing different things, too," says Cathy. "Even in Smith's article, I was aware of his writing in a way I never was before..."

I quietly join another group.

"...that brief conversation between the teacher and a child. I wonder about taking that much control."

"It certainly seems awfully directive," Leslie says.

"But you know," interrupts Norma, "often my resource students, particularly at the beginning of the year, are very reluctant to write anything. My taking that kind of lead would certainly help them get something down. The question is whether a kid would think it was his own writing."

"Smith mentions 'when they are done the child feels responsible for the entire story...' I'm not so sure a child would," Leslie replies.

"I agree," says Earl, "I think I'd feel it was the teacher's story..."

I move on.

"...haven't really thought about how to connect reading and writing," Barb is saying. "I do writing with the kids and we read books but I haven't been tying the two together at all."

"I haven't either," says Michael. "I have no idea how to put what Smith says here on page 564 into practice:

> The author becomes an unwitting collaborator. Everything the learner would want to spell the author spells. Everything the learner would want to punctuate the author punctuates. Every nuance of expression, every relevant syntactic device, every turn of phrase, the author and learner write together.

I certainly don't notice that kind of stuff when I'm reading. I can't believe kids would."

This would be an ideal moment to ask "How did Serebrin help his students connect with authors and the inherent demonstrations in their writing?" However, I'm trying to stay out of the small group conversation for a while. There will be opportunities to make that connection later.

I join Bruce, Susan, Maggie, and Shelagh. As I eavesdrop, I notice that while everyone is engrossed, no one is keeping track of the conversation. I think this an apt time to mention thinking, talking, and reading with a pencil in hand.

"Let me interrupt you for a moment. I've been watching you work and I want to suggest a strategy you may find useful. Most of you, I've noticed, don't seem to be listening or talking (or reading for that matter) with a pencil in your hand. Some of you have taken 'notes' (I gesture 'quotes' with both hands as I say the word) when I've had something to say, but I haven't seen you keeping track of your own or other people's contributions which are equally, if not more, valuable. Why haven't you been recording what you and others have said?"

A moment of silence, then Bruce offers a response.

"I suppose we're just used to taking down what the teacher says."

"Why is it important to keep track of other people's contributions or of connections between their experience and yours?"

"So we can learn directly from one another," says Norma.

"I was going to suggest we report back on our conversations to the whole group but I've decided against that. What often happens with group reporting is that one person assumes the role of scribe and nobody else bothers to monitor the discussion.

Instead, I think we should inkshed after talking about Smith—first we'll freewrite about the article and how the conversation affected your interpretation then we'll respond to one another's reactions. How will doing something like that affect your note-making?"

"Knowing I'm going to have to respond to the discussion creates a definite purpose for making notes," Penny comments.

"While you're talking think about ways of setting up similar purposes in your own classroom."

I jot in my notebook:
   inkshed—response to Smith
to remind me to bring the discussion to a close with some reflective writing.

Collaboration is at the heart of any enterprise-based curriculum. For collaboration to work people have to value the contribution of other students. To nurture that valuing I have to make the students' contribution an integral part of what's going on. It's not enough to pay lip service to collaboration. I have to create situations which foster working together.

I also have to be a participant in the collaborative process. One way I try to accomplish that is via my daily reflection letters to the class. I make a point of sharing comments which have served as critical moments for me. I also try to practice what I preach—I listen with a pencil in my hand whenever I'm a group participant. I often refer to my notes publicly so people can see how their observations, comments, and questions feed into the overall orchestration of the learning event.

This negotiating of the curriculum is a major difference between a collaborative learning situation and what many people are calling 'co-operative' learning. That became very apparent to me during a day-long session on co-operative learning which I attended at the International Federation for the Teaching of English Conference in Ottawa, May 1986. I remember, clearly, how very uncomfortable I became when one speaker in particular presented his list of teacher responsibilities:

- when assigning a task, the teacher should be sure to state and have the students restate the purpose of the assignment
- be sure to note time limits
- praise, support, create enthusiasm
- energize the group when motivation is low
- summarize and suggest
- teach students process skills by direct lessons and systematic group practice

It was obvious that in this co-operative model the teacher controls the agenda and retains an 'expert' status with regard to what is being learned. Very different from the coaching role Schön describes. For me, this list misses the essence of what I would describe as collaboration: teachers learning both alongside and from their students. There are no surprises for teachers in this learning model. There is no place for anything unexpected to occur. Teaching is directed specifically at eliminating the unpredictable. What it boils down to is students learning traditional factual content—just being forced to do it together.

I discussed my concerns with a colleague afterward.

"I'm really uncomfortable with the role of the teacher in this co-operative learning model. The teacher is outside the endeavor, not a learner at all. She's only instituting these co-operative structures so students can produce fancier projects or achieve higher test marks but the teacher is not really learning anything from what the students are going through; the teacher has everything sorted out in advance. The teacher definitely isn't part of the learning community."

"You're right about that but I like how they structure the groups —assigning different roles to group members."

"The problem with assigning roles is that people don't monitor what other people are doing. Think about what happens when one person becomes recorder and someone else time-keeper. You know that if you take the notes and write up the synopsis of a meeting, it's your meaning the group is forced to accept. In fact, sometimes, when the outcome of a meeting matters to me, I purposely agree to take minutes so I can shape the group's thinking on issues.

"Well, I think everybody should learn how to keep a record of what's going on so they can think about it from their own point of view. I want people to learn to think with a pen or pencil in their hand, to keep a running record of what's

---

Your example of co-operative vs collaborative learning and your ensuing conversation with a colleague made me think about how important it is for those students in my grade 5 class who seldom, if ever, willingly participate and who are only too eager to relinquish the duty to the 'group leader' who is usually the same volunteer. I have wondered how to draw these reluctant ones into the conversation; my efforts have felt heavy-handed. I think the listening with pencil in hand is really worth trying and I plan to have them try it tomorrow when we get together for follow-up discussions about what we're working on. I can't help but think of Greg who's afraid to say anything. He blushes if asked for his opinion, clearly embarrassed and uncomfortable with being put on the spot. He frequently blurts out anything he thinks will get him off the hook—no personal empowerment here. I think the responsibility to monitor what others are doing by writing some of it down might reduce his anxiety.

Linda Cook

connecting for them, and not rely on someone else's connections. I don't want to assign a time-keeping role, or a chairperson's role either. At least not most of the time. I want everyone to be responsible for sustaining a focus and for keeping an eye on the clock."

There clearly are situations where it's more efficient to divide up a task and have individuals deal with some specific aspect of it. However, in an enterprise-based learning situation, with everyone contributing to everyone else's learning, people need to be aware of, and responsible for, all aspects of group function. People are not good at sustaining a focused discussion at first, but I keep mentioning the strategy of talking (or reading) with a pencil in hand and I make a point of doing it myself so I can refer back to what someone has said when I ask a question or make a suggestion.

Yet, when I review that list of teacher responsibilities I can see how I do many of the things on it. I do propose specific tasks. I open the discussion so people can talk about various ways of exploring ideas and issues. On occasion I offer specific directions, particularly if I sense a need for enlarging people's repertoire of strategies. I suggest approximate time limits, but time is definitely flexible—some groups may need longer, some groups may focus quickly and need less time. I provide opportunities for people to pull an experience together and to discuss what they've learned. I monitor group activity, offering support when group engagement seems to have dropped. I offer procedural suggestions, I ask questions, I mention resources, and I invite input from the learners themselves.

What's different, though, is that while I'm ready to offer guidance, to organize the learning experience, I'm also using what's going on to help me learn about the learners. By initiating a learning activity, by setting an experience in motion and giving people room to engage, I find out what strategies they have at their disposal, what insights and knowledge they can bring to the situation, what organizational tactics they can employ.

There are always surprises. Frequently, I find learners know more than I think they do. Sometimes I find they know less. I discover how to teach by letting people show me what they know and how they control their own learning.

At this moment I have a second purpose for introducing the 'talking with a pencil in hand' strategy. What I'm attempting is some incidental learning with regard to note-making.

What the co-operative learning model ignores, as does most traditional transmission teaching, is that we develop the variety of skills we do, not as ends in themselves but as by-products of living in a community. As Russ Hunt (1989) explains:

> We don't learn language by having our errors pointed out and corrected; we learn as a by-product of using language in order to do things we care about doing. (pp.82-83)

At this point in the Institute, I'm trying to create a situation in which note-making is learned, not by formal instruction in note-making, but by engaging in some kind of recording that isn't the focus of the activity but a by-product of it. Rather like the way Mr Miyagi, in the film **Karate Kid**, teaches Daniel karate.

I've seen the film four times. Each time I was fascinated by the teaching example it offers. Remember how it goes? Daniel wants to date one of the cute cheerleaders at his new high school. However, he runs afoul of the macho bully and his cronies as a result of his interest in the girl. Mr Miyagi, the retiring Japanese gardener who looks after the landscaping at the apartment building where Daniel lives, comes to his aid when the guys beat him up. The bully is a karate student at one of the local karate schools. Mr Miyagi, outraged by the way in which these students use their knowledge of karate to bully other kids, confronts their karate teacher. A challenge results: Daniel vs the bully.

The problem is, Daniel doesn't know karate. Mr Miyagi undertakes to teach him. He starts by having Daniel polish his fleet of antique cars. 'Wax on, wax off' he shows him—right hand working in clockwise circles; left hand counterclockwise. Second lesson: 'Sand the floor'—right hand moving counterclockwise; left hand clockwise. Next lesson: 'Paint the fence'—right hand down-up; left hand down-up. Fourth lesson: 'Paint the house'—right hand out-in; left hand out-in. Each day, Daniel is given something new to do. Unlike the dojo students who have been doing repetitive drills, Daniel has been engaged in productive work. Each task is an intact, purposeful project, but it is also an indirect preparation for something larger.

Daniel grows in strength and control, but he himself sees no connection to his desired goal. By the fourth day he rebels. That's the point at which Mr Miyagi shows him what he has actually been learning. He demonstrates how the separate activities he's been doing consolidate to become something else—integrated karate movements.

'Wax on, wax off' is powerful metaphor. It high-lights incidental learning. It forces me to consider

There's a limitation with this metaphor, though. Daniel became angry because he had no sense of the larger picture. Miyagi didn't share it with him. Foreshadowing is a useful idea, but I think students do have to see how what they're doing fits into some larger whole.

Linda Swinwood

ways of establishing experiences that foreshadow what will come. I am trying to introduce note-making, but not teach it directly. I want to set up the discussion in such a way that note-making becomes an integral aspect of what is going on. I'll initiate some reflection about what effects the note-making is having on their learning in a couple of days. Right now, I'm just aiming to establish a real purpose for encouraging them to try it out.

We return to Smith's "Reading Like a Writer." I join Penny, Janice, Debra, Hanna, and Cathy. I listen to their conversation for a while.

"I don't know what to do with spelling," says Penny. "I'm torn between helping the kids get ideas down and teaching them spelling rules."

"Everyone's saying we shouldn't be teaching spelling," ventures Janice. "But if you can't spell how can you write?"

I read aloud something I've highlighted in Smith's article:

...knowledge of all the conventions of writing gets into our head like much of our knowledge of spoken language and indeed of the world in general, without awareness of the learning that is taking place. The learning is unconscious, effortless, incidental, vicarious, and essentially collaborative. It is incidental because we learn when learning is not our primary intention, vicarious because we learn from what someone else does, and collaborative because we learn through others helping us to achieve our own ends. (p.561)

A powerful statement of the importance of incidental learning. I don't have to deliver a lecture on it. Smith raises the question for us to examine.

"How do you react to that?" I ask.

"I marked it, too," says Penny.

"Why?"

"I guess I was uncomfortable with Smith's contention that learning is unconscious, incidental, and whatever the other things he mentions are. I really see a need for some things to be taught explicitly."

"How do the rest of you react?"

"I can see how Smith is using the example of how children learn to talk to build his argument, that no one explicitly teaches little children to talk," says Debra, "but I feel the same way Penny does, I'm not sure everything is learned that way."

"This might be a good place to consider your own learning. Let's start something here. Later, when you have a moment, think about something you like doing and try to remember how you learned to do it. For example I love building and flying kites, I enjoy sewing, I do lots of other things. When you have a chance today, think about something you know how to do and try freewriting about how you learned to do it. Let me suggest four questions to help you focus:

> Why did you decide to learn it?
> How did you go about it?
> What roles did other people play?
> How could you tell you were learning?

Keep Smith's arguments in mind as you write. We'll talk about this tomorrow."

I scribble:

Thurs.—learning stories

to remind myself to mention this activity to the rest of the class before the end of the day. I hadn't planned on making a foray into personal learning stories with this class but a teachable moment has presented itself. People's reservations about learning being 'unconscious, effortless, incidental, vicarious, and essentially collaborative' need to be brought into the open. This may be a useful way of dealing with their concerns and for helping them draw comparisons between learning outside school and in the classroom.

The small groups have been discussing issues raised by Smith's article for about half an hour. We could go on productively for longer but I think if we're going to keep our writing moving we need to begin talking about what people have written. I draw discussion to a close by suggesting a freewrite.

"What's one thing Smith helps you question about your own teaching?"

A difficult question because most teachers, in my experience, don't approach professional reading in terms of questions it raises about their assumptions and teaching practices. Most read for 'tips.' Even teachers who have taken courses with me before find it difficult. I'm not expecting penetrating questions at this point, but it's important to ask the reflective

*question. My asking it will begin to influence the
teachers' reading stance. In a couple of days I know
questions will begin appearing in the journals and
logs.*

I write for about five minutes myself, wait a little, then ask
people to finish the sentence they're on. As soon as everyone
stops writing I suggest we swap what we've written and
respond to one another's questions. We decide to pass our
writing to the person on our left. I receive Penny's:

> Smith says teachers should try to protect themselves and
> children from the effects of evaluation. He's arguing
> people learn to write by writing not by being graded on
> their writing or by having their errors pointed out to
> them. But if I take his argument seriously what do I do
> about evaluating, about grading? What do I do if I don't
> point out the kids' mistakes to them? How are they going
> to learn about writing conventions? Something as simple
> as letter formation with my first graders. How are they
> going to learn how to print letters if I don't point out
> their mistakes to them?

> *Although Penny begins with questions about marking
> and grading I see in her final query an opportunity to
> redirect her attention to curriculum, specifically to the
> relationship between writing and reading. I react in the
> space below her writing:*

> These are important questions. I struggled with them
> myself for a long time before I was able to see some way
> out of the problem. It took me a long time to really
> understand Smith's connection between reading and
> writing. Once I saw how an author could teach me
> something I wanted to know how to do, I was able to
> see ways of setting up situations that would help people
> learn what they 'needed' to learn by directing them to
> reading. Can you see ways in which I have been doing
> that with you here? How could you do something
> similar with your first-graders to help them learn about
> letters and about symbol-sound relationships? Talking
> about what you've discovered is also an important
> ingredient. How have I been helping you use talk to
> make conscious what you've been learning from
> reading? How could you do the same with your
> students? Do your answers to your questions help you
> think about this issue of 'marking mistakes'?

The beginnings of another possible written conver-
sation. I don't expect Penny to answer my questions
right now although she might choose to later. I've
asked them to help her watch more closely what's
happening in this learning situation and to think about
connections she can see to her own teaching situation
with first graders.

It's now past ten o'clock. We should move on to sharing our
writing. Time to bring Elbow into the conversation.

I get everyone's attention, take out **Writing Without
Teachers** and read:

> To improve your writing you don't need advice about what changes to
> make; you don't need theories of what is good and bad writing. You
> need movies of people's minds while they read your words.... And you
> need to keep getting it (feedback) from the **same** people so that they
> get better at transmitting their experience and you get better at hearing
> them. (p. 77)

"Elbow discusses whether you should hand out copies of
your writing to be read or whether you should read your stuff
aloud. As he says, there are merits to both. I find when a piece
is short, listening to it read aloud works well. Once it become
three or four pages long I prefer reading silently."

Today, I suggest they read aloud.

Next, I read Elbow's suggestions for 'giving movies of your
mind.'

"I really like this metaphor because it helps me remember I
am trying to show the writer what happened to me when I heard
or read his or her words. Elbow offers several tactics for giving
movies of your mind. He mentions

pointing—talk about the words or phrases which catch
   your attention;
summarizing—

> ...tell quickly what you found to be the main points, main feelings, or
> centers of gravity;

telling—share personal connections the writing evoked;
   and
showing—reflect the reaction you had to the writing.

"Elbow makes a distinction between telling and showing in
an interesting way. 'Telling,' " he writes,

is like looking inside yourself to see what you can report. Showing is like installing a window in the top of your head and then taking a bow so the writer can see for himself. (p. 92)

Then I skip to you are always right and always wrong (p.100).

"As listeners/readers," Elbow says, "we're always right because what we're sharing is our experiences of the writing. He believes the most valuable thing listeners/readers can do for writers is tell them what we really see and how we really react. On the other hand, we're always wrong in that we never see accurately enough. There are always things in the words we can't get.

"To writers he says: **Be quiet and listen.** If you talk, he warns us, you'll keep readers from telling you important reactions. He cautions us against giving introductions, apologies, and so on. They'll only interfere with readers' reactions, he contends. After people have had a chance to talk then we can ask them about aspects of the writing we particularly want to know about or explain about our intentions.

> **Don't reject what readers tell you....But don't be tyrannized by what they say....**Remember who has what job. It's their job to give you their experience. It's your job to decide what to do next. If you start putting decision-making power into their hands, you push yourself out of the picture.
>
> **You're always right and always wrong....**You're always right in that your decision about the writing is always final....But you are always wrong in that you can never quarrel with their experience—never quarrel even with their report of their experience. (p. 106)

There's a great deal more in this chapter but I don't read any more. I've simply wanted to set the stage for responding to writing. Giving movies of our mind is a powerful metaphor. It should help people begin listening and responding to one another in other than a traditional teacherish fashion.

"Before we move to responding to the writing, let's talk quickly about what's been happening here."

I want to raise the notion of 'mini-lesson'. Mini-lesson is the current jargon term for a brief moment of focused teacher input. A number of authors talk about mini-lessons. Both Atwell (1987) and Calkins (1986) discuss them.

For me, mini-lesssons serve a variety of functions. In whole class situations I may take a few moments at the beginning of an activity to offer a strategy or suggest a focus for what follows. I also sometimes interrupt a class in the middle of something to raise questions about procedure, to draw to everyone's attention an issue that's been raised in a small group, or to sustain or focus engagement. I often close a discussion by inviting people to comment on what they've experienced and to help them summarize and draw conclusions.

At this particular moment, I've taken a little time at the beginning of our discussion about their writing to offer a responding strategy. I decide to do that based on my prior experience. Many people, teachers, in particular, have trouble responding to one another's writing. By asking what's been happening here, I'm trying to nudge people to consider how I've shared a strategy—not by putting a list of directions on the blackboard or overhead projector, but by reading from someone who has a useful suggestion to offer. I want the teachers to consider how setting the stage in this way can affect what will come. I know that a good deal of their conversation will still be about changing the writing, but when I join a group I'll be able to listen for a while, share movies of my mind, and then ask about what I've done.

Although this has been a formal lesson, it has, nevertheless, also been a foreshadowing. It's purpose has been to set up a metaphor I think we'll all find useful in a variety of unexpected ways.

"Even though I made notes while you were reading Elbow to us, I don't have any real sense of what he's saying. I need to read the chapter and maybe some of the rest of the book myself," Bruce interjects.

"I agree, I've read that stuff before," says Shelagh, "but I certainly need to read it again."

"If any of you own Elbow's book, could you bring it in? I'll leave mine on the table so you can copy the chapter if you want to."

"This 'giving movies of your mind' is an interesting idea," Cathy remarks, "but doesn't Graves say the writer should tell about the writing before we react to it?"

"The more you read about writing," I respond, "the more you'll discover there is no one right way of doing anything. There are no failsafe strategies for writing, no foolproof tactics for responding. One vital thing, as a writer, is learning to judge whether talking about your writing or listening to readers' reactions is likely to be more useful given how far your writing has evolved. There aren't any rules to follow.

"Right now, I'd like you to try giving movies of your mind. It would be interesting to compare what Graves and Elbow say about writing conversations. Why don't we read chapters 11 to 14 in **Writing: Teachers and Children at Work** tonight, then we can talk about Graves's ideas and try them out tomorrow. The book is in the class library, I know some of you own it, and there are copies in the bookstore."

I hadn't planned on going in this direction but since Cathy has raised the contradiction it's a good idea to explore it.

"In the meantime, how do you want to go about discussing your writing? Do you want to work with the others who are trying the same kind of writing you are, or do you want to work with the people you're with now?"

The consensus is to work within genre groups.

We haven't dealt with mini-lessons. Cathy's question was a response to the content of my intervention, not the process. Now I have to decide whether to ask my question again or to raise mini-lessons another time. I glance at the clock and elect to postpone the discussion until later. I make a note to myself, though, before I forget it.

As people regroup, I go to the blackboard and at the top, right-hand corner write **Writing Conversations**.

"Sign up if you want to talk to me about your writing."

I also start a **Discussion Topics** list. I write

Thurs:—Graves

under the heading, as a public reminder to read Graves's chapters.

I have a couple of other items I want to add to **Discussion Topics** *but I'll wait until this afternoon to include them. On the first morning I handed six short stories and some poetry. We need to explore ways of responding to literature as readers as well as to consider how that responding affects the writing we're doing. I write*

short stories—Thursday—**Discussion Topics**

in my notebook to remind me to add it to the blackboard list later. I also note

mini-lessons.

*I don't know whether I'll get a chance to bring that
issue up later today or not; I can always raise it in my
letter for tomorrow if we don't get to talk about it
today.*

While I'm writing in my notebook, Maggie puts her name
and Shelagh's on the **Writing Conversations** list. She
mentions on her way past the table that she and Shelagh want to
chat with me. When I finish writing, I look around to see how
people are settling in. Everyone looks engaged so I join Shelagh
and Maggie.

"How're things going?" I ask as I bring a chair to the table.

*I notice Bruce is busy writing. He looks up briefly
then resumes what he's doing.*

"Shelagh and I have decided we want to write about
evaluation," Maggie says. "We both had a difficult time with
grading last year. Neither of us could keep up with the amount
of work the kids produced. We want to sort out the problems we
had."

"Share with me what happened yesterday."

"Well, we talked to Susan about the writing workshop in our
classrooms. I don't think we ever got a handle on the situation.
We had the kids doing a lot of writing, and grading all of it
became a nightmare," says Shelagh.

"What came from your discussion yesterday?"

"Susan helped us lay out some of what we were doing,"
says Maggie. "We talked about the reading logs and the journal
writing."

"Um-hmm."

"But I don't know how to take that conversation and begin
writing," Shelagh says.

"Tell me a story," I say to her.

Shelagh looks at me.

"Tell me a story about something that made you aware of a
problem you were having."

Shelagh continues looking at me silently.

I turn to Maggie. "Can you describe an event that highlights
one of your concerns?"

Maggie, too, sits silently.

*We now have Bruce's attention. He sits, pencil sus-
pended, watching the three of us on the other side of
the table.*

"For example," I turn back to Shelagh, "Do you remember
telling me about an occasion when you found yourself at the
dining room table in floods of tears? Tell me that story again."

I know from previous courses both Maggie and Shelagh have considerable difficulty writing anything other than terse expository prose. Shelagh, in particular, has found it difficult to use writing for looking at herself with a critical eye. What I'm trying to do in this conversation is help her tell about a moment when she realizes she's got a problem so she can bring some theoretical insight to the situation. I'm trying to nudge her beyond a safe description of her program to writing about her uncertainties. I read her silence as fear. She's not consciously blocking her vulnerability, she has talked to me before about difficulties she's had. But writing about them? That's another matter altogether.

"What happened at your dining room table?" I prompt her.

"I guess it was early in the new year and I was feeling overwhelmed. It was Sunday afternoon and I was exhausted. I'd been steadily marking, reading logs and novel responses for more than a day and a half, and I still wasn't through the pile. I wasn't dressed yet, hadn't done any house work all weekend. Arthur came through the dining room. I was so frustrated I just burst into tears."

"A nice incident. From this vantage point, why is that an important moment for you?"

"I suppose that was the moment when I realized I couldn't sustain what I was trying to do."

"You might find it useful to write about that incident. My guess is, once you begin exploring your frustration, the concerns you have about evaluation and grading will become clearer. Remember, you don't have to have your story completely worked out before you can begin writing. You know," I turn to include Maggie, and Bruce who's eavesdropping, "you can start with a strong moment and see where it leads. Recall how Murray (1980) talks about 'writing finding its own meaning.' Here's a chance to let that happen."

I turn to Maggie.

"Let's hear your story."

"I'm less concerned about the quantity of work than Shelagh is, I have fewer students to deal with than she does, but I have a lot of unanswered questions about my mandating specific assignments. I began thinking about that issue last fall when it became apparent some of the students were writing simply to comply with my requirements—I had asked the students to complete four pieces of writing for their first term grade. Melissa's folder, for example, had three pieces that she'd worked on, but the fourth was obviously a last minute effort. I began wondering about setting requirements like that."

"Sounds like you've got a story to tell, as well. My suggestion to you is the same one I offered Shelagh. Try writing about that moment. I think you'll find a story will emerge."

I'm trying to encourage each of the workshop participants to explore new writing genres. I know Shelagh and Maggie are uncomfortable with personal narrative, hence my suggestion to start there. They may not be able to sustain the genre; the writing may well evolve into exposition. However, whether they stick with it or not, by attempting personal narrative they will learn something about writing in that genre that should prove useful both for them and their students.

I get up to leave the table but sit down again.

I've been watching Bruce eavesdropping. I want to find out what he's learned from our exchange.

I ask the now familiar question: "What's been happening here?" I look at each of them in turn.

"You began," Bruce says, "by asking them to talk about what they'd done so far. You listened to Maggie tell about their discussion yesterday."

"Maggie didn't have anything on paper to share, so what did I do?"

"You asked her to tell you a story."

"Why did I do that?" I turn to the others.

"I suppose you were trying to get me started," replies Maggie.

"That's right. Why did I ask you to tell a story?" I look at Shelagh.

"Well, the personal incidents we related are manageable. We should be able to write something quite quickly."

"Why is it useful to write quickly?"

"Once we have something on paper we'll feel some control over the writing. I can see that until we get something on paper we can't stand back and look at what the writing is doing."

"So talk about the kind of help I offered you."

Your constantly asking 'What's happening here?' forces the teachers to think about your pedagogy and by extension, their own. Maybe that is what is missing from our teacher education endeavors, both preservice and inservice. We may work to set up environments in which teachers experience the kind of instruction we think is supportive of learning but we don't take it further than that. Consequently the teachers aren't made aware of how the teaching and learning is occurring so can't easily draw upon their own learning experiences when back in the classroom. We need to ask your question to help them make that connection.

Susan Church

Bruce responds. "You asked them to tell a story. You accepted the story and said it was a good idea to get it down. You affirmed that it was alright to begin before everything was worked out. You didn't say anything about the content, did you? You only made suggestions about how to proceed. Am I right?"

"Yes, that's perceptive. At this point, I'm trying to help them get started. Both of you," I nod to Maggie and Shelagh, "need to get something on paper so you can explore your ideas. Writing is kind of like doing a jigsaw puzzle only you haven't got any pieces to work with yet. You have to create some pieces before you can move them around.

"Now I didn't give any movies of my mind. Why was that?"

Bruce again. "Because there wasn't any text yet to respond to."

"I've a question I'm going to leave you with: 'What issues has this brief conversation raised about your own teaching?'"

I've asked the question to initiate some critical reflection. Bruce writes in his notebook. There may well be a response in his journal later.

I check the **Writing Conversation** list. There are several names listed now: Earl, Connie, Carmina, Debra, Penny, and Norma.

I'm pleased to see some of the new folks have signed up. I was afraid they might be too intimidated to share their writing with me this soon. I guess I've done something right. I'll have to remember to ask about that.

Earl's next. I locate him in the corridor and join him on the sofa. He's sitting with a blank page. I invite him to talk.

"I don't know what to write," he says.

"That's OK. Let's chat a bit and see what happens. Talk to me about some things you care about."

"Well, I've been thinking about my father. He died last Christmas and I'd like to write something about him but I don't know if that's appropriate or not."

"Of course it's appropriate," I reply. "If I remember you decided to try a short story, right?"

"Right."

"I'm sure you have a lot of stories to relate about your father that can come together into something interesting. You just have to start in. Share an incident with me."

"My dad had a good sense of humor."

"Um-hmm."

"I recall one time, I must have been fourteen or so, my older brother and I were driving somewhere with him and we ended up having the only conversation about sex that I ever remember us having. It was totally unexpected and it left me and my dad laughing helplessly. Billy, though, he was terribly embarrassed."

"Sounds like a good place to begin," I encourage him. "Why don't you head for the computer and see what comes out. We'll talk again after you have something on paper."

Earl departs after we chat briefly about what's been happening in our conversation.

I think Earl is underway. I had the feeling his story was strong enough to take him into some interesting writing. I'll check on him later.

Next on the list: Connie. I find her working with Diane, Norma, and Lorna. She's just about to read what she's written to the group so I join them and listen.

Jimmy signed up for T-ball and had got his uniform. When I saw him wearing it, it was all I could do to keep from laughing aloud. "Kentville Fire Department" was stencilled on the front of the large T-shirt but when he put on the whole uniform only "Kentville" showed. The rest was tucked inside the long white pants that made his skinny legs look like picket fence posts. The way he stuck out his six-year-old chest you could tell he considered himself a real player in the majors.

Then the first practice. By 8:50 all ten players had arrived at the field but there was no sign of the coaches. The kids soon tired of tossing pebbles, kicking at ants, and telling each other how far they could hit the ball. Suddenly one blond head streaked toward first base. The rest followed in hot pursuit till ten sets of legs rounded the bases. If you can imagine a giant green and white centipede you'd get the picture.

At home plate chaos occurred. The first runner made a brave attempt at a Pete Rose slide. There was no hesitation as the rest came in for similar landings. Ten shouting voices and then ten sets of arms and legs finally separated into ten small bodies. After a mutual dusting-off, another leader suddenly dashed off to continue their new game. Again they formed the centipede, leaving a trail of small sneaker prints and a cloud of dust settling around home plate.

Connie stops reading and looks at us.

"Any movies of our minds?" I ask.

"I can just picture that centipede," laughs Norma. "And the noise, I can hear the kids shouting."

"I can also feel their discomfort at the beginning," adds Lorna. "I never joined a sports team as a kid, there wasn't anything for girls to play, but like the first day of class, when you don't know anyone and you're waiting around for things to begin, it feels like that."

"I could see the picture of the kid standing there in his uniform—it being way too big and only the first line of the team name visible above his waist," Diane says.

"Although you don't describe the dust much, I can smell it. There's such a lot of nice description," I comment, "that the hints of other aspects of the situation are enough for me to fill them in. Can you tell us more about your story?"

"I thought I'd write about my nephew. A couple of weeks ago I attended a practice and I saw that episode. We all nearly died laughing it was so funny."

"Is this going to be a baseball story, or is it about your nephew?" Norma asks.

"I'm not sure yet. I haven't seen him play in a lot of games so it may have to be about other things," Connie answers.

"You've got a terrific vignette here, where do you think you'll go next?" I ask Connie.

"I though I might try writing a couple of other episodes and see what happens."

"Good idea. Anything you want to ask us about?"

"No. I tried being really descriptive when I was writing and your reactions have told me it worked. So I guess I need to write about some other situations and see what happens."

Connie has a piece on the go. Her description is effective. I'll be interested to see how her story unfolds.

I turn to the others. "I find it helpful to think about writing in the same way I think about photography. I try to visualize the scene as if I'm seeing it through a camera. I try to think about whether I want a close-up shot, a distance shot, or a middle-range shot. Sometimes I think in terms of a video camera; I think about panning a scene or zooming-in. I can see that centipede, for example, as a nice middle-range shot while the description of the child in his uniform could be closer-in view. It's useful to remember that a good photo essay contains a mixture of shots. You might, in fact, want to watch a bit of TV this evening and see how the camera is used in creating a story."

*A brief lesson. The metaphor might just help some of
them conceptualize the situations they're writing about
a bit more clearly.*

Then I join Michael, Carmina, Barb, and Theresa.

> 'Discipline' has become less and less an
> issue for me. I think there are many
> reasons. Even though I teach inner-city
> kids who have a reputation for
> 'misbehaving,' I have less trouble with
> my six year olds now. I think the
> biggest change has been in the greater
> responsibility I give the kids for
> decisions about learning. Some people
> would say discipline is just not such a
> problem with younger kids anyway. I
> agree. I think younger kids are naturally
> active learners and respond to a learning
> environment which supports that. Older
> kids can come to expect passive
> learning and not know how to deal with
> a more open learning context.
>
> Lynn Moody

Carmina is concerned about discipline. This past year, her first year teaching, she has found it difficult keeping her first-grade students involved in "their work." What she's trying to sort out for herself is how to maintain control so the children complete assignments. "How do I get them to do the work? How do I handle discipline?" she wants to know.

"I'm not concerned about discipline and control," I respond, "but about building social relationships and engagement."

"But don't you have to make sure everyone does the assignments?" Carmina asks.

"Think about this situation. What have I been doing to help you work?"

"You asked us to choose something we wanted to try writing. But if I did that with my grade ones, half of them wouldn't do anything."

"What am I doing to help you get started?"

"Well, you're talking to us. But I don't see how that would help with my students. I have to threaten some of them before they'll begin working."

"I don't worry about controlling students, but engaging them. My gaze is on curriculum, on the activities and experiences I'm offering, and whether they are drawing students' interest."

"But what do you do if students aren't interested?"

"Students are either involved or they're not. If they're not, I don't ask myself 'What's wrong with **them**? How can I **make** them do this?' Instead, I examine the situation to see how I might change what's going on so people can become more engaged. If they're not involved, quite likely the problem resides in my curriculum. You have to think about what you see me doing to help you become involved here."

*Carmina, like a lot of teachers, sees teaching as
policing and control—I don't; I see my role in the*

classroom in terms of initiating a variety of learning endeavors and then following along and supporting individual learners' efforts. I am trying to say to Carmina, from my perspective, discipline is a matter of looking at what's not working, then altering the situation to make it more conducive for learners to become engaged. Rather than coerce students, I work to lower the barriers they've erected against learning. I try making it possible for people to take risks and thereby find things out for themselves.

Carmina looks at me with considerable skepticism.

To illustrate my point, I relate a teaching experience from a number of years ago.

"I remember a two-day inservice with an elementary school staff. The first day, I worked with the teachers. The second day, with the teachers observing, I did similar activities with twenty-eight five and six year olds.

"I'd spent a couple of hours the evening before setting up a working space in this large open-area classroom. I'd prepared a number of activities, based on materials I found in the primary grade area, which I thought the children would be able to handle independently: making patterns with beads, exploring shapes with geoboards, building with lego, browsing through picture books, drawing with crayons, and painting at an easel. I'd laid out these independent activities so I could work with a small group and be fairly certain the other children would be engaged productively. I set up each activity at a separate location in the room.

"Then, I prepared a number of reading and writing experiences to demonstrate ways of extending the children's strategies without resorting to basal readers, workbooks, and drill exercises. I positioned a round table, front and centre, so the teachers could observe me as I worked with each small group of children.

"First thing that morning I introduced myself to the twenty-eight children while the teachers looked on. I invited the children to examine the work area and we talked about the activities I had laid out. I explained they would all have a chance to work with me at the table but most of the morning they would be doing these other activities without me. Because I would be busy, I told them, if anything went wrong they would have to solve whatever problems arose by themselves.

'What kinds of things could go wrong?' I asked.

'We could knock the paint over.'

'What would you do if that happened?'

'We could wipe it up.'

'Do you know where to find paper towel?' Yes, in the cupboard right there.

'What else could happen?' People could fight.

'What could you do about that?' Tell them to stop fighting; tell them to share.

'What if there are too many people at one of the activities?' Somebody could choose something else for a while.

'Those seem like good ways to solve those problems,' I reassured the children.

'Just remember, if I'm busy you figure out what to do on your own.'

With that, I selected four children and initiated a reading/writing activity at the table.

Not ten minutes later I was interrupted by a little girl tugging on my skirt.

'I'm busy,' I said to her quietly. 'See if you can solve your problem by yourself.' I turned back to the group and resumed our activity. A few minutes later she returned. 'I'm still busy.' I repeated to her. 'You look after your problem yourself.' Again she turned away and I continued with the group at the table. A third time the child interrupted me. 'You solve your problem yourself,' I said to her. Could she talk to Mrs Gordon she wanted to know. 'Of course you can,' I replied. And I thought no further about the incident.

After lunch the teachers and I met to discuss what had transpired during the morning's activities. Mrs Gordon began by telling me about Madeline needing to go to the bathroom.

'But isn't the bathroom right here in the classroom?' I asked.

'Yes it is,' she said, 'but we can't let the children go to the bathroom whenever they want to because they just play in there.'

'If the children find playing in the bathroom more interesting than being in the classroom, that tells you something about your curriculum, doesn't it?' I responded. 'I'd be inclined to use the children's interest in the bathroom as a barometer for judging their engagement—the more interesting I succeeded in making the in-class activities, the less they'd want to play in the bathroom, right?'

"It was a tactless response," I admit. "And needless to say, it instantly killed my rapport with those teachers."

However, I can tell from their faces the point of my story isn't lost on Carmina or the others at the table. I think they've understood what I'm saying about the relationship between behavior and engagement—if students are productively involved, they don't need to be controlled.

"But isn't it a lot of work to set up and sustain an activity-based classroom?" Carmina asks.

> Last year with my grade 10 students, I set up a small-group study of *Romeo and Juliet*. Because I had never approached the play in this manner before, I spent hours and hours preparing so that nothing would go wrong. In fact, I over-prepared; I erred on the side of too much teacher-based structure, but the six weeks my classes spent studying the play were the most wonderful of the entire year. For me, one of the greatest rewards was listening to my students doing all the talking about the play instead of holding stage myself.
>
> Patricia Whidden

"I don't find it is," I say. "The work involved is different. I don't spend hours on repetitive boring marking. I spend that time reading interesting and individual journal responses, stories, and so on. I don't spend time preparing lectures; I read professional material to keep current and to select what I think might be useful resources for people to read. I prepare activities, I read and write myself to experience the problems that everyone else may be having to deal with. I do put in lots of time, but that time is enjoyable, not drudgery. I don't spend time trying to control behavior, I use indications of a lack of engagement to think about strengthening the curricular experience."

We chat for a bit longer about control versus engagement before I leave the group.

That was an important conversation. Although I've considered the discipline versus engagement issue many times before, I hadn't thought about whether implementing a whole language, enterprise-based curriculum was more work or not. Interesting to realize that I don't feel it is. There certainly is a lot to do. I spend a lot of time preparing and responding but I find all of it interesting. I learn a lot about my students and about my teaching through our written conversations.

Next I check the **Writing Conversations** list. I haven't yet met with Debra, Penny, or Norma. I find each of them in turn and we chat about their writing.

When Norma and I are finished, it's nearly lunchtime. I tour the hall, classroom, and computer room reminding everyone about lunch and letting them know I'll be available for more conversation this afternoon.

There's no point having the class meet as a group after lunch. There's nothing specific wanting attention. People need time to continue writing and reading. I make sure that time is available. Timing is an important aspect of juggling—sensing when to intervene and when to stay away. This is a stay-out-of-the-way time.

After lunch I chat with people as they return to the classroom. I cross out (but don't erase) the names on the **Writing Conversations** list.

I realize if I leave the evolving list unerased on the board I can use it to keep track of who has and who has not talked with me.

No new names have been added, so I pick up my copy of Dewey's **Experience and Education** and find a comfortable spot to read.

I haven't put Dewey on our agenda yet. It's still a bit too soon for the teachers to explore a transactional theory of learning/teaching. We haven't done enough as a community for them to be able to discuss connections between Dewey's arguments about the role of experience and community in learning and what's happening in our workshop.

I read quickly, highlighting new ideas as I go along. While flipping through chapter four on social control I notice the following:

…weakness in control…is likely to arise from failure to arrange in advance for the kind of work (by which I mean all kinds of activities engaged in) which will create situations that of themselves tend to exercise control over what this, that, and the other pupil does and how [she] does it. This failure most often goes back to lack of sufficiently thoughtful planning in advance (Dewey 1938, p.57).

I missed this passage when I read the book a couple of weeks ago. At that time, I was reading for an overview of Dewey's argument and didn't pay attention to this discussion of curriculum/control. With Carmina's concerns in mind, however, I notice Dewey's comments.

I read the entire chapter, then I search for Carmina to show it to her. On my way past the library materials, I pick up an article by Edelsky, Draper & Smith (1983) "Hooken' 'em in at the start of school in a 'Whole Language' classroom." I think Carmina might find it interesting reading, as well. Discipline isn't a focal issue in that article, but it offers a useful discussion of values, rules, roles, and cues which might help redirect her questions about discipline.

I'm trying to let the readings raise issues and conflicting theoretical perspectives. Rather than confront the teachers with my beliefs directly, I keep offering them something to read which may lead them to question their personal assumptions.

After my brief conversation with Carmina I visit Penny. She's in the corridor reading **Creating Classrooms for Authors** (Harste & Short, 1988). We discuss the book.

"There are lots of useful suggestions for setting up a reading/ writing classroom in it," she says.

"I agree there are some interesting curriculum ideas in it, but I have some reservations about the book," I reply. "In a context like this one, where people are reading a variety of arguments, this book is very useful. You begin to understand some subtle differences in the instructional implementation of various researchers. But if this is **the** textbook, the only reference source people have access to, then I'm concerned because it doesn't allude to any of the mess that teachers have to deal with."

"But this morning, when you were talking about your teaching with Carmina, you made it seem very smooth, very simple, very straightforward. I didn't get the sense of you having to contend with any mess," Penny remarks.

That stops me. I didn't realize Penny had been eavesdropping on that conversation. Her comment suddenly lets me see I've become so accustomed to the mess and uncertainty of the kind of teaching I do that I don't even notice it any longer. In fact, it's the mess that signals to me it's time to stop and talk about what's going on—to invite people to examine the problems they're having and to think about ways of handling them.

"Good gracious, my classroom is very messy," I reply. "We're juggling several enterprises and I'm constantly having to keep track of a lot of different interests. Because I'm trying to foster a **just try** environment I'm encouraging people to take some big risks and that means helping you become comfortable with messing around."

"I can see the mess," she responds, "but you didn't talk about it. What you said made it seem as if it were never messy!"

"We better talk about that as a group, huh?"

"Well, I think the others would find it interesting to hear you talk about the mess of teaching. Most of the stuff I have read implies that this kind of teaching is tidy. But my efforts are bordering on the chaotic. So, yes, I think we should discuss it."

I write

　　mess

in my notebook before I leave Penny. It's probably a good issue to raise in my reflection this evening. By handling it this way, I'm foreshadowing a discussion. People will have thought about the issue before we talk about it.

Janice, Leslie, and Norma are talking quietly around the corner. I listen as I slowly walk past.

"...What I'm still wondering though," says Leslie, "is do you find when you're reading the piece yourself you concentrate too much on the 'can't'?"

"Yes, if it's a content conference, I don't read it," says Norma. "The kids know what they have written so I find they read it better than I can. I stumble over their spelling and handwriting. And since at that point I'm really just trying to help with the flow of the story, I don't want to be distracted by the surface stuff."

"What is the point of them reading rather than retelling the story, then?" Leslie asks.

"I don't think it matters," Norma answers. "It accomplishes the same thing, don't you think?"

"So that's another option, then," says Janice.

"But there's one thing that might happen." Norma says, "Take the kid who's not quite good at writing what she intends, she means one thing and the reader gets a totally different idea— if she's retelling she might not discover that the reader doesn't understand what she's actually written."

"But one advantage retelling has is that if you look at the writing you might think the child has little sense of story while their retelling is coherent," says Janice.

"So maybe it depends on the kid..."

*That's an interesting question. Do I read students'
writing, do I ask them to read it to me or do I invite
them to retell what they've done so far. In my
experience it's a judgement call. What I decide to do
depends on who the writer is, what I know about his
or her writing, how far the writing has progressed,
why it's being written in the first place.*

Bruce, Maggie, and Shelagh are also deep in conversation.

"...so that's one assumption. Create an environment that
fosters a sense of self-worth, one that's sort of safe and
predictable that will let them take risks," says Bruce.

"That's also assuming this is a very social age and their
peers are important to them and that if they're allowed to work
with their peers it will foster the writing," adds Maggie.

"Not just at that age. At any age," says Bruce.

"But she's directing her arguments toward grade 8," Shelagh
asserts.

"So then there's the assumption that learning is social?" asks
Bruce.

"There's a difference between assuming writing is social and
that everyone has ideas they can put into writing, isn't there?"
says Shelagh.

"Well, isn't Judith trying to show us a connection between
these two? Aren't we finding things to write about because we
are talking to each other about our ideas?" Maggie asks....

*Sounds like they're discussing Atwell. Interesting that
they're trying to ferret out her underlying assumptions
and connect them to what I'm doing here in the
Institute.*

I tour the premises, touching base when I sense it might be
useful, leaving well enough alone when I think people are doing
just fine without my input.

I remember to look for Earl to find out how his writing's
going. He's been at the computer for a large part of the day. He
shows me a lengthy printout.

"Look at this mess," he complains. "What I've written so far
has been repeated **five** times. I can't figure out what I'm doing
but every time I save and then retrieve it I seem to be copying
everything again. How do I get rid of the extra junk?"

"Let me have a look," I offer.

I sit at his computer and start reading. I figure out what Earl's been doing wrong. He's been saving his text and then retrieving it into the writing currently in memory. He doesn't need to retrieve after a save in order to resume writing. I show him what his problem is and help him clean up the mess.

Susan is also at a computer. We talk a bit about what's happening for her. She's finding it very useful, she says, to be part of these conversations. The teachers' concerns are helping her think about some projects she might undertake with teachers in her school district this fall.

I talk briefly with the others in the computer lab, then head back to the classroom.

The group reassembles at 3:30. We take a few moments to do a reflective freewrite: 'What's one thing I've learned today?' as a way of recapping what's gone on. People share their experiences. There's mention of how talking about what they're reading and about their writing has relieved anxiety considerably. Norma raises the issue of structure. She's been watching me closely, she says. She's become very aware of the intricacy of the structure I've been creating.

"You're going to be working with senior high resource students in September, aren't you?" I ask. "You need to think about what you're learning from your experience here and how you can apply it. Try drawing up a list of observations. We'll talk about it soon."

*Norma's comments serve as a cue. I have forgotten my **Discussion Topics** list on the blackboard. This is the moment to use it again.*

I scribble

— Structure

under **Discussion Topics,** extending the invitation to the group as a whole,

"Think about what you're learning here and what questions that's raising about your own teaching.

"There's something else I'd like you to try for tomorrow. This morning, while I was meeting with one of the groups we discussed an activity I think we should all try. Please take a bit of time to freewrite this evening about something you like to do, why you decided to learn whatever it was, how you went about it, what other people did to help you, and how you could tell you were learning?"

"Wait a minute," says Michael. "Pass that by me again. How about writing the questions on the board?"

"Good idea."

I write down the four questions:

- why you decided to learn whatever it was?
- how did you go about it?
- what role did other people play?
- how you could tell you were learning?

and add

Thursday—learning experiences

to the **Discussion Topics** list.

"There are some other topics we should add to this list. Remember the short stories and poetry I handed out the first morning? I know some of you have read them. I think we should have a response session on the short stories tomorrow morning. Those of you who are interested, please read the stories and react in your reading log tonight." I write

Thurs. — short stories

"How about a poetry discussion on Friday?" I ask as I write

Fri. — poetry.

"What about **Dead Poet's Society**? You've asked us all to see the film. How about Monday to talk about it?" Leslie suggests.

That's right. I haven't forgotten my request—there just hasn't been time so far to get back to it. I'm glad Leslie raises it.

I add

Mon. — DPS

"I'd like to talk about children's books sometime," says Diane.

"Good idea," agrees Cathy.

"When?" I ask.

"How about Tuesday?" offers Bruce.

I write

Tues. — Children's Books

Now we're cooking. Our agenda is filling up. The major themes and issues I was hoping would surface have emerged. The trick will be dealing with all of them in the time we have available. We've just concluded our third day; seven days left in which to discuss the specific issues they've decided to focus on individually, to bring a piece of writing to completion, to talk about writing/reading connections, as well as deal with these other important concerns. I'm beginning to feel some pressure. Will I be able to orchestrate this event to a comfortable closure? I hope so. In any case, it's still too early to panic.

That brings the afternoon to a close.

Later in the evening I read and respond to journals. There are lots of interesting reflections:

Connie writes:

It was helpful for you to stop at our table. The mini-lesson about ways of visualizing situations helped me think about my writing. It is now becoming clearer to me what my role as collaborator might involve. I can see that intervention or touching base while students are in the process of writing is important, more so, perhaps, than at the end of a piece.

[I reply: I wasn't sure whether that metaphor would be helpful or not. Glad it was.]

Diane shares as well:

This reflective writing is beginning to link things together for me. Some of my preconceptions are crumbling. Connections with things I've been reading and hearing about the last few years are beginning to lose their sterility and are becoming more relevant to me personally.

[I write: If writing reflectively is useful for you, can you see some way you might use it with your third graders?]

Norma comments:

It is most interesting to watch this juggling in action. To see how long you wait before rescuing someone. What seems to happen is that while you're holding back very often someone from the group jumps in—which pushes them further along toward taking responsibility. What happens when you miscalculate and the rescue does not come quickly enough? What do you do to shore up the learner at that point?

[My response: Fortunately, my miscalculations aren't as devastating as they might be if I were an authoritarian teacher simply because I have many more opportunities to respond to what's going on and, as you point out, other people jump into the breach. I also try to be open about my blunders so people don't take things too personally.]

There are some interesting reactions to the reflection letter I wrote last night as well. Lorna responded to my comments about not waiting until a piece of writing is complete before sharing. She has written

I'm glad I shared my writing today. I was tempted to hold back until I thought I had really created something. But talking about it with the group answered many of the questions I had about what I was trying to say. I was able to return to the writing full of new ideas.

Leslie picked up on my question 'Were you aware that my questions, touching base, offering suggestions were writing conferences?' with her response

Not consciously, but I can see now they most definitely were. Seeing this in action is a big help for me. I have often wondered how will I ever get to talk (conference) with every student—and of course I couldn't in any formal, scheduled way.

After reading and responding to what the teachers have written I write my own reflection/letter for the next day. I decide to explore the mess of teaching.

I had an interesting conversation with Penny this afternoon about the mess of teaching. She pointed out that when I talk about a whole language classroom I make it seem very tidy. That's not at all how things are, however. Let's look at some of the mess of our situation. Having helped you start on individual writing projects, and having got our multiple 'conversations' going, I am now faced with having to orchestrate this juggling act. I have lots of on-the-spot decisions to make: Do I decide to sit with this group and listen to the discussion about some writing, keeping an eye out for an opportunity to throw in a mini-lesson? Or should I take a group and read poetry in order to demonstrate some ways of handling response to literature? Perhaps I should be doing some individual writing conferences?

Maybe my help is needed in the computer room? Or maybe I should stay out of everyone's way until I'm asked for help? But if I don't hover on the edges, eavesdropping, how do I know what's going on? Do I need to know what's going on?

Anyone else walking into this workshop expecting to find a teacher-led discussion of the whole class, or even of small groups, would certainly be aware of the mess of this situation. Half of you aren't anywhere in sight. You're off working on your own or with a couple of other people. I try to keep tabs on who's doing what but on the whole I stay out of your way as much as I can because I trust you will come find me if you need help. But I also can't quite leave the learning enterprise entirely up to you since you're not always aware that you could use help, but if I come around and ask "How's it going?" you might just ask me a question or make a comment which helps you see new connections.

I guess part of the reason I can handle this apparent lack of traditional structure, this **mess**, is that I trust each of you to find some way to become involved with what you're doing. The range of possible activity is sufficiently broad that if some work isn't going well, or you tire of doing it, you know there are other things to turn to. And I know I can usually handle most situations I might be presented with (although I have had students who have had me flummoxed, and I do make judgements which backfire); not because I have answers to every possible problem, but because I'm not uncomfortable acknowledging I haven't any idea about whatever it is you've raised and inviting you to discuss the situation. I know that as a group we will come up with a reasonable course of action. So I guess I'm asking you to think about the mess of what you're experiencing and to share with me your reactions about how my handling of it is affecting you.

Next, I review my notes:
    — listening and talking with a pencil in hand.
I check that one off.
    — freewrite - response to Smith.
We did that.
    — Thurs. - Learning Stories.
I did manage to remember to ask people to do that. Haven't written anything myself. I'll do it before I leave in the morning.

— Thurs. - Graves.

Damn. I forgot about that. I better do it right now. I take my copy of **Writing: Teachers and Children at Work** and prepare to reread the section on "Making the Writing Conference Work."

— Thurs. - Short Stories.

That's OK.

— Mini-lessons.

Still have to raise that. I better write a post-it note and put it on the computer. I must remember to write about that tomorrow evening.

Yesterday was slow. People were getting started. Today we've moved ahead full steam. Now that we're rolling there's lots to juggle. We've got writing on the go. We are having both group and individual conversations about writing. People are reading to answer some of their own questions. We are engaging in a number of written conversations. I've introduced what I hope will be a couple of useful strategies and metaphors which should come into play as we work along.

Our agenda is shaping up and here's where commitment becomes important. The teachers are going to have to make some real choices about where they want to direct their energies. There's now too much happening for people to take part in everything. That has been intentional on my part; by getting many different enterprises off the ground I've made sure people can find something to capture their interest. My concern now becomes one of juggling the entire effort. That means keeping a close watch on individual learners.

Flying Kites

from up here it looks easy
even effortless
i ride on the breeze
going where i need to go
i have my freedom

i am bound to the kite flyer
by a thread so thin
many people cannot tell
that we are attached

but without the thread
i would be lost
carried god knows where
at the whim of any wind

the kite flyer has to know
when to pull in on the line
and when to pay out more

the kite flyer has to know
how to keep me from becoming
ensnared in wires
entangled in trees

it is a delicate thing
keeping a kite aloft

Larry Bent

By the fourth day I am completely engrossed in flying kites. Our enterprise is well underway. Everyone has begun a piece of writing. People are reading widely: professional books and periodicals, poetry, short stories, children's books, my letters and responses to them, and one another's writing. We are engaging in a variety of interesting discussions. I try paying out as much line as people need so they can use the breeze to best advantage but at the same time I have to keep a close watch on the tension making sure it's adequate to keep each kite soaring.

I am up early this morning working on my learning assignment in preparation for the class discussion. I decide to explore how I became involved in building and flying kites. I write:

Where did my interest in kites come from? I started kite flying when my two-and-a-half-year-old nephew Robbie (now sixteen) arrived for a ten-day visit in the country bringing his tricycle, a soccer ball, his fishing gear, and his kite with him. I had never flown a kite before, but wind conditions on that coastal shore were perfect and on our first attempt we succeeded in getting the kite airborne.

We flew his kite nearly every day of Robbie's visit. After he left I decided I wanted a kite of my own. When I couldn't buy one I decided to make one. Built of light-weight clothing nylon and 1/4" wood dowel, my red and yellow delta wouldn't fly at first. It took a while to sort out the construction problems, but once I had, I flew that kite often. Then one late November day a gusty wind snapped the line and my kite disappeared. I immediately built another.

Over the years I've made many different kinds of kites. Some I have kept. Many I have given away in an effort to entice other people to become fliers. By and large, however, I have indulged my interest alone. I keep kites in my car, ready for any inviting wind. I travel with at least one kite and I seek out kite stores so I can chat with other enthusiasts about kite design, construction, and flying.

Like most serious single-line fliers, I've developed an interest in dual-line kites. But I haven't been very successful flying them. Last year in Honolulu, however, I had a chance to watch some experts. One young man, Rusty, was flying a pair of stunt kites. He positioned them on the ground, then, holding the lines taut, back away from the kites and pulled—the kites would lift off. He manoeuvred his kites with ease—right-angled turns, loop-the-loops in one direction then back in the other, swooping dives which just avoided ending in a crash. His stunt repertoire was intriguing to watch. I particularly noticed his arm position: nearly straight, by his sides, not bent at his waist. I could see why—he had much better control that way. I had been holding the lines at waist-height and finding it difficult to sustain the flight left and right. We talked a lot about controlling the movement. I learned a lot about how to manoeuvre the kite from watching how he did it.

Later I got to watch a stunt kite competition. Each competitor flew two, or more, four-line kites in formation to music. It was amazing. I now have a better idea of what stunts are possible and although I am nowhere close to being able to perform like those competitors, I know what I'm aiming toward!

How did I go about learning? I learned by trying things out myself. I built kites and flew them. Each new kite taught me more about the wind and the aerodynamics of kites. I consulted books and magazines for ideas and hints. I subscribed to **Kitelines**, a quarterly periodical. My learning was also collaborative. I talked with other fliers whenever I had the chance. Each conversation broadened my understanding of kite construction and flying technique. Although I didn't have opportunities to fly with other experienced fliers very often, what conversation I did have answered my current questions and I was able to go further. My learning was always under my control. I chose when to initiate any further exploration. I decided when to give up for a while. And I have been learning for a long time—almost fourteen years now.

What role did other people play? People shared their experience. They talked with me about their kites. They answered my questions, offered suggestions, shared their interest and excitement. If there was any formal instruction, it came as 'I do it this way' in response to my questions.

How could I tell I was learning? I have become a reasonably skilled flier. I am able to launch kites in light or gusty conditions. And although I occasionally lose a kite to a kite-eating tree, I can usually extricate it, repair it, and fly again. My kite construction has become more sophisticated. I am able to solve design problems without having to consult reference materials. I am able to help less experienced fliers. No tests, other than flying successfully, time after time.

My reflection is far from complete. However, it's time to leave; so I save and print out my file, turn off the computer, and head for the university.

❖

I begin the morning by preparing the environment for the day. I leave my reflection/letter on the table by the door. I straighten up the books and periodicals on the back table and sort through the borrower cards to see who has been reading what. I clear away garbage left on the tables.

I must remind people to be responsible for that themselves. While I have no difficulty coping with ambiguity in the teaching situation, physical mess like this irritates me.

I check the **Writing Conversations** list taking note of names left over from yesterday. I collect responses to my yesterday's letter and remind people to swap journals with one another.

I'm trying to establish a multi-faceted written dialogue among members of the workshop. Encouraging them to respond to one another's journals is one more way of keeping issues on the table and conversation going.

"There are several tasks which follow on from yesterday. I was up early this morning writing about some learning of my own. I think we should discuss these learning experiences. Also, yesterday, when we were talking about Elbow's 'giving movies of our mind', Cathy asked about Don Graves's ideas for holding writing conferences, right? We want to talk about that sometime today. I'd also like to talk about the short stories and how you responded to them.

"At this point, though, I want to make something clear. I'm not expecting everyone to participate in every discussion. You're free to join those that interest you. What's happening here, of course, is that as we become more involved, more issues are coming up and there's more and more to talk about. You still want to keep a healthy chunk of time free during the day for writing, for reading, and for responding. I don't want to swallow up the entire day with class discussions and push those other activities over into homework. Writing and reading, in fact, are still the focus of our agenda and I want to make sure you have time to write and to read during the day. So you'll have to make some choices."

"The trouble is," says Norma, "everything is so interesting. I want to be part of the Graves discussion and last evening I read the short stories and I want to hear how other people reacted to them. I also worked some more on my story and have to talk about where to go next with someone and I need to discuss the issues that are emerging from the professional reading."

"I want to talk about the professional stuff, too," says Diane. "I started out reading about getting ideas on paper but that led me to revising and editing and responding to other people's writing and I need to talk about these ideas. The reflective journal is very helpful because it lets me record my reactions and questions, and I look forward to reading your written comments and those of other people, but I need to talk about the issues as well."

"How about the rest of you?"

Just about everyone nods in agreement.

"Well, how would you like to work that out?"

Hanna makes a suggestion. "We could begin a new list on the board called **Issues**, decide on some topics, and put our names beside the one that interests us."

"Sounds fine. Any other ideas?"

"I think Hanna's suggestion is a good one. The only thing is," says Janice, "there's already so much to do we may have a problem fitting it all in."

I hear murmurs of assent.

"We're talking choices here," I remind them. "One of the things about an enterprise-based learning situation is that new interests are continually being generated. Part of my responsibility is to keep various enterprises from getting out of hand, but at the same time I want to help you sustain your own interests. I think we can work something out here. Do we need to schedule a time when the whole class discusses **Issues** or is there some other way we could operate?"

I've been launching kites for a couple of days, testing the wind with different kites, now it's time to pay out more line. I want to hand over some of the decision-making to the participants. We have some structures in place and it's time for people to improvise with what we've created. Norma and Diane have offered a teachable moment. I could take charge and schedule another discussion session, cutting into our already fairly full time. It seems to me, though, the teachers need to make some decisions for themselves.

"Why don't we begin by listing some issues?" Connie suggests.

I move to the blackboard and write **Issues.**

"Well, I want to talk about revising and editing," says Diane. "I'm reading about that stuff but I'm also beginning to need to do it with my own writing. I want to talk about Smith's (1982) and Murray's (1984) and Perl's (1983) and Mayher's (1985) ideas about writing. They're not all saying quite the same thing, I don't think."

I write under **Issues**

Revising and Editing

and wait.

"I know we're going to talk about Graves as a whole group but I need to talk about various ways of responding to writing a lot more," says Theresa.

I add

Responding to Writing

"I'm intrigued by how people see reading feeding into writing and writing into reading," says Bruce. "I need to talk about Smith's 'reading like a writer' notion again in relation to some of the other stuff I've been reading."

I write

Reading/Writing Relationships

on the list and wait again. No one offers else anything immediately.

"Perhaps three topics is enough to start with," I say.

I realize I'm cutting off the issue-generating process with my speculation. If I waited a bit longer I know more issues would surface but our agenda is certainly becoming full and we're going to have to come up with a scheme for meeting and talking about these issues.

"Any suggestions for how to proceed from here?"

"Obviously, now we need to sign up and then as a group decide when to get together," says Norma.

I could have guessed Norma would be the one to suggest a procedure. She doesn't hesitate to take a leadership role. If I'm not careful I could come to depend on her to be 'teacher.' She's done a lot of reflecting on her teaching these past several years and so she sees alternate ways of going about something. But I think it may be time to have a private word with her about what's happening and help her see she might find it useful to take a leadership role not by offering solutions herself but by helping others work things out. I know, from conversations we've had in our monthly study group, she's been struggling to move away from 'teaching by telling' as Don Murray (1982) describes it. Here's an opportunity for her to work at teaching by what Gordon Wells (1986) calls 'leading from behind.'

"How about this: sign up if you're interested in any of the **Issues** topics during the morning. At noon we can get together briefly in those groups and decide when to meet. Will that work, do you think?" I ask.

I see agreement. "Fine, then let's do that."

Now, do we want to begin with the discussion of Graves or the learning experiences? Whichever we don't do now, we'll get to either later today or tomorrow. I could make the decision myself. In fact, I'm tempted to do just that. I would prefer to open with the discussion of learning experiences. Although I suspect the teachers see this as a peripheral matter, I want to use it to set up a contrast for us to pursue later. By comparing our various learning experiences we'll be able to articulate similarities and differences in why we chose to learn what we did, how we went about it, the roles other people played, and how we could tell we were learning. That list of similarities and differences would invite a comparison with what goes on in our classrooms. It would give me the opportunity to ask people to reflect on the kinds of factors that support them as learners and to think about how to build them into their classrooms.

I know what I'd like people to see: their learning in the real world is under their control and it takes time. Smith's list applies here, too: 'learning is unconscious, effortless, incidental, vicarious, and essentially collaborative.' These various factors are the foundation of the experience I'm attempting to create. I want people to think about how I've gone about setting that up.

I also want to use that discussion to focus, once again, on the 'talking and listening with a pencil in hand' strategy I introduced earlier. To really explore these different learning experiences it'll be necessary for everyone to keep track of the different aspects of people's stories. We could create a group list and photocopy it, but it's their different ways of making notes that I want to highlight later. That diversity will actually be helpful for articulating similarities and differences.

*However, I suspect that to do the discussion justice
we'd need at least an hour and I'd rather not take up
that much time at this point in the morning so I decide
to let people choose. I'm betting they'll want to talk
about Graves. We'll set aside time this afternoon to
talk about the learning experiences.*

"Which do you want to do now: explore your learning
experiences or discuss Graves' ideas about responding to
writing?" I ask.

"I'd like to talk about Graves," says Cathy. "I've been trying
very hard to help my teachers institute process writing in their
classrooms. I think I would find it helpful to talk about what he
says."

*There's that jargon phrase: 'process writing.
Teachers locally, and across the continent, are
throwing it around freely as if it meant something. It's
become a catch-all signifying
anything from having the kids
keep journals, which some
teachers conscientiously mark
with red pens, to having
every piece of writing rigidly
go through three, or five,
editing stages. The problem is
that the phrase distracts
teachers' gaze from where it
ought to be: on learning from
and with their students.
They're focusing instead on
some arbitrary set of writing
rituals—the new orthodoxy.*

Guilty! Guilty! Guilty! I too used to think the phrase 'process writing' meant something. My first foray into whole language was à la Nancie Atwell. I devoured *In the Middle* and then I implemented her process approach in my senior high classes. I nearly killed myself trying to keep up with the work, and I hounded my students to adhere to the process. When I started to write more actively myself, I discovered that process is dependent on the needs of the writer and the piece being written. There is no magic formula; some pieces need little revision, others aren't worth revising. My students knew that, but at that time they were writers and I wasn't.

Patricia Whidden

*Do I say something about
it here or let it go for the
moment? I decide to let the phrase pass. I'll get the
chance to say something about it in the small groups.
If not I can add it to the list of things to raise in my
reflection/letter this evening. I make a note for myself:*
mention 'process writing'

"What's the consensus?" I ask.

"Well, we had a glimpse at Elbow yesterday. It might be
useful to look at Graves today," says Earl.

"What do the rest of you think?"

Nods of agreement. Looks like I guessed correctly.

"OK. How do you want to go about it?"

I could easily suggest a comparison matrix here:

	Elbow	Graves
Role of writer		
Role of reader		
etc.		

but if I do that, I lose the opportunity for discovering which of them uses the strategy already. I also want to find out if anyone will suggest inkshedding as a tactic. There's no need for each group to use the same focusing strategy. In fact it might be interesting if they use different ones because that will allow us to discuss the relative merits of various tactics.

"What I'd like to do," offers Bruce, "is list Graves's suggestions and then see how Elbow compares."

"That's certainly a useful way of approaching the task. You'll need to work out a basis for comparing them."

"Are there any other ideas about how to proceed?" I ask.

Part of what I'm coming to see is my need to make 'personal sense' of what various authors are trying to work through but in a critical way which helps me explore what I think about it all and how I might translate those beliefs into personal and classroom practice. Rather than buying into their 'how-to's, I see myself 'writing' and constantly 'revising' my own practices. In some instances I'll be very aware that something I'm doing with the kids has been influenced by something I've read. I'll be very aware of who I connected with in a particular context. In others, I'll have no idea when someone else's ideas have become my own.

Lynn Moody

I wait, but no volunteers. The comparison suggestion is an obvious choice; it's a typical school activity. They don't see doing something as apparently unstructured as inkshedding as applicable in this kind of situation. I think it's important to suggest the possibility, though.

"What about inkshedding, here? You read and responded to Graves yesterday, right? You could swap your writing and react to one another. I suspect something interesting would come from that."

An interesting dilemma. The teacher has suggested a direction. Is it a decree? Are they expected to follow it? I better say something about choice again.

"Just because I've made the suggestion doesn't mean you have to comply. I've tossed it out so that you can see there's more than one way of approaching the task, that's all. It's up to you as a group to decide how you want to conduct your discussion."

With that I get out of their way.

❖

I watch for a while to see what the groups decide to do. Shelagh, Maggie, and Bruce have taken a blank piece of paper and divided it into two columns. What they haven't done is create a column for category labels. I stop and we talk about why it's important to make the bases for comparison explicit by identifying specific aspects of the arguments being compared. I take a new sheet of paper and invite the three of them to begin brainstorming ideas for categories.

Not a simple comparison to make as it turns out. It would be much easier if we were discussing either just Elbow or Graves, but because their arguments are so different we have difficulty coming up with categories that apply readily to the particular chapters we've read.

I write

role of teacher

simply to get something on paper. We may decide later to subdivide that category, or we might want to eliminate it altogether, but we need to begin somewhere. Shelagh suggests

responsibilities of students.

Bruce adds

types of feedback.

A bit more conversation leads to

timing of feedback.

"That should give you something to work with. Don't feel restricted to these categories," I caution. "Change them if they don't work. Add, delete, do whatever seems appropriate as your discussion proceeds. It's also a good idea for each of you to be keeping track of the conversation individually, right?"

A direct reminder to think and talk with a pencil in hand.

Before leaving the group I ask "What's just happened here?" They laugh at me.

I don't wait for an answer when I see Bruce reach for his notebook.

❖

Next I visit Hanna, Debra, Cathy, Janice, and Penny. They haven't begun to focus their discussion at all yet.

I've noticed this group is generally slow to do that. Learning to move directly to a focused conversation is a skill that takes time to develop. I don't want to intrude too directly too soon. They might be talking about something more valuable for them. So I listen for a few moments in order to find out what's going on.

They're telling stories about their difficulties with writing conferences.

Telling stories serves an important social function for a group. It builds a common experience and helps establish trust. However, storytelling on its own will take them only so far. They need to engage in some analysis of their assumptions if they're going to effect any change in their instructional practice. I listen for an opportunity to bring Graves into the conversation.

> I find deciding whether to participate or just eavesdrop incredibly difficult. I'm really having to fight my transmission teacher beliefs all the time. When I join a group I think it would have been better if I'd stayed out; when I stay out I think I've missed some important opportunities. I know you say we just have to try, but this just trying makes me uncomfortable.
>
> Linda Cook

"I have such a hard time knowing what to say," says Debra. "I find I want to be helping the kids make their stories more coherent. I keep asking questions about parts that are missing. But it doesn't seem to have much effect with my first graders. They never want to change anything."

"My grade fives are the same. I haven't been able to find a good way to engage them in revising. When I suggest any changes the typical response is 'Do we have to?'" complains Hanna. "I've tried peer conferencing and author circles but that doesn't seem to be helpful either. The kids respond to what they like in the writing and ask questions about parts they don't understand, but not much gets changed."

"I've experimented with having my fourth graders read their stories to the primary children, figuring the younger children would let them know where their writing didn't make sense to them. But that hasn't worked very well. The young ones just accept the stories as wonderful and there's no pressure to reconsider the writing," says Janice.

"What really frustrates me," declares Hanna, "is how so much of the kids' writing is TV cartoon fantasy. It's no wonder the stories don't make a lot of sense. Every time I have to read about Ninja turtles, I want to scream. I just don't know how to help them connect real events and experiences. I've tried suggesting personal narrative but I don't seem to get anywhere with it."

This might be a good place to jump in.

"Was Graves of any help to you?" I ask.

"I thought his response on page 147 about what to do when I think the piece needs a lot of work and the kid doesn't was helpful," says Hanna. "I have to admit I never thought of asking a child why she thinks her piece of writing is good. I can see that it would give me a chance to find out how the child views the writing. It would, I suppose, also give me an opportunity to ask if there was anything she wasn't entirely satisfied with. I'm terrified the child will think everything is fine. I saw that Graves did ask questions when there was a problem with the meaning of a piece even if the child thought it was good. But I find that so hard to do. When the child is satisfied I feel like I'm confronting a brick wall and have nowhere to turn."

"Here's where being a writer yourself is invaluable," I comment. "Being a writer allows me to bring my writing into the conversation. The most useful sharing times are when I'm stuck, or not sure about what direction to take, or when I sense something's wrong but I'm not sure what. That lets me show people the kinds of problems that can arise and we can discuss ways of handling them. If the kids are asking me questions about my writing, then I'm able to ask them questions about theirs in a way I couldn't otherwise."

"I haven't been a writer with the kids," Hanna replies, "but I can see how it would help."

"Was there anything else in Graves that raised questions about your writing conversations with the kids?" I ask.

"Graves is definitely saying the children should speak first," comments Cathy. "I really was surprised yesterday when you made a point of having us give reactions. Why did you do that?"

It was Cathy's comment yesterday that made me suggest we read Graves so we could compare his and Elbow's positions on responding to writing.

"The danger in the classroom is that instruction can quickly turn into ritual. That's what's happening with Graves's work. You hear so many people say 'I'm **doing** process writing'—a fair indication that they've grabbed on to some surface features of the complex process he or Atwell (1987) or Calkins (1986) describe without engaging in the personal reflection that's an integral component of their arguments. Graves (1984) himself cautions us about the dangers of orthodoxy.

"It's important to remember there's no single right way of doing anything in the classroom. What instruction we choose to offer is affected by a large number of factors. When it comes to writing, how you respond as teacher depends on what you already know about a particular student's writing history, about her repertoire of writing strategies, about how developed the particular piece of writing is, why it's being done, for example. There's no one right thing to do. I know most of you have at least heard of Graves if you haven't read him extensively. But how many of you know of Elbow's arguments? I thought it would be useful to introduce a strategy that I find very helpful and one I suspect you're unfamiliar with. 'Giving movies of our minds' isn't the only way of responding to writing, but it is generally an informative response. I thought it might be a useful first strategy to offer."

"But isn't there a danger in telling a child how you respond to her writing?" Cathy persists.

"What's the danger you see?"

"Well, it sounds like what we've always done—tell the child what's wrong with the writing. It seems to me it's just the same old stuff."

"It depends on what you tell and how you tell it, doesn't it?" I ask her. "You might find it useful to have a look at how Harste and Short (1988) describe what happens in what they call 'Authors' Circle.' They suggest the children begin by commenting on what they heard in another child's story, what connections they made. Isn't that similar to 'giving movies of our mind'?"

I don't want to challenge Graves's ideas directly myself. Instead, I want Harste/Short to help Cathy examine her assumptions about writing instruction. I'm sensing she has an investment in Graves. She seems to be reluctant to look at his work with a critical eye. I think I need to talk with her about what she's been working on with her staff. I may have to help her think about 'It depends' a bit more. I make a note to remind me to bring her my copy of **Creating Classrooms for Authors** *and I must remember to chat with her over lunch, if I can.*

"Any other connections?" I wonder.

"I found Graves's categories of questions useful. I hadn't thought about 'opening' questions, or 'following' or 'process' ones," offers Debra.

She may not have thought about names for the categories, but she uses these various kinds of questions every time she has a conversation with anyone. Do I bring that to her attention? If I do, will I get a 'yes, but...'?

"A problem with calling conversations about writing 'conferences'," I comment, "is that it makes us think there's something special and mysterious about it. The fact is, you all know about opening, following, process, etc., kinds of questions. You use them every time you have a conversation with anyone. Watch yourself on the phone, for example, or when you start a conversation at lunch. See how you handle the talk. The only thing about having conversations about writing with our students is we think we're supposed to be teaching. If, instead, we approach the conversation the way we would a conversation with a friend, we'd listen to what they have to say, share our reactions, and not worry about 'how do I make this better'. Not that we wouldn't keep an eye out for an opportunity to ask a question that might help the writer view her writing differently, but on the whole, if we're having a conversation, responding pretty much takes care of itself."

"I can see your point," concedes Debra, "but I find it so hard to know what to say to the kids."

"You have conversations with your own children at home, don't you? How do you know what to say?" I ask her. "Watch yourself this evening. After the kids have gone to bed reflect in your log about what went on. See what you can learn.

"It might be a useful thing for the rest of you to try, too. See what you find out," I invite them.

Quite likely it's a good idea to invite the whole class to monitor a couple of conversations in the next twenty-four hours. I'm sure we'd learn a great deal. I make a note to remind myself to mention it. But now I glance at the clock and see time is zooming along. Better make tracks for another group.

"So far, you've identified three aspects of Graves's work that were useful: asking the children what they like about a piece of writing, letting the children talk first, and the different types of questions he suggests. This might be a good point to begin recording your discussion in some way so that you can refer to what you've discussed later," I suggest.

Although I've worked with Cathy and Hanna before, the other three are new to me. I still don't know much about their backgrounds or their strategies yet. I can see I'm going to need to help this group learn how to develop and sustain an analytic focus. My hint about recording their discussion may help them continue making connections with Graves and Elbow; on the other hand they may not have heard me. I'll have to see how they fare.

❖

As I attempt to join the next group I encounter an interesting problem. Theresa, Barb, Connie, Michael, and Carmina have taken me up on my inkshedding suggestion. They're busy responding to one another's writing. I'm the odd person out here.

The question is, do I try to slip into the flow of reading and responding or do I leave them alone? I'm curious to see how the inkshedding is going. I also want to find out whether the conversation in the rest of the class is disturbing for this group, so I join in.

I pull up a chair and sit quietly until Barb, beside me, finishes reacting to the response she's reading. I take my reaction to Graves from the pocket in my notebook, hand it to her, and pick up the one she's just finished. I read:

I'm definitely struck by the differences between Graves's 'rules of thumb' and Elbow's. They're nearly opposite. With Elbow, rule #1 is that the writer listens, the readers share their experiences of the writing. With Graves, the teacher (reader) listens while the writer talks. Graves really is insistent that the writer must talk first. Why the difference? Is it because we're talking about writers of different ages? Graves is writing about young kids and Elbow is obviously writing about college students and adults.

Barb has written in the margin here:

I was wondering the same thing myself. I have a difficult time imagining children responding in the way Elbow is suggesting.

I add:

Perhaps Graves is insistent that the writer talk first because as teachers we're so preoccupied with "telling" and "correcting." If we force ourselves to listen we might find we learn something about the student we wouldn't get to learn otherwise.

I read on.

I felt Graves made conferencing seem quite prescriptive with his lists of questions. However, the key to questioning, I realize, is in the listening. REAL LISTENING—which is something I have a problem with. Because conferencing is something new for me, I grabbed right on to the questions provided by Calkins to use during a conference time. Now after reading Graves, I was gently reminded about the use of questioning and how questions should be appropriate for where a particular student is.

I respond:

Because people give it a fancy name 'conferencing' you think it's something you don't know how to do. But think about it. You know how to have a conversation. You have lots of conversations every day. You know how to listen. Why do you believe these conversations about writing are different?

Graves says, 'Mrs. Altman didn't acquire these conference skills overnight.' But that's what many teachers are looking to do at in-services or when they read these articles. I think that the rigid time outline on page 142 for conducting "The Writing Period" is unfortunate. Things rarely fall into place as neatly as Graves implies here. And when I have a mess on my hands I'm not likely to say to myself, 'Graves is too prescriptive,' I'm likely to wonder 'What's wrong with me that I can't do it the way he's outlined it?'

I continue:

People have the idea that if they're given 'tips' they're all set. It doesn't work that way, though, does it? In the end it all comes down to understanding why we make the decisions we do.

I finish reading this freewrite and react to a second before I feel I should move on. I'll come back later and retrieve mine. It's now pushing ten o'clock. Doesn't look like I'll make it to the fourth group.

I make a note reminding myself to start with Norma, Lorna, Diane, Helen, Leslie, and Earl next time. It's not crucial that I visit each group every time so long as I touch base regularly enough to know whether people are having problems or not.

I watch the fourth group for a moment and I can see there's productive engagement there. Elbows are on the table, faces are animated. I eavesdrop on the conversation from a distance and can hear connections being made between their own experiences and the reading they've done. They're OK without me.

❖

I want to bring the whole class together briefly now to establish closure before moving on. I want to share the various ways the discussion has been tackled—to make the point that everyone doesn't have to do things the same way for an experience to be productive. Besides, there's writing to continue, short stories to talk about, reading and responding to be done. Our agenda is becoming full. On the one hand, it's wonderful; but on the other, it's getting more complicated to orchestrate.

"Talk to me about what's been going on."

Conversation dies down.

"We've been reading and responding to one another's freewrites," volunteers Michael.

"How did that work?" I ask.

"I thought I would be bothered by the conversation in the rest of the class but I became engaged enough with the reading that I realize I didn't hear it," he comments.

"I wondered about that, which is why I joined you," I remark. "I found the same thing. I think I was aware of the talk in the rest of the room when I stopped to ponder what to write, but once I began scribbling I forgot about it again. What about the rest of you?"

Murmurs of agreement from the others.

"What did you learn from the reading/responding?"

"I was surprised at the different ways people reacted to what Graves had to say," says Barb. "I don't know why I expected we'd all respond to the same thing. I like reading other people's reactions. I sometimes find it hard to know what to write back, though."

"It might be interesting to think about whether there's any commonality to the kinds of responses and connections which invoke comment and those which don't. I'd be interested in any generalizations you might find."

Years of responding to students journal/freewrites suggests there are some useful generalizations. I find it hard, for example, to respond when the writer has taken no risk in the writing, when there's no personal exploration, no examination of self. I wonder if they'll find the same thing.

"We decided not to inkshed," says Maggie. "We preferred to use Bruce's idea of making a direct comparison between Graves and Elbow. It wasn't easy though because their positions are diametrically opposed, I would say."

"You might find it interesting to read an article I wrote about their conflicting views (Newman, 1985). Someone remind me to dig it out for you."

> *I rarely remember to do things like this unless I have a written reminder. That's why the notes to myself in my notebook and publicly on the blackboard. I usually make a point of having people write me notes, and of writing notes to them, from the very beginning of a course. Because we're spending so much time together during the Institute, there really hasn't been a need for a message board which is something I inaugurate with most of my classes (actually we use e-mail on the mainframe computer to send notes to one another).*

"What did you find by doing the comparison?"

"I think we confirmed there are a number of different ways of going about conferencing," laughs Shelagh.

"Why was that interesting?" I inquire.

"I guess it forces us to recognize there isn't one way of instituting a writing workshop. I've been trying to follow Atwell's guidelines pretty closely but running into lots of difficulty. Our discussion of Graves and Elbow made me realize I have to stop trying to be Atwell and learn how to take my lead from where the students are."

> *An important insight, I'd say. I've been trying to nudge Shelagh to let go for nearly two years. This is the first time I've heard her say she needs to look beyond the experts for **the answer.***

> *No need to belabor the discussion. A couple of useful insights have been shared. That's plenty for now.*

I suggest we reread Hunt's "Could you put in lots of holes?" and Wayne Serebrin's "A Writer and an Author Collaborate."

"These articles add interesting dimensions to our conversation about writing. We'll discuss them tomorrow, OK?"

First, I make a note in my book:

Friday AM—Hunt/Serebrin

then I write a reminder on the blackboard under the **Discussion Topics** list.

"It's now just past ten o'clock. Here's how I'd like to run the rest of the day."

I move to the blackboard and write **Thursday** boldly near the top of the left-hand panel. Beneath I write

10 - 10:45 Short Stories

followed by

2:45 - 3:30 Learning Experiences

Between I put

10 - 3:30 Writing, Reading, Responding, Writing
   Conversations

"Anything I've forgotten?"

"You have a time overlap in there. Did you mean it?" asks Bruce.

"Yes, I did. I am scheduling in some specific discussions but you can choose to participate, or not. That decision really is yours. We need to keep the writing progressing because I'd like us to produce a class book by next Friday. So we're operating with a deadline. How you get there is up to you. If you prefer to write in the evening, that's fine.

"Also, I would like to keep in touch with what you're doing. I've had my eye on the **Writing Conversations** list. I'd like to chat with each of you every couple of days. Will that be OK?"

"Hmm," Bruce replies. We all laugh.

It makes me nervous to have the kids off in several different directions at the same time but when I try it I'm surprised by how well they handle themselves. It really is connected to choice and engagement, isn't it? I mean, when they have some say in what they're doing they're much more committed to it. Nevertheless, I worry that they're goofing off, that we won't get the curriculum 'covered,' that the principal will have a fit.

Linda Swinwood

Bruce is very engaged in what's going on and doesn't want to miss anything. His expression is one of frustration. His comment reflects the difficulty the teachers are having taking control of their own learning. They'd be much happier if I made all the decisions. Of course it would be easier for them, but a lot less interesting.

❖

"OK, who's interested in discussing the short stories? Help me move some tables so we can sit together."

We quickly rearrange the furniture, moving people's belongings to the side of the room. Some of the teachers have moved to the corridor to write. Others have gone to the computer room. Twelve of us squeeze ourselves around this square table and I make a note of who's present.

*I keep a record of who's participated in which
conversations so I know what connections to try
building with whom.*

"How do we want to proceed?" I open.

There's a silence. I wait. The silence continues.

"I take it you want me to offer some direction."

*I look around the table at the faces. The bodies aren't
pulled back but I sense caution. I'm not surprised.
Talking about stories in an instructional setting like
this usually means having the teacher tell you what the
story is about. However, what I'm trying to do here is
create a reader response situation. I want the teachers
to share what Louise Rosenblatt (1978) refers to as
their 'lived through experience.' I want them to discover what they were experiencing while reading these
stories. Even further, I'd like to encourage them to
explore how these stories let them 'read themselves.'
Seeing* **ourselves** *in new ways, taking a new
perspective on our own life circumstances, Margaret
(Meek) Spencer (1987) contends, is the real purpose
of a literary experience.*

"I think we might find it useful if we explore the movies of
our mind these stories have evoked. Remember Elbow's
suggestions: pointing, summarizing, telling, and showing?
Let's react as if these authors were here, wanting to know how
their writing affected us."

*I have an ulterior motive. Not only am I interested in
helping people respond to stories more personally,
I'm also trying to keep my sights on the writing that's
going on. I want to help the teachers learn to be more
responsive to how writing makes them feel so that
they can respond to one another's writing more
spontaneously. Another instance of 'wax on, wax
off'. And of course, I'm wanting them to see
connections between what they experience here and
what their students experience.*

"Someone start."

"OK," offers Barb. "'The Last Wife'[1] was the story in the
collection I liked best."

---

[1] "The Last Wife," by Marian Engel (1985), is a story about a housewife in her
late thirties, early forties, who confronts her contented, peaceful, domestic
life with her husband. Never divorced, still at home looking after the family,
Pat allows a phone conversation with her long-time friend, Marina, to instill a
pinch of guilt about giving up her career as a commercial artist to become a

"How about reading something from your reading log," I invite her.

"I don't know if it'll make any sense."

"That's alright. We all understand you were writing a spontaneous reaction," I reassure her.

Barb takes a big breath and reads:

> I have trouble connecting with the main character Pat. I feel a closer affinity, I think, with Marina, her friend. Oh, not the details of Marina's life, but the rushing, the compartmentalization. I certainly don't long for Pat's balanced equanimity. The crusading, the uproar which are central to Marina, feel more like me. And yet, there are times when my internal 'mother' is very strong and I'd love to be nurturing someone.

"Talk about your reaction a bit," I invite her.

"I identified with Marina. I feel my life is like that: more of a hectic pace. I'm having to deal with the family, with the teaching, with taking courses. Generally I feel like I'm on a roller coaster. There are moments when I wish my life were simpler, more like Pat's."

"I think I saw more of myself in Pat," says Janice. "I am more of the plain stolid one, rather than the rushing-through-life kind of person Marina is. I recently experienced the same sort of shock Pat describes of not feeling very different now than I was twenty years ago, yet I know I must be changing just as everyone else is. I look in the mirror and see a different person there. The kids are growing up so I must be changing too."

"I connected with the Canadian bits in the story, the 'eh?'s, for example. It was funny to see that there. I haven't read very much Canadian writing, so those Canadian bits jumped out at me," reflects Maggie.

"What questions does that raise about the reading your students are doing?" I ask her.

"I guess I can understand why we need to find material that lets them see themselves in the stories more. I became aware of a special affinity I felt with these two women. I don't think I feel alienated by the lack of Canadian contact, but finding it in the story certainly made me feel closer in some way."

"There's that lovely comment Pat makes on page 16 about Marina being like an eggbeater," says Hanna. "I could just see

---

wife and mother. In an argument with her husband she reveals a snippet of her secret inner life which disconcerts him. His discomfort comforts her, for her perfectly calm life now contains a flaw.

her whirling. I think what's interesting, though, is that to a lot of people, Pat's life would seem similar. In the middle of plastering her son's room she's rushing to answer the phone, deal with people at the door. She's coping with the kids various activities, doing errands for her husband, just keeping the family going. Pat may not see her life as chaotic, but it could be seen that way."

I'm enjoying this discussion a great deal. I'm not having to say anything because they are carrying the conversation themselves. I'm not sure they're aware of just how probing their responses are. So far no comments from the two men in the group. I invite a reaction.

"So far we've heard from some of the women. I'm curious about how the story affects a male reader."

Michael responds. "I don't think the fact that the central character is a woman matters a whole lot. I didn't identify with either character, but the story did make me think about how I see my own life. I don't do that very often but I happened to write in my log:

That bit about 'the whole world was upset and she was happy' has made me stop for a moment and ask myself how I'm feeling right now. I think I feel a comfortable satisfaction with what I'm doing. I'm enjoying teaching. The family is growing up. We're not dealing with any crises at the moment. I certainly don't feel uncomfortable about feeling comfortable.

"Look what Engel does with the very next line: 'She cut herself grating the carrots,'" laughs Maggie. "It's wonderful. The irony implied by that sentence. That's what Pat remembers as the big event of her day."

"Did you find the stories talking to one another?" I ask.

"Oh, now that's an interesting idea," remarks Bruce. "I wouldn't have ever thought about stories talking to one another but they can, can't they?"

I'm a bit surprised by the question myself; I've never asked it before but the diversity of conversation we've been having: within small groups, as a large group, between me and individuals, among the teachers, with many different authors, orally and in writing, and I suddenly see the potential for stories to talk to one another, too.

"Well, I found 'The Last Wife' affected how I reacted to 'Prue,'[2] says Shelagh. "I felt strong similarities between the two women. Both of them were really quite happy with their lives. Prue wasn't unhappy with her affair with Gordon. What probably pushed her to leave him was simply the silly way he tried to deal with the cafuffle over his fight with his other girl friend. I think she finally saw how foolish he really was. I mean, standing there with the overnight bag which the other woman had just flung at him clutched to his chest and asking Prue to marry him (in a few years time, of course)."

"I wondered about that paragraph at the end about the stuff she'd stolen from Gordon, the enamelled dish, a sterling-silver salt spoon, a crystal fish, a single cufflink. The story felt unfinished to me," Theresa says.

"I thought Munro handled that in a nicely ironic way," replies Bruce. He reads:

> She doesn't do it in a daze and she doesn't seem to be under a
> compulsion. She just takes something, every now and then, and puts it
> away in the dark of the old tobacco tin, and more or less forgets about
> it.

You know that for years every time she's been unsatisfied, been short changed by him, she has taken something from him, nothing important but something that leaves his life a little less complete. He probably doesn't even notice these things are gone. But that doesn't really matter. Prue has found a way to get her own back."

"Thinking about Prue's story in conjunction with 'The Last Wife' the ending takes on a different meaning for me," I reflect. "I think I felt a bit like Theresa, at first, the story ended abruptly. But I think I now see Prue taking that part of her life and stashing it away in the tobacco tin, with other parts of her life, and more or less forgetting about it. The act of taking the cufflink is like Pat's inconsequential argument with her husband—another small flaw in her life that gives her some secret pleasure. I wondered about the secret stories each of those other objects implied. Talking about a secret life, I think 'Miss

---

[2]"Prue," by Alice Munro (1983), is a story of a middle-aged woman's termination of her affair with a wealthy, sometimes-married neurologist. Not unhappy with her life with him, she ends the affair, however, with his proposal of marriage ("In a few years time," he says) when his current amour interrupts Prue and Gordon's intimate dinner for two by throwing his belongings in his face.

Manning's Angelic Moment'[3] is another story about a person's secret inner life. You know, I didn't see these three stories as connected when I put the collection together; I chose them simply because I liked them and they were all very short. Secret inner life, I have to think about that idea some more. I recently read a novel about people's secret inner lives. I can't recall the title or the author but I remember wondering about my own secret inner life because of that book."

We weave connections among the six stories in the collection. People reveal personal experiences and relate them to events and feelings depicted in the stories. References to novels, other short stories are woven into the fabric of our conversation. Feelings, images, connections abound. A very rich interchange.

I keep the conversation going with an eye on the clock. I want people to feel they've had adequate time to explore the stories but I don't want to leave the discussion at just the level of the stories—I want to forge connections between being readers and writers. That connection will become more explicit tomorrow after we've read and discussed Serebrin's 'A Writer and an Author Collaborate,' but I want to foreshadow that conversation a little, if I can.

"Time for my usual question: 'What's been happening here?'"

The group grows quiet; the conversation shifts gears.

I'm teacher again, asking them to reflect on the experience. That reflection is still not coming easily; I suspect it never really does. Part of the problem is not having a familiar language with which to talk about the learning/teaching episode. Part of the problem, too, is not having sufficient distance to consider the implied contrast with their own teaching. Although these teachers are open and enthusiastic, it's still uncomfortable being critical of your own practice and I realize that everything I try to do with them sets up

---

3 "Miss Manning's Angelic Moment" (Maitland, 1987) tells of an English spinster shopkeeper and her observing an embrace between the Vicar and the young man from the polytechnic, one of the acolytes on Sundays, who she at first takes to be an angel. Rather than being shocked by the homosexual embrace, however, she feels a sense of glee because she now knows one private thing about the Vicar, which makes him real like her, and which he doesn't know she knows.

*that implied comparison. My question 'What's just
happened here?' makes that comparison explicit.*

We talk about the way I participated in the discussion. We
discuss literature as a lived through experience and how stories
let us read ourselves. I mention Louise Rosenblatt's and
Margaret Meek Spencer's work.

*I write a reminder to add some of their writing to the
library.*

I point out differences in interpretation and mention the personal
connections people have made.

*No one mentions **intertextuality**, though, and I
think the teachers need to consider how reading
involves weaving connections between what we're
currently reading and all the stories we've ever read as
well as with our past and present lives. I'd like them
to think about how I set the situation up so this kind of
conversation was likely to occur. Again, I want to
make explicit the implied comparison between the way
we have just dealt with the stories and how they deal
with stories with their students. However, I don't
think I want to push it right now. We've raised
enough issues for the moment; I'll save this one for
another time.*

I turn to writing.

*I didn't plan a lesson but I sense an opportunity worth
capturing.*

I pick up the collection of stories and read the beginning of
'Miss Manning's Angelic Moment':

> When she had closed the shop Miss Manning decided on the spur of the
> moment to go to Mass. She very seldom went during the week, but
> this was mainly because she kept the shop open late; it made things
> easier for the wives who worked all day and for the men coming home
> who wanted cigarettes and things like that, and because she could not
> bear it when people said that the Asians were harder working than
> English people.

I turn to 'The Last Wife':

> Pat was up on a ladder shoving plaster into the hole in Nick's ceiling
> when the telephone rang. She had been putting off the job for the
> longest time, had indeed had an estimate from a plasterer, then decided
> that six small holes left from the rewiring were something she could
> handle herself. She was, in fact, enjoying pushing the squishy stuff into
> the crevices when the telephone summoned her.

Then I read aloud from 'Prue':

Prue used to live with Gordon. This was after Gordon had left his wife and before he went back to her—a year and four months in all. Some time later, he and his wife were divorced. After that came a period of indecision, of living together off and on; then the wife went away to New Zealand, most likely for good.

Prue did not go back to Vancouver Island, where Gordon had met her when she was working as a dining-room hostess in a resort hotel. She got a job in Toronto...

I choose one more:

When I was just a kid, my father Paul Ermineskin, took off for the city, and I only seen him a few times in the last ten years. He hang around the bars and missions in the city and the last time I seen him he was in bad shape and I didn't figure he had long left to live. So it sure is a surprise when he come walking into the Hobbema Pool Hall one afternoon.

"Hey, Silas," he say to me, and give my hand a shake. There is something sneaky about Pa, maybe it is the way he walks kind of sideways, with his eyes always darting all over the place....[4]

"It's interesting to look at how authors begin their stories. You're all writing something and need to think about your opening. Let's talk about how these stories start out."

"They all seem to start off in the middle of something right away," says Leslie.

"There has to be something at the beginning that grabs the reader, I mean, everything is there for a reason. They introduce you to some characters but they don't just do that, though, do they? They give more than just the setting, they're hinting at some kind of conflict situation," Maggie comments.

"Yes, like in 'The Bottle Queen' the father is described as sneaky," says Bruce. "Or in 'The Last Wife' the phone rings."

"They leave you knowing something is going to happen," says Connie.

"It would be interesting to know whether these openings were written later after the story had evolved," remarks Shelagh.

"It's impossible to know, but they could very well have been," I respond.

"It might be fun to try writing an opening ourselves," I say. "You don't have to have a story worked out in advance, I've

---

4 "The Bottle Queen" (Kinsella, 1983) is a story, told by his son Silas, of the time when Paul Ermineskin, down and out yet again, cons his ten-year-old daughter Delores out of the three hundred dollars which she's painstakingly accumulated (for a new Indian dancing costume) by collecting and selling roadside bottles.

discovered when I tried this on other occasions; interesting things happen when you simply start writing."

"Oh, yeah!" laughs Leslie. There are chuckles from the others.

"Let's just try and see what happens."

We each take paper and pencil and begin writing. I freewrite:

Elizabeth sat swinging on the worn tire hanging from the old apple tree in the front yard. Slowly she leaned back to propel herself forward then bent forward to make the swing move backward. Back and forth, back and forth. Watching her you'd have said she was just enjoying the clear, warm day—not a care in the world. But that wasn't the case.

I stop and look up, waiting for the others to stop, too.

"Let me read mine," I offer.

"Hmm," someone responds when I've finished.

"My description doesn't quite work yet. I'm trying to capture the movements you make to get a tire swinging."

"'Watching her you'd have said she was just enjoying the clear, warm day—not a care in the world. But that wasn't the case'," reads Theresa from beside me.

"Yes, there it is—suddenly I have a story. I have a bit of the setting but now I have to consider what's happening in her life. Who is Elizabeth and what is she thinking about?"

I invite someone else to share.

Maggie offers. "I didn't get anywhere, really." She reads:

Sun was streaming in the window, creating rainbows all over the walls and ceiling from the crystals hanging there. She was lying in bed wondering what to do.

"I didn't have any idea where this is going. I don't know what's she's wondering about."

"That's OK, but you've got me wondering. That's what an opening is supposed to do," I comment.

Connie reads next:

Finally it was over! This tantrum had lasted ten entire minutes. His face was purple, he was gasping for air, his hands shaking. The sobs gradually subsided.

"I don't care," she thought to herself. "He's alive, isn't he. These fits aren't going to kill him but they will kill me if I don't do something."

"You've caught me," says Leslie. "I'd love to keep reading."

"Any idea what was going on?" I ask Connie.

"It's a mother and her son in the middle of the supermarket. These two have got to lock horns and there's got to be a change. The problem would be to work out how she decides to deal with the situation."

"I couldn't see anything when I was writing which is why I didn't write any more," says Shelagh.

"I'm not sure what the problem is for Elizabeth, either," I add. "I haven't even decided how old she is. Is she an adult, a young child, or an adolescent? I could hint at her age by describing what she's wearing."

"Do you always get characters introduced at the start?" Leslie asks.

"That's a good question," I answer her. "I don't know. In the six stories I gave you they do, but that may not be always true. We should have a look at a variety of things to see what we can find out.

"Did you learn anything useful from what we've just done?"

"I didn't believe I would be able to write anything," says Shelagh, "but I can see I actually could create a story from this beginning."

"I want to see how much variety there is in the way authors start out," says Bruce.

"I'll be interested in what you discover," I reply.

"I can see I need to think about my own opening again," says Connie. "I began with straight description but now I'll have to think about how to hint at the conflict to come."

"I want to comment about something quite different," Bruce says. "It's been very interesting watching the dynamics of what's been happening at the table. Because everyone is able to make eye contact with everyone else, there's been a lot of conversation among us, not just with you."

A nice spontaneous reflection! Looks as if Bruce has internalized my 'What's happening here?' question.

"Yes, that's true. I learned about needing to see people's faces, in order to have conversation, in my mother's living room. It's a very unsociable room. She has an eleven foot sofa! Six people can sit side by side on it but you can't talk. I have a vivid memory of that sofa from last year when we were going through the mourning period after my father died. I see the six old men sitting silently in a row with their feet firmly planted on the floor, their hands comfortably folded in their laps, waiting for prayers to begin. It was an interesting vignette and I wanted to photograph them but my mother was scandalized. I'm sure it would have offended the men's sense of the occasion, too, but I really wanted to record the scene because it just said so much."

"Have you written about it?" Maggie asks me.

"No, I haven't. Actually, I've been feeling guilty about not working on a piece of writing along with everyone. I haven't really had time to get anything started. Perhaps, however, I'll try a poem about the sofa and see what happens."

With a bit more chatter we end our discussion. I ask people to help me restore the furniture and we retrieve the belongings we moved aside earlier. Time to move on to other work.

This furniture is proving more useful than I realized. I've not been able to get successful large group discussions going in my winter classes and I suddenly see why: the round tables in the Resources Centre are heavy and don't fit together well so we haven't bothered to move the furniture to accommodate a single large group. People stay seated in their small groups and can't establish eye contact with people across the room so those conversations are directed at me. What's been happening here has been quite different. Although the twelve of us have been packed around the table people have been able to talk directly to one another. And now with our conversation over we're able to put the furniture back without much hassle. I'm going to have to think some more about moving furniture to foster different kinds of engagement in my winter classes.

During the hour before lunch people work at whatever they wish to. At this point most of them are choosing to write. I use this time to chat with those who have signed up for a writing conversation.

Penny and I talk about her poems.

She shows me one:

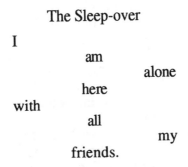

The Sleep-over

I

am

alone

here

with

all

my

friends.

"I really like what you've done with this," I tell her. "I can definitely feel the separateness of being in the middle of a crowd with the way you've spaced the words out. Very effective. Talk to me about how you decided to do that."

"Originally I'd written the poem just as two lines—here let me show you." She hands me a sheet of paper.

The Sleep-over

I am alone here
with all my friends.

"And then when I was discussing it with Janice and Cathy, and some of the others, someone had the idea that I should space the words out. I tried doing it a number of different ways but that layout seemed to work best."

"It works very well. Very effective. You've got another poem there, do you want to talk about it?"

Penny hands me a second short poem. I read it to myself, then I read it aloud:

Piano Recital

what if
I don't do it
perfectly
my fingers won't
stop
shaking
I know it
I practiced it
I did
why can't I
do it now

"Can I ever remember that sinking feeling," I say to Penny. "I recall one occasion when I was giving a guitar recital. I got a couple of lines into the Allemande of a Bach cello suite and then went blank. I felt an incredible moment of panic. I just could not remember what came next."

"What did you do?"

"I started at the beginning again. I felt just like you've described here."

"This actually happened to me at the Music Festival when I was in my teens," Penny says.

"I can tell it did. You couldn't have captured precisely that feeling if it hadn't. Here's something you might want to think about, though. I sense two different time references—the first three lines before the recital, and the rest during. I find that a bit jarring. Perhaps I'm just thinking about my own experience but I wonder, in fact, whether you need the first three lines."

Penny and I talk a little longer about her poems.

"These are wonderful. I think you've got the beginning of a collection of small poems here. Keep it up. I'm eager to see what will come out next."

She hasn't written poetry before, she's told me. Well, if these are any indication, there's certainly potential here. Penny's captured some powerful feelings in those two short pieces. My role here is simply to keep her going.

After Penny and I finish, I look for Hanna, who's next on the list. Then I meet with Connie and Diane.

The writing is coming along amazingly well. I don't think I've ever experienced the kind of energy with which these teachers are generating material. I'm convinced it has a lot to do with the social community we've managed to establish. They're not relying just on input from me. In fact, my contribution is relatively insignificant—I simply can't get around to everyone fast enough. They're learning most from the conversations they're having with one another.

Just before lunch I visit the computer room to see how people have been getting along there. I help deal with a number of technical concerns. It's interesting to observe the kinds of questions people are asking at this point. They're over the initial bumbling around. They have enough understanding of the operating system and of how the word processor works to boot up and create documents. Their attention has turned, now, to editing ('How do you delete from here to the end?'), formatting ('There must be some way of double spacing this on the screen so it's easier to read.') and printing ('How do you abort a document?'). I can answer some of their questions but I have to check the documentation for solutions to others. I'm having to learn along with them.

There's an enormous amount of learning occurring without my direct intervention. That's exactly what I was hoping would happen. I want the teachers to discover how much they can help each other solve problems as they arise. I'm just trying to monitor the activity enough to avert disasters. There are a couple of people—Debra and Carmina in particular—still having difficulty with their writing. I'm keeping a watch on what they're doing. I want to stay out of their way for a bit longer. I'm hoping their conversations with the others may still get them over the hump.

❖

At lunch I remember to track down Norma to chat with her about teaching by setting up experiences.

"Oh, you mean I'm talking too much," she laughs.

"You're welcome to talk. I appreciate your contributions to the large group discussions. But I think you would learn more, right now, if you watched for opportunities, not to tell what you're learning yourself, but to see if you can help some of the others sort out their assumptions and reach similar insights."

This experience is helping her put a lot together and she's excited about it. Her active participation is revealing just what's going on inside her head. I don't want to cut her off completely. I suspect I can't anyway. But I think she's progressed to the point as a teacher (she's done quite a lot of inservice work) where she might find it interesting to think about helping people experience what she's discovered for herself.

Next Cathy. I walk back from lunch with her. As we saunter down the shaded path past the new Communications building, we talk about what's been happening in her school. She tells me about the inservice thrust she's been trying to initiate. Her staff of fifteen elementary teachers have been dabbling with process writing and she has been trying to help them give the children greater freedom to choose writing topics, to help them be less concerned about the children having everything right on first try.

As a result of some district workshops she had participated in herself, she had ordered several copies of Graves's **Writing: Teachers and Children at Work** and given them to her staff to read. Since last spring they'd been taking some time at each staff meeting to talk about writing. She had asked the teachers to keep a folder on a couple of children in their class and they were using these children's samples as the basis for some of their discussion.

Cathy and I talk of the difficulties she's been experiencing with the teachers, about the questions they've been asking, the concerns they've been raising. I begin to understand Cathy's insecurity and her attachment to Graves. She herself hasn't read much besides this book although she has read Graves a couple of times. She's only barely begun feeling comfortable with his idea of a writing classroom. She's not sure she's ready to step into a wider world.

Our conversation has been helpful for me. It's allowed me to have a clearer understanding of Cathy's concerns and her purpose for coming to the Institute. I have a better sense of what kind of writing support to offer her and how to help her connect this experience with what she's attempting to accomplish with her staff.

❖

After lunch we meet briefly to organize **Issues** groups. The 'Responding to Writing' group decide to have lunch together for the next few days. The teachers interested in 'Revising and Editing' agree to meet at 8:30 the following morning. 'The Reading/Writing Relationships' people, however, have some difficulty arranging a convenient time to get together. They finally arrange to meet over lunch as well. I write the meeting times and locations on the blackboard beside each group so people can refer to it if they need to.

This learning situation is becoming more and more like our real world lives. There are a variety of tasks to be accomplished, responsibilities to be met, meetings to attend, and not enough time to do it all. It means we have to think about organizing our time and developing more effective strategies for doing what we want to get done. People have to establish priorities, decide what's most important to them, and invest their efforts and energy on those tasks. I've been dealing with organizational strategies incidentally, waiting for an appropriate moment to bring them up for discussion. I'm anticipating we'll need to talk about structure and organization by the middle of next week.

During the early part of the afternoon people work on their own and in small groups. I continue my conversations with the teachers on the **Writing Conversations** list while monitoring the various other conversations that are going on, just as I have for the past three days. The atmosphere is relaxed. People move between the computer room downstairs and the

> Something that's just struck me about your teaching is how 'on the edge' it is. One of your responsibilities is to keep everything from flying apart—I'm reminded of a black hole holding galaxies together—you're the gravity keeping these many different activities flowing.
>
> Ron Hodder

comfortable furniture in the corridor. Some people work quietly in the classroom. I move from situation to situation, asking 'How are things going?' Chatting for a few moments if invited to, moving on if the response is 'Fine.'

I overhear Bruce, Connie, and Lorna discussing collaboration.

"...All learning is social, isn't it; isn't collaboration just another way of saying learning together?" asks Lorna.

"I think 'collaborative' means people are involved in one another's ideas," says Connie.

"There's a lot of social learning going on without there necessarily being active collaboration," says Bruce. "Collaboration suggests to me at least two people working together toward some specific common goal."

"So in these writing workshops, that's not collaborative learning then?" Lorna wants to know.

"There's collaborative learning going on because there's talking among the students, asking questions, giving feedback," Bruce responds. "They're all working toward finished pieces of writing. But when you're a kid learning language, that's not necessarily collaborative learning; that's learning in a social setting."

"I would say," says Connie, "there's collaborative learning going on when kids are working together in a peer group and they're talking about what they're doing and learning from each other...."

> *It's easy to use the slogans, much more difficult to make sense of what they're describing. What does 'learning is social' mean? What does 'collaboration' refer to? Bruce's observation that learning in a social situation is not necessarily collaborative is provocative. Clearly collaboration is social, but the social setting is not necessarily collaborative.*

Norma, Leslie, Theresa, and Barb are also engaged in conversation.

"...Do you think the stuff on the walls outside the classroom needs to be in conventional writing?" Barb wonders.

"We had an incident in our district last winter where we were told we weren't allowed to submit anything to the district publication of kids' work which wasn't spelled conventionally. That bothered me. I thought that was a contradiction in philosophy. On the one hand we're telling kids it's OK to use functional spelling and on the other rejecting their work when they do," says Leslie.

"I had this very conversation not long ago about publishing my first graders' stuff on the computer," Theresa comments.

"You publish it transcribing it into conventional spelling?" Leslie asks.

"Um-hmm. I do if it's going into the class library in a published form."

"When I'm working with the younger kids," says Norma, "I just explain that everybody will have an easier time reading their story."

"One of the articles I read, I can't remember which, the author said something about transcribing the kid's writing and I couldn't tell if she wrote right on the child's paper or if she wrote the transcription somewhere else," says Barb. "I know sometimes I can't remember what they've written..."

"Here it is," says Norma. She reads: 'On more than one occasion she [the child] abandoned her own words and read her teacher's transcription instead.' "

"But it doesn't say where she put her translation."

"It was there in the book."

"On the child's book?"

"I have the children do the snack order themselves and I don't worry whether it's spelled conventionally or not," Leslie comments.

"That's another kind of issue," says Norma. "If the order is understood by the person responsible for getting the snacks then it has served it's purpose."

"That's something different," Barb interjects as well.

"If it's a published book and it's out there for the public to read, then the public has to be able to read it," says Norma.

"And it has to be correct, I mean conventional," says Barb.

"But within the process of trying to get the kids— I don't mean to keep sounding like I'm the one making them do it—but while encouraging them to write more," says Leslie, "I feel I have to not interfere. Like if what the kid has written is indecipherable, and I write on the paper, I'm afraid he'd feel that what he wrote had no meaning."

"I keep some foolscap stapled on the inside cover of the kids' journals," says Theresa. "That's where I keep my notes. I use it for any transcriptions but I also record observations there, too—what the child has done independently, what she did with someone else's help, and so on. When the kids ask what I'm doing I explain, 'These are my notes to help me remember what you're learning and they're for your mom, to help her read your stories if you're not here.' On their books and things I use post-it notes at the back."

*A complex issue this. Where and when do conven-
tions matter and when can we be lax? Beth Hendry
has an unusual way of helping her kids understand
this decision. In the file box where she keeps
addresses of people the children might like to write to
she has included the Queen of England's address.
Beth repeatedly asks the children 'Who are you writing to? If it's the Queen it has to be perfect,' she says.
For me, this is another 'it depends' issue; it depends
on who is doing the writing, how experienced and
fluent they are, who they're writing to, for what
purpose, and how far along the writing has progressed. It's not a simple black and white issue; the
factors which enter into the decision about whether to
deal with writing conventions depends on a complex
of factors. Writing conventions will come into play
here in the Institute later next week as we work to
complete our collaborative class book.*

❖

At 3:00 we meet as a large group to explore our learning
experiences. The teachers position themselves in what seems to
have become their working groups: Bruce with Shelagh and
Maggie; Michael, Carmina, Connie, Barb, and Theresa together;
Hanna, Cathy, Janice, and Penny at the same table (Susan has
joined them); and Earl working with Leslie, Norma, Helen,
Diane, and Lorna.

"How are we going to conduct this conversation?" I ask.

"You gave us four questions to consider. They're still there
on the board and I think we could use them for comparing our
experiences," offers Lorna.

*That's the first time she's ventured a suggestion in the
large group, I notice, an indication perhaps that she's
feeling reasonably at home now.*

"Sounds like a good idea. Try it and see what happens. By
the way, this is definitely a situation where you'll find it helpful
to talk and listen with a pencil in your hand. Remember to keep
your pencil working."

I dig out the description of learning to build and fly kites I
wrote this morning and join Earl, Leslie, Norma, Helen, Diane,
and Lorna. I pull up a chair beside Earl and listen to him talk
about how he learned to drive a car.

*As he talks I turn to a new page in my notebook and at
the top I write*
Why

about half way down I write
  How
at the top of the next page I put
  Role of Other People
and mid-way I write
  Evaluation of Learning
As I listen to his story I make notes under each heading.

Earl says he wanted to learn to drive because the other guys his age and a bit older were learning. He describes the first time his father took him to a nearby parking lot, stopped the car and turned the ignition off, then told Earl to sit behind the wheel. He wasn't quite sixteen yet, he said, and although he'd desperately wanted to know how to drive, he was suddenly afraid. He describes turning the key, hearing this awful screeching sound, and not knowing what to do.

Earl's story wends its way through a series of outings with his father and an uncle and how the two adults handled the teaching/learning situation differently. As he talks, I make notes about his experience. He initiated the experience, pestering his dad to teach him until his father gave in. It was a hands-on learning situation. A more experienced person was with him, giving directions and offering advice when the situation called for it. There were interesting differences in the way Earl's dad and his uncle taught. Earl's dad talked a lot, confusing him with a lot of information, more than he could deal with. His uncle, on the other hand, was much more relaxed. He just sat back and let Earl drive, occasionally cautioning him to go a bit more slowly, pointing out hazards to notice, but not overwhelming him with instructions.

"What about the other kids? Did you discuss driving with them?" I wondered.

"I talked about driving with my older brother. In fact, there were a couple of occasions, while I was learning, when we were going somewhere in the car and I talked him into letting me drive for a bit. He was the best teacher of all. He wasn't scared about what could happen and because he wasn't terrified of my driving I felt less anxious about it. I'd miss a stop sign, or come up behind another car too quickly and he'd tease me about it, but I felt more like a driver on those occasions than I did with the adults."

"How could you tell you were learning?" I asked.

"I passed the driver's exam!" he laughs.

"Right," I respond, "but before the test, could you tell you were learning?"

"Sure. I was learning on an old standard transmission Dodge Dart. The steering was tight like an old ten-ton truck. At first I had an awful time managing the clutch and the gas. The car was leaping around the lot like a crazy jackrabbit. It was the second or third time I was out that I began getting the hang of it. I think it was the leaping about that unnerved my dad."

"So how could you tell you were learning?"

"I could see I was gaining more control."

This conversation is just between Earl and me, and I'm the only one making notes from his story. I decide to point that out.

"I notice I'm the only one asking questions and keeping track of those aspects of Earl's experience we want to know about. How come?"

Giggles and sheepish looks around the table.

"Why do I want you to make notes from the stories?" I ask.

"So we can compare the details," volunteers Norma.

"How're you going to compare them without any data? You're conducting interviews here, right? You need to record some of the responses so you have data to work with later. If you don't make notes, no data. Why is it useful if you all make notes at the same time?"

"I guess we can then compare to see if we interpreted things the same way," says Leslie.

"Of course, it's a check on the data. Carry on with your stories and keep track of the responses. Remember you're trying to determine just how similar your experiences have been, right? So keep an eye on the questions. Did you notice how I did that by putting headings on my page? I'm sure you can work out a way of keeping your interviews on track yourselves." With that rather direct lesson I move to another group.

I offer the same lesson to each group in turn. I want the teachers to experience 'writing to learn.' They all nod in agreement when I mention the value of using writing to make sense of an experience but their own writing to learn strategies are not well developed. Putting pencil to paper during a conversation is not something most of these teachers do spontaneously even when there's clearly a need to document what's going on because there's some follow-up to come. How are they going to help their students learn the strategy when they don't value it for themselves? That's part of the issue I'm trying to raise here: we can only teach others to do what we value ourselves. If we don't use writing to learn in a variety of different ways

*in our own lives, we can't help students learn how to
do it in any meaningful way.*

As each group completes the storytelling, I watch to see
which of them begins to compare the elements of their
experiences on their own. Two groups quite naturally take a
blank sheet of paper and divide it in two down the centre:
Similarities / Differences. Referring to their data they begin
identifying both common and disparate aspects of their
experiences. Two groups drift to less focused chatter. I offer a
short lesson to both of them.

"You have some data, right? What are you going to do
next?"

"Compare them."

"How are you going to go about that?"

No answer.

"You all know how to set up a comparison. I'm not after
something mystical. How do you handle a comparison on
paper?"

"You divide the paper in two with the headings: Same,
Different."

"Of course. Go ahead."

I've never really thought about the connection between learning in school and out. Your discussion here has made me think about it and about some of the contradictions I must be setting up for my sixth graders. I'm an avid reader and I generally read very fast. However if I'm reading difficult material, be it fiction or non-fiction, I read slowly and carefully, making sure I understand before going on. That's how I was taught! I know I should push ahead; I find I understand much more with a couple of fast reads but it's so hard to break old habits. And what's worse I know I've been telling the kids to slow down when reading difficult material.

Linda Swinwood

The challenge for me as teacher is judging when to step in and when to wait. I'm trying to raise an important issue here. I believe learning in school should be like the learning we do in the everyday world outside of school. I'm trying to collect evidence so the teachers can see for themselves that learning which has mattered in their lives has some common features. I want them to identify those features and to think about how we might set up classroom in-struction to incorporate as many of them as we can. Along the way, I'm also trying to make the teachers conscious of their existing strategies as well as extend them.

So in this situation I'm prepared to take quite a bit of procedural control, leaving the sense-making to them. It's true that I know what I'd like them to discover but I'm not going to put my list of characteristics on the blackboard; nor am I going to give them a prepared handout. I will accept whatever it is they find from their investigation and only act as scribe during the pulling-together discussion. I'm trusting their experiences have been sufficiently like mine that the similarities and differences I'd like them to discover are going to emerge from the discussion. If they don't, I'll have to create another experience to raise the questions I want them to think about.

I chat with the groups as they explore similarities and differences. Then I move to the overhead projector to record the conversation:

Similarities	**Differences**

reasons:

- had a need
- somebody asked me to try
- wanted to be part of a group
- to help someone else
- saw someone doing it
- read about it

how:

Similarities	Differences
• generally initiated by learner	• sometimes initiated
• discussion with 'experts'	by others
- read books	• sometimes others
-watched people with	took control
experience	
-asked questions	
• discussion with peers	• misinformation
-offered another point of view	
-clarified own understanding	
-provided empathy—not alone	
with difficulties	
• the learner initiated and	
controlled the duration of the	
practice and of the learning	
• lots of practice; lots of time	

evaluation of the learning:

Similarities	Differences
• some success	• some tasks required
• some end product	technique to build on
• encouragement from others	

- feeling of satisfaction
- sharing successes and failures
- becoming innovative— leading to improved technique

- some tasks were more sequential, most were more holistic, not sequential learning

A reasonable list to work from. Now for some reflective questions. I invite the teachers to think about two things over the next few days:

First, in what ways have I tried taking these factors into account in setting up this experience for them?

Second, what has this exercise helped them question about their own teaching?

I record my request in my notebook. I really mustn't forget to return to this conversation. Although we're ostensibly exploring writing/reading connections in this Institute workshop, this covert agenda is equally, if not more, important. I intend making it explicit before we finish.

Time to bring the day to a close. We check the blackboard to see what's on the agenda for tomorrow: the poetry discussion in the morning. I also have a reminder in my book about the Hunt/Serebrin discussion. They've writing to work on and **Issues** discussion groups to prepare for. I remind people I would like to keep tabs on each of them personally so I ask them to write me a reflection/letter if they haven't already done so in the last day or so.

Later that evening I respond to the reflections I collected during the day. As tired as I am, I enjoy reading what the teachers write. They all have interesting things to say. I find our written reflective conversation a powerful vehicle for getting to know people better. Take Cathy's letter:

I'm sitting at the computer and quite frankly I'm not at all sure what I'm going to write. I'm sitting here with a lot of mixed up feelings that I want to try to "write through" but I don't know where to begin and what is even worse is the fact that I'm feeling more than a little threatened about putting those jumbled incoherent thoughts on paper. But I must do it. For some time now I've been struggling with the gap that exists between theory and practice. As a principal I'm not seeing dramatic shifts in what the majority of the teachers are doing. Of course, there are a couple of them doing more "whole language" activities than the others. But on the whole, I'm not seeing the kind of change occurring that the talk I hear would suggest. Related to that is something that is just becoming apparent to me. While teachers are being inserviced about process writing and whole language, for the most part, information is being transmitted through traditional teacher-directed activities. The degree of engagement by a lot of teachers at most inservices is indeed minimal. My point here is not to criticize the administrators giving the inservice. I realize inservice is a complex undertaking with many variables coming into play. Rather I am simply struggling with the gap between what teachers are being told to do and what is being demonstrated. Frank Smith (1981) perhaps has most clearly expressed what is bothering me when he argues that what students learn may be quite different from what we think they are learning. That's often the case with teachers at inservices. I wonder if they aren't learning that the very people advocating a holistic approach to language would have great difficulty implementing their ideas in a classroom of thirty children since they don't seem to do it effectively with adults. Is the message "It can't be done?"

I'm taken with the insightfulness of Cathy's response. She's gone to the heart of the issue and is raising something I struggle with myself. I constantly wonder whether I'm managing to create a learning situation which allows teachers to experience what taking control of their own learning feels like. I respond to Cathy's discussion with some comments about my personal concern.
Bruce relates an interesting incident:

I remember the old pitch barrel in the field down by the shore. It had been left by the construction crew when they paved the road through our village in '54. We passed by it every day on our way to school. On hot days when we looked into the barrel we saw a sticky mass of tar. When the weather was cool it was hard and shiny. A warm rain made it pliable. After a time we could predict its probable character by the weather. We didn't know its name or its utility but someone mentioned it was safe to chew. One day we chipped off a piece and chewed it. It was great! The taste wasn't objectionable and it didn't get tough like bubble gum. We'd found use number one. Use number two was revealed to us by Old Martin who we found at the pitch barrel one hot June day filling a pot with the gooey, black stuff. We stood around the barrel silently watching Martin scoop the pitch into his pot. We couldn't figure a grown-up chewing that much gum.

"What's this stuff called, Martin?" someone asked.

"This is pitch," he answered, not volunteering any further facts.

"What's it used for, Martin?" each of us knowing that the barrel of pitch hadn't been left by the chewing gum fairy.

"Pitch can draw splinters and disease out of your body," Martin replied, touching the sore on his lip.

We ran off to school hoping that somewhere along the way someone would get a splinter so we could try out this miracle cure. Only later did we find out that Martin had lip cancer and had cured himself with a pitch poultice. We found out soon enough that warm pitch is the greatest thing for deep splinters, too!

I'm not at all surprised that Martin and the pitch barrel would come back to me sometime in my life, but I would never have predicted that it would be in relation to Frank Smith. When I finished **Joining the Literacy Club** (Smith, 1988), looked at the web of notes I'd built, and reflected on how Smith's writing connects with me, I came to this conclusion: Smith, more than most writer, draws out learning incidents and connections that would have otherwise remained hidden. Some are deep in time and others recent but somehow unseen. I searched for a metaphor to picture this 'drawing out'—Martin and the pitch barrel leaped out. An unexpected connection of this metaphor to 'joining the literacy club,' one that didn't present itself until I had written it down, is that Martin helped us become literate about pitch.

A very insightful reflection. What is literacy? How do we become literate? Bruce has certainly under-stood Smith's argument about learning and about us becoming members of the club.

Then I look at responses to my reflection/letter. Several people have commented on the 'mess' issue I raised. Theresa has written:

What you've called a "mess" isn't a mess at all from the inside. On the inside as a student, learning is taking place although from the outside it looks like mass confusion or chaos. For me as a teacher, I still feel intimidated by what the outsider sees.

Moment-to-moment decision-making is beginning to take over my daily plans more and more. I feel the purpose of the mess and the importance of the teachable moments. These would not be possible in a content-oriented classroom.

As has Diane:

My personal "mess" is beginning to sort itself out. I am beginning to feel comfortable on the freewrite responses, a new adventure for me. I'm struggling with the daily log, which has become a reading diary, a hodgepodge of notes to myself, ideas for my short story, and more deliberate thoughts on the readings for my response journal. I still feel like I'm in a time warp, however. One day blends with another, and I get confused about what happened when.

Earl reacts:

"The mess." It's nice to know that other teachers have messes. It gives me confidence to keep on going.

And Maggie:

...the problem has to do with control and letting go. I know I can go to you at any time for a short chat or a long conference and I think that contributes to my understanding of how the "mess" works.

They're thinking about the issue, exploring its ramifications in our learning situation. Now to help them think about it in connection with their own teaching.

As I read the teachers' journals and their responses to my reflection I record some of the issues mentioned. I incorporate them as I write:

OK. Let me respond to some of the issues you mentioned in your journals today. Structure. That's something I know some of you have been discussing at various points. What are you learning about structure from your experiences? What are some of the various kinds of structure I've been building into our situation? I know at first glance this class with people roaming all over the place with the teacher heaven's knows where doesn't appear to have much structure, but that's one of the myths about whole language, right? Think about some contrasts between the kind of structure I've been trying to create and the sort of structure more traditional classrooms are organized around. My next question to you, of course, is what questions about your own teaching has the kinds of structure I've been working to develop raised for you?

Then there's negotiation. While I have some curricular goals in mind for us to work toward, I've opened up the details to you. How does this negotiation work? What responsibilities do I assume? How about you as students? What effect on your learning has this negotiation had? What is the range of things we negotiate about? Again, what questions about your own teaching does this negotiation raise?

And there's the issue of homework. How has the kind of homework I've asked you to do compare with more traditional kinds of homework? What is its function? Of what does it consist? What about how it is done? What are the consequences of not having done it?

And how many different kinds of conversations are we having? What are they about? What functions do they serve?

I want to ask about journals. What function are the journals serving? Yours? Mine? How do these journals compare to the kind of journal writing that is occurring in a lot of classrooms?

I'm raising this host of questions about the learning/teaching context because it isn't enough to read about how different people think we might create it. I believe it is necessary to experience it, and to reflect on that experience. More and more I've come to realize the shortcomings of my teaching when I don't put my own teaching on the table and invite us to look at it. By the way, it's important to discuss when something isn't working for you. I need to hear when something has interfered with your learning so I can decide what to try instead. It's important to discover how experiences affect different learners. I'm not looking only for confirmation about the 'good' stuff. The 'bad' is equally informative; perhaps even more valuable. So don't be reluctant to speak up if something that's going on is wrong for you.

I have another question to ask as well: How did the discussion of Elbow's ways of responding to writing and your trying them out yourself serve as a fore-shadowing for the short story session this morning? How do you anticipate it will serve for our discussion of poetry and children's books?

I've counted them—twenty-four questions in this letter and I still haven't dealt with mini-lessons. I dare not mention one more issue. I'm simply going to have to wait for another time. Again this isn't a personal reflection but an invitation to the teachers to reflect on our learning/teaching situation and to consider what questions about their own teaching are being raised by the experience they are having here.

Kite flying and teaching. Lots of similarities. A constant tension on the line. Keeping your eye on the kite, reading its response to the wind. Many small adjustments—a little line out slowly, a quick hauling in trying to avoid a tangled mess. Ever watchful of students' responses—their faces, their bodies, their comments to one another. Kite fliers have to be risk-takers; so do teachers.

Serious kiters never go flying with only one kite. You have to have several on hand, each designed for different wind conditions. Kite flyer or teacher, you have to be willing to find the right kite for the situation. Sometime it takes several tries before you find a match. But that's the adventure of teaching. You have to be willing to take several stabs at getting a kite aloft. You have to learn to read the wind. And you have to know when it's time to haul in and go home!

You're Always Right and You're Always Wrong

7

I awake early this morning with the glimmerings of a poem going through my head. I lie in bed a while composing but realize that if I don't get something on paper the ideas will vanish.

I get up and try writing on the computer but I get nowhere so I move to the armchair to doodle.

I freewrite:

> The Sofa
> I remember it covered with plastic and hating to sit on it—plastic to keep it from wearing out. The greenish color, the length—six people side by side—so long it had to be moved into the apartment with a crane.

I stop. This isn't what I want to say. I record in my reading/writing log book:

> July 29
> The idea for a poem came from class yesterday.
> Situation: twelve of us were discussing short stories.
> Bruce commented, "When we get together we set it up so we have eye contact." I replied, "I learned that in my mother's living room—her eleven foot sofa seats six in a row but conversation is impossible on it." That led to the image of the six old men seated there during Shiva and how I wanted to photograph them. Maggie wondered whether I had tried a poem.
> I have just tried freewriting but nothing wants to come. I have no idea what the poem wants to be about—I have to let this percolate.

After breakfast I return to the study, turn to a fresh page, and start again:

> I hated that sofa
> covered in plastic
> to keep it from being used

I stop once more and write in my log:

> I've picked up the pad again—no go—nothing of significance—I can barely force myself to put words on paper—I'll just have to put it aside for now.

I shower and dress. When I return to the study I write:

> Six in a row; side by side on that exceptionally long sofa
> Little old men, clean shaven
>> with their (I cross out *their*) gnarled hands clasped
>>> (cross out *clasped*)
>> resting on solid pot bellies
> Legs wide, feet planted
> Skull caps (insert *black* in front of *skull*) on grey
>> (cross out *grey*) bald heads
> Seated there to mumble prayers
>> for my now dead father.
> (A comfort?)
> Their presence no comfort
> but enhancing my alienation
> A ritual to console
> A connection with (cross out *a connection with*)
>> Offer community and continuity
> But we women are excluded—
> Unwelcome at the (cross out *at the*) to participate
>> in their prayers.

I read what I've written, go back and insert some names after 'six in a row.' I read it a couple of times again. Now I move to the computer to see what I have. I type:

> ### The Sofa
>
> Six in a row.
> Mr. Cuperfine, Mr. Goldfarb, Mr. Kaplan,
> Mr. Yablon, Mr. Cohen, and Mr. Scholossberg.
> Side by side on that eleven foot sofa.
> Six little old men
> Clean shaven
> Gnarled hands resting on solid pot bellies
> Black skull-caps perched on shiny bald heads.
> Waiting to mumble prayers.
> A ritual to console,
> To offer community and continuity.
> But their presence is no comfort;
> It adds to the alienation—
> We women are excluded.
> Unwelcome to participate
> In their prayers for my now dead father.

Interesting. This isn't the poem I expected. I reflect in my log:

I no sooner stepped into the shower when a line popped into my head: 'six in a row.' I can't quite recall what else, I just know that words started coming quite unexpectedly—images I'd thought about, about the men, not the sofa. I was quite surprised when I got to the point where I realized I was writing about alienation—my distance from the Jewish community—from the family—heightened during Shiva, focusing on the exclusion of women from the morning and evening prayers.

The initial drafting in pencil seems necessary. In this case, a poem came quite quickly, about fifteen minutes. Then with the move to the computer I could see ways of realigning the bits, the phrase 'for my now dead father' fell into place as a last line. I'm trying to capture images of the men. Not satisfied with the description of their bodies, and the bit about alienation is important but not right, yet. I'm not happy with the names either.

That's all I have time for right now. I feel better about having a piece of writing to bring to the workshop. I felt I was missing a valuable opportunity to discuss strategies if I wasn't working on something myself. I wanted to be part of the writing community but with the complexity of keeping everyone else moving, I didn't think I'd find time to write myself. Now I can be a legitimate participant.

With some writing underway I turn to a second matter that arose yesterday. In her reflection/letter which she handed me late in the afternoon Shelagh wrote the following:

In your article "Sharing Journals: Conversational Mirrors for Seeing Ourselves as Learners, Writers, and Teachers" (Newman, 1988) you wrote about Pam and how she let you know that you undermined her confidence re: her story. Well this afternoon when I received your note about my writing, I felt the same way. Your note said "the writing felt detached", that you didn't "feel me in the narrative." I was devastated for a moment. As an inexperienced writer, willing to take risks after feeling some trust, I felt my writing was in vain. I have invested a lot of myself in what I've written so far. As Pam felt, I was given no recognition for my efforts. I discussed how I was feeling with Maggie. She and I talked about your note and my reaction to it. I don't object to comments and constructive criticism; what I am upset about is how you said it perhaps. I guess I wanted some recognition of the effort I'd expended....

A tricky moment. Shelagh has taken a very big risk here by letting me know just how my response to her writing has affected her. I have to write her back but I'm not sure exactly what to say. She had handed me her writing and asked me to read and respond to it just before lunch. I wrote what I thought was an Elbow-like response to her couple of pages of narrative because I had wanted her to see how her words were affecting me as a reader. The problem is I handed my written response back to her without having had a conversation about it.

While her writing had glimmers of an emerging voice, I hadn't really sensed her presence in it until, perhaps, the last paragraph. The anguish I know she was experiencing in the situation she's trying to capture didn't reach me. I said that in the note. For a couple of years now I've been trying to nudge Shelagh to hold a mirror to herself, to help her become a more reflective teacher. A lot of her difficulty in the classroom stems from her need for rigid structure and control. Here she's writing about being swamped by an overwhelming marking load but not looking at how she herself has created the problem. I thought she would be able to handle my written reaction. Looks like I was wrong, however. She is obviously more insecure about her writing and,

This note from Shelagh regarding your response to her writing made me think of one of my fifth graders. Brendan is bright but he's been very reticent about sharing his writing. So as he stood in front of me with his piece about his trip to New York in hand I understood what he was risking by making this move to seek me out. However, as he began reading I realized I had a tough decision to make—his narration read like a travel brochure. How was I going to save his feelings and yet let him know that I couldn't connect with his story? When he got to the end I took a deep breath and said, "I get a picture of your drive into New York, but where are you? I want to know how you feel about arriving in the city." He looked discouraged, but not exactly surprised. "I think perhaps you had better give this some thought," I said. "Do you want me to know what New York is like by describing the buildings and sights? Or do you want to say something about how you feel about the experience of visiting the city?" Just as you did with Shelagh, I can see I pushed, no I shoved, Brendan toward thinking about what he was writing. As uncomfortable as my response made him, however, I believe he deserved to be challenged.

Linda Cook

perhaps more important, about her teaching than I sensed she was.

I think about the situation and I write her:

Let me explain why I chose to respond as I did. I could see the situation you were describing but the feelings you were attempting to convey didn't reach me. I could have sympathized with your plight by commenting on similar experiences I have had, but I didn't think that would help you consider how your words were affecting me as a reader. Nor did I think that kind of a response would help you examine the contradictions which had brought you to that impasse. So I decided to be honest about what I experienced as I was reading what you've written so far.

I know first hand it's not easy when readers say this or that doesn't work. When my friend Marlene told me the original opening of that article you mentioned was awful and should be thrown away, I, too, had a sinking feeling, but I knew she was right and so I went back and worked on it some more. Good writing demands honesty. That means learning to tell one another the truth about what's working and what isn't. That's hard on both the writer and the responder but definitely worthwhile.

I want you to know I appreciate the risk you took by writing to me. I'm glad you told me how you felt. What you've let me see is that my nudge was more like a shove. I apologize for that. We should have talked about the writing and what effect it was having on me before I handed you my written reactions. I'll try to remember that next time.

I think about adding one more question: Can you identify some of the demonstrations I was trying to create by responding to your story as I did? I decide not to. That question would reestablish me as teacher and right now I need to be more of a colleague.

Shelagh's letter is an important incident. It forces me to reflect on Elbow's contention 'You're always right and you're always wrong.' Elbow is referring to our reactions as readers and writers but his notion applies equally forcefully to teaching.

No matter what I do in the classroom, what decision I make, I'm always right and I'm always wrong. That is, everything I offer will be right for some students and wrong for others. I wrote about an instance of 'you're always right and you're always wrong' not long ago (Newman, 1990).

> I had just finished a writing conference with Greg. I'd listened to him read his piece. I'd encouraged him to talk about the difficulties he felt he was still having deciding where his writing should go. He felt the piece was unfinished and detached but he wasn't sure what to do about it. As I listened to him I recalled something he'd done with his own students which he'd described during one of our class discussions. I wondered aloud whether he mightn't actually use that experience as an opening.
>
> "That's a possibility," he said, so I sent him off to write. Not long afterward, however, I heard him telling his group "Judith said I should...."
>
> What did I learn from Greg's comment? I was confronted with evidence of how difficult it is to step outside an authoritarian role, and it raised for me some of the problems of holding writing conferences with students. I had no clearly worked out notion of how Greg's writing should go. I was simply trying to help him bring more of himself into the piece. I'd offered him back his own story so he could see how he'd already shared with us some incidents which illustrated what I sensed was the point of his writing. But my tentative connection had the force of a directive—not "Judith thought I might," but "Judith said I should." I'd inadvertently taken charge of Greg's writing. Only then did I realize I might have asked him whether he could think of something he'd done in his own classroom that illustrated what he was writing about and then asked him where he might use it effectively.
>
> And yet, offering a suggestion isn't wrong either. My conversation with Debbie, which followed immediately after the conference with Greg, helped me see that. I could tell from Debbie's face and voice she didn't feel comfortable with what she'd written. She sounded tentative and looked perplexed when I asked if she could sum up what she'd done so far:
>
> "Tell me more about the situation," I prompted. As she talked I asked questions, I kept watching for signs of animation and authority which would let me know she was on to something. She finally began telling about her own recent experiences with writing -- the furrow between her eyebrows disappeared, her face relaxed.
>
> "Here's where she's comfortable," I thought to myself, "this is where she should be able to write. How do I help her see that?"
>
> "Why are you hesitant to write about yourself?" I asked. She gave a couple of reasons: she didn't think her own experiences were interesting enough; besides, she thought I was expecting her to try fiction.
> "Why don't you try writing the incident as a personal narrative?" I suggested. At that her face changed. I could see the tension dissipate as she left to resume writing.
>
> This conversation made me aware that one of my roles during a writing conference, particularly when the writing is just starting out, is to help the writer make contact with what she's trying to convey. In addition, these two conversations juxtaposed allowed me to see there is

no one way to assist student and teacher writers. While Debbie was able to accept a suggestion and make it her own, in Greg's case my connection was made too directly. His response to my input showed me I needed to keep out of the decision-making at least until he is more willing to trust his own ability. Offering him the suggestion wasn't a bad thing to have done, though; it let me learn more about how to support Greg's learning and writing (pp. 19-20).

The inescapable conflict—the inevitable dilemma of teaching: no matter what I try, what activity or strategy I offer, what comment I make, it will be helpful for some and yet may interfere for others. In other words, I'm always right and I'm always wrong.

Frank Smith (1981) discusses the problem of students' interpretations of teachers' intentions in his important **Language Arts** article "Demonstrations, Engagement and Sensitivity." He argues students are learning all the time but that what they could be learning may not be what we think we're teaching. My conversation with Greg and Debbie made it very clear to me just how differently my responses can be interpreted.

This notion of demonstrations, engagement, and sensitivity is very complex. It links with Vygotsky's notion of **zone of proximal development** (Vygotsky, 1978). Vygotsky contends we learn from seeing how others do things and by trying them out with whatever assistance is available and thereby become able to do many things autonomously. That's why the collaborative context is crucial if we want learning to occur. We are learning from each other all the time. Making that learning conscious is a crucial aspect of creating a learning-focused environment.

Demonstrations and **engagement** are difficult concepts. As Maggie commented in one journal last winter:

It's been very helpful for me in sorting out what I believe to think about pedagogical decisions in terms of 'you're always right and you're always wrong' and 'it depends.' It's relieved me of the burden of trying to figure out the one right way to do things. It's also freed me to change my mind and to think much more about the context in which I'm operating. Many teachers really don't like to hear that sort of answer when they ask me, an acknowledge 'expert,' some version of "Am I doing this right?" I think we've helped to perpetuate the notion that teaching is simple and straightforward by the kind of usual answers we give and through the various curriculum guides and instructional materials we produce. Teachers have come to expect there's a right way of doing things and get very frustrated by this whole language philosophy which seems so difficult to pin down. The ones who are comfortable with ambiguity have stopped trying to pin things down and have shifted to a reflective stance through which they'll never stop learning about teaching. What do I do to help the others?

Susan Church

I think that I am just now beginning to see the significance of the concept Smith is presenting. It seems that our colloquial understanding of a 'demonstration' is limited to showing how someone does something...a gymnastics demonstration, a demonstration of Indian basket weaving or of quilting. What Smith seems to bring to the meaning of this word is the presence and stance of the potential learner....When I checked a dictionary for a definition of 'demonstration', I found 'the act of making clear, esp. by practical exposition.' The operative words here seem to be **making clear.** Only Smith sees 'the clarity' as **having to occur in the learner through engagement**.

Then there's the question of how this idea of **demonstration** differs from **modelling**. ...When we see others doing things and we imagine ourselves doing these things with pleasure or effect, they become demonstrations for us. It's an active transactional process, not passive. [A learner] doesn't simply copy the demonstration but selectively chooses what she wants to synthesize.... Modelling doesn't account for interpretation on the part of the learner.

As I see it, learners create demonstrations for themselves from the potential inherent in the instructional setting. As teachers we have no way of controlling what learners will take from any situation. Different people will engage with the same potential demonstrations differently. That means in order to learn what's working for whom, what's interfering for whom, we have to be engaging with our students' demonstrations. There is, or should be, engagement in both directions. From a transactional, uncommon sense, perspective we teachers must be learners, too.

It's time, I think, to raise these important issues in the workshop. However, I'm not yet sure how to go about it. I'm waiting for the teachers to present me with an opening.

❖

The Responding/Editing **Issues** group are already meeting in the hallway when I arrive this morning. I don't join their conversation. I chat, instead, with some of the others as they socialize in the classroom and I prepare for the day's agenda: a discussion of the Hunt and Serebrin articles and a poetry circle.

At 9:00 I invite small group discussion about the Hunt and Serebrin articles.

I want to establish connections between what these researchers are arguing and what Elbow and Graves have said about writing conversations.

"Let me raise a strategic concern here," I open. "People in the winter classes seem to find it difficult to make connections among the various readings. The tendency is to 'memorize' what each author is saying rather than consider similarities and differences among the arguments they advance. I'd like you to think about how Hunt's and Serebrin's ideas connect with Elbow's and Graves's."

With my year-long classes I wait until someone complains they can't keep track of all the stuff they've read. That's when I suggest they 'interview' the authors/researchers and compare their theoretical positions. It usually happens somewhere about the eighth week of term. Then I suggest the teachers reread everything they've read so far (twenty or more articles/chapters/books) and in groups figure out a scheme for comparing the various arguments. But here in the Institute I'm starting to feel some time pressure so I elect to be a bit more directive.

This morning, we talk about ways of doing a comparison. Bruce thinks he'd like to take the matrix he, Shelagh, and Maggie developed yesterday for Graves and Elbow and add Hunt and Serebrin.

"Try it and see how it works. You'll probably find your categories need some revision," I encourage them.

"We didn't do a matrix yesterday," says Norma, "so we'd have to start from scratch. Bruce, would you be willing to share your categories with us?"

There's no reason for me to insist each group invent their own categories. Bruce's represent a good starting point .

"Why don't you put Bruce's categories on the overhead so we can all see them?" Michael asks.

That's the second time Michael has suggested something of this kind. Was it yesterday, no the day before, when he asked me to write my focusing questions for the learning stories on the board? It's a good suggestion but I must talk about it with him. I'd like him to see that I go public with a list, or whatever, primarily when the request comes from them and that what appears on a transparency, the blackboard, or chart paper are their ideas, not my prepackaged information. I'm making a guess that Michael does a lot of prior organizing for his kids; I could be wrong about that. But I think I need to touch base; there could be a potential teaching moment here. I write a reminder —

discuss 'lists on the board' with Michael.

At this point, I could hand Bruce a transparency and a pen and ask him to list their categories from yesterday but that would mean the rest of us would have to wait for him to get it done. It's faster if I put a transparency on the overhead, quickly sketch a matrix and have him, Maggie, and Shelagh dictate the headings to me. That way, people can be engaged as I write; no waiting required, and the momentum of the situation is maintained. Sustaining momentum is important. Situations die when people have to wait around so I'm always watching for ways to keep activities in high gear.

Yes, teacher organization is faster, but is it useful? I've discovered most painfully that when I do the organizing I short change the kids. I prevent them from developing their own understanding. They are trying to build on foreign ideas (mine). I've invalidated their prior knowledge and how can I expect them to build on anything else? The results are less than satisfactory and I have only encouraged them to memorize my patterns of meaning.

Pat Kidd

We quickly talk our way through the category headings:

role of teacher
responsibilities of students
types of feedback
timing of feedback

and then the groups get to work.

I join Theresa, Michael, Connie, Barb, and Carmina. I listen as they talk about the articles.

"I'm not sure how Serebrin contributes to conferencing. I mean, he didn't have much of a conversation with Kristin, did he?" comments Carmina.

"It's true he didn't," responds Barb, "but that single question he asked (she scans the article to find it), 'How would one of your favorite authors make Olga and Boris seem funny?' was very powerful. It sent Kristin to explore writing through reading. You're doing that with us, aren't you?" she says to me.

"Talk a bit more about that," I invite her.

"Well, you kind of did that yesterday when we talked about the short stories."

"But she didn't ask us anything about connecting with our own writing," argues Carmina.

"Not directly," Barb answers her. "But she did read the beginnings from those stories to us and had us write an opening ourselves. Last night I reread the stories looking at the openings more closely and then tried a new beginning for my own story. I guess I did what Kristin, in Serebrin's article, did."

"What did you find out?" I ask.

"I'm reading the short stories, poems, children's books, even the professional articles differently. I'm noticing how various authors do things and our talking about it is makes me look at my own writing with different eyes."

This is a nice example of what Smith means by 'reading like a writer.' The fact that Barb is engaged in writing is affecting how she's reading.

"What about your beginning?"

"I suddenly saw a way of introducing the characters and the situation. Here let me read what I wrote:

The table was littered—readings from my courses at the Mount, finished papers, papers in progress, blank paper, crumpled paper, magazines, flyers, bills, and my son's grade 9 report card. I picked it up. A milestone had been reached—the end of Junior High. Senior High was on the doorstep. I was proud of him. But..."

"I see the mess on your table; just like mine," says Connie, "and you draw me into some conflict right away with the 'but'."

"That was what I was trying to do. Before, I had a lengthy explanation about who I was and what the problem was. I could see a reader wouldn't want to be bothered with all that stuff before finding out what was going on, but I didn't know how to get right into the story. Playing with beginnings yesterday was quite helpful."

"It worked for you?"

"It certainly did. I just didn't know how to start off and after that writing session yesterday I could see some possibilities I hadn't thought about before."

I look from Barb to the others in the group. "Can we connect back to Serebrin? How do those category headings help you think about what Serebrin did?"

As they begin discussing 'role of teacher' I move to another group.

Norma, Earl, Diane, Leslie, and Lorna are talking about writing conventions.

I can see how that issue grows out of a conversation about conferencing—Hunt raises it with his 'mockingbird' responses. I listen for a while.

"I still think I have some responsibility for teaching kids how to spell," insists Earl.

"Of course you do," Norma responds, "but you have to think about spelling in relation to the larger thing you're trying to accomplish which is help the kids develop some fluency as writers. If they don't like writing and won't write much because they're worried about spelling correctly, then it seems to me we're undermining them as writers, aren't we?"

"So how do I deal with spelling? What do I do about it when we're publishing, for example?" he asks me.

I don't have a definitive answer for him; there isn't one. It depends. Besides, if I gave Earl an answer I wouldn't be helping him think through the issue on his own. If I gave him tips, if I told him what to do, I'd just be sustaining his reliance on 'experts' and not helping him become more reflective, more independent. When he has other questions he'd continue looking for authoritative answers and not take the time to consider his choices and what effect each might have on his students. So I ask the group a question.

"Why do you want the children to write? Why do you want to publish some of their writing?"
I'm hoping no one will say "That's what we're being told to do!"

Diane explains, "I think writing is important. It gives the children a chance to think through their ideas, and publishing it lets them share their ideas with other people. Publishing some of their stuff also creates a little pressure for the children to be concerned about spelling, punctuation, layout, and the like."

"How does publishing create that pressure?" I ask her.

"It sets up a situation where there are other readers. If the writing doesn't make sense then the other children aren't going

---

Six-year-old Alicia and I were sitting side-by-side both writing stories and Alicia wanted to know how to spell 'beautiful.' "Just give it your best shot," I said as I often do. Ignoring my suggestion, Alicia craned her neck to look at my writing, commenting, "you're writing about the country, too, so it must be here somewhere!" Concerned that Alicia wasn't attempting to spell independently, I asked her, "What would you do if I weren't here?" She looked at me, grabbed her paper, skipped into the den where my twelve year old was using the computer, "Robyn, how do you spell 'beautiful'?" This incident forced me to take a look at some beliefs and actions operating here. My intended message was 'spell as best you can.' What Alicia demonstrated to me was that she was aware of other strategies for learning to spell that she, undaunted by my efforts to restrict her to one strategy, wanted to try. Her awareness of the usefulness of collaborating with others as a strategy for learning to spell forced me to re-examine my actions. In my zeal to encourage her independence, I was inadvertently undermining collaborating with others as a legitimate strategy for her.

Lynn Moody

to make sense of it. If the words aren't decipherable it's going to be difficult to figure out what the author is trying to convey. When we're publishing a piece I raise these problems with the kids."

"Anything else?" I look around the table.

"Well, by publishing some of the children's writing, we can draw their attention to published books and the conventions authors and publishers use. They can discuss why words are spelled in particular ways, what function punctuation serves, and so on. We can help children see connections between the writing of professional authors and their own," offers Leslie. "I'm beginning to see how looking at various children's books is helping me figure out what to do with my story."

"Those are important by-products of publishing. You get to be read, you have to think about what your audience expects, you begin reading with a different eye. So how do you go about creating that kind of context?" I ask the group.

There is no right way of achieving those ends. It's always a matter of judgement. How much attention should be paid to revising and editing, to spelling and grammar, depends on a particular child's writing fluency, how much writing the children have done in the past, who will be reading what they are currently writing, what particular books and stories they have read recently, what the parents expect their child's writing should look like, and so on. My judgement about what constitutes appropriate pressure for conventional writing is going to be different for each writer and for each piece of writing.

We discuss the dilemmas facing us.

"I feel I'm always under pressure when it comes to the children writing," says Lorna. "No one has said anything but I know the parents expect me to correct the children's spelling."

"I've had parents come in upset about the invented spelling in their child's journal wondering what's going on," Leslie adds.

*I dislike the word 'invented'—it masks the underlying relationship between people's approximate spellings and conventional forms. I prefer Carolyn Burke's term **functional** which highlights that connection. I decide it's too fine a distinction, however, to raise at this moment.*

"Is there anything you can do to help parents understand?" I ask her.

"I suppose I could write parents, explaining what I'm trying to do."

"I've had parent meetings where I've shown them how the kids' writing progresses as we work on it," says Diane. "Sometimes I've even had the parents do some writing themselves so they experience a little of what the children are doing. That has helped a lot."

"How has it helped?"

"Well, having the parents write opened the conversation to their own anxiety about writing. They talked about not having anything to say, about worrying whether grammar and spelling are correct. That's when I brought out a child's writing folder to show them how writing unfolds if ideas are dealt with first. When I did that, the parents could understand what I was trying to do with the kids. They could see where concern for spelling and grammar came in."

"Something one of the teachers in my school tried," says Norma, "was have her kids and their parents in to 'workshop' together. It was quite amazing—what happened is that the kids jumped into the writing and the parents simply followed along. They couldn't not write when the kids were engaging so easily."

"But what about the provincial guidelines which tell us we have to teach spelling?" Earl asks. "Our school district is definitely stressing conventional spelling. I think there's a real contradiction there. On the one hand, in the stuff I'm reading we're being told not to correct spelling and on the other we're told we're expected to teach it. What **are** we supposed to do?"

"You're describing the kinds of contradictions we face in the classroom every day," I comment. "No expert can tell me precisely what to do, what decision to make. My decisions have to be based on my assumptions about teaching, on what my long range instructional intentions are, on what I know about my students and on what I sense might be useful for an individual or a group of students at a particular time. I find out whether the judgements I have made have been useful, not from the assurances of outside experts but from how you, my students, react and engage."

In a collaborative and learning-focused context students are continually commenting on procedures, making connections, questioning decisions, asking for information. Their questions and comments have potential for letting me learn both about them and about my teaching. Through my students' engagement I learn about their interests, their strategies, and their difficulties. By following their lead, I allow them to show me new directions to pursue. Every teaching encounter becomes an opportunity for me to discover new things both about learning and about how to assist them. I become a learner, too.

I describe an instance of letting my students lead me that occurred last winter.

"I had invited the teachers to think about something they liked to do, to consider how the learning had happened, who had determined its direction, what sorts of rewards had been available, and so on, just as we did yesterday. Then we freewrote about our accomplishments. After the freewrite, Trish confronted me: 'What has any of this got to do with writing and teaching children about spelling, punctuation, and grammar?'

"Until that moment I had intended no direct connection. But as we talked it occurred to me we could use these descriptions of learning to craft stories which would let us discover something about how and where writing conventions become important. Story writing hadn't been a part of my original plan. However, Trish's question presented an opportunity which allowed me to develop my agenda and at the same time help her explore her concerns."

"Is that what Garth Boomer (1982) means when he talks about negotating the curriculum?" asks Norma.

"By negotiating the curriculum I think Boomer means deliberately inviting students to contribute to, and modify, the instructional program so they have a real investment both in the learning journey and in the outcomes. In that instance, while I didn't deliberately ask students for input, Trish's questions certainly reshaped what happened, " I answer.

"So what you're saying is students should have input into what's going on in the classroom," says Norma.

"Let me leave you with this question, "How am I negotiating our curriculum here?"

I've probably talked too much but it's important for people to think about how we're negotiating this curriculum. My overarching intentions are constantly being revised based on input I'm receiving from them. In a learning-focused environment, I have to recognize that no sooner will I think I have some aspect of our learning enterprise worked out when something will happen to raise new questions and we will have to rethink the situation. There are few absolute answers to questions about teaching. Every question has to be answered 'It depends.'

Hanna wrote in her journal the other day:

> On my way home today I decided to take the MicMac
> Rotary rather than use the 107 Bypass as I usually do.
> The Rotary is still under construction and to be avoided
> at all cost. I'm not sure why I took it, except as I
> approached the traffic circle I noticed that the fog was
> becoming denser. I had been replaying our conversation
> this afternoon and I found myself thinking about how
> navigating the Rotary in its present state and teaching are
> somehow analogous.
>
> With the Rotary, the roads are still there, the
> direction I'm taking is still the same, but the routes are
> not as clearly marked as before. The paths keep
> changing; they are continually being altered slightly.
> There are more risks using the Rotary now—I need to
> slow down and watch the signs and other drivers more
> carefully. The fog adds to the challenge.
>
> While my goals for teaching are still fairly clear, I'm
> not as certain of the route as I was when I first started
> teaching, or even a few years ago. I need to move
> cautiously through the fog, reflect more, and be ready to
> change lanes if I find I'm heading in the 'wrong'
> direction.

Hanna is beginning to appreciate there are no certain routes. Her
classroom is like the Rotary under construction—the paths keep
changing, continuously being altered slightly—and she needs to
be more observant as she travels. She's beginning to know there
are no infallible answers; instead, 'it depends'.

I glance at the clock—9:45; time to reconvene the large
group.

"What do we learn by comparing these four ways of
responding to writing?"

"They are all different aren't they," says Barb. "Graves is
talking about teacher responses, Elbow about peers responding.
Hunt, like Elbow, is making an important distinction between
responses which let writers discover what readers experience
from the writing, and Serebrin is arguing we need to help
writers learn through reading."

"The question about timing is interesting," Maggie says.
"Serebrin didn't wait until a draft was completed or until Kristin

came to ask him for help. He sensed Kristin was having difficulty and asked her what was wrong. The responding Hunt is talking about seems to come at the request of the writer. The bat asks for reactions when he's finished his poem, although I can see I'm now asking for reactions as I draft each part. I suppose I could even ask for help if I were stuck and not sure where to go next, couldn't I?"

"Of course you could; you can ask for a reaction at any point in the writing. You can even let your reader know what kind of help you're looking for. There are situations, for example, where mockingbird feedback is desirable. Sometimes you're looking for technical support. You can look for it in published writing, if you know the specific question you're asking, like 'how do people open stories?' But sometimes you're not sure what the problem is and you may just need someone to say 'Oh, what you're trying to do is — —, let me show you how to do that.'"

We talk around the issues for another few minutes and I record their comments on a comparison matrix.

I need to be alert for opportunities to use various responding strategies when I talk with people about their writing today.

Ten o'clock. Time for the poetry response group. As we rearrange the furniture several people leave to work on other things. This morning, fourteen of us squeeze around the table.

"Who'd like to begin?"

"Well, I want to talk about 'Inside Out'," insists Norma.

"Me, too" chimes in Leslie, "I couldn't make any sense of that poem."

"I must have read it half-a-dozen times," adds Connie. "It was really frustrating."

"Not me," laughs Earl. "I read it, had no idea what it was about, so I quit and tried another one."

"How did you approach the poem?" I ask. "Did you attempt any freewriting about the images, connections, etc., the words generated for you?"

"I didn't try that," says Norma. "I just read and reread it, but I couldn't see what the poet was getting at."

"Did any of you read it with a pencil in hand?"

It appears nobody did.

"That might be worth trying right now. Let's take a few minutes to read the poem and write whatever comes to mind while you're reading it."

"Inside Out" is a complex poem. I shared it with one of my classes last winter because I had no idea myself what it was about. We ended up with three plausible interpretations, but I sense the poem will yield even more which is why I included it in the Institute collection.

Gordon Pradl believes we need to help students deal with poetry 'at point of utterance' by allowing them to see us struggling with interpretation ourselves (Pradl, 1987). I'm struggling with "Inside Out". Using it to open discussion will allow me to explore the poem along with the teachers. It will let me demonstrate, in Frank Smith's sense, that a poem, like any text, is an answer in search of questions (Pradl, 1987).

I silently read the poem again:

Inside Out

I walk the purple carpet into your eye
carrying the silver butter server
but a truck rumbles by,
               leaving its black tire prints on my foot
and old images   the sound of banging screen doors on hot
                                 afternoons
        and a fly buzzing over the Kool-Aid spilled on the sink
flicker, as reflections on the metal surface.

Come in, you said,
inside your paintings, inside the blood factory, inside the
old songs that line your hands, inside
eyes that change like a snowflake every second,
inside spinach leaves holding that one piece of gravel,
inside the whiskers of a cat,
inside your old hat, and most of all inside your mouth where
                              you
grind the pigments with your teeth, painting
with an ostrich feather on the moon that rolls out of my
                         mouth.

You cannot let me walk inside you too long inside
the veins where my small feet touch
bottom.
You must reach inside and pull me
like a silver bullet
from your arm.

                           Diane Wakoski

The poem is still a mystery to me. I really don't know what it's about. I start at the beginning once more, jotting thoughts and ideas as they surface:

I still feel hallucinatory images but the more I read the poem the more I'm certain it's <u>not</u> about a drug experience. I see a relationship of some kind but I'm not certain whether it's between two people or within a single individual. Could be about a woman and a man, or a person and her past—'and old images flicker: the sound of banging screen doors on hot afternoons and a fly buzzing over the Kool-Aid spilled on the sink.' Walking the purple carpet into your eye—do I take that literally, can I create a scenario where that would make any sense? A modern painting? (There are other references to paintings, pigments, here)—or is it metaphoric? Is it referring to my trying to get inside this 'other' person or self? 'Come in you said'—an invitation extended, but inside what? Inside his being (I feel the person talking is male, can't say why but it feels like that), the shared memories ('the old songs that line your hands')? Then I sense a change of speaker: 'You cannot let me walk inside you too long—small feet'— a woman? A child to a parent? A student to a teacher? A plea to the other to help 'I' grow from dependence to independence?

I haven't made a coherent whole from this reading, but I have seen new images I missed in earlier readings. A painter and his muse? Could be.

I put my pencil down and wait quietly for the others to finish writing.

"Well?"

Norma speaks first, "I saw more this time. I just let myself respond to the images without worrying about what the poem is about. So while I wasn't making sense of the whole, I was touched by more: 'the whiskers of a cat'—a fleeting, tickling sensation; 'your old hat'—comfortable, like an old shoe; 'spinach leaves holding that one piece of gravel'—an unexpected, unpleasant encounter."

"It feels to me like someone taking drugs," insists Earl.

"Talk more about that," I invite him.

"It's all those disjointed images, and the bit at the end about pulling me like a silver bullet from your arm—I see a needle," he says.

"I didn't see that at all," Connie comments. "I felt it was someone remembering their childhood—screen door banging, flies buzzing, old songs. 'You can't let me walk inside you too long'—I can't dwell in the past too long."

"I was struck by those flickering images of the past as well," says Diane. "It took me a while to see them as memories, though. It happened when I read: 'and old images...flicker' leaving out the images themselves, then I could see them there."

"I don't know what to make of the silver butter server," says Carmina. "Someone is carrying it, but I don't know why."

"What could that be about?" I ask.

"Well, a silver server represents luxury compared to a plastic one, say. And butter is rich, lots of calories," Norma muses. "Is 'I' bringing wealth to this other person, does it represent an abundance of something, if so, what?"

No one responds to her question.

Bruce, sitting beside me, has been silent. The high school English teacher in the group, I expected he'd try to interpret the poem for the others; I was wrong. He's been engaged, though. He's been writing as people talk; from where I'm sitting it looks like he's recording people's impressions. I think I want to nudge him.

"What do you make of the poem, Bruce?" I ask him.

"In some ways, I think the poem could be a metaphor for this experience we're having right now, for the workshop.

Now that's an unexpected connection. Once he says it, I can see it myself. It certainly wasn't an intentional juxtaposition on my part!

"'Come in, you said.' That's what you've said to us. You've invited us to look at your 'paintings'—readings, stories, poems, your writing— to share old familiar songs, to examine our own experiences. But you can't let us stay too long. You can't let us become dependent on you. You have to pull us out, help us stand on our own."

"So you see the poem as a metaphor for teaching?"

"I guess so," he answers.

"I like that—I think you're right, the poem captures elements of the experience I've been trying to set up for you. My own interpretation this time is somewhat different. As I was reading it I was suddenly very aware of the many references to painting. The scenario I found myself constructing was of a painter and his muse; it could be her muse. The muse comes as the magi, bearing rich gifts: 'I walk the purple carpet into your eye, carrying the silver butter server.'"

"All I can think of is drugs," laughs Earl.

"There are certainly elements in the poem which can be interpreted that way, aren't there? What I find so interesting about this poem," I continue, "is how open the text is. It evokes a lot of discussion and there is clearly no single interpretation. The more I talk about it with people, the more I see in it."

As I'm talking I also see connections between this poem and some of the stories we talked about yesterday. Several of the stories were about a secret inner life. This poem could be a metaphor for that inner world. I also wonder what connections the teachers see between this and the other poems.

"What connections do you make between this poem and others in the collection?" I ask.

Connie reads aloud another poem and we move in a new direction.

The conversation weaves connections among the poems, between the poems and paintings we've seen, stories we've read, experiences we've had. Like our conversation yesterday about the short stories, the experience we construct together is far richer than our individual interpretations alone.

We wander these poetic paths for an hour before I ask, "What's been going on here?"

I want the teachers to compare what we've been doing with how they handle poetry in their own classrooms. I'd like them to examine the role I took, how the situation affected the way they read, connections with the story discussion we had yesterday, and what implications this experience holds for them as teachers.

I take a moment to come back again to Elbow's 'giving movies of our mind.' That's been our principle mode of response to the poetry. We've shared images, feelings, experiences evoked by the words on the page.

"How has our discussion this past hour helped you think about responding to one another's writing?" I ask.

Silence for a moment, then Bruce offers a comment, "What you're trying to get us to see is that we ought to be dealing with one another's writing as evoking feelings, images, etc. You're implying that we need to respond to students' writing in the same way."

Bruce has definitely internalized my agenda. He's now seeing this learning experience in terms of its implications for his own teaching.

"That's exactly what I'm trying to help you see. There is no difference between responding to the writing of published authors and to our own, or to our students'. That's Hunt's contention, I think: that we need to be **heard**, not corrected; chipmunk responses, not condescending, kindly mockingbird advice. One of the ways we can help students learn how to respond to other people's writing is by encouraging them to give movies of their minds in response to published works. That's one of the important reading/writing connections I believe we have to learn how to forge."

To make my point about responding to our writing in the same way we respond to the writing of professional writers I take a risk—I decide to share my poem 'The Sofa' with the group. I didn't write the poem with this intention in mind. I wrote it because it wanted to come out. But I can see this is another of those potential teaching/learning moments too important to pass up.

"Let's test out what we've just been exploring."

I take out "The Sofa" and read it aloud:

Six in a row.
Mr. Cuperfine, Mr. Goldfarb, Mr. Kaplan,
Mr. Yablon, Mr. Cohen, and Mr. Scholossberg.
Side by side on that eleven foot sofa.
Six little old men
Clean shaven
Gnarled hands resting on solid pot bellies
Black skull-caps perched on shiny bald heads.
Waiting to mumble prayers.
A ritual to console,
To offer community and continuity.
But their presence is no comfort;
It adds to the alienation—
We women are excluded.
Unwelcome to participate
In their prayers for my now dead father.

"You call it 'The Sofa' but it's about what happened after your father died? Why have you called it that?" asks Maggie.

"That sofa symbolizes alienation for me. I think it always has. When we were young my mother had it covered with plastic to keep people off. Even uncovered, however, it didn't foster a sense of community; it was too long to allow conversation. The image of those six men, sitting there, not talking, just waiting to perform their rituals, it left me with a real feeling of being cut off."

"The poem is like a photograph for me. I can see the six old men sitting there, comfortable, sure of themselves. You're not in the picture, though. How come you decided to leave yourself out?" Leslie asks.

"I started out intending to describe the men. But those words 'we women are excluded' popped out and once they did I was suddenly present through my exclusion. I found it interesting how that actually happened."

"Read the poem again," Bruce says.

I do.

"I was surprised by the 'clean shaven'," says Barb. "I had expected them to have beards. I can't say why, it must connect with images from my past."

"The line 'But their presence is no comfort' reminds me of my grandfather lying in a hospital bed dying of cancer and the jobs of the nurses (and it took four of them to move him) was to comfort him. He believed they just wanted to torture him. They offered him no comfort," comments Theresa.

"I get a sense of anger and bitterness from the poem. 'We women are excluded'," Janice remarks. "Do you think that efforts by women to become part of the religious mainstream, to participate fully in religious ritual, will ever come about?"

"Not easily," I reply.

"While there's anger there, I also feel a snort of humor, a sort of secret like Miss Manning's," says Bruce.

"Talk about that a bit more."

"The description of those old men is funny. You're mocking their serious intent, rejecting it. Pillars of the community with their badges of position, their skull caps, askew. You women may be excluded from their rituals but you know something they don't—their rituals don't really ease the pain."

We talk about death and dying, mourning and alienation, and about women in the community.

The conversation offers me further insight into my feelings about the experience. I make notes as I listen. I shared the poem precisely because it doesn't feel done. I wanted to hear reactions so I could begin seeing it through other people's eyes. I can't say there have been any flashes of insight but it was helpful hearing people's reactions. My perspective has been broadened.

"Before we move on to writing, reading, and responding let me mention a couple of books about exploring poetry with children: Russell Hazzard's **It scares me but I like it**; Amy McClure's **Sunrises and Songs**; and Georgia Heard's **For the Good of the Earth and Sun**. I've brought them in and put them in the library. Have a look; I found them interesting."

For the remainder of the morning I chat with people about their evolving writing. Although her name isn't on the **Writing Conversations** list, I make a point of tracking down Shelagh. She and I need to chat.

I find her in the corridor with Earl. They're discussing his story about his father. I listen while Earl reads.

"Roll up your window Billie. Dad, tell him to roll up his window." The smell of day old fish drifted through the car as the window went up. I took a quick look around and sized up my surroundings. A 1962 Dodge Dart with a stick shift, black bucket seats and a red exterior. I could hardly wait 'till I got my license.

A rather trim and strong looking forty-seven-year-old man was driving the car. He had a proud look about him. He had worked long hard hours to buy this car.

Sitting next to him was my older brother, Billie. I liked this quiet, nineteen-year-old. He, too, seemed to be developing the trait of working hard for a living. He had just finished high school and was working for the summer at the fish plant until something better came along. Not much work around this year.

Dad seemed a bit uncomfortable this morning. Something was on his mind. He looked at me through the rear view mirror, glancing shyly towards Billie. He repeated the motion once more then shifted the gears. What was he up to? Had he heard something about me? No, who could have told him? Marg and I were seeing each other steady and I really like her a lot. We were getting along quite well. She liked walking 'the tracks.' Marg always smelled nice and had soft skin. Yeah, I really liked her. Billie was seeing a girl who had just moved over from Newfoundland. I didn't know her too well. She worked at the grocery store where Mom shopped. She'd speak to us and was really nice to me.

Once again Dad shifted uncomfortably in his seat, glancing from me to Billy. What was he up to? Clearing his throat, he started to speak.

"Oh, Bill"—pause—"umm...Earl, you know, you two boys have been seeing steady girls for some time now and I think it's time we had a little talk."

I sat up immediately.

Dad was really nervous as he moved his hands around the steering wheel. He put his hand in his red plaid shirt pocket looking for the Hollywood butt he had left there just after breakfast. Fumbling to light his cigarette, he once again began to speak. I hung on his every word. Gosh, this was something. Dad was really going to tell me—us, about SEX! No, he wouldn't, would he? I looked towards the back of Billie's head. He seemed to be slipping slowly into the seat. What was wrong with him? I thought this was extraordinary. Come on...come on, say something. By this time we were rounding the corner to Front Street and only a few minutes to work. I leaned forward and listened, not daring to urge him on....

Earl finishes reading. I wait for Shelagh to respond; she sits silently. So I begin.

"I can visualize the situation with your dad and brother in the front seat of the car and you in back. You were what—fourteen, fifteen at the time?"

"I'm four years younger than Billie so I was fifteen."

"And I can imagine you there with a wide grin on your face, your poor dad flustered and Billie mortified."

"I can feel your amazement, is he really going to say something about sex?" Shelagh laughs .

"I like what you've done since yesterday. That bit about your dad being uncomfortable, you've worked on that and now I can feel his discomfort. He glances at you in the rear-view mirror, his conversation is halting. You've created his tension through his actions and his words."

"And Billie's embarrassment—his slipping lower in the seat," says Shelagh.

"When you started out you said you wanted to write about your dad's death. This incident is a delightful one. Do you see yourself working it into something larger about your dad?"

"I'd like to but I've never done anything like that—I mean, write something in separate parts and then bring them together."

"You might find it useful to reread the short stories in the collection with an eye to noticing how those authors take small incidents and weave them together to create something larger. My hunch is this amusing story about your dad's foray into sex education with you guys will work as a flashback quite well. If you try that, you'll have to think about when the main story is taking place and how to lead up to the flashback. Have a look at the short stories to see how those authors do that."

I don't have the short stories with me at the moment or I'd dig them out and we could look at how these authors create larger stories by weaving many smaller elements together. At this moment, I'm explaining to Earl (and to Shelagh, too) a tactic which short story writers use and directing him to some authors to see how they use it.

"Do either of you have the short stories here?"

"Mine are at home," says Shelagh.

"Mine, too, I don't have them with me today," Earl answers.

"My copies are somewhere in the classroom. I'll get them for you when we're finished so you can look at them."

I turn to Shelagh to see if she perceives any connection between Earl's writing situation and her own.

"How has Earl's writing helped you think about your own?" I ask her.

"His description is more detailed than mine."

"In what way?"

"He's showing through his father's and Billie's actions how they're feeling. He has his dad digging around in his shirt pocket for an old cigarette butt, he has the fragmented speech. That helps the reader feel the tension in the situation."

"Do you think you could try the same kind of thing."

"Right here at the beginning, I guess, where I'm sitting at the dining room table buried under mountains of marking."

"How could you convey the pressure you're feeling?"

"I could describe what the table looks like, the fact that I'm still in my housecoat at 2:30 on a Sunday afternoon."

"Why don't you try that?" I encourage her. "Put what you've done aside for the moment and try writing a paragraph or two of description to see what happens. Keep in mind that you're trying to create a photograph for us. You're using words to make a detailed picture so we can visualize the situation."

Just before I leave I ask: "What's been happening here?"

They describe how we've responded to Earl's emerging story, talked about the feelings evoked by the description, thought about where to go from here, mention the connection I tried building between Earl's writing and Shelagh's and the short stories we've been reading.

"Think about the four researchers we've compared so far: Elbow, Graves, Serebrin, and Hunt. Whose ideas were we using in this conversation?"

"Well, your suggestion to go back to the short stories is like Serebrin's question "How would one of your favorite authors do whatever?" Earl comments.

"And we responded to Earl's story by sharing movies of our minds," adds Shelagh. "We were giving chipmunk responses, telling how the writing affected us, and not really discussing the technical stuff except to see how published authors do what we're trying to do."

"Did we do anything Graves suggests?" I ask.

"You asked me a couple of open questions—'How did Earl's writing help me think about my own?' 'How could I convey what I was feeling?'" Shelagh responds.

"So what are you learning about conversations about writing?"

"That there's **no** one way of conducting them," says Earl. You're listening to us and responding based on what you're hearing."

The challenge for me is setting things up so people can experience various kinds of productive writing conversations. It's difficult because I don't want to get heavily into teacher-student conferencing with people. I want to keep our emphasis on peer-responses. For two reasons:

First, I think we all need to learn what kinds of feedback are useful for writers; that means sharing images, feelings, words which get through—learning not to get sucked into offering advice (which we can so easily slip into) but not avoiding it if that's what wants to come out.

Second, I want people to discover how much they learn about solving their writing problems from seeing how other people solve theirs. That aspect of learning about writing is completely lost when teacher-student conferences are the predominant sort of feedback students have. This latter by-product of the talking about writing doesn't become apparent until pieces are comfortably underway but I've come to believe this outgrowth of peer conferencing is the most valuable contribution of sharing writing.

What should come out of a writing conversation? It seems to me a writing conversation should do at least one of several possible things:

> *1) allow the writer to experience his or her words read aloud;*
>
> *2) give the writer an opportunity to explain the intentions behind the writing—(really so he or she can hear him or herself);*
>
> *3) let the writer hear readers' interpretations in relation to his or her intentions;*
>
> *4) set a challenge—one the writer can't actually answer at that moment but which will lurk and guide the writing in unexpected ways;*
>
> *5) help sort out a problem by allowing the writer to consider alternative ways of proceeding.*

Which of these possibilities is most useful depends to a large extent on how developed the writing is (whether it's just starting out or begun to have a clear structure and style) and on how experienced the writer is (whether the writer is comfortably fluent or still struggling to put ideas and words on paper). Any writing conversation should focus on no more than one aspect of the writing at a time—a conversation can't solve every problem; subsequent drafts and subsequent conversations will take care of other aspects of the writing.

*Mayher, Lester, and Pradl's **fluency, clarity, correctness** continuum (Mayher, Lester, & Pradl, 1983) is very useful for helping me decide just how to support a writer. They contend*

> The best way to understand and encourage the interaction between the child's growing linguistic system and her emerging ability to write is to see the latter as a developmental process, which first emphasizes **fluency**, then **clarity**, and finally **correctness**. In stressing **fluency**, the goal is to build a sense of comfort, confidence, and control in the growing writer. Young [I would say *inexperienced*] writers must feel that they have ideas and a language system in their heads and that they can combine these to fill up blank sheets of paper. Only when words fill the page can we emphasize **clarity**: does the writing make sense to others? The final concern is whether or not the text conforms to the

conventions of standard written English and is, therefore, correct. These three dimensions, of course, continually overlap; even the youngest writers must engage in some struggles for clarity and correctness, and even the most experienced writer has frequent problems with fluency—particularly when writing on a new topic or in a new genre (p. 4).

If I'm dealing with building fluency, getting writing flowing, then having the writer talk is what I'm after—to give the writer an opportunity to work out aloud what it is she's trying to do. If the writer is no longer having difficulty with fluency then it may be time to be somewhat more directive. I think there are several ways to be directive: letting reading directly affect the writing by examining books or stories to find out what authors do in given situations and trying something like that ourselves (writing story beginnings, for example), exploring what options might be possible in a particular writing situation, or considering specific questions about audience and purpose.

*Most teachers, in my experience, are not sure just how to go about having writing conversations with students. One way for them to become comfortable with conferencing is to develop a reasonably strong sense of what helps them write; then there's less uncertainty about what questions to ask, whether to get the writer to speak or listen first, whether the conference should be formal or informal. They're better able to 'read' the writer based on their own writing experiences and have a better sense of whether what's going on is helping the writer see where to go or what to do next. Because that's all a writing conversation should be trying to do—**keep the writer going**.*

I remember an incident which occurred during a writing inservice workshop a year or so ago. I was holding a group conversation with three teachers, a couple of other people were onlookers. We were sharing their postcard stories[1], now nearing some

---

[1] I discovered postcard stories from a wonderful collection *Leaping Up Sliding Away* by Kent Thompson (1986). Thompson describes postcard stories in the following way: "I call them postcard stories because many of them were written originally on postcards purchased at various art galleries....Having

kind of completion, discussing the difficulty of creating a balance between not providing too much context (after all the recipient of a postcard would have much of the background, right?), yet giving the reader enough to be able to see the point of the brief story. I was asking directive questions—since the person she was 'writing to' knew the individuals in the 'story', what detail could she eliminate?

"But aren't you interfering in her story?" blurted one of the onlookers horrified. "According to Jane Hansen, we're not supposed to interfere in the writing," she said.

*Her reaction made me reflect on two issues: first, the teacher's role in helping students craft their writing; and second, the power of an authoritarian orthodoxy. This teacher has interpreted Hansen to be saying we mustn't be directive about students' writing, so in her view any suggestions or questions intended to help students focus attention on particular aspects of their writing are **wrong**. No making a judgement about whether the writer might be interested in how to craft something and offering that specific help or information—instead, a blanket response.*

Now, the teacher who had been sharing her story had expressed dissatisfaction with her writing but wasn't sure what wasn't working. To me, as teacher, her problem seemed to be one of tone, she had written a narrative, not a postcard story—I was trying to help her visualize the difference. In fact, her face had lit up in response to my probing and when we discussed how she felt about my question in response to the onlooker's concern, she seemed surprised at the vehemence of the other teacher's reaction.

When I thought about the incident over lunch that day I realized, once again, how the distinction between fluency, clarity, and correctness helps me think about responding to students' writing. When

---

bought the postcards, I wanted to send them to friends—but I didn't know what to say. There's not enough space on a postcard to discuss anything. And a postcard is a peculiarly public form of communication—you assume that everyone who handles the postcard will read it—the recipient's spouse or lover, children, certainly the postman. So I decided to write little stories to surprise the readers. I wanted to make the postman walk from my friend's address in wonder—and you too."

students are struggling for fluency I try to encourage and support their writing, but I refrain from offering any suggestions. With non-fluent writers (of any age) I want to help them get their ideas flowing. In this particular situation, however, the writer had fluency well in hand and was working on clarity and style, precisely the point where some specific suggestions could help her craft her writing.

As it happened, I had spent a little time during the morning browsing through some books published by the children in the school—what I saw was mostly first draft writing in those fourth, fifth, and sixth graders efforts. It was evident the teachers had got the hang of fostering fluency. Seemed to me, though, they now needed to bring reading to bear on writing and start helping their students with crafting.

I made this point to the teachers after lunch. Again I stressed that there are no sure techniques here—we have to keep our eye on each individual writer to judge when it might be useful to offer specific input and when to leave well enough alone.

When I come to you asking for advice on my writing, I would be very upset if you offered me less than you could because of your allegiance to some new orthodoxy!

Linda Swinwood

I suddenly thought of an analogy: I bake reasonably competently but I have trouble with meringues; they always fail. I've tried a variety of recipes without much success. One day I finally called my mother to ask her advice. Can you imagine how I'd have reacted if she'd asked "What do you think you would work?" I expected her to tell me what I was doing wrong and what I should try instead.

There comes a point, I believe, where it's legitimate to offer our writing expertise to our students. Many teachers haven't thought beyond fluency; it's time we began considering clarity and beyond clarity, correctness.

❖

Back to Shelagh.
Do I discuss her angry response before she departs or should I wait until she's played with a descriptive paragraph or two? I think I want to wait. If she's learned anything from the conversation with Earl, as I

think she may have, then we'll be able to talk about
what I was trying to help her see in her own writing.

I leave her to fetch my copies of the short stories for Earl. Then I make a tour of the classroom, touching base to see how people are getting on. A brief conversation with one group, a question to another.

After fifteen minutes or so I look for Shelagh again.

"How's it going?" I ask.

"Here's what I've written:"

> "Where can I go? What can I do? I just can't keep this up. I hate it and I want to quit."
>
> "But you love teaching," says Arthur. "What's going on anyway?"
>
> "It's all this $@!+& marking. I can't get away from it. Look at me. I'm a mess. It's 2:30 on Sunday and I haven't even showered yet. I've been up since 7:30 and all I've done is mark, mark, mark—and this is the weekend. We don't do anything anymore. Friday nights I'm so exhausted and Saturday and Sundays are spent marking and then it's Monday again with more of this $@!+& marking every night. There's no end to it!..."

"Much stronger, don't you think?" I comment. "Your anger and frustration are tangible now. I can see you at that table, feel your exasperation. The swearing tells me you're definitely miserable. Talk to me about writing this."

"I could see how Earl's description worked to convey something about his characters. Your comment about photographs made me close my eyes and visualize the scene. All I did was write down what I saw and felt."

"I think it works. Now I can hear your voice loud and clear. I wasn't feeling that in what you handed me yesterday and I was simply trying to reflect that back to you. Are you still angry with me?"

"Yes, I am," she replies.

"Talk about that."

"Well, you could have been more sensitive about how I would feel when you said the writing felt detached."

"I definitely misjudged how you'd react. Remember what Elbow says: 'You're always right and you're always wrong.' As a writer the decisions about what to do with the writing are your responsibility, but you can't quarrel with my reactions to it. My reactions as a reader are my reactions. I felt the writing was lifeless and looking at Earl's writing has helped you see how you can show us what you were experiencing, but I wonder if you would have engaged with his description if I hadn't reacted candidly to your writing. We can't know of course. I didn't intend my comments to be unfeeling. When I read your reply I realized that we should have had a face-to-face conversation."

"Talking about it would have helped. At least then I would have been able to ask you questions to explore what you had to say."

"Have you anything you'd like to ask now?"

"No, not at the moment. I can see how some description of how I was feeling makes the picture more vivid. I feel the writing is stronger."

"What questions about your own teaching has this whole experience—my responding, the conversation with Earl and your recasting—raised for you?"

"It certainly has let me know I have to be awfully sensitive to my students' feelings."

"Um-hmm."

"I guess it also makes me look at the sharing differently. If you hadn't asked me what I'd learned about my own writing from what Earl had done, I might not have thought about the description. I suppose I'll have to think about how to help students connect with one another's writing better. That's another kind of 'reading like a writer'."

"Do you think you can carry on now?"

"I think so."

"Good. Go to it."

This idea that you're always right and you're always wrong is crucial. Each learner's engagement with the multitude of intentional and inadvertent demonstrations in the classroom is complex. I can't know for certain that what will be supportive for one will be helpful for another. Yes, there are some principles to guide decision-making but in the end it comes down to making judgements. I have to be sensitive to how each student responds and to make judgements based on that reading.

We spend the afternoon engaged in writing, reading, and conversation. I keep on the move. "Do you need help? What do you need help doing?" The writing progresses steadily.

Actually, I'm concerned about Debra and about Carmina. I've been aware from our few conversations that both women have been struggling. If the Institute continued a third week I might wait a bit longer, but if they're going to manage to produce some kind of finished product along with everyone else I've got to make sure they have something beginning to shape up over the weekend. I've been standing back allowing their contact with the others to influence what they're doing but I think it's time now for me to offer more explicit input into their writing.

First I find Debra.

"How's the writing going?"

"Not great."

"Time we talked about it?"

"I guess so."

"Let's hear what you've been doing."

"Well, my idea for a kid's story was this. My son hates cleaning his room and he always gets exasperated with me when he asks me something and I go into what he considers an unnecessarily long explanation. In the story I thought I could combine those two ideas."

"Sounds interesting."

"So I thought the story could be about a boy who asked his mother things like 'Can I go out to play?' and she gives him a list of reasons why not, why he has to clean his room, for example."

"Yes."

"Well, I've been trying to write it but all I've got so far is a few situations worked out."

"Share them with me."

"I thought the boy could want to go out to play but his mother wanted him to clean up his room. He asks if he can have a snack and she tells him not until he cleans his room up. He wants his friend David to come over; mother says not until his room is clean."

"All good ideas. You might need a few more situations to make up a book. Have you asked you son to help you with this?"

"Ask my son for help?" Debra laughs. "I have to tell you. I happened to read Norma Mikkelsen's article (Mikkelsen, 1984) again last evening and I nearly choked. She talks about trying to buy a story from her son—I actually did that," she says.

Debra finds the article and reads me something she's highlighted:

My ten-year-old son was constantly creating stories of fantasy creatures. His latest was a blue mouse. I ransacked his head for details, even paid him a dollar to tell me more. But the rewards weren't in it—for me. He

had been turning himself into a mouse for weeks now. I had only one
night, at best.

   My mother-in-law kept a writing journal, I discovered next. And
she was delighted to share it with me. What personal narratives she had!
I took pages of notes, enought for a novel, only to find myself sinking
into fiction quicksand—plots, sub-plots, characters, conflicts that
weren't even mine. I jumped out just in time.... (p.704)

"I've been going through exactly the same thing!" she
laughs. "I tried to get a story from my son. I asked people in the
class for ideas. I just couldn't find anything to write about. Then
yesterday, Bruce helped me brainstorm about things that
happened around home."

   "Looks like Bruce was a help. I think you're ready now to
get some help from your son. At this point you're not looking
for his stories. You're looking for specific details for your own.
I bet he'd be able to describe lots of situations where he's asked
you questions and you've come back with lengthy
explanations," I explain. "Have you given any thought to the
form of the story?"

   "I think I want this to be a predictable book."

   "What kind of predictability do you want to build in?"

   "Are there different kinds?"

   "There are. Let's look at a few examples to see what we
find."

   Our investigations reveal that children's books build in
predictability by using some natural progression of everyday
experience: by following a sequence of days, or hours, or
seasons, or common family routines. They achieve predictability
by repeating elements of the text at frequent intervals. Some
children's authors do both.

   "I was thinking about using repetition of some kind with this
story. I can't see how I'd follow any kind of sequence."

   "I think you're right. Have you played with anything yet?"

   "Actually, I have. Here." Debra reads:

Andrew's mom walked into his room and she couldn't
believe the mess. Andrew had just dumped his entire toy
box out into the middle of the room.

   "Andrew clean this room up!"

   Andrew reluctantly began to clean his room with
heavy dragging feet, when he heard David playing just
across the street. He carefully approached his mom and
made one small request.

   "Can I go play outside with David? He's just across
the street."

His mother sighed and then replied,

"Grammie's coming next week. This place is such a mess. I want you to finish cleaning up your room instead."

Andrew stamped his feet and marched back to his room and slammed the door shut.

"Why can't she just say yes or no instead of all that stuff?"

Andrew once again began to clean his room with heavy dragging feet. But soon his stomach began to growl for something good to eat. He carefully approached his mom and make one small request....

"That's a great beginning. I see lots of potential for using repetitive refrains. You've already begun doing that. I also like the bit of rhyme you've used. The rhythm of what you've written really reminds me of **It Didn't Frighten Me** (Goss & Harste, 1981)."

"Actually, I was using the book as a model."

"Why didn't you mention that?"

"Well, I didn't want to be copying another book."

"When it's done your book will be your book, not anyone else's. You've read Smith's 'Reading like a writer.' What you're doing here is reading like a writer. You're using what you see another writer doing and trying it out yourself. That's OK. When you have more experience you'll be able to rely on other people's work less. Anyway, I think what you've done works well. It'll need refining, but don't worry about that yet. Try another couple of situations and see what you get. Will you be OK?"

"I think so."

"If you get stuck ask your son for help."

Debra laughs.

Next I track down Carmina.

"How's it going?"

"Well, I think I'm beginning to get somewhere. Norma, Barb, and Bruce have all been helping me quite a bit. Norma got me going on a story."

"Let's hear."

"I've been trying to understand discipline. I was really shocked by your response the other day when I asked you about it. But then talking to the others helped me think about situations which I could have handled differently. Norma thought I should write some of them down. So I've been working at that."

She reads:

When I first came into this course, I wanted to know
what role discipline had in a whole language classroom.
I hadn't seen much written on it and it was an important
issue for me. I thought I would ask Judith about it. Her
annoying resonse was, "In a whole language classroom
discipline is not an issue!" I didn't say anything but I
sure didn't agree. So, I read different articles that Judith
recommended. The term 'structure' started to pop up.
What was meant by structure and more importantly how
was it related to eliminating what I perceived as
discipline problems in my classroom?

As I started to freewrite, I discovered that I was
writing about problems that were directly related to
structures that existed in my room. I was slowly
beginning to make the connections between behaviour
difficulties and structures. Perhaps Judith was right.
Discipline isn't an issue in a whole language classroom if
the structures are set up properly. But I had to find this
out through my own reflections.

I remember one of the many confrontations I had
with an argumentative little girl names Larissa. It had
been the fifth day in a row that Larissa had been first in
line to go to the bathroom. As usual there was pushing
and shoving in line but the real hard pushing was at the
front of the line where the stakes were the highest. "I'm
tired of this!" I thought.

"Larissa, stop pushing and shoving!" I said.

"But Ms. Cluett, I was here first!"

"Larissa, move to the end of the line."

"But, but..."

"No, buts. Just move it!" She sulkingly went to the
end of the line.

Can you believe I created this situation at least three
times a day? I can't....

"You're rolling. Where are you going to go from here?"

"I think I want to explain what I learned from that situation. I
suddenly could see how I was setting up the problem myself.
When you told us that story about the bathroom I could see how
I was doing the same thing."

"You've got a solid piece underway. Keep at it and see how
it unfolds. Do you have any questions for me?"

"I don't like the way I started out. Have you any suggestions
for a different beginning?"

"My advice at this point is not to worry about a beginning but to keep moving on. In my own writing, I start wherever it wants to start. Sometimes that's at the beginning; more often it's in the middle somewhere. Often I don't write a beginning until I've finished the whole thing. So don't worry about a beginning right now, just keep writing."

"OK."

One product of our traditional writing instruction is an overwhelming desire to have everything right as it goes down on paper. We haven't done a good job of allowing people to discover how writing can find its own meaning. By encouraging Carmina to carry on I'm trying to help her find her own meaning—an opening will come later when she has a better idea of what she's writing about.

I touch base with a number of others during what's left of the afternoon. For the last twenty minutes we reassemble to discuss what's happened so far. I make sure everyone is comfortable with where they are going. I suggest we reread the Harmon/Edelsky article for Monday morning.

I'm hoping the article will allow some of the educational issues to surface when people reflect on **Dead Poets Society** *which is also on Monday's agenda.*

With the ongoing business attended to we disband until Monday.

I breathe a sigh of relief. Thank God for the weekend. We've worked at a feverish pace all week long. I'm ready for a break. I know everyone else is, too. Although I have work to do myself: a poem to rethink, some rereading, reflections to react to, a reflection/letter of my own to write, it's time for a breather. I'll get to those tasks Sunday afternoon.

Later, I think about "You're always right and you're always wrong." Today's instance is a mild one. I may have inadvertently trampled Shelagh's feelings but we'll be able to reestablish a working relationship. However, that isn't always the case. Sometimes my being wrong has had far more devastating effects.

I remember an incident which occurred during a three-day inservice workshop with twenty teachers who had been meeting monthly as a group for close to a year and a half. Because we were working under tight time constraints I had chosen to use a somewhat confrontational initiating activity: I asked each teacher to list all the writing, reading, listening, and talking he or she had done in the past week and the purpose of each instance. We followed that with a similar list for our students. As people shared their own and the students' literacy and language experiences, I recorded collective lists on an overhead projector. Then, in small groups, we compared the two lists.

In four of five groups, discussion focused on differences. The teachers saw that despite their efforts to make learning more participatory, much of the reading, writing, and talking their students did was still being done for the teacher as an examiner. In one group, however, conversation veered toward similarities.

Our sharing in the large group began with similarities: both students and teachers made notes, we read notices, we wrote lists. To help the teachers see beyond surface commonality I asked them to consider the purposes served by these various examples of language activity. In the large group people addressed the issue of teacher as examiner and how it played out in their classrooms. One teacher, however, was uncomfortable with those differences and what they implied about her teaching. Copying notes from the board was the same as recording highlights from a lecture, she insisted.

An interesting moment. I acknowledged there were certainly similarities between our language use as adults and students' language use in school. In fact, our goal was to eliminate as many differences as we could. But I knew as a teacher there were still important contradictions in my own classroom and it was looking at differences that helped me change.

With that I directed the group conversation to an articulation of the differences the teachers could perceive. A little while later when I joined her small group I quickly became aware of that teacher's hostility. Her back was definitely turned in my direction. The others and I were chatting, their elbows on the table, bodies leaning forward. Attempts to bring the fourth into our conversation were unsuccessful. I finally asked her directly what was wrong.

> You've mentioned watching for the expression on people's faces, their body language, the tone of their voices several times. This is all an important aspect of assessment. Interesting, though, that when people talk about assessment, 'faces lighting up' or 'elbows on the table' are never on the list!
>
> Diane Stephens

"You made me feel like I was stupid. You aren't caring. You don't want to help. You're not a teacher, you don't know how to connect with people's feelings," she exploded.

"What did I do?" I asked her.

"You rejected our contribution to the discussion, you refused to consider what we had to say."

"Do the rest of you feel the same way?" I asked them. "I need to know because I can't go any further until we've sorted out what's happened here."

As I looked at each of the other three I read embarrassment but not lack of engagement.

"No, I didn't react that way," offered one.

"Nor I," said a second shyly.

"And you?" I asked the third.

"I think there are similarities but I could see why you wanted us to consider differences," he replied.

"So you didn't all react vehemently to my pushing you to think about differences."

At that, the fourth abruptly arose and stomped from the room.

You're always right and you're always wrong. While my invitation to examine contradictions made many of those teachers uncomfortable, they were willing to go along with me to see how the session would play itself out. But for one of them, my confrontation inadvertently turned out to be much too direct. I'd chosen a frontal assault because the background I'd been given about this group of teachers, the fact that they'd been meeting to discuss ideas about change regularly for more than a year, led me to assume they would be able to face inconsistencies in their teaching. And that was true for nineteen of the teachers. But for one, my nudge was too overpowering. Her defenses slammed into play, cutting us off from one another. Although she returned to the workshop the following day, we remained antagonists.

I've thought about that workshop a lot. As a consultant I've chosen the role of questioner. I feel it is imperative to help people confront contradictions in belief and practice. Consequently the inservice workshops I offer put people in a position of some vulnerability. I can't always predict who will engage and who will defend.

And I am vulnerable, too. I lay my beliefs on the line each time I meet a group of teachers. I, too, have to face the contradictions of my inadvertent demonstrations. I know no matter what I try, it will be useful some people but interfere for others.

As teachers we are constantly having to deal with the unexpected, to accept surprise. As Don Murray (1989) argues what is certain is change. We must expect unexpectedness. If we are to teach our students responsibility, we must prepare them to make use of change. (p. x)

I recently read the following in **The Royal Bank Newsletter** (1989):

> If a doctor, lawyer or dentist had 40 people in his office at one time, all of whom had different needs, and some of whom didn't want to be there and were causing trouble, and the doctor, lawyer or dentist, without assistance, had to treat them all with professional excellence for nine months, then he might have some conception of a classroom teacher's job.

Teaching is a daunting job. The best we can ever do is just try.

Interlude

8

What a joy. A whole day to myself. And it's sunny, too. I savor the moment. I don't have anything particularly pressing for the day. Other than a couple of housekeeping chores, the only thing on my agenda is my poem.

After breakfast, I pick up the poem and begin what Don Murray (1984) calls a 'third read'—a careful line by line consideration of what I've written.

> Six in a row.
> Mr. Cuperfine, Mr. Goldfarb, Mr. Kaplan,
>> These names are wrong. The last name should be just a
>> single syllable: *Kirsch* perhaps?
> Mr. Yablon, Mr. Cohen, and Mr. Scholossberg.
>> Same thing here, too many syllables. Previous line the
>> names are 3,2,1. Should this line be the same?
> Side by side on that eleven foot sofa.
>> *that* too emphatic, should just be *the*
> Six little old men
>> They weren't all little; in fact some of them were
>> 'substantial'.
> Clean shaven
>> Yesterday Barb said something about the clean shaven being
>> a surprise. They weren't bearded, any of them. I think even
>> if that image is jarring, it stays.
> Gnarled hands resting on solid pot bellies
>> I can see the hands neatly folded.   The bellies aren't just
>> round, they're solid!
> Black skull-caps perched on shiny bald heads.
>> Their yalmakas are never straight, they're always askew. A
>> single image per line here would be stronger:
>>> Clean Shaven
>>> Gnarled hands folded
>>> Resting on solid pot bellies....
> Waiting to mumble prayers.
> A ritual to console,
> To offer community and continuity.
>> It's really consolation they're selling.
> But their presence is no comfort;
> (It adds to the alienation—)
>> This line should go. The next line 'we women are excluded'
>> makes the alienation explicit.

We women are excluded.
Unwelcome to participate

> Those prayers are supposed to be a public acknowledgement of mourning. Yet, here we are, now a family of women, and we're cut off from own grief.

In their prayers for my now dead father.

I retype the poem and set it aside for a while.

Later in the day I take the poem to my friend Marlene. She's a candid, yet supportive reader.

Although I can see it so clearly, I'm finding it difficult to capture succinctly the image of the men leaning slightly back, legs wide, feet on the floor, one hand resting on top of the other. We talk about the men's body positions.

> Gnarled hands ~~resting~~ **folded**
> On solid pot bellies

Marlene also suggests I change 'solid' to 'full.' Do I know, she asks me, that the word 'full' in Hebrew means 'peace' as well? I didn't know that. I like the play on meaning; in addition, the rhythm of the single syllable 'full' is stronger; I make the change.

As we talk Marlene says something about the men being comfortable but not offering comfort although that's why they're there. I record her phrase 'comfortable, they offer no comfort' to think about later.

During the evening I work on the poem again. The names are still bothering me. The rhythm isn't right. As I play with them a possible pattern emerges: two two-syllable names and a single syllable name. I try a number of variations; I end with:

> Mr. Waxler, Mr. Goldfarb, Mr. Kirsch,
> Mr. Freeman, Rabbi Pritzker, Mr. Cohen.

Next: Comfortable, they offer no comfort. I slip the line in after the bit about prayers.

> Waiting **silently** to mumble prayers.
> A ritual ~~to console,~~
> To offer ~~community and continuity~~ **consolation.**
> ~~But their presence is no comfort;~~
> **Comfortable, they offer no comfort.**

I print the poem out once again.

I make it halfway down stairs and the ending, going through my head, changes.

We women are excluded.
Unwelcome to participate
In their prayers for my now dead father.

The last line should be just 'for my now dead father.' I come back to the computer. 'Morn' has to be there just ahead. That single word is necessary to foreshadow the statement about death.

Comfortable, they offer no comfort.
We women are excluded.
Unwelcome **to morn**
~~For~~ My now dead father.

Next, punctuation catches my attention. I vary it, changing things around until the relationship among images feels right.

The poem feels done now. The images are compact and the 'comfortable, they offer no comfort...' has become the pivotal point; the reflective moment.

The Sofa

Six in a row:
Mr. Waxler, Mr. Goldfarb, Mr. Kirsch,
Mr. Freeman, Rabbi Pritzker, Mr. Cohen
Settled side by side on the eleven foot sofa.
Six old men
Clean shaven
Gnarled hands folded
On full pot bellies
Legs wide, feet firmly planted
Black skull-caps askew.
There for business
Waiting silently to mumble prayers,
A ritual
To offer consolation.
Comfortable, they offer no comfort—
We women are excluded.
Unwelcome to morn
My now dead father.

I record in my writing log:

Writing this poem has been very difficult. I'm now past tears, but I cried through the writing of much of it. I'm not exactly sure why the tears—were they for Father or for myself?

I'll include the 'third read' and the revised poem in my reflection letter for Monday to see what responses I get.

Sunday evening it's back to work. I read and respond to people's journals. Again, interesting issues emerge. Leslie writes:

> I am beginning to realize that I have assumptions which affect other people although I may often be unaware of these underlying beliefs myself. I am also beginning to see how difficult they are to recognize and confront. Your article "Learning to Teach by Uncovering Our Assumptions" (Newman, 1987) really hit it on the head. It's the small things, like a kid's comment you overhear, that can help you see the contradictions between belief and practice. If we can recognize these contradictions and tease them out into the open we have a chance of becoming better teachers.

In my marginal response to Leslie I offer her encouragement:

> This is a crucial point of departure—realizing there are contradictions and that we can do something about them. That's the exciting part of becoming what I call a 'learning' teacher.

Barb has written:

> You asked what demonstrations I'm engaging with. Well, I started off asking you questions expecting direct answers. Now I know that if you think I can answer the question myself you will encourage me to do so. Consequently, I'm beginning to try to answer my own questions. I've stopped looking for tips. What I'm looking for now is my own theory of learning and writing so I can develop instructional ideas for myself and stop trying to copy someone else's.

I confirm her observation:

> Yes, I am trying to help you articulate and answer your own questions, to help you become more self-reliant as a teacher and less dependent on experts. You have lots of experience yourself. You need to value it.

Hanna reflects as well:

I saw a close connection between your assumptions article and Harste, Woodward, and Burke's (1984b). The point is, we mustn't be afraid of examining our experiences with students even if we feel we've done the wrong thing. This is the only way we can fully appreciate how negative assumptions are still playing a large role in our teaching. We can't get rid of them if we don't know they exist. We have to remember "the assumptions we make limit what can be learned. Alter those assumptions and the potential for learning expands" (Harst, p. 106).

I nudge her to go a bit further:

You might find it useful to try writing a brief story about some situation you're uncomfortable about. My guess is through the writing you'd reveal some of your assumptions and see new ways of handling situations like that.

I am really taken with Bruce's reflection.

It's always dark under the stairs. I keep saying to Sharon, my wife, we should have a light installed but it never gets any further than that. Perhaps I don't want the kinds of things I keep under here to be readily seen. I'm looking for a box, a blue box…ah, there it is, way over in the corner. I wrestle the old vacuum cleaner out of the way, stack the Christmas decorations in an already crowded corner and drag the box into the hall. I snap back the flaps to reveal a dozen red covered plan books—a record of my classroom activities since the mid-seventies.

This investigation has a purpose: I want to see how I've evaluated writing over the years. I sit on the carpet and leaf through '76, slowly at first but then with more urgency and agitation. '77, '78, '79. Enough! I pick up 1980 and go straight to the marks in the back. Nothing. This is unnerving. This is it! I've found it—1982. But only two classes? Funny title I used for those lesson— 'writing with a purpose'—and underneath my reminders to give three topic choices: bedtime at our house, noon hour in the cafeteria, and the interior of our church. Whose purpose, I thought. I repacked the plan books, unsettled, wondering why I'd saved them.

The above story is true. I set out to investigate how my practice of evaluating writing had changed only to find out there was no authentic writing to evaluate. I found instances where I allowed a couple of classes, both grade 10s, to write about what interested them. Yes, there were paragraph assignments, and a bit about opening sentences, and lots of tests on compound sentences, but not much real writing.

This is where reading Hunt, Romano and Atwell got me on Saturday. It was sobering at first but I feel good about it now. If ever I needed to see examples of inauthentic writing, this was it! I thought I valued writing and I know I marked every assignment partly for the way it was written (I always set aside 10 points or so for writing). But what was I doing in class to make writing real? Nothing, that I could see if my plan books are accurate. There was no organized approach to helping the kids develop their writing. The few instances I mentioned earlier where the students chose their topic were simply examples of letting them loose for a period or two; a freewrite I guess.

What can I say! I write:

A wonderful critical incident. You've made me wonder about my own pile of plan books (they're all hidden in the basement)!"

The real agenda of this Institute workshop is to help these teachers become more reflective practitioners. Everything I've done has been directed at using our ostensible agenda— exploring writing/reading—to help them question what they do in their own classrooms. Looks like my reflective message is getting through. I'm excited about that.

I read and respond to the other journals then write a reflection/letter of my own:

Let me begin with DPS (**Dead Poets Society**)[1]. I saw it again Friday evening. That's when I realized the

---

[1] **Dead Poets Society** is a film about a New England private boys school in the late 1950s. In it, John Keating, an English teacher, attempts to engage his senior high school class in seeing the world from a broadened, non-conventional perspective. He invites the boys into an exploration of poetry and cultural values both in class and out. When the boys, upon uncovering Keating's yearbook entry and a mysterious reference to a 'Dead Poets Society,' indicate interest in the clandestine society, Keating slips his well worn poetry anthology into Neil's desk. That gesture, while opening doors for some of the

focal character in the film is Todd, not Neil. When I first saw the film a month ago I wondered a lot about Todd's story but my gaze was on Neil and his suicide. I was puzzled about Todd, though. Although he seemed to be hovering on the fringe, I could also see how things happened which changed him. This time I thought the film was really about Todd and the experiences that drive him to assert himself and protest Keating's dismissal by being the first to stand on his desk. It was to Todd that Keating winks as he departs.

In fact, the matter of the wink escaped me until I read Theresa's response. She wrote:

> The wink was the all-important event of the movie; it stood for hope that what was considered radically wrong with transactional teaching in that traditional school would survive the dismissal of the progressive teacher, Mr Keating.

More than half of those boys were affected by Keating and their involvement in the Dead Poet Society. While we know they were forced to 'play the game' in order to complete their school year, I came away feeling the boys who protested weren't likely to forget the experience. They learned some truths about power and control and in that final confrontation may have uncovered some unexpected personal strength and values.

I'm looking forward to our discussion to see what else I can learn about the film. I know I'll have to go back a third time after we've talked about it.

Then the issue of conversations. It's been clear from much of what the teachers were saying about conferencing last week that they visualize this pedagogical tool as something formidable. A big part of the problem with conferencing is the term itself. I mentioned it in a small group conversation on Thursday; time to raise it with the whole group, I think.

I also want to make a point about the term **conversation** as opposed to **conference.** A mystique has grown up around the term *writing conference.* That has made it something big and intimidating. A *conference* is just a conversation. What

---

boys to find themselves, has unexpected and serious consequences for everyone, including Keating himself.

we're trying to do in these writing and reading conversations is to chat about our experiences as writers and readers.

Conference is really just another unnecessary buzzword. It ritualizes something that we all know how to do in real-life situations. When a friend calls and asks me how to do something, the conversation naturally flows from her questions to my descriptions, from my questions to her clarifications, etc.

Now we introduce this new thing *conferencing* into the classroom. Yes, it's a departure from having the teacher talk all the time, but by introducing a new bit of jargon for something we all know how to do (except, perhaps, in the classroom) we create a whole new set of rituals, a new orthodoxy which is hardly of any more value to students than what we've been doing in the past.

That's why we have to read what these various researchers have to say about conferencing critically. So many of the discussions come close to offering prescriptions. Many teachers certainly treat what these people have written as if it were a magic recipe. In fact, it's all too easy to turn a conversation into a conference and thereby assume control of the writing. The important thing about writing conversations is to hear what students are trying to say and to be supportive; to share our 'expertise' but without smothering their efforts. Tom Romano (1988) does that as well as any of them. You might want to look at his book **Clearing the Way**.

And as for conversations, watch what goes on during your conversations at lunch and at other times when you're not actually 'conferencing'. What is happening? What roles are you taking? What does this mean for carrying on learning conversations?

In the same vein, how has our discussion of poetry and the short stories set you up for discussing writing? I didn't intend those experiences to be isolated events. I was trying to build on what I'd read you from Elbow earlier, and to help you respond to one another's writing more personally. I also was trying to use those discussions to nudge you into reading like writers, to help you see how writers solve the very same problems you're experiencing. So although you may be writing prose, the imagery in the poetry, for example, might have helped you think about ways of showing and not telling in your writing. What other interconnections can you identify?

I think I want to raise the issue of **mini-lesson** here as well. It's another of those prevalent jargon terms. I dislike it a great deal because it puts the emphasis in the wrong place, seems to me. It conveys a formality, a teacher-centred focus, that I think is misleading. More appropriate is the idea of **teachable moment.** (I'm sure others have written about the idea, but I can't cite anyone in particular, can you help me out?) Teachable moment is an aspect of negotiating the curriculum. It involves me responding spontaneously to opportunities which you present me. There were many teachable moments last week, both in the large group, in small groups, and with individuals. Can you describe an instance which affected you as a learner?

Let me end with my revised poem for your reactions.

> I don't like 'teachable moment'. Let me think about why. I don't like it because it suggests there are teaching times and learning times. It seems to stop time, to segment it, to say that **NOW** you should teach somebody something. Teaching was occurring when you were sitting and reading Schön during the first or second day of class. Is there any reason to label one particular demonstration *teaching* or *teachable* and another not? It also seems to privilege your coming to centre stage. It makes it seem like teaching = talking! It's a teachable moment when you stay out of it, too. The critical incident idea is much better I think. It keeps the perspective where it should be—on the learner.
>
> Diane Stephens

I append both the 'third read' and the revised poem, then I sit back and consider the week. We've been very productive. Everyone has some writing on the go (even me). It's not unreasonable now to think most folks will have a piece more or less completed by late Tuesday. That will give us Wednesday and Thursday for recasting, revising, and doing a third read; Friday for printing out well formatted copies. I won't have time to retype anything before compiling the class publication, so I must remember to ask the Computer Centre to install new ribbons on the printers so we'll get dark copies.

The responding to writing is coming along, too. Giving movies of our minds has been a useful strategy. Having done that with the short stories and poetry, people are finding it easier to share how other people's writing makes them feel and what connections it evokes.

Not quite ready, though, for more focused feedback yet. Nevertheless, I do want to get to Murray's careful third read kind of responding both for themselves and for one another. Everyone will receive a copy of my own third read for "The Sofa" tomorrow. I think I also better make sure they all have a copy of Murray's "Clarify" chapter from **Write to Learn** (1984) before Wednesday so they can start thinking about handling fine detail. Focus and organization have been evolving as the writing has unfolded for just about everyone. As their writing falls into place I'll now have to help them shift their attention to clarity and correctness.

Aside from my inadvertently being too candid about Shelagh's writing, I think the others are all feeling comfortably engaged. I've watched Bruce recording connections through the week. I'd love to read his personal log book but he hasn't offered it to me. That's OK, but snoop that I am, it would be fun to have a peek. Actually, he's mentioned a number of issues in conversation, so I know he's been watching what I've been doing and thinking about what questions it raises for his own teaching.

Maggie, too, has been reflecting. I know that this past year she stuck very closely to Nancie Atwell's writing workshop but she's made a couple of comments which lead me to think she's considering how to broaden what she does with her students.

Carmina's been interesting. I didn't expect her insightful reflection. She started out focused on grammar and discipline but that has changed. The last day or so her writing has shifted direction; she's starting to look at herself.

Lorna and Janice, I noticed, have both overcome their discomfort about assuming responsibility for their own learning. Their responses to my reflection/letters have started to become more questioning.

I'll need to keep a close watch on Shelagh for the next few days. I want to stay close at hand, to touch base with her frequently, but at the same time give her a lot of room to feel her way. I think revealing herself in that bit of writing she did Friday may be an opening. She might just be willing to start looking at her inadvertent classroom demonstrations, to face some of the contradictions in her teaching. I need to keep questioning her, but oh so gently.

I spend a bit of time with Schön's books, again. Schön describes three coaching strategies: joint experimentation, Follow me!, and hall of mirrors, which have helped me think about ways of responding to students. Schön discusses how in joint experimentation the coach's skill comes first to bear on the task of helping the student formulate the qualities she wants to achieve and then, by demonstration or description, explore different ways of producing them....

From her side, the student's artistery consists in her ability and willingness to step into a situation. She risks declaring what effects she wants to produce and risks experimenting with an unfamiliar kind of experimentation.

The coach works at creating and sustaining a process of collaborative inquiry. Paradoxically, the more he knows about the problem, the harder it is for him to do this. He must resist the temptation to tell a student how to solve the problem or solve it for her, but he must not pretend to know less than he does, for by deceiving her, he risks undermining her commitment to their collaborative venture. One way of resolving this dilemma is for the coach to put his...knowledge to work by generating a variety of solutions to the problem, leaving the student free to choose and produce new possibilities for action (Schön, 1987, p.296).

> Schön's description of joint experimentation is interesting, I don't like the last line, however. I can see that by providing the students with various people's ideas about response/writing etc. you are in a way providing a variety of solutions to the problem...but saying it the way Schön does makes it seem too fixed, too neat, too without input from the learner.
>
> Diane Stephens

I've been trying mainly to implement a 'joint experimentation' context. Our various enterprises—to write something and explore a number of issues—leave the problem of what educational issues to examine and how to examine them, of what to write and how to write about it, up to the teachers themselves. During the early part of the week I had to get a variety of initiatives off the ground but then I was forced to wait—to wait until people had something going on which we could then jointly experiment. I used to describe my role as 'leading from behind' (Wells, 1986). However, that metaphor conveys more implicit control on my part than I'm now comfortable with. I'm beginning to see my role more in terms of Schön's coach engaged in joint experimentation with students.

But joint experimentation isn't the only way I engage with students. I also use another of Schön's coaching tactics: Follow me! With this strategy

the coach's artistry consists in his capacity to improvise a whole designlike performance and, within it, to execute local units of reflection-in-action.... Beginning with a holistic image of performance

[I want to say of writing and of reading], a skillful coach disposes of many ways of breaking it into parts and unraveling its various aspects, each of which he treats in turn...

...an important part of a coach's artistry consists in his ability to draw on an extensive repertoire of media, languages, and methods of description in order to represent his ideas in many different ways, searching for the images that will "click" with this particular student. And the student's artistry consists in her ability to keep many possible meanings alive in her mind, putting her own intentions and objectives into temporary abeyance as she observes the coach and tries to follow him. She does as she has seen him do, reproducing his responses, testing by further words and actions how the means she has constructed are like or unlike his (Schön, 1987, p.297).

A number of the strategies I offer the group as a whole could be thought of as instances of Follow me! My suggesting people 'read fast' or 'talk with a pencil in hand', for example. However, the difference between my proferring strategies and the tactics used by the practitioners Schön describes is that immediate imitation is neither required nor expected. I'm really offering a strategy and suggesting the students just try. On the whole, I carry on actively reading and writing myself, and reflecting publicly on what's happening to me as I read and write, at the same time, depending on other members of our learning community to impart many strategies that would never occur to me.

In Schön's third coaching strategy, hall of mirrors,

student and coach continually shift perspective. They see their interaction at one moment as a reenactment of some aspect of the student's practice; at another, as a dialogue about it; and at still another, as a modeling of its redesign. ... In this process, there is a premium on the coach's ability to surface his own confusions. To the extent that he can do so authentically, he [demonstrates] for his student a new way of seeing error and 'failure' as opportunities for learning.

But a hall of mirrors can be created only...when coaching resembles the interpersonal practice to be learned, when...the kind of inquiry established in the practicum resembles the inquiry that students seek to exemplify in their practice (Schön, 1987, p.297).

"What's going on here?" is my attempt to make our instructional interaction an object for reflection. The question forces the teachers to stand back from what they're doing, think about factors that are both supporting and interfering with their learning, and to consider implications this personal experience has for

their teaching. Our hall of mirrors conversation goes on in many tacit ways as well—through our written conversations, when we chat about all sorts of things. What's particularly difficult with what I attempt as a teacher is that I'm rarely coaching a single student! I have a whole class I'm trying to help become more reflective practitioners.

Schön sums it up nicely:

...when [coach and student] do their jobs well, [they] function not only as practitioners but also as on-line researchers, each inquiring more or less consciously into his own and the other's changing understandings. But they inquire under difficult conditions. The behavioural world of the practicum is complex, variable, and resistent to control. At any given time, concurrent processes are underway, any one of which might cause a change in understanding. And some of the most important kinds of learning are of the background variety, revealing themselves only when a student moves out of the practicum into another setting (pp.298-299).

...When a coach reflects aloud on his own knowing-in-action and encourages his students to reflect aloud on theirs, both parties are more likely to become aware of gaps in their descriptions and understandings. Such a coach...(and in this respect all reflective practicums involve 'Follow me!') demonstrates a mode of inquiry that students can mirror by joining him in reflective dialogue (p. 301).

But engaging in that reflective dialogue has political consequences. The more the teachers and I question our assumptions the stronger our challenge to prevailing, commonsense, transmission views of teaching. It changes our consciousness of what schooling is about; it changes our perception of our roles and responsibilities. Our reflection, our changing practice brings us into open conflict with colleagues and with students and with a large portion of the community outside of school.

We are going to have to discuss what happens when we make such a shift in the way we teach.

Coming week? It'll be mostly a matter of keeping the juggling act going—offering a supportive ear to this person, asking a probing question of that one, nudging another, and pushing a few, all with an eye on the clock. Friday is going to come very quickly and I would like to be able to orchestrate the workshop to some kind of comfortable closure for everyone. That means getting our writing revised, edited, and printed, having discussion on a number of remaining issues, and spending time talking about questions this experience raised about their own teaching.

We have to devote the better part of Friday to such reflection or most of the experience will simply evaporate. Everything I will have done during the two weeks has been intended to provide the teachers with data so we can have that conversation. That's where this all comes together. I'll be interested to see if we can pull it off.

Letting Go 9 ❖

Week two begins. Last week I was concerned about getting our different enterprises—writing something, reading on a variety of educational issues, talking about teaching—underway. Now, my role is to sustain what we've got going, to direct people to new resources (both books and other people), to challenge their beliefs about learning and teaching, to help them keep their writing moving, to sustain their learning engagement.

We have a number of agenda items which were initiated last week, and I'll try to see those through, but on the whole I'm trying to vacate centre stage. There will be more large group conversation, small group discussion, and talk between and among individuals in which I will take part; however, at this point I'm making a concerted effort to let go.

Monday morning we form one group around a single large table and discuss **Dead Poets Society.**

"I was struck last night when I started my response," begins Hanna, "how things came to me that I hadn't been aware of at all. I realized as I wrote that I felt very manipulated by the film's metaphors. The boys themselves were very stereotyped, each one there for the purpose of portraying a particular character type, I thought. I was very bothered by how black and white the issues seemed. I wrote about that."

"That sense of having been manipulated came to you as you wrote?" I ask.

"Yes," she replies.

"Did Neil have to kill himself?" Lorna wonders.

"What are some options the writers had at that point?" I ask. *I'd like people to consider how creating a film and writing involve similar decision-making processes.*

"Neil could have just gone ahead and done what his father wanted him to," Michael replies.

"If it had been even five years later it might have been drugs," says Penny, "but in the fifties, I don't know what other options there were."

"He couldn't just leave home and live on the street the way kids did a bit later, I don't think," Norma says.

"Neil still could have tried discussing it with his father," insists Michael. "He could have tried persuading his father to see how he felt about acting."

"There was that moment in the living room after his father pulled him out of the school when I thought he was going to talk to his parents about his feelings, but they were so adamant about not listening to him that Neil backed down. I ached for him at that moment," responds Penny.

"I was really surprised by Neil's mother. She did absolutely nothing to help him," says Barb. "She just sat there smoking and saying nothing. I was furious with her."

"She didn't even bother to listen to Neil after his father announced he would be sent to a military school. I thought at least she'd let him talk after his father had stomped from the room but she didn't. I don't think she even touched Neil before she left the room herself," says Norma.

"I can't remember whether she put her hand briefly on his shoulder or not," I comment.

"Did Neil have any other options?" asks Bruce.

"That's the crucial question," I reply. "You know, by the way, I don't think I see Neil as the central character in the film. The more I've thought about it, the more I think Todd is the focal character."

An unfortunate misdirection on my part. I should have let Bruce and the others explore Neil's options further. Instead, I've shifted the conversation to Todd. There are times to add my two cents and times to listen; I should have listened here.

"In the overall picture I'd say Todd was," argues Connie, "but Neil had an important role. My attention was certainly on Neil as I was watching the story unfold."

"I think I felt I was watching events through Todd's eyes," Hanna comments. "Neil was an important person in his life."

"You know, I felt Todd died, too," reflects Maggie. "Not suddenly, but slowly, in bits. When his parents sent him another desk set for his birthday and in that scene where he is forced to sign the accusation against Mr Keating. I think at that point his capitulation must have felt dreadful."

"I've been wondering why Todd was the one to make the gesture to Keating—to stand on the desk," Penny says. "It could have been a number of the other boys, Knox, or Charlie (no I guess Charlie was expelled by then, wasn't he). I was surprised it was Todd."

"Oh, I think it had to be Todd," Norma jumps in. "The film's about Todd's unfolding. At the beginning, he's timid, uncertain, insecure. He's as cut off from himself by his family as Neil is. Remember how at the beginning he's introduced as so-and-so's brother and all of his brother's accomplishments are touted by his parents and the headmaster? But I think living and working with the other boys, particularly rooming with Neil, in class with Keating, and the Dead Poets Society all help him begin to value himself. That scene where Keating helps him create a poem in class and says to him, 'Remember this experience.' That's an important moment for Todd."

Norma's raising the issue of Todd's alienation and the experiences that help him take some control for himself.

"I think having Keating come back to the classroom to collect his belongings was the turning point for Todd," says Maggie. "I mean, the look on Todd's face; he looked so abandoned. I think that was when he summoned the courage to stand on the desk. If you watched his face, he just looked so bereft."

"I wonder, had Keating been in the office when Todd was forced to sign the accusation, if he wouldn't have taken a stand then," Connie comments. "He started to say 'It wasn't that way,' but his father insisted he sign the document. His parents weren't interested in anything he had to say."

"Do you think they were just as controlling even when they weren't there?" Leslie asks.

"I suspect both Neil and Todd felt their parents' pressure all the time. The difference between the two boys, I think," says Norma, "is Todd finally throws over their control and takes a stand which affirms himself. Neil, on the other hand, although he's been able to make decisions for himself in spite of his parents expectations, now finds himself so completely trapped he believes his only way out is suicide."

That connection between being able to make choices and having control is important. Lots of times the teachers feel they have no control because they don't perceive they have any choices.

"I wonder what would have happened to Todd if he had been Cameron's roommate," Bruce comments.

"Given that Cameron's the kid who sets Keating up as scapegoat," says Norma, "we can only guess he wouldn't have changed much. Cameron was one for towing the line and sucking up to authority. I think it's Neil's finding his own way in spite of the roadblocks his family and the school keep putting up that lets Todd see it is possible to make decisions for himself."

"What did you make of the poetry?" I ask.

I'm trying to draw attention back to the instructional context in the film and to the role poetry played.

Bruce responds. "I found it interesting that most of the poetry was shared outside of the classroom without Keating's presence at all. The poetry was used to give insight into characterization. But we don't actually get to see Keating using poetry in class other than that one time when he had the boys reading the poems they've composed themselves."

"Mostly all we get are a few glimpses of Keating doing something outrageous to engage the boys. There's the bit with him having the boys tear out the introduction to the poetry textbook, or the class where he invites the boys to stand on his desk so they can take a different perspective on the world," says Hanna.

"I felt he was still a transmission teacher," Norma says. "Certainly doing unusual things in comparison with the other teachers in that private school, but still very much in charge."

"I thought, actually, the most useful thing Keating did as a teacher happened inadvertently," points out Maggie. "When the boys found the note in the school yearbook about Keating and the Dead Poets Society he was non-committal about it. All he did was slip his old poetry anthology, with the quote from Thoreau—'*carpe diem*' (seize the day)—on the flyleaf, into Neil's desk. That started the whole thing off."

"I wondered how the book got into Neil's desk. I don't remember Keating putting it there," comments Theresa.

"I assumed Keating put it there," answers Maggie.

"That's interesting," Theresa replies, "it makes Keating's manipulation more direct than I had though it was."

> I didn't like the movie much. I felt it wasn't very real; that it lacked depth. Williams as Keating seemed hollow—and his naivete annoyed me, perhaps because I didn't see him as believable. I thought it was interesting that you thought the script writers believed they were dealing with a radical teacher. Trouble was, Keating wasn't radically good—or bad.
>
> Diane Stephens

"He definitely manipulated the boys. Although I don't think he thought of the possible consequences of what he was doing," Bruce remarks.

"I wondered why Keating didn't actually turn the class into a Dead Poets Society," remarks Norma.

"I imagine that never crossed the script writers' minds. I would wager they thought they were offering a picture of a very far out teacher." I say.

Again, I'm trying to connect film-making and writing.

"Do you think the DPS could have ever happened in a classroom?" asks Diane. "Wasn't that whole business in the cave—the boy's smoking, horsing around in the dead of night—really about adolescents exploring boundaries for themselves? It wouldn't have been the same if Keating had tried to encourage that kind of exploration in the classroom. He would have been in charge. The point was this was something the boys decided to do on their own. Keating could pretend he knew nothing about it, yet sustain it in the subtle ways that he did."

This is an appropriate moment to raise the Harman/ Edelsky article, I think.

"How does the film talk to the Harman/Edelsky article or vice versa how does the article talk to the film?" I ask.

"I thought the connection was a very direct one—addressing alienation," says Barb. "The boys were alienated from their families and by the school. Keating himself was alienated; he certainly didn't connect with the other faculty."

"I took the point of the article to be that however alienating traditional schooling might be, a more open, progressive education could be even more alienating because it's more seductive," asserts Penny. "That's what happened to Neil. As he found his own voice through the poetry and the play he came into conflict with his parents' values and their pressure to conform was more than he could handle. His alienation was so intense he felt he had no way out."

"The child or adult who has put one foot into the exciting new world where language is power may feel a strong tug on other foot from those left behind. Family and friends may express resentment, jealousy, abandonment, or simply incomprehension at their loved one's movement away from them" (Harman/ Edelsky, p.399), Norma quotes. "I've been feeling some of that myself since I began changing as a teacher. I have moved into an exciting new world and I'm finding myself cut off from the other people in my school. They don't understand what I'm trying to do.

> I hadn't thought about the political aspects of what I've been doing with my inner-city five year olds. I've been so busy fighting the alienation which pre-packaged, prescriptive, skills-based curriculum forces on these kids that I never stopped to wonder about the impact of the kind of environment I've been trying to create for them. I suppose I've been so excited about how well the kids have been doing that I never considered that there might be hazards in my instructional efforts, too. Obviously, I need to think about it.
>
> Lynn Moody

They don't agree with my new values. I find it hard often to talk about the kids and what I'm doing with them in the resource room because the teachers don't want to know about it. My sense is they are feeling threatened by what I'm trying to do."

*An interesting moment for me here. Norma is artic-
ulating what was for me the focal connection of the
Harman/Edelsky article. Here's a freewrite I did after
reading it for the first time:*

> The Harman/Edelsky article raises some interesting
> questions about my own teaching for me. What are
> the risks for teachers in terms of alienation if I am
> successful in engaging them in my instructional
> experience? What are some 'unanticipated
> repercussions' for them as a result of the
> experience? I have become very aware of the
> political consequences of what I'm doing as a
> teacher. I've had phone calls from several former
> students who have gone on to study elsewhere
> about mid-October wailing "What have you done to
> me!" They find our experiences which have
> allowed them to assume control over their own
> learning now make it difficult for them to perform
> in more traditional transmission, teacher-controlled
> contexts. There are clearly ways of dealing with
> those situations and we discuss them, but their
> comments have made me very aware that I have
> some responsibility to raise the political issues
> more openly than I have in the past.

*Norma has raised precisely that concern: teacher
alienation. I decide to expand upon it with everyone.*

"How about the rest of you?" I ask the group. "Have any of
you experienced that sense of alienation Norma is describing?"

Maggie responds first. "It hasn't been the courses so much
as my actually trying to teach differently that's opened a gulf
between me and the others on my staff. As I tried implementing
a writing workshop in the junior high I was immediately at odds
with the other English teachers. Fortunately, I was teaching all
three grade 7 classes and didn't have to accommodate another
teacher's curriculum but I still had to deal with the grade 8 and 9
teachers. As I move further into a more open classroom it's
become harder and harder to talk curriculum or anything else
with the others."

"I'm experiencing some sense of alienation as a principal,"
adds Cathy.

"Talk about that," I encourage her.

"Well, it's affecting me in two ways I think, in school and
among the administrative group. In school, I'm trying to initiate
some change among the teachers but they are responding

somewhat defensively. I can see they regard my questions as an intrusion. They're not comfortable with me wanting them to examine what they're doing and to think about alternatives. I'm not exactly isolated among the other principals—there are a couple of others who are trying things with their teachers, too— but while we've now got a couple of district curriculum policy documents that support the direction I'd like to see us take, I hear a lot of 'Yes, but...'s in response to my questions at principals' meetings."

"Anyone else?" I ask.

"The high school is a nightmare," Bruce remarks. "I'm constantly teetering between going my own way and having to negotiate with the other teachers. I don't have any large group of students to myself. I don't, for example, teach only grade 10 English. I have a mixture of classes and that means I'm forced to a large extent to live in the communal world. I can try some writing workshop ideas, but the fact that my students write a common exam with content questions set by other teachers means I have to 'teach' (he gestures the quotes) the short story, I have to make sure we've done some poetry. I'm just not sure how to move away from transmission teaching in that situation. That's why **Dead Poets Society** fascinated me. I found myself thinking about how Keating taught and wondering what lessons were in it for me."

The film and the article serve as mirrors, reflecting our beliefs and practices back to us, making them visible and open for discussion.

"That's the dilemma we're all facing," I say to him. "John Mayher in his book **Uncommon Sense** (1990) frames the debate in a helpful way. You might like to have a look at it. It's a tough choice to make. You've begun to experience the sense of excitement that taking charge of your own learning brings and yet when it comes to letting go in our own classrooms it's another matter. There are lots of different forces working to maintain the status quo. It's very hard swimming against the current particularly if you're the lone teacher in your situation trying to explore learning-focused education."

One of the teachers last winter wrote a very insightful reflection about fighting the status quo:

> I'm rereading "Critical Professional Inquiry" by
> Lester and Mayher (1987). On this second reading
> I'm relating it much more to my own experience
> particularly after having begun to reflect on my
> own teaching.

I like the lead paragraph where they ask: "how can we, as teachers, become more responsible for our own teaching?" They recognize the reality that we teachers are not autonomous, free of political or institutional constraints. It's an important question if I'm not going to be thrown out of the system or be driven out by frustration. Their idea of working within the system toward more responsible teaching I see as a constant challenge.

The five basic reasons schools have remained virtually unchanged in our century which they cite from Cuban (1984) touched home. I could see myself caught up in the first reason: school is a means of social control and sorting. I was supervised by my VP this term and what he was most concerned about was students' obedience and my control, or in his eyes, the lack of it. He wrote in the supervision report that I should never proceed to give directions unless I have the attention of all the students. What he was referring to was a split second decision I happened to make while he was present in the class. I had decided to take the risk and just be myself during that super-vision rather than orchestrating the kind of performance I thought he might want to see. I had done a math patterning mini-lesson where I had the complete attention of the class. The kids were now off to do some independent follow-up on their own when I thought of something else to tell them. I realized, however, when I tried getting their attention and didn't succeed, that they were now engrossed with what they were doing. I could have insisted on their attention and made them listen to me but in a successful moment of being a reflective practitioner I decided to let go, realizing that it was something they would probably figure out on their own if I gave them the chance. And where did that decision get me? A written demerit. All over such a momentary interval of time. It made me see clearly why the system is so slow to change. Although I had the self confidence not to be crushed by this administrator's lack of understand-ing of, or appreciation for, what I was trying to do, my gut feeling is to play it safe next time—to orchestrate what he wants to see: the teacher in

I can certainly understand this teacher's decision to play it safe next time but the more I read about gender, race, and class issues and how these inequalities play themselves out in power relationships in society and in schools, the more I realize I can't play it safe. I'm beginning to understand that although I have been paying lip-service to personal meaning-making, I have been ignoring the socio-political ramifications of what this means for my students and me. Because the inequalities and contradictions are so much a part of the lives of the inner-city students I teach, they cannot be ignored or silenced by my inaction. If I truly want school life to be meaningful for these children and their families I have to help them (and myself) see the contradictions and obstacles they might face and help them develop strategies for dealing with these barriers.

Lynn Moody

uncontested control. Sadly, I can now see where a lot of teacher conformity comes from.

There are a lot of constraints working against this teacher's efforts. The school structure, the culture of teaching, the deeply embedded beliefs of people around her, poorly thought out attempts at reform within the district all impede her personal development as a learning-focused teacher. The pressure is always there to comply rather than resist.

Dead Poets Society raised precisely those kinds of questions for me, as did the Harman/Edelsky article. How do I deal with the consequences of my teaching when those consequences involve the potential alienation of my students, in this case teachers themselves, from their community?

I draw this conversation to a close. During our discussion I tried taking a peripheral role, letting the teachers' interpretations and interests direct our conversation. I did ask some focusing questions, but on the whole I was trying to hold back so I could discover what connections they were making between the film, the Harman/Edelsky article, and their own experiences.

The issue of letting go is something I'm struggling with right now. Letting go is hard. I have a lot of useful research and teaching experience to pass on, but I've discovered that the teachers learn more when they explore their problems themselves. That means that within the communal enterprise I have to provide a lot of room for people to find a way for themselves. I find myself constantly having to hold back, to refrain from telling everything I know, allowing situations to evolve even though they might not unfold in the way I though they should. The Dead Poets conversation was useful, I think. We haven't really resolved any of these tough issues—they aren't really resolvable. We've just raised more questions, important concerns, however, for all of us to think about.

❖

The rest of my morning is taken up with writing conversations and the like. Some conversations are very brief, just enough to sustain the writer through a tough moment. Others are much lengthier discussions of issues. The longer conversations seem to invite eavesdroppers and turn into impromptu small group discussions with people exploring issues about writing, about reading, about writing/reading relationships, and about teaching in general.

People have scattered throughout the building. I move from one small group to another, listening and asking questions, making comments, offering suggestions, suggesting resources, and telling stories. As teacher, my intentions for the day are primarily to sustain work in progress. I watch for opportunities to ask "Do you need help?" If the answer is "Yes," I then ask "What do you need help doing?"

I learned to ask that pair of questions a long time ago from my then six-year-old friend Danny who hated having people tell him things or do things for him when he didn't want or need them done. His tantrums taught me how to leave control in his hands. I learned to watch and listen before barging in and offering advice. I learned to ask him what help he wanted. Letting the learner direct the teaching is an important aspect of letting go.

I find it interesting that "What do you need help doing?" is a tough question for many of the teachers in the Institute workshop to answer. They are not used to identifying and describing problems they are having. So I have to be patient and give people time to respond.

I ask that question of Norma when she joins me to talk about her short story.

"How's it going?"

"I think I need help," she replies.

"What do you need help with?"

"God, I don't know. I don't have any idea where to go next."

"What are you trying to do at this point in your writing?"

"Well, I've got as far as Robert having described his family and a bit of his school history. I've tried to make it clear that he was a capable student but that it was his feeling cut off from the other kids by how he was dressed and by his father's refusal to buy him anything new that made him so unhappy and angry."

"What's the problem you're having?"

"I don't think I want to tell the story in chronological order; there's no suspense in that. I think I want to open at the point where Robert commits his fateful act."

"Sounds fine."

"But I don't think I know how to do it."

"Can you think of an author who does what you're wanting to do?"

This is the first time I've actually asked Serebrin's question of anyone in the Institute workshop!

" No, I don't think so. None of the short stories you gave us does that, begin at the end, I mean."

"I think your idea about beginning at the end would work. It would draw readers in and leave us wondering why this person did what he did. Let's look at some of the short story anthologies in the class library."

A moment of joint experimentation. Norma has an idea about what she wants to do with her story—it's my role to help her do it. In this instance I choose to assist by putting her in touch with some published authors so she can discover some conventional ways of accomplishing her intentions. I help by reading along with her.

We both go to the library at the back of the room and glance at some short stories. I pick up **A Quiver Full of Arrows** (Archer, 1980). We discuss the beginning of "The Chinese Statue" which is followed by a flashback.

Norma selects **As Birds Bring Forth the Sun** (MacLeod, 1986). She turns to the story "To Every Thing There is a Season."

She reads:

> I am speaking here of a time when I was eleven and lived with my
> family on our small farm on the west coast of Cape Breton. My family
> had been there for a long, long time and so it seemed had I. And much
> of that time seems like the proverbial yesterday. Yet when I speak on
> this Christmas 1977, I am not sure how much I speak with the voice of
> that time or how much in the voice of what I have since become.

"I can see Robert saying something like that," she says. "He's relating his story with the insight of an adult but he could begin with something like this."

"Um-hmm. Here's another one. I read briefly from "Hard Luck Stories" in **The Moons of Jupiter** (Munro, 1982).

> Julie is wearing a pink-and-white-striped shirtwaist dress, and a hat of
> lacy beige straw, with a pink rose under the brim. I noticed the hat first,

when she came striding along the street. For a moment I didn't realize it was Julie. Over the last couple of years I have experienced moments of disbelief when I meet my friends in public. They look older than I think they should....

We have not seen each other for two months, not since the conference in May....

When the conference last May had ended and the buses were standing at the door of the summer hotel, waiting to take people back to Toronto or to the airport, I went into Julie's room and found her doing up her backpack....

"I think I can write an opening now," Norma says to me.

"Good. Have a try and see what happens. I'll be happy to respond when you have something."

While I'm at the library table, I do some tidying up. Then I tour the hallway.

Debra, Susan, and Lorna are chatting.

"...what happened," says Debra, "is that Jamie, my nine-year-old, had to do a poem based on one they'd read in school. I was really impressed with what he'd written. I told him that. However, he pressed me to help him fix it. He wanted to know if there was anything that could be better. His second last line I thought could use some improving, so I mentioned it to him— and that was it—his face fell—I knew as soon as I opened my mouth it was the wrong thing to do—I couldn't take it back, I couldn't undo it, the damage had been done. Jamie went and changed the line, but I knew he was now unhappy with his poem."

"We're exactly the same," says Lorna. "When someone else suggests changes it may make the writing stronger, I know it's better, but then I feel it's no longer mine."

"It's still yours," Susan asserts. "I think you have to redefine what you mean by ownership because there are no ideas in your head that weren't influenced by other people's ideas."

"Yes..."

"What makes them yours," she continues, "is that they're part of your experience."

"Yes..."

"I think there's a real fuzzy line between what's yours and what's someone else's particularly with regard to ideas that are discussed during a writing conversation."

"I know, " says Debra, "that only a single line was changed but boy did it ever make a difference. Jamie wasn't happy with my suggestion but he refused to change it back."

"It's the belief that you're supposed to do everything by yourself otherwise it's cheating," says Susan, "that makes you feel uncomfortable about incorporating other people's ideas into your writing, isn't it?..."

Two issues are lurking in this conversation: the first is the problem of what kind of response to make when students request help; the second has to do with whose writing is it if other people have helped shape it. I can't offer Debra any fool-proof advice about offering feedback to her students; I've learned I can only respond and see what happens. If the student backs away then I know I have to approach her differently next time. I make a note to raise the issue of 'ownership' with the whole group soon.

I notice Maggie, Hanna, and Leslie engaged in conversation nearby. I eavesdrop for a while:

"I happened to catch an interview with an author on the radio last evening," says Maggie. "I wasn't really paying attention. But all of a sudden what they were saying was really interesting. The author, I can't remember who he was, writes both children's and adult stories. The interviewer was interested in audience and wanted to know whether he wrote with audience in mind. And he said, 'I can't. All I worry about is whether the publisher is going to like it.' That seemed contradictory to a lot of stuff we've been reading."

"I thought you were going to say he writes for himself," says Hanna.

"Well he did say that, too. But he said he just writes the story and hopes the publisher is going to like it and publish it. He said he doesn't really think about who's going to read it while he's writing it. He seemed to be writing and not really worrying about an audience. Is Judith really worried more about audience because her writing has an informative content?"

"Because her purpose is to inform rather than entertain?" Hanna asks.

"Right. That's what struck me," continues Maggie. "She seems to be very concerned about audience and yet this guy certainly didn't appear to be."

"Isn't she concerned about different stages of audience?" Leslie wonders. "The publisher is one stage of audience. You have to get past a publisher before you reach a wider public."

"If you think about writing for submission to a particular journal, you have to have both things in mind—the journal and the ultimate audience. You know specific journals publish certain kinds of things and they're not going to publish it if it's not..."

"...catchy or..." interjects Leslie.

"Well, if it doesn't fit with what they're publishing. You have to know what that journal publishes and then you craft whatever it is you have to say to fit what you think the editor is looking for. So, yes, you have a wider audience in mind but you also have a concern about this preliminary step..."

"You've got to get past the editor and reviewers," says Maggie. "Maybe it's what you've said Hanna, a difference between writing for entertainment and writing to inform. Maybe they're two different things."

"I'm not sure I agree," says Hanna. "I can't say why I don't agree, but I don't think they're different kinds of writing...."

An interesting conversation. It reminds me of an article by Peter Elbow (1987)—"Closing My Eyes as I Speak: An Argument for Ignoring Audience." In it he describes

> ...many different entities called audience: a) the actual readers to whom the text will be given; b) the writer's conception of those readers—which may be mistaken...; c) the audience that the text implies—which may be different still...; d) the discourse community or even genre addressed or implied by the text..., e) ghost or phantom 'readers in the head' that the writer may unconsciously address or try to please...(p. 50).

Something I'm trying to help teachers and students learn is how to recognize the constraints which purpose and audience place on our decision-making and then to set those constraints aside temporarily while the writing is finding its own meaning.

After lunch Norma returns with an opening for me to read:

I watch as his eyes scan the room. Desperately, I sink lower in my seat.

"Robert, come up to the board and do the next problem."

A familiar wave of despair washes over me.

"Bastard," I say to myself, "bloody bastard."

I do not move. He stares down at me. He is not sure how to handle this unexpected insurrection.

"Well...?"

Behind me, I know all eyes have turned in my direction. Acutely embarrassed, I am aware of my mud-covered shoes and cheap pants.

Still I do not move. I finger the stink bomb in my pocket.

"Well..." louder and more threatening this time.

All year I've been waiting to get Butt, to pay him back. The year is almost over, I've already graded. There's nothing he can do to me now.

Egged on by this false sense of bravado I pull the stink bomb out of my pocket and hurl it at the blackboard.

This incident which occurred over thirty years ago marked the end of my school career.

"I like what you've done. I can feel Robert's anger."
I think about taking a risk here. Norma certainly has done what she's set out to do—begin her story at the end and then flashback to the beginning. With some of the less experienced writers in the group I'd probably celebrate the effort and leave my response at that but Norma has written before and we have a long-standing relationship so I decide to nudge her a bit further.

"I think I would feel his emotion even more strongly, however, if I could picture both Robert and the teacher more clearly. You're not exactly telling me what he's feeling, but I suspect a bit more showing would make the impact stronger."

"You mean, you think I should give more description?"

" 'Desperately, I sink lower in my seat....' " I read. "Why does Robert do that, what's going through his head?"

"He's trying to make himself less visible."

"You might want to say that."

"OK, I see what you're saying. OK, I'll try elaborating the picture."

"Have a go."

A half-hour later, Norma is back.

I watch as his eyes scan the room, seeking a victim, circling, coming in for the kill. Desperately, I sink lower in my seat, hoping to be a less visible target. Without realizing it, I hold my breath.

"Robert, come up to the board and do the next problem."

A familiar wave of despair washes over me. I feel powerless, sick to my stomach. I try to steel myself against the humiliation sure to follow.

"Bastard," I say to myself. "Bloody bastard."

I do not move. He stares down at me, his bulk shifting uneasily. He is not sure how to handle this unexpected insurrection. His thin, humorless mouth tightens. His eyes focus on me as if I were some sort of insect, making me squirm.

"Well...?" The ominous tone is a warning to me.

Behind me, I know all eyes have turned in my direction. Mick, with his air of snooty superiority, stares and snickers.

Acutely embarrassed, I am aware of my mud-covered shoes and cheap pants riding a good two inches above my ankles. Jesus, if only they had been jeans, it would have made all the difference.

Still, I do not move. I finger the stink bomb in my pocket.

"Well..." louder and more threatening this time.

All year I've been waiting to get Butt, to pay him back for all the shit he's put me through, for all the times he's singled me out, making me a laughing stock, making me feel small. The year is almost over, I've already graded. There's nothing he can do to me now.

Egged on by this false sense of bravado as much as by a desire to get even, I make the fateful decision. Quickly, before my wiser self can intervene, I pull the stink bomb out of my picket and hurl it at the blackboard.

This incident which occurred over thirty years ago marked the end of my school career....

"Now I definitely feel Robert's tension and anger. I can really put myself in his place as the teacher scans the room looking for someone to pick next. It doesn't matter if the teacher is really picking on him or not. But I can feel that Robert believes he is."

"That was hard to write."

"Talk about it," I encourage her.

"I could close my eyes and see the pictures but I had a hard time finding words to describe what I was seeing."

"I can't tell that when I read it, though. The pictures are vivid. I feel the knot begin to form in the pit of my stomach just as Robert does."

"I think I'm beginning to understand what this show not tell business is all about."

"You might now want to reread the rest of what you've written to see whether you want to elaborate the images or not."

"I'll work on that tomorrow."

"Great."

Before Norma leaves I ask her to talk a bit about what she's just learned. She pauses before answering.

I'm trying to help Norma shift perspective, to allow her to stand back from our conversation and her writing to think about what was happening and what questions it raises for her about her own teaching.

"I've never written anything where I wrote a large part of the middle before tackling the beginning. I always thought you had to write the beginning first."

"That was a surprise for me, too. When I began using a computer for writing, I discovered I could begin writing anywhere and assemble the parts later. It was very liberating."

"I'm also intrigued that you didn't tell me what to do but together we looked at a couple of books and I saw for myself some things I could try."

"Now you need to think about what those two insights might mean for you as a teacher."

An important part of letting go, I'm learning, is to refrain from doing all the teaching myself. I'm finding out that authors can do a great deal of my teaching for me. "What do you need help doing?" I ask, and in response I listen for opportunities to connect the writer with some familiar text or other.

These days I also find myself teaching by telling stories. As I talk with people about writing, reading, and teaching, rather than delivering an authoritative theoretical dissertation, I find myself recounting some personal incident that makes a point indirectly about some problem or other the teachers are grappling with.

For example, after lunch as Carmina and I chat about her evolving piece, her reflections trigger a story. I describe how many years ago when I was creating a series of videotape programs for the N.S. Department of Education (Newman, 1978) I found myself in the midst of a conflict with the eighth-grade students we were filming. I'd been working with the class for several weeks, conducting lessons in science, math, social studies, and language arts, to develop a reading across the curriculum presentation. During this time, although I was conducting whole class lessons, I made sure the students were free to work with the people they wanted to. However, by the third day of shooting, I was extremely tired so to avoid any hassle I assigned working groups.

The videotape recorded what happened next. The rapport between the students and me deteriorated steadily as the morning progressed. By the third period, social studies I believe, I had open rebellion from a number of students—total resistance to anything I wanted them to try. The incident which blew my patience was trivial. However, suddenly very angry, I stomped from the room and cursed my way down the hall to the closet where the production crew was housed. I called a halt to the day's videotaping session and the crew began packing up.

When I returned to the classroom, I told the kids I was exhausted and exasperated. We were supposed to tape again the following day but I was prepared to close down if they really weren't interested in what we were doing. They had a decision to make: we could carry on with the videotaping, but if they chose to do that, they would have to be more co-operative than they had been that morning. I left the room once more to allow the kids to discuss what they wanted to do. (I learned later from the cameramen that the kids organized a secret ballot and voted on the matter.) When I returned they told me they thought we should proceed with the final taping.

I left the school in a turmoil. While the cost of production was a fraction of any professional effort, it was substantial in terms of anything the Department of Education had ever attempted. I was furious with the kids for wasting our time. I ranted to anyone who would listen throughout the afternoon and early evening.

Insight came for me later that evening while describing the incident to my friend Marlene on the phone. Her laughter, and her questions, as I described what had happened, suddenly helped me see how I'd caused the situation myself. I was now very aware of how my decision to take control of the grouping had established a me/them confrontation that morning. My decision had had predictable consequences: if I was taking charge, then they were going to play 'make me.'

> 'Have you ever thought, Ms. K., that maybe we behave the way we do because of how the teachers treat us?' Tammy's voice, desperate, clear, eloquent, unravelled part of the reason her class had been uncontrollable for well over a month. Why had it taken me that long to do what I did with other classes: ask, listen, and turn the problem over to them to solve? Why had I substituted control (unsuccessfully) for listening?
>
> Pat Kidd

> *I have related this story to Carmina as a way of nudging her to look at her role in what she perceives as the kids' misbehavior.*

"What I learned from those kids," I say to her, "was that my structures and restrictions had a lot to do with how they behaved. I could no longer look at students, children or adult, and not recognize that my classroom rules and requirements played a large part in determining engagement."

> *What I'm saying to Carmina is 'Here's what I learned on this occasion, think about how my experience might help you view your own situation differently.'*

This story, and the many others I've been sharing, are what I call **critical incidents**. They are moments which have forced me to stand back and examine my beliefs and my teaching critically. Significant learning moments don't only occur in the classroom. Something I read may force me to take stock. An overheard comment sometimes makes me wonder. Noticing how someone else is doing something I've always taken for granted, or suddenly seeing my own learning strategies with new eyes, helps me learn more about my teaching. Whatever their source, latent critical incidents are everywhere and they offer important opportunities for Schön's reflection-in-action. First, however, I have to become aware of those moments and the potential they offer.

The idea of critical incidents began evolving for me a number of years ago when teachers in a curriculum implementation class and I started looking at our own teaching reflectively. One of the things we discovered was how difficult it was to keep running field notes on what was happening while we were teaching. But we could manage to capture a couple of brief highlights every day if we were alert.

We played with a number of ways of recording our experiences. The easiest and most effective we found was simply to jot a phrase or sentence on one side of a 3 x 5 index card—just enough to allow us to reconstruct the situation later. We began sharing our classroom stories, looking for complementary themes and discussing implications for our teaching. Later we recorded insights evoked by the incident on the other side of the card. Sometimes the incidents confirmed what we believed; more often, however, we were forced to reappraise our assumptions. These critical incidents often revealed a surprising gap between what we said we believed about learning and teaching (our 'espoused' beliefs) and what our actions were conveying (Newman, 1987).

As I began recording critical incidents from my own teaching I discovered something rather interesting: the incidents which were helping me examine my teaching weren't monumental events; they were small, seemingly insignificant occurrences. I recorded in my log at the time:

> I can see many learning opportunities come from
> comments made in passing, from a statement overheard,
> from something a student might write in a journal, or
> from something I might read either because it confirms
> my experience or because I disagree and have to consider
> what I believe instead, or because it opens possibilities I
> haven't thought about before.

I also realized that the learning often remains tacit unless we teachers have an opportunity to make it explicit. Writing the stories down became an important aspect of becoming reflective; it forced us to explain these contradictory and surprising events and situations to ourselves.

Vito Perrone (1991) explains why reflecting in writing is important:

> Maintaining a journal is, without question, very
> difficult....because we don't see ourselves as writers, or we
> don't really believe we need to write to reflect on our
> work....[Just thinking about what we do] is never as
> productive as thinking *and* writing. Teachers who engage in
> journal writing...do become better observers of their students
> and their practices. They also become more reflective and
> grow in their ability to speak clearly and authoritatively about
> their craft. (p.87)

The teachers and I found, however, that engaging in this kind of analysis wasn't easy. We evolved some questions to help us focus:

why do I remember this incident?
what makes it significant?
what do I learn from it?
what is one question it raises about my teaching?

Answering these questions became a regular part of our class discussion.

I've actually been telling critical incident stories from the beginning of this Institute workshop. I was particularly aware today of the number of times I responded to a question with such a story. The power of these stories, it seems to me, is that they afford me

*an opportunity to state my theoretical position but to
diminish its power of authority; I'm simply relating
something that's happened to me and allowing subsequent conversation to explore its point.*

*What I've noticed, however, is that other people
aren't being drawn into similar analytic story telling.
There has been story swapping, but not the analytic
reflection that would make the stories critical
incidents. It's time, I feel, for some class discussion.*

I need to bring critical incidents onstage.

We regroup at the end of the afternoon for an impromptu
meeting to discuss critical incidents.

"I've been relating critical incident stories for several days
now. Time, I think, to deal explicitly with what a critical incident
is.

"Let me start by sharing a brief critical incident that occurred
during an inservice workshop a few years ago. I was introducing what we were going to do, explaining to the teachers that
in order to change we need to be willing to look at ourselves, to
examine our teaching. One woman responded immediately.

'I don't want to leave here today feeling everything I'm
doing is wrong. What I'm doing is just fine. I'm happy with my
teaching,' she said.

'If you're happy with your teaching then this is not the
session for you,' I replied. 'There are several other session
going on down the hall, please feel free to leave and find
something that interests you.'

"She didn't leave, but she didn't really engage in our
discussions either.

"Later I thought about the implications of what she'd said.
Her comment made me realize that nothing I offer teachers is
going to make a difference if people are comfortable with their
teaching. The only way I'm liable to have any impact at all is if
people are interested in examining what they're doing and
willing to consider changing it. Even experiences which might
let them reflect on their own learning are of little value if people
aren't prepared to be critical of their teaching.

"That teacher's comment, and the reflection it engendered,
represents what I call a critical incident."

*I've given an example of a critical incident, now they
need to try creating a personal example.*

"How about everyone trying a freewrite about a nightmare in
your classroom?"

*I'm aware that not all critical incidents are nightmares,
nor do all reflective moments necessarily involve*

events in the classroom; a potential critical incident can
occur anywhere. However, by casting critical in-
cidents as 'nightmares' I'm trying to draw the
teachers' attention to situations that were uncomfort-
able ones.

I freewrite for six or seven minutes, shaping another brief
incident. Once I see the point of what I'm writing I stop and ask
people to finish the sentence they're on. I wait.

"How do we want to go about this?" I ask.

"I think it would be useful for us to discuss our nightmares
in small groups," says Bruce.

"Why do you think that tactic would be useful?" I inquire.

"First, it would give everyone a chance to share their story.
Then it would let us have a chance to discuss them all."

"What other options are there?"

Leslie responds. "We could pass our stories around the
small group and people could respond to them."

"Some version of an inkshedding, you mean?" I ask.

"Yup," she answers.

"Some of us could read or tell our stories in the large group
and people could discuss them," suggests Earl.

"But we wouldn't all get a chance to explore our individual
stories that way," blurts Diane. "I might not feel comfortable
sharing my story with everyone but be happy reading what I've
written in the smaller group."

"Looks like small group sharing would work best here,"
Penny says.

"Sounds fine. Let's try."

As I move from group to group I listen to people's stories.
Cathy's story is about a first-grade teacher from Toronto she met
during the spring who informed her that she had set up her
writing centre with only lined paper.

> When I asked her why she had done that, she told how a
> friend of hers had attended a workshop Judith had given
> during the winter. The friend had been concerned
> because her kindergarten children weren't doing much
> writing. Apparently Judith had asked her if she'd tried
> putting lined paper in the writing centre. Both teachers, it
> seems, went back to their classrooms and removed all
> unlined paper, substituted only lined paper, and began
> teaching the kids to stay within the lines!

"I was astounded at their misinterpretation, at their blind
acceptance of a suggestion without any reflection," Cathy
remarks.

She turns to me and asks, "You didn't say they should use only lined paper with the children, did you?"

"No, of course not. I simply said it might be interesting to include lined paper as an option to see what the children would do with it.

"That incident makes me realize I have to keep a close watch on my own staff whenever I suggest anything. So often just mentioning an idea gives it the force of a directive when all I'm trying to do is broaden someone's options."

In the next group I listen to Lorna read her freewrite:

Near the end of the year, while the rest of the class was getting ready for recess, Jeffrey, a bright but shy boy, came to me and asked very seriously,

"Ms. MacLean, do you think I am an author?"

"Yes," I answered, "for sure you're an author, Jeffrey."

"How do you know?" he challenged me.

"Well, you've been writing good stories, haven't you?"

"Yes."

"And you find it easier to write more now than you did when you came into this class, don't you?"

He screwed up his face as he thought about that. "I guess I do," he replied.

"And you always have stories you want to tell us, right?"

"Sure, telling stories is fun."

"And we've published three of your stories now, haven't we?"

"Yup."

"Well, people who have lots of stories to tell, who write them down and have them made into books are authors, aren't they?"

"I guess so."

"So wouldn't you say you're an author, Jeffrey?"

A beaming smile crossed his face. Then he returned to what he'd been doing.

"When we began the year Jeffrey was a very hesitant writer," Lorna explains. "I remember one occasion when he spent twenty minutes thinking about what to write in his journal. His page was a blank. When I asked, he said he had nothing to write about. I reminded him he could write about anything he wanted to. He asked if he could write a story. I'd told him he could. By recess that day he was so engrossed in the writing that he asked to stay in class to continue. That was the beginning. He started writing more and more easily after that. I guess I was really taken aback when he asked me whether I thought he was an author. I thought by spring he believed himself a writer. Clearly he still needed some reassurance. His question made me realize that I can't take the kids' feelings about themselves for granted."

"Interesting story, Lorna," I comment. "It's so easy to underestimate people's feelings of insecurity."

"I guess I see it in my classes, too," adds Leslie. "The fifth graders can go along for weeks writing comfortably; then suddenly, for no apparent reason, it seems to become hard again."

"I suspect it's a sign that they're undergoing some growth," I say. "We tend to think that growth happens when things are going along smoothly but it's actually when it seems hard again, when we're confused and trying out new things, that growing is going on."

"I've never thought about it that way," Leslie remarks.

"Think about your own experiences here in the Institute." I glance at everyone around the table. "Where have you seen your own growth occurring? How can you tell something is happening?" I ask.

"I can't answer you right now," Earl says.

"Let it percolate," I respond to him. "You might find it useful to freewrite about it this evening."

I join a third group. Connie is discussing an experience she had last winter.

"I got lots of flack from the other teachers about the fact that I wasn't producing lovely displays of everyone's snowman story, or everyone's poem about snowflakes. So at one point I tried to get the kids all to do a worksheet about the books they were reading, what they liked about them, what they didn't like. I was going to use them to make a bulletin board about favorite books. Well, the kids did the worksheets but they were really a mess. There was very little talk, the level of caring was remarkably low, and lots of 'OK, I'm finished. Can I write now?' "

"What did you learn from that experience?" I ask her.

"I certainly saw how I can force the kids to do something but I can't make them like it or do it well, either."

"It is interesting how compliance doesn't necessarily produce engagement, isn't it?" Barb comments.

"How about the rest of you? What questions about your own teaching does Connie's story raise for you?"

Michael responds. "I've had the same thing happen in my classroom, too. I've just never stopped to think about what the kids are saying to me. I can see I have to listen to them more closely."

"Graduate students don't always rebel so obviously," I reflect. "I find I have to keep a close watch on body language. Often I can read compliance there, although if I ask people how they feel about what they're doing, they'll say they're fine."

The critical incident story is an important reflective tool. I've been helping teachers explore their own stories for a couple of years now and as we begin telling them to one another significant questions about teaching always arise.

For example, last winter, a teacher wrote the following story:

> I guess it was when I first read "Demonstrations, Engagement, and Sensitivity" (Smith, 1981) that I began to question what the kids in my class were learning. Until then I thought my students were learning what I was explicitly teaching. Smith helped me see my students were engaging with and learning from clusters of demonstrations, many of them unconscious, that I offered them....It was then I began asking myself, "What are my kids learning right now?" Later, I learned to involve the kids in discussions about this same question. I'll bet not a single day goes by that I don't ask them this question. And still things slip by....
>
> I have been trying to make it possible for my kids to take control of a lot of the things that go on in the classroom. My kids and I talk a lot about the constraints of curriculum, of time, of space. We talk about expectations: what the school board expects of me, what parents expect of them and of me, what they expect of school and of me and of themselves, and what I expect of them, collectively and individually. We make decisions based on these discussions. More important still, my students, knowing the constraints that exist, make independent decisions about their own learning.
>
> I was feeling quite good about how our 'communications' exploration was proceeding until some students asked me if they could work on a specific topic or use a particular format. True,

some like David simply informed me about what they were planning do. Others, however, came seeking permission. Even after all the things I had said and done to show them they could make their own decisions, they still came seeking permission. Obviously, they saw the power residing with me. Had I taught them this inadvertently, I wondered.

As I thought about what I could have done to cause this problem, I realized there was another smaller, related, problem in our classroom. At the beginning of the academic year we, my students and I, had established a procedure so people could leave the room, without permission, when they needed to. Then five months into the year, I was suddenly aware that most of the kids were checking with me before leaving.

Here was another example of them not making their own decisions. So I called a class meeting and asked what was going on. And they told me. They told me they had noticed that if I was about to talk to the class as a whole, make an announcement or discuss homework, I would ask a person about to leave to wait a minute or two until I had had my say. They had decided it was best to check with me, just in case.

Here I was. Teaching something I hadn't intended to teach—that I still held the power in the classroom. Because I questioned what was happening and because I talked with my students, I discovered what I had been teaching.

Becoming a reflective practitioner is a risky business. It's inevitable that we'll find lots of contradictions between what we say we believe and what our actions and comments are saying to students. Critical incident stories are powerful mirrors. They let us examine those contradictions. By turning our reflective gaze on ourselves we can begin to glimpse the effects our teaching might be having.

Monday evening, after reading and responding to journals, I write my reflection/letter.

I'm beginning to think about some kind of timetable for getting us to the end of the Institute. I mentioned this afternoon in class that I thought it would be useful to have a completed draft of something by Wednesday morning if we could. The reason for that is we will need to explore revision and editing some before Friday. Revision and editing are not the same process—revision refers to re-vision…to seeing again, to recasting and reconceptualizing a text; attention to style, organization, and flow. Editing refers to the more focal kinds of attention to a piece of writing—to the careful examination of words, phrases, spelling, punctuation, and the like. Have a glance at Donald Murray's **Write to Learn**, Chapter 6, on clarifying. He introduces a useful idea: the **third read.** It typifies for me what editing is about. The third read is the point at which attention to all the little details become crucial. It's the last step before some kind of publication. It's what copy editors do. (I must remember to bring in the copy edited manuscript for **Finding Our Own Way** so you can see how the copy editor handled it.) However, there are lots of situations where we don't have access to copy editors and besides we do have to learn to do our own third read; we each have to take responsibility for how our text finally appears. One thing I wish we had time for would be to set up an editorial review committee to screen the almost finished pieces for attention to conventions. We'd need another couple of days to accomplish that, however. But in a classroom it's a useful idea to think about implementing.

What else? I guess I want to draw your attention again to our overarching agenda: reading/writing/talking relationships. What have you learned about how reading feeds into writing, writing feeds into reading, talking benefits both? How have you found conversations about published writing similar to our conversations about our own writing? How has the reading you've done affected what and how you have been writing? The relationship is very complex, it seems to me. It goes on a number of levels at the same time. That's why it doesn't make sense to talk about reading instruction or writing instruction as separate activities; they are closely interwoven and it often isn't possible to tell when you are learning what.

It's appropriate to say something about letting go, here as well, I think. I was struck this afternoon by how many of the critical incidents were about letting go, about situations where we didn't give students sufficient room

to manoeuvre so we could learn how to teach them. I
find it a constant struggle to wait for teachable moments
to occur spontaneously. I keep barging in and telling too
much too soon to too many people. I keep forgetting
what I learned years ago during the Rubik's cube craze:
when people want to learn something they approach the
problems directly and look for solutions themselves. I
was a compulsive member of the Rubik's cube club
myself, constantly seeking out kids who knew more
about ways of solving the cube than I did so I could
learn from them. Tactics for solving the cube spread like
wildfire without adult direction because it was something
kids wanted to know about. Within six months there
wasn't a kid in my sphere who couldn't solve the cube
(they didn't all understand the topological mathematics
underlying the solutions, nor did I, really, but we had
learned a number of heuristics for solving the puzzle).
That experience held an important lesson about teaching
for me: **the need to know** is what drives genuine
learning. I have to keep reminding myself I need to let go
enough so learners can show me what they need to
know, what questions they're currently asking, what
experiments are engaging their attention.

The truly artistic teacher...perceives the focus of responsibility for
learning to be in the learner; he conscientiously suppresses his own
compulsion to teach what he knows his students ought to learn in favor
of helping his students learn for themselves what they want to learn
(Malcolm Knowles, *The Modern Practice of Adult Education*, in
Wilson, 1976, p. 144).

Holding In   10 ❖

To instruct calls for energy, and to remain almost silent, but watchful and helpful, while students instruct themselves, calls for even greater energy...because holding in is more demanding than crying out. (p. 87)
Robertson Davies, 1982

We begin Tuesday morning with our discussion of children's books. In anticipation of our conversation I'd asked people to read Margaret Meek's article "How Texts Teach What Readers Learn" (Meek, 1988) which I'd handed out the first day. In it, she raises interesting questions about how stories relate to one another, about how many, if not most, of the important lessons we learn as readers we learn from texts themselves.

Again we form one large group. The number of people has grown; nearly everyone has chosen to participate this time. Although I have tried making it clear these discussion sessions are optional, the teachers are afraid they'll miss something. So it's a tight squeeze around our big table.

"Where would you like to begin?" I ask.

"With Meek's article, I think," says Helen. "She helped me see reading is more than handling a lot of printed words."

"She made me think about how important it is to let children choose their own books," adds Leslie. "I know last year I started letting the kids choose their own books and chatting with them about them. I started asking 'Why did you choose this book?' Then the kids started asking questions themselves. Meek's article made me feel better about what I was doing. I think I can now explain why it's important to let kids choose their own reading material."

Should I pursue Leslie's insight further? I decide to listen instead.

"I really enjoyed Meek's discussion of **Rosie's Walk** (Hutchins, 1969)," says Norma. "It's one of my favorite books. I've used it with the young children in the resource room. They choose it again and again. There's so much to deal with in that book and the kids have lots to say about what's happening in the story."

*I have several copies of **Rosie's Walk** in the class library. I could get them and we could do a close reading as Meek does, but that would take us in* *another direction. I sit quietly letting the conversation unfold.*

"I also liked what Meek points out about the things we don't read, like the publishing information, the date, the author and her question about when did we learn not to read that stuff," adds Leslie.

"I don't think I ever remember having that information pointed out to me in school," comments Theresa. "I don't remember looking at that stuff until I had to do a research paper in high school."

I could point out how this is a good example of incidental learning.

"Maybe that's because the only reading we did was from the readers," says Penny. "We never read books and such. We read stories out of the readers and that was it."

"What other books does **Rosie's Walk** evoke for you?" I inquire.

"It reminded me of **Who's Got the Apple?** (Lööf, 1975)," Janice says reaching for a copy of the book. "Here it's telling about the principal's car running into the fence," she says, opening the book to the appropriate page, "but there's an entirely different story going on in the background; there's a robbery taking place and this character, the crook, shows up later on. It took me many readings before I caught on. I didn't see the robber in the classroom behind the large chart for a long time. And there's no reference to the crook in the text except later when the policeman asks the children whether they've seen him. There he is hiding in the classroom and the children aren't aware of it either."

"**Charlie Needs a Cloak** (de Paola, 1974) is like that too," says Leslie opening a copy of the book. "It's about Charlie making a woolen cloak for himself. The story is really about where wool comes from and how it's processed. There's also the substory about a mouse which isn't mentioned in the text at all. If you watch the mouse, you see it collecting everything Charlie's using. Here it has the scissors from the shearing." She turns to that page and points to the mouse. "And here it has the soap from when Charlie washed the wool. Then it's taking some of the wool and the pokeberries to dye the wool. Here at the end you see the mouse in its house with the collection it has used to furnish it."

"Mercer Mayer's books are like that, as well," says Earl. "The children get into the Mercer Mayer series and the first thing they look for in a new book is the cricket and the spider."

"So what lessons, both about reading and writing, do these books teach us?" I ask.

This is Margaret Meek's question. Her point is similar to Frank Smith's—we learn to write by reading like writers. I want the teachers to think about that relationship.

"That there's more to a story than the print," says Theresa, "or even the pictures or what the print says about the pictures."

"So much emphasis in my teaching has been on words," remarks Penny. "Can you turn the pages quickly, pronounce the words correctly. It's never been on stopping and looking at the pictures and what's going on and how it connects to the children's experiences."

I could ask "How have our experiences here helped you think about your teaching differently?" I don't.

"Like often at story time I'd sit and read, (God, I did this for years)," comments Leslie, "I'd be reading to the kids and they'd want to say something and I'd be going 'Shhh, this is story time, everyone has to be quiet.' I didn't realize how much the discussion is an important part of what should be going on."

> This is not unlike the tyranny of S.S.R. "Shh. This is sustained silent reading time," I hear myself. Too often, the loud stage whisper has cut off a delighted meaning-maker's sharing a link, a connection, or her enjoyment with a neighbor. Perhaps it's really the tyranny of an unthinking teacher.
>
> Pat Kidd

"I liked what Margaret Meek refers to as the 'intertextuality' of books," says Diane. "I had never thought about how books contain references, sometimes overt, sometimes quite subtle, to other stories."

I was hoping, if I waited, someone would raise this.

"Yes, her description of **The Jolly Postman** (Ahlberg, 1986) really made me think about that book very differently. I came in and looked at it again early this morning. I could see so much more in it," Leslie remarks.

"It really is incredible," says Penny. "Imagine dreaming up a book that consists mainly of other people's letters, complete with envelopes, written from one fairy tale character to another. I really love the witch's flyer with the little boy pie mix the best."

"I found children missed that. It seemed to be the most difficult piece of mail for them to understand," Janice says. "They didn't seem to catch on to it until I explained it."

"Well, I don't think kids read a lot of flyers," says Penny.

Do I ask about all the other kinds of print kids don't have much experience reading?

"Now my kids didn't have any trouble with it," says Theresa. "They all have G.I. Joe flyers that come with the dolls, or the transformer ones. They were constantly looking at them checking for how many points they needed to send away for this or that. They all seemed to get the connection with that particular piece of mail right away."

"It points out the need to bring junk mail into the classroom," says Norma. "so we get a chance to talk about why people send flyers, what's on them, and help kids make connections with this one."

Should I mention that we should have a great deal more non-fiction of all kinds in the classroom? I decide to come back to intertextuality.

"I'm looking for the postcard," I say leafing through the book. "This is it: to Mr. V. Bigg, Jack in the Beanstock's giant. There's one picture reference I don't understand on it. I recognize 'The Old Woman in the Shoe' in the part captioned 'First Class Hotels', 'Hey Diddle Diddle' in the 'Music and Dancing' picture, 'Simple Simon' in the 'Fun and Food' picture, but I can't think of a nursery rhyme that 'Fabulous Beaches' refers to. Does that picture of the mermaid lounging on the beach eating an ice cream cone with a sea serpent loping in the waves offshore ring a bell for any of you?"

"The Little Mermaid," offers Diane.

"Um-hmm, there is the Hans Christian Anderson story. But the other three pictures all clearly refer to nursery rhymes which makes me think this one should too, but I don't know one about mermaids."

"It was the little mermaid that I thought about when I looked at the postcard," Diane says.

"Unless it's an English nursery rhyme none of us knows," laughs Penny.

"Could very well be."

*John Mayher (1990) uses **The Jolly Postman** to flesh out this idea of **intertextuality**—a crucial concept if we're to understand a meaning-centred perspective on reading. He points out*

> The reader must be familiar in advance not only with the characters but also with their stories so that when as in the first letter, Goldilocks writes to apologize to the Three Bears, we understand what she is apologizing for and can supply the context with our own remembered version of their story. If we are unfamiliar with the adventures of Goldilocks and the Three Bears, we just won't know what is going on, and we certainly won't think it is funny. This is a key aspect of the

transactional nature of the reading process, but it plays a role in writing as well, since clearly the shared meanings that the Ahlbergs hope will be built between them and their readers depend on shared textural, as well as cultural and linguistic, contexts of childhood (p. 169).

"Look at this one," laughs Bruce, "from Meeny, Miny, Mo & Co., Solicitors to 'Dear Mr. Wolf.'

We are writing to you on behalf of our client, Miss Riding-Hood, concerning her grandma. Miss Hood tells us that you are presently occupying her grandma's cottage and wearing her grandma's clothes without this lady's permission.

Please understand that if this harassment does not cease, we will call in the Official Woodcutter, and — if necessary — all the King's horses and all the King's men.

On a separate matter, we must inform you that Messers. Three Little Pigs Ltd. are now firmly resolved to sue for damages. Your offer of shares in a turnip or apple-picking business is declined, and all this huffing and puffing will get you nowhere.

Yours sincerely,
H Meeny

"I'm fascinated by the way these fairy tales talk to one another," Bruce continues. "Just mentioning the characters in this new context evokes the stories in their entirety."

"This is another facet of books and stories talking to one another, isn't it?" asks Leslie.

"Talk about that a bit more," I encourage her.

We need to delve a bit deeper here, I think.

"Well, it's not just recognizing underlying connections between books. We saw how we could build relationships among the short stories we read and among the poems, too. Some stories, like this one, actually openly play at evoking connections with other texts."

"Meek makes a powerful point about that for me," I comment. I flip through my copy of her article looking for something I've highlighted. I read:

> "'On the surface intertext can seem to be a kind of literary joke; underneath it is a very serious business, part of the whole intricate network of words which mean more than they say....This intertextuality cannot be a feature of the reading scheme [she means a basal reader program], which offers words to be read only in order to reinforce lessons that are taught **about** reading rather than learned **by** reading' (p.95).

Meek's arguing, I think, that a crucial lesson which books like this teach us is that all texts have the potential to talk to other texts in a similar way. So what questions about books did Meek raise for you?"

"The value of rereading," says Michael. "That's something I've been guilty of, discouraging the kids from rereading. 'If you've read this before, get something else,' and I can see now I shouldn't have been doing that. I guess I'm more aware that there is significant value in rereading; it can be a whole new experience. And I honestly didn't encourage it."

I reread a lot. I've read some books over and over again. Should I say something about it? I remain quiet.

"I've been guilty of that with myself," Hanna adds. "I don't reread books at all. Yet I'm not like that with the children in school as much as I used to be. But I haven't valued rereading for myself."

> People borrow my books and keep them for long periods of time. I'm beginning to think they don't realize I **use** my books all the time—I re-read parts, even whole texts. Does that mean other people only read their books once? Do they think I'm 'done' with mine when I lend them?
>
> Diane Stephens

"This conversation has made me more aware of connections among texts," Maggie remarks. "I think I understand better how I might begin with one text, using it as a jump off for a lot of exploring. I can see I have to rethink how I can help my junior high students build connections among texts and their own experiences better."

A shift in direction; I'm curious to see where it will lead.

"I'm beginning to appreciate how important it is to juxtapose a lot of texts," Bruce offers. "In the senior high we often read a single story and then discuss it to death. What I've experienced here is how much richer the discussion becomes when more texts are brought into the conversation. I have to think about ways of broadening the offerings. I can foresee a real problem though—the students aren't used to reading a lot of stuff fast. We've been able to talk about so much here because we've been reading at top speed. I'm not sure how to go about helping students handle the amount we'd need to read in order to have this kind of conversation. I've put the question on my list of things to think about."

"How does this notion of intertextuality affect you as writers?" I ask.

"When I was trying to come up with an idea for a children's story," Helen says, "I was going through these books for ideas, finding things that I could connect with. What's surprised me is how while the books gave me a place to start, my story isn't like any of them. What's come out is totally different from anything I read. I didn't realize that maybe encouraging kids to go to books for ideas would be a useful thing to do. I was always afraid they'd simply copy stuff. What I've learned through my own story is that what comes out isn't copied. What I ended up with is my own."

I don't say anything; having voiced her insight, I
believe, Helen will be better able to use books to help
her students develop as writers.

"I'm beginning to sense my writing lacks something," says Leslie, "because I'm focusing mainly on getting my story out. I've not been consciously thinking about making any connections with other books or stories."

"I don't think it's a matter of always making overt connections," I respond. "The more writing I do, the more I find myself wondering 'How has this author done this?' and 'Why does that seem a good way to have done it?' or 'How might I have done this differently?' So I've become much more actively engaged with the text as a writer and when I'm working on my own writing I find myself thinking about other texts I've read and drawing on those to take my writing further. At that point the boundaries between the lessons I have learned from writing and the lessons from reading blur—the distinction vanishes."

"As I wrote the beginning of my children's story about the loose tooth I was quite surprised by the connection with **The Carrot Seed** (Krauss, 1984) that emerged," says Theresa. I didn't plan it; in fact I didn't notice it until I'd written a page or so. 'I wiggled it and jiggled it, but it wouldn't come out.' I thought afterward that I'd probably used 'But it wouldn't come out' a bit too often so I removed some of them. But I knew I wanted to keep the potential connection there for the kids. I found it quite surprising how the connection happened without my planning it."

The texts we read can teach us a lot about how to be writers. The conversations we have about books and about writing are also crucial for learning about writing. However, many of the connections we make between what we've read and our own writing are tacit, as it was for Theresa. I could say something about that but I leave Theresa with the last word.

The rest of the day is again spent writing, responding to one another's writing, reading, reacting to the professional articles, talking about learning and teaching.

I'm trying to hold in, to stay out of people's way as much as possible, to let them show me what lessons might be opportune. I participate in conversations about specific writing problems, respond to questions about reading/ writing instruction, ask questions of my own about the connections people are making from this learning experience, always being as careful as I can be to follow the learner's lead.

I keep a watch on the **Writing Conversations** list, meeting with people as soon as they sign up. In these conversations I make a concerted effort to affirm what the writer is attempting, to sustain the emerging writing rather than worry about coherence or correctness. We'll be getting to those concerns very soon but before we can talk about fine tuning the teachers have to have some kind of beginning, middle, and end in place.

My chat with Norma is a typical conversation.

She tracks me down just before lunch to discuss her story.

"I don't know where to go, again," she tells me.

"What have you done so far?"

"Well, I've been working on building some background so the reader can understand why Robert did what he did."

"Talk to me about it."

I want to find out what's happening in Norma's head; I need to learn more about her intentions and what she's struggling with.

"Shall I read what I've written?"

"If you want to."

My education began in a one-room school where thirty kids from grades primary to 7 vied for the

teacher's attention and learned what they could. I found
school very easy and when I finished my work I would
listen in on what the others were doing so I was never
bored. I also remember getting lots of attention from the
teacher for being smart. She would give me extra things
to do and would often call on me to help those who were
having difficulty. The teacher made me feel special and
school was a sustaining experience; it helped make my
unhappy home life more bearable.

When I was thirteen, however, I switched to the high
school—a huge consolidated plant, a good three-mile
walk from my house. At least a thousand kids went
there. I became just another statistic.

Lots of solid description.

The sheer size of the place was, of course, a
contributing factor to my ultimate demise. But of far
greater significance was the drop in social status I
experienced with the move.

I was suddenly one of the poor kids. My shabby
clothes set me apart and assured my place among the
losers—a rag-tag band of n'er-do-wells who sat at the
back of the class and waged their particular form of
guerilla warfare against the teachers. Not that I fitted in
with them either. They tolerated my presence but did not
include me in their fun.

I wait for Norma to resume conversation.

"You remember one of the reasons Robert decided to get
expelled from school was because he felt so different from the
other kids; he was particularly sensitive about how he was
dressed," Norma says. "I'm trying, here, to fill in some
background about that."

"My sense of Robert is certainly extended. I have a stronger
sense of how he feels about himself."

She continues reading.

I didn't work on the school newspaper or sing in the
glee club or go to school dances. I didn't get invited to
parties. It's not that anything was said…it was simply
understood.

Thinking back, I cannot recall a single incident where
I was teased because of my appearance. Perhaps it was
because my embarrassment was so obvious they had the
decency not to make it worse. I suspect, however, it was
simply because I did not matter.

I remember the shoes I was forced to wear...black-vinyl hand-me-downs, a size too large, badly scuffed and worn through at the soles. I fitted them with cardboard insoles in a vain effort to keep the mud from seeping through on the long trek from home.

One day, in particular, comes to mind when I think of those shoes. There had been a vicious rainstorm the previous night, so by the time I arrived at school my shoes were caked with mud and soaked through to the inside. I walked into the classroom, my shoes making soft squishing noises, leaving a trail of mud in my wake. Not long before that, Johnson had decided to move me to a front seat. He felt I was being distracted by the rowdy bunch around me. I had objected strenuously but to no avail. So on that day I was forced to walk up to the front, feet squishing, to sit in full view of the class. I wanted to die.

"I love your pictures. The showing is working very well," I respond.

"I've been keeping what you said about the first part in mind while I've been writing. I've been trying to visualize the situations, almost as if I were watching a film. It's getting easier to do."

"So far you've said nothing about Robert's family. Have you thought about that at all?"

"I haven't much."

"I'm wondering why Robert is so badly dressed. Was the family poor?"

I share a question that occurred to me while I was listening.

"I'll have to think about that. I don't know any of the details about the real Robert's life. So I guess I'll have to make all of that up."

"What you're experiencing is how fiction unfolds from real experience. You're going to have to draw on your own life, your own feelings, as you work out what happens with Robert. Don't worry about whether it all fits together right now. Just keep writing. The story will unfold for you."

I have a hunch Norma's story is going to turn into something rather longer than most of the other pieces. The incident she began with has lots of potential for expansion both forward and backward in time. I suspect she may not be able to work out the entire narrative before the end of the Institute. I will have to help her find a reasonable place to stop. But at the moment, I'm trying to encourage her to explore the story further.

After lunch Norma wants to talk about her writing again.
"I've gone back and written something about Robert's family."

> It has been said that where you are born in a family
> has a lot to do with how you turn out. Well, I think in
> my case it was probably true. There were already five
> girls in my family when I came along, ten years after the
> youngest girl.
> By that time my mother had become a pale, worn
> reflection of the person my sisters remembered. The light
> in her eyes and the lightness of her step had
> disappeared—destroyed by years of unrelenting
> hardship.

A strong image.

> That must have been the case because my sisters are
> constantly surprised by my memories of my mother
> which contrast so sharply with theirs.
> I don't ever recall her telling me she loved me or that
> I was special in any way. Not that she ever mistreated
> me; she certainly attended to my basic needs. It's just
> that she had given up trying to make the best of things.
> There was no joy left in her to share with me.

Again, I wait for Norma to take the lead.
Norma pauses.
"I'm trying here to paint a picture, not of neglect, but of a mother too tired to give much to this child," she says.
"I think what you've written is working. I can see the mother without energy or much life to her, and I can sense Robert's longing for more attention. What about his father?"
"I wrote about him next."

> I can never remember hearing a kind word from my
> father. It wasn't until years later I learned he was about
> to leave my mother when he discovered she was
> pregnant. My coming into the world was not a welcome
> event. I bore the brunt of my father's shattered dreams.
> I have few clear memories of my first five years. I do
> know I learned early to stay out of my father's way.

I had my first lesson when I was about three. My
father ran a small convenience store attached to our
house. A door from the kitchen led directly into the
store. Usually this door was kept shut. However, on that
particular day my father had left it open without
intending to. Quite innocently, and with the curiosity of a
young child, I wandered, unattended, through the door
into the store.

The penny candy was displayed behind the
counter—the boxes arranged so that the customers could
easily see what was available. It wasn't long before I
discovered this cache of delights. I proceeded to help
myself, oblivious to the boxes I knocked to the floor in
the process.

I can guess what's coming.

By the time my father discovered me, I was happily
seated in the middle of a pile of candy, mouth full, totally
engrossed in the pleasure of the moment.

I glanced up when I heard a sudden noise, only to
see him advancing toward me, face purple with rage. I
can still remember as though it were yesterday, the
terrifying fear I experienced as he reached over to grab
me with one hand while using the other like a hammer—
smashing into my small frame over and over again.

My anguished cries alerted my mother who
attempted, unsuccessfully, to intervene. His unleashed
temper ran its course.

My badly bruised body recovered, eventually, but
after that my view of the world was forever altered. I lost
the innocence and trust of childhood. I became old
before my time.

To this day, I can't eat penny candy—the very sight
of it brings me back to that awful day and fills me with
such anger and sadness I can hardly bear it.

After that incident, I became quite skilled at avoiding
my father. I learned to live in the shadows, asking for
little, expecting nothing and counting myself lucky when
I succeeded in going unnoticed.

"The family you're painting explains why Robert is as angry
and as isolated as he is."

"He's emerging for me as a child on the edge," Norma says.
"Some of the kids I teach in resource are like that—you don't
know a lot about the families but you wonder if there isn't
neglect and abuse there. I don't think I realized I was actually

drawing on my students as I wrote this but I can think of a couple of kids who could be Roberts. Interesting."

"Writers draw on whatever experience they have. The skill in writing fiction is learning to put yourself in the situation you've created for your characters and imagining what it would feel like based on things that have happened to you. I think you're doing that marvellously well, here. Your pictures are very rich. Keep on writing."

"I'm worried I won't be able to finish before Friday."

"That's OK. We'll find a place to stop so you can have something to contribute to our anthology but don't worry about stopping yet. What you're writing is very strong. It may not need much revising. Just keep writing and see how far you can get. Have you any idea where you want to go next?"

"I think I want to pick up after the stink-bomb episode and work out what happens to Robert after he's expelled from school."

"That's a good idea."

"I think I can write about how Robert feels when he realizes he has to tell his parents, especially his father, what's happened."

"Go ahead."

As teacher, I could make all kinds of suggestions about how Norma might shape her story but I hold back. The elements she's written so far are very powerful. She doesn't need my help with this unfolding narrative. She really just needs my encouragement to keep writing.

Later in the afternoon as I move from group to group I happen to overhear an interesting conversation between Maggie, Bruce, Norma, and Earl.

"...this is your short story—you've written all of this?" Earl asks in amazement.

"I don't think I know now what a short story really is," Bruce replies. "I suddenly realized..."

"You wrote all of this," Maggie comments.

"This is the one about your mum?" Norma asks.

"But now it's no longer entirely true. I have changed the point of view. It's no longer me talking, it's my sister, and it's more about relationships between children and mothers."

"What are these breaks here?" Earl asks. "I know I haven't read it..."

"Those were points when I wondered if I should have stopped."

"Like chapters?"

"Well, sort of...I guess...it's a different episode. It starts out very much my sister and my mother, but there's a lot I've made up..."

"It's not true, you mean?" Earl wonders.

"After sharing the bit I started with last week I had a number of ideas about how the story could unfold. They weren't all my ideas—various people made suggestions. That's when I began to see the possibility of going beyond the actual facts."

A nice lesson on the relationship between personal narrative and fiction going on here.

"You wrote that incident first about your mother then you thought about other things to write?" Maggie inquires.

"Yes. The story is about family relationships—but it's no longer **my** family. It's a fictionalized family. In fact, taking the point of view of my sister helped me do that," Bruce says.

Interesting how the shift in perspective has helped Bruce go beyond the specific details of the event and begin creating a fictional account.

"But how could you take the point of view of your sister?" Earl asks.

"The very best fiction captures some kind of universality about the human experience, doesn't it," Norma reflects. "You're taking an experience you've had and you're stepping back. It doesn't all have to be true, you can elaborate this detail or emphasize some other things. What you're doing is trying to evoke for me as reader the same feelings you had when you were experiencing this whole thing with your mother."

This learning from each other is at the heart of an enterprise-based curriculum.

"That's what I'd like to be able to do with my story," says Maggie, "but I just don't seem able to step aside. You've really worked at it."

"Yes."

"You can tell."

"Now did it all come out at once or did you go back and forth with it?" Maggie asks.

Now Maggie is looking for some strategies for herself.

"By 'all coming out' do you mean..."

"Did you sit down and just write it?"

"Well, I got going at the end of the week and worked at it a lot over the weekend. It was interesting, because there were times when I thought I would never be able to make connections, and yet when I just let myself write, developments came from the writing itself. One of the things I did was read a lot—I reread Alice Munro's book and looked at Alistair MacLeod."

"The reading helps, doesn't it," says Norma.

"It does in some ways."

"How does it help?" asks Earl.

I notice how Earl pushes for clarification.

"I learned a lot about attention to small details...description," Bruce says.

"Have you reread the complete piece?" Maggie asks.

"Once, but not really to sit down and look at it as a reader and I should."

"Well, maybe you're just tired, after getting it all out, I mean," Maggie comments.

"There's another thing—with this writing it's been like getting all this garbage out of the way and hoping I'm writing my way into something and finally on the third page I thought, 'Oh yeah, this is where I should start!' I kept thinking I've got to somehow expand it a lot more. I don't know whether I've created something worthwhile or not."

"You're not feeling terrific about this?" Earl asks surprised.

"I think Maggie's probably right—I need some time to detach myself from what I've written, read it as a reader instead of a writer and say 'OK, this is working...'"

Time to join them. By eavesdropping, I've learned that Bruce has had a lot of useful experiences while doing this writing. And the others, I hope, will have been helped to take similar risks as a result of Bruce's experience and his insight into what he's discovered.

Our full class meeting that afternoon is brief. I remind people to read, or reread, Murray's chapter on clarifying and to look again at the third read I did on my poem in preparation for tomorrow.

Not everyone is ready for a third read but our deadline is fast approaching. If I had more time, I'd let the need for clarity evolve on its own. But we have just three days left to the Institute. I'm now feeling a lot of pressure to help everyone to closure. So I opt for the lesson, ready or not.

During the evening as I write my reflection/letter to the class, I find myself raising the fluency—clarity—correctness issue. We're at a point where clarity and correctness are becoming our focus and I want the teachers to think about what's involved in moving beyond fluency.

Mayher (in **Uncommon Sense**) raises an important issue:

> The commonsense approach to writing instruction has been based on an implicit developmental model which moves from
>
> **correctness** (in the sense of conformity to the conventions and rules of standard written English—SWE) to
>
> **clarity** (in the sense of making one's meaning as transparent as possible...) to
>
> **fluency** (in the sense of talented performance—a level of achievement that the commonsense position believes only those born with special talents are likely to achieve).

The uncommonsense position, in effect, turns this developmental model on its head by arguing that development should proceed from:

> **fluency** (in the more expansive sense of a feeling of comfort, confidence, and control of the writing process...) to
>
> **clarity** (in the sense that through the struggle, and the nearly inevitable internal and external revisions that it involves, writers can become clearer about what they mean...) to
>
> **correctness** (in much the same meaning as in commonsense, but with the recognition that the conventions of SWE are means to the end of meaningful dialogue, not ends to be sought in themselves, and they are there properly subordinate to and supportive of the processes of meaning making. [p. 229]

I raise this issue because this notion of **fluency — clarity — correctness** has been very helpful to me when it comes to making decisions about how to react during a writing/reading conversation. That is, I try to decide whether the writer is needing experience with just getting ideas on paper—fluency. If that's the case, then my conversation is directed toward helping them talk about their ideas and encouraging them to **just try**. If I think the writing has begun to flow, then I may raise some questions about the coherence of the writing, the connectedness of the story or argument. When there is a beginning, middle, and end, then it may become useful to talk about conventions: pointing out ways of formatting, or using particular punctuation (in the middle of a sentence an ellipsis is three dots...; at the end of a sentence it's four....). Here's where teachable moments come into play, I think, most effectively. "How do I make the writing talk?" asks a child, and I show her there and then.

In any given class there will be people working to achieve fluency, others able to focus on clarity, and a few ready to tackle correctness. Within a given piece of writing a writer often starts out struggling for fluency, working toward clarity, and finally dealing with correctness. And what's interesting about this progression, is that as a teacher I find I move from a relatively open kind of questioning and support for helping fluency along to a quite directive kind of teaching when correctness comes into play. Of course, it's always a judgement call: is this writer sufficiently in control of the writing to be able to think about clarity? Or do I just reflect back the movies of my mind as a way of sustaining the writing and the writer? As our writing has moved along, I'm sure you've noticed that I've become more directive. In what ways has that been of help to you? How has it interfered? How has it helped you think about teaching writing with your own students?

Another day gone. What did I learn today, I wonder? Our conversation about children's books tied in more closely with some of our other conversations than I expected. I really didn't have to take as strong a lead as I thought I might have to. People are looking for connections more independently.

While I'm sensing a good deal of pressure to start tying ends together, I was able to leave room for people to work at what-ever they felt they needed to. I can remember how uncomfortable I used to feel when people would get on with their own agendas and I didn't have anything teacherish to do. I used to feel quite useless. Our ongoing **Writing Conversations** list has alleviated quite a lot of that. The list has kept me involved and out of people's hair; there's always someone who wants to talk about something. Although I make rounds periodi-

> Your revealing your discomfort when people would get on with their own agendas and you didn't have anything teacherish to do helped me realize one source of discomfort I've been feeling. Sometimes I get so busy I end up spinning my wheels and it's difficult to see the forest for the trees. Sometimes it's simply a comfort to learn you're not the only one with those feelings. Somehow that makes them more acceptable and therefore easier to deal with rather than deny.
>
> Lynn Sawyer

cally to see what's going on and to interject questions if they seem warranted, I'm learning to stand back.

There are occasions, however, when I'm not successful at holding in, when I can't let students get lost and sort out their own problems themselves.

One unfortunate incident occurred in my curriculum implementation class last winter. After several weeks of indecision most of the teachers had finally decided upon some aspect of their own teaching to explore. Becky, however, was fighting my attempts to engage her in reflective writing. She was determined to read for tips.

Years of experience have shown me tips don't affect teachers' instructional practices, so I argued with Becky, trying to get her to write a few critical incidents for the next class. Her arms folded firmly across her chest informed me of the futility of my efforts and I backed off.

After class I wrote in my own journal:

> Becky poses an interesting dilemma. Still comfortable
> with her commonsense beliefs—not really willing to
> look at herself critically. Is it because if she documents
> her efforts she will have to face her contradictions? I
> realize I was pushing her too hard this evening. Was that
> because time is flying and her lack of commitment is
> holding up the rest of the class? The others have done
> enough now so that working groups are forming. What
> do I do about Becky? If I leave her on her own she
> won't have the social learning experience I'm trying to
> create. It'll be me pushing her—not the others, and there
> will be no one for her to interact with during class. From
> here on in the teachers will be talking to one another
> about their research. Perhaps I should just let her become
> isolated and then help her confront the problem.

I wasn't comfortable, however, leaving Becky isolated. Instead of holding in and letting her flounder, I took control. The following class I teamed Becky up with two other people who were also struggling. I offered the three of them some suggestions to help them examine their teaching. Becky resisted. I explained why writing was essential for examining her practices and assumptions. She flatly refused—she'd tried keeping a journal before and it had been useless. We tangled once more when I finally insisted she record a few classroom observations.

In the end Becky complied, but my coercion brought disengagement. Yes, she produced a few critical incidents, but she didn't really learn from them. From then on she went through the motions, but I could tell, from her scanty weekly reflections, she had opted out. In her final reflection she was very angry; she attacked me and my teaching. In large measure Becky was right. By not holding in, by not giving her a chance to learn from her own mistakes, I had robbed her of an opportunity to confront her beliefs and grow as a teacher.

The next couple of days should be a challenge. I'd judge that only about half of the writing pieces are anywhere near clarity. I'm going to have to intervene in some of the more slowly evolving pieces—against my better judgement, though. I really have to think about how the third read lesson can involve those who are farther along instructing the others.

Time is always a problem. An enterprise-based curriculum requires an open agenda, but at some point there have to be deadlines and enterprises need to be brought to closure. With people engaged in different experiences and moving at different speeds, establishing closure is sometimes difficult. I find myself pushing a few, who are not yet ready, to be finished.

Teachable Moments 11 ❖

Teachable Moment

"How can I?"
    I ask.
"Watch me,"
    she said.
"Do I want to?"
    I ask.
"It's your choice,"
    she said.
"Will it work?"
    I ask.
"Try it,"
    she said.
"Will I make a mistake?"
    I ask.
"You might,"
    she said.
"Why take the risk?"
    I ask.
"Why not?"
    she said.

Marion Anderson

"What's the difference between the teacher standing up and doing a telling lesson and teachable moments?" I was asked not long ago.

The differences are these, I think. Transmission teaching takes little notice of what students want to know. In a traditional teaching-by-telling situation the course of study is planned and the instruction organized by the teacher or some outside agency without consulting the learners involved. In a transmission situation students are given information, factual or strategic, whether they can use it or not, whether it makes sense to individual learners at that particular time or not.

A teachable moment could well involve teaching by telling, in fact, it often does. One difference, however, is that information is volunteered in response to what students are actually doing; questions are asked or suggestions are made to those particular individuals for whom they are likely to prove immediately helpful. Letting go and holding in don't mean backing away from teaching altogether.

Another difference is that information can come from sources other than the teacher or the textbook. As a teacher my response to a teachable moment may be to refrain from doing the telling myself and to suggest a resource instead. Students are certainly capable of giving one another relevant information when it's needed or when it's apropos. Books and other printed sources are available to provide useful input. Artifacts themselves are teachers. Whenever I do a kite-making workshop, I make sure I have kites in various stages of assembly on hand. That way, people can find out for themselves how to do something. In the same way, during a writing workshop I make sure lots of different kinds of published writing are around.

I also respond to a teachable moment, not by telling how to do something but by setting up an experience which will let learners discover for themselves what does and doesn't work in a particular situation. Regularly, I respond **'Just try'** to students' questions. I also frequently answer requests for information with another question: 'How could you find out about that?' If the student doesn't know, and I'm not sure myself, I often respond, 'Let's find out.'

A crucial component of teaching is the talk about 'what's going on here?', 'what are we learning from what we're doing?' It's the conversation about the connections people are making, about their discoveries, that makes the learning conscious. Sharing individual discoveries makes that information and those strategies potentially available to anyone else for whom it could be relevant.

I have experienced teachable moments which have legitimately included the entire class. My attempts at foreshadowing during the early part of the institute were directed at the entire class with me maintaining a watchful eye in order to discover who was making connections and who wasn't. I structured those whole class lessons primarily to offer strategic information; that is, they were invitations to try out a particular way of working.

I rely heavily on whole group instruction at the beginning of a course when I don't know much about my students and they don't know much about me. As our relationship builds and we begin trusting one another, however, I quickly shift what I do, providing input when people request it or when I perceive opportunities to help them shape their learning experience.

The thing about teachable moment lessons is that they're usually brief. A single comment, a question, a metaphor, a story

I have trouble with this teachable moment stuff. I guess because it's called 'teachable' and because you discuss it as involving a decision on your part, I feel like teachable moments are about you; yet I feel that the experimenting that goes on is about everyone. Indeed, so do you.

Let's try it this way—you say that every teachable moment is an experiment and I read 'for the teacher.' Then you tell me about experiments that I think are for everyone but feel like you're talking about you. Then you say that teachable moments constitute the primary learning vehicle—which means for everyone. How can the moments in which you consciously make teaching decisions be learning vehicles for everyone else? How can you even assume they are? Aren't critical incidents moments that learners are self-consciously learning? Because you identify the time as 'teachable' doesn't necessarily mean that's when learning occurs.

Diane Stephens

can all serve to make a point, to help a student or a group of students see a connection. These lessons aren't lengthy teacher lectures. They don't always occur at the beginning of an activity and I can't prepare for most of them. **Teachable moments are unpredictable.** I just have to be alert so I can capitalize on opportunities when they present themselves.

The best teachable moment lessons are often inadvertent ones —when someone recognizes a way of proceeding for themselves in what someone else is doing. As a teacher I have no control over those moments, but I do need to legitimize them.

Cheating is a deeply ingrained taboo. Taking good ideas where you find them makes many people, particularly teachers, nervous. Yet most of my best learning has occurred either when I've watched other people do things I'm interested in and talked to them about what they're doing, or they've offered suggestions in response to problems I'm trying to solve.

Furthermore, teachable moments are two-way streets. Every time I offer a support, ask a question, or share a strategy I'm learning, too. I learn more about the students and about my teaching. **Every teachable moment is an experiment.**

Schön (1983) contends reflection-in-action necessarily involves experimentation. For the practitioner

> to experiment is to act in order to see what the action leads to. The most fundamental experimental question is, "What if?" (p. 145)

Schön details several kinds of experiments in which we practitioners engage:
exploratory experiments—when action is taken to see what follows, without accompanying predictions or expectations.

Exploratory experiment is the probing, playful activity by which we get a feel for things. It succeeds when it leads to the discovery of something there (p. 145);

move-testing experiments—*when we take action in order to produce an intended change.*

Any deliberate action undertaken with an end in mind is, in this sense, an experiment. ...the test...is not only Do you get what you intend? but Do you like what you get? (p.146);

hypothesis testing—*when we try to produce conditions that disconfirm a number of competing hypotheses*

...[The practitioner] puts forward hypotheses and, within the limits of the constraining features of the practice context, tries to discriminate among them—taking as disconfirmation of a hypothesis the failure to get the consequences predicted from it (p.147).

As Schön explains

When the practitioner reflects-in-action in a [situation] he perceives as unique, paying attention to phenomena and surfacing his intuitive understanding of them, **his experimenting is at once exploratory, move-testing, and hypothesis testing. The three functions are fulfilled by the very same actions** [emphasis mine] (p.147.) ...The inquirer's relation to this situation is **transactional**. He shapes the situation, but in conversation with it, so that his own models and appreciations are also shaped by the situation....He understands the situation by trying to change it, and considers the resulting changes not as a defect of experimental method but as the essence of its success (p.151).

Experimenting can occur in many different kinds of teaching situations, but they constitute the primary learning vehicle in an enterprise-based classroom. It's precisely by responding to the immediate problems and questions that present themselves in the on-going situation that extends both the students' repertoire of strategies and my understanding of what's happening.

Wednesday morning we launch small group discussions about Don Murray's idea of a third read. I engage in conversation with first one group, then another, alert for potential teachable moments.

The following conversation ensues with Lorna, Earl, Diane, Norma, Leslie and Helen.

"A lot of what Murray describes as doing a first and second read have been happening during our conversations about writing with you and with one another, it seems to me," Norma asserts.

"What do you mean?" I ask her.

"Take his question 'Does the reader need more information?' I've been getting feedback on that from readers directly. 'Does the writing go off on tangents that can be cut out?' Same thing. Having other people read my story and then talking to them about it has helped me focus on a lot of the same concerns Murray raises."

" 'What does this piece of writing mean?' " quotes Helen. " 'Is it too long or too short?' I've been working that kind of stuff out as my writing has unfolded."

"The same with the second read questions: 'Does the lead catch the reader in three seconds or less? Does the draft show as well as tell?' In the conversations I've been having we've discussed a lot of those questions as we've gone along," Lorna adds.

"I get the feeling from Murray's chapter that you're only supposed to engage in these revising and editing processes after you've a finished piece of writing. While here in the Institute, you've been encouraging us to recast and rework as we've gone along," observes Earl.

"It's not exactly a matter of one or the other, I don't think," I reply. "Murray is a very experienced writer and I imagine he is generally able to push through to a draft quickly without much input from anyone else. I'm not so skilled and I find I can use help at various points along the way. In fact, I'm more receptive to feedback when I know the writing is still unfolding than when I feel some kind of closure has occurred. Personally, I find it very hard to re-work a piece of writing once it seems finished. I think whether the writer attempts a complete draft before looking at a piece of writing or solicits input along the way depends on the piece and the circumstances under which it is being written. I do draft some things completely before looking for input; with other stuff I ask for reaction all the way along."

> Is this what Follow Me! is about? That I demonstrate a whole for which I have already thought about the parts so that I can help people with the parts within the whole; I can facilitate their learning of the whole and the parts?
>
> Diane Stephens

A teachable moment. Earl's question about differences between Murray's way of working toward clarity and

mine allows me to describe my experiences as a
writer. I can let people see the range of strategies I use
and help them think about whether they want to try
any of them.

"Now, as a teacher I'm trying to help you sustain your writing. So sometimes I've suggested people keep moving and not think about whether the organization or the details are the way you want them until later; other times, I've sensed you might find it more useful to stop and rework a portion before carrying on. A judgement call—but both strategies are intended to keep your writing moving."

"I know I found it useful not to worry about an opening until I was well underway," Diane comments. "Before, I always agonized over how to start. You helped me see I could start anywhere and once I had some writing a beginning would emerge. It did. It really surprised me how it happened. It sneaked up on me and, quite unexpectedly, as I was rereading what I'd done, I suddenly had an idea for how to start the piece. I didn't have an ending at that point. What I found was that once I knew how the story began I found it easier writing the rest. But the amazing thing is I couldn't have written the beginning at the beginning when I was just starting to write. I had to write four or five pages before I sensed where I was going."

"I went through the same thing," Earl says.

"I did, too," says Norma.

"That's why I encouraged you to just start. That happens regularly in my own writing and I've learned just to write and then work with what I have later. Generally beginnings come once I have a sense of what I'm writing about. I shared with you how that happened with my poem, right?" I remark.

Diane's remarks about what she's learned about
writing from this writing experience puts a voice to
what some of the others have experienced as well. I'm
trying to validate the experience they've had.

"So is anyone ready to tackle a third read here?" I ask.

An opportunity for some joint experimentation. My
intention is to help one member of the group take a
close, detached look at his or her piece so the others
can see how to handle their own writing.

There's silence for a moment and I wait, glancing
from face to face, not trying to pressure any individual
but to judge whether anyone in the group is secure
enough to have his or her writing examined in public.

Lorna moves to retrieve her writing from her briefcase. "I think my story about 'Bubba's Birthday' is done. I mean, I think I now have a beginning, a middle, and an end. So I guess I'm ready to look at it carefully."

"Have you tried a third read yourself yet?"

"No, I read Murray's chapter but I didn't try it out on my own story."

"Would it be all right if we did a third read here as a group?"

I watch her closely as she responds. I don't want to put her in too stressful a situation.

"I think so. I'm curious to see what happens with editing."

I suggest Lorna read her story to us. She does.

I wait for the others in the group to say something. No responses. People are waiting for me to react.

"What are we trying to do here?"

My question turns the conversation back to them.

"Murray sure has a long checklist for a third read," Earl remarks.

"What are some questions he asks?"

"Is the piece built on the subject-verb-object sentence?" reads Leslie.

"What does he mean?" Earl questions.

"Can anyone answer Earl?"

"Murray believes strong writing is based on active rather than passive sentences," Norma explains. She leans to her left to read from the paper in front of Lorna, "'It was Friday and Rachael decided to stop at her Bubba's house on her way home from school.' It's an active sentence—subject-verb-object. 'Rachael stopped at Bubba's house.' I'm not sure I can turn it into a passive. Here let me try: 'On Friday, Bubba's house was visited by Rachael on her way home from school.' God, that's awkward," she laughs. She continues reading, "Bubba's house was just about half way between the school and her house so Rachael often visited."

"Let's try something here," I interject. "Lorna, why don't you read us the first paragraph or two and we'll copy them down as you read. Then we can look at the writing in pairs."

Murray includes among his third read questions:

> Is each word the right word?
> Is each word the simplest word?
> Have unnecessary adverbs been eliminated?
> Are the tenses consistent?

It's often hard to answer those questions about your own writing; it's easier with someone else's.

If this were my piece, I'd take a red or green or purple pen (something that shows brightly on the

*page) and begin marking it up. Quite likely I wouldn't
follow Murray's questions. I'd read for how the
writing feels, for its flow and rhythm, for the presence
and absence of details. I'm about to suggest we work
in pairs on these couple of paragraphs to see what
people come up with.*
Lorna reads to us:

It was Friday and Rachael decided to stop at her
Bubba's house on her way home from school. Bubba's
house was just about half way between the school and
her house so Rachael often visited. Today was special. It
was Rachael's seventh birthday and Bubba was baking
bread for the dinner at Rachael's house that evening.

When Rachael arrived, Bubba was busy baking
bread. Rachael often helped her Bubba make bread for
the Friday night dinner. This week they were taking
particular care with the preparations because the whole
family would be there. Mum and Dad, Rachael's older
sister Marta and her brother David. Her Aunt Golda and
Uncle Ben, their children Mark, Michael, and Sara, her
Aunt Mim and Uncle Jack were all coming. And so, of
course, was her Bubba Brina.

*If this had been a prepared lesson, rather than a
teachable moment, I would have had some writing of
my own for people to work on. That's one of the
reasons I always write along with the class. I want to
be able to use my writing to discuss strategies,
decision-making about content, and so on. I did that
with my poem and I shared my third read in my
reflection/letter. I can now see it probably would have
been better if I had waited and used my poem to help
the teachers at this point but the poem was pushing
me. It took on a life of its own and I simply had to
follow it along. On the other hand, sharing my third
read in advance has provided people with a glimpse of
what I'm expecting them to do with their own writing.
It won't be such a shock to think about writing all
over a completed draft.*

*Again, had this been a prepared lesson, I might
have been tempted to bring an editing handout or use
an overhead I'd developed in advance. I thought about
both those possibilities last evening but decided to let
the teachable moments look after themselves. The*

*thing I have to be careful about, though, is not
allowing us to trample all over Lorna's text.*

I'm sitting beside Diane. Norma buddies up with Lorna. The
others take partners. I purposely don't move to sit beside Lorna;
I work with Diane, instead.

*I don't want my response to Lorna's writing to carry
more weight than anyone else's. It will anyway, of
course, but I'm trying, nevertheless, to minimize the
authority of my expertise.*

I invite Diane to follow along as I read the two paragraphs
aloud.

"Is there anything that feels awkward to you?" I ask her after
I finish.

"I didn't realize until Lorna was into her story that Bubba
was her grandmother. I think that relationship should be made
clear in the first sentence. She takes her pencil and crosses out
Bubba and writes in 'grandmother's.'

It was Friday and Rachael decided to stop at
her ~~Bubba~~ Grandmother's house on her way home from

school.

"I'd be inclined to change 'decided to stop' to 'stopped.'
We don't need all those words," I add.

It was Friday and Rachael ~~decided to stop~~ stopped at
her ~~Bubba~~ Grandmother's house on her way home from

school.

Together Diane and I puzzle over the two paragraphs,
discussing the whole story, making decisions about wording,
about various deletions, substitutions, and additions. In a couple
of minutes we have:

(It was Friday) ~~and~~ Rachael ~~decided to stop~~ stopped at
her ~~Bubba~~ Grandmother's house on her way home from

school. Bubba's ~~house was~~ lived just about half way

between the school and her house so Rachael

often visited. ~~Today was special. It was~~

~~Rachael's seventh birthday and Bubba was~~

~~baking bread for the dinner at~~

~~Rachael's house that evening.~~

| | Could be deleted since the same information is in the next paragraph. |

It was Friday today and

~~When Rachael arrived,~~ Bubba was busy baking

bread. Rachael ~~often~~ usually helped her ~~Bubba~~ make bread for

the Friday night dinner. This week they were taking

particular care with the preparations because it was Rachael's birthday and the whole

family ~~would be there.~~ was coming to celebrate. ~~Mum and Dad, her older sister~~

~~Marta and her brother David. Her~~	Feels like too many names. Does the family need to be introduced yet?
~~Aunt Golda and Uncle Ben, their~~	
~~children Mark, Michael, and Sara,~~	

~~her Aunt Mim and Uncle Jack were all coming.~~

~~And so, of course, was her Bubba Brina.~~

I draw the group together to discuss what's been happening. *My reason for inviting everyone into this third read is that I find it a great deal easier to function as editor on someone else's writing than on my own. When my own writing is ready for a third read I give it to a few specific friends and colleagues whom I've grown to trust as careful editors. I respect their sense of my writing and their feeling for flow, rhythm, and word choice. So while I do my own third reading, I solicit third (and often fourth) readings from others as well.*

Here I'm trying to help the teachers distance themselves from their own writing so they can begin to see it with a reader's detached eye. We aren't going to do a careful editing on Lorna's entire story, just these few paragraphs. I'm trying to make everyone a little more aware of how picky we need to be as our writing nears completion.

The reason for this is one I alluded to earlier— many teachers locally have become successful at helping their students develop fluency but clarity and correctness have gone by the boards. By engaging people in a third read of their own and their friends' writing I'm inviting them to consider ways of engaging students in a similar scrutiny of writing.

"Let's talk about what we've been doing."

I'm trying to initiate some reflection-in-action—What decisions were we making?

"I felt very uncomfortable working on Lorna's story," says Leslie.

"Say more," I request.

"I was very reluctant to change what she'd written. I mean, it was her writing and I didn't feel I had the right to change anything."

*The ownership issue again—writing as private enterprise; rather than collaborative venture. Fortunately, I've saved the copy-edited manuscript from **Finding Our Own Way**. I remembered last evening to put it among the stuff I needed for today. I hoped there might be an opportunity to show it to people. This feels like the moment to bring it out.*

I pass around several chapters of the copy-edited manuscript so each person can examine one. I point out what the copy editor did with my introduction to the book, pointing out the insertions, deletions, and rearrangements she suggested. I indicate her comments in the margins about questions or suggestions she had. I want them to see how a copy editor functions.

An important by-product of being a publishing writer —I have piles of mess from my own writing projects to show people. It lets teachers see that I have to work at being a writer, just like they do.

"She really did read this carefully, didn't she?" says Leslie. "I can't believe she wrote all over the text the way she did."

"She didn't just deal with spelling and punctuation," notes Earl.

"No, she didn't. She reworked sentences, paragraphs, and queried things we'd said. Here, for example, she wonders about my use of the word 'inservice':

> Au: [that means author] Is 'inservice' a noun that educators use? Or an adjective. If it has become a noun since it was introduced perhaps start off by using 'inservice workshop' to clarify, and then use 'inservice' alone. If it is an adjective, however, it needs to be replaced w/ [that means with] a term like <u>workshop</u> when used as a noun.

I thought about her comment quite carefully and decided in the end to change that first usage to workshop as she suggested."

"This is fascinating," says Norma. "I've never seen a copy-edited manuscript. I had no idea people would actually do this with someone's text."

"As author I get a chance to respond to what the copy editor has done. Generally I find her changes more than acceptable; after all it's her business to know about punctuation, word usage, and so on. Furthermore, the copy editor is an outsider so she's able to read my text with detachment. Her questions alert me to possible confusion about what I've written. There are times when I disagree and then I take a stand—times when I mean what I've said in the way I've said it; then I override what the copy editor has done."

"There are a lot of other marks I don't recognize," says Helen.

"Those are instructions to the typesetter about print style and size, spacing, indenting, and so on.

> Recently, I've been avoiding what I call butting into the learning experience. 'Respect the learner's vulnerability, learning preferences and space' have been my watchwords. However, in my fear of violating the learner's space have I merely demonstrated isolation rather than collaboration, and lack of teacher interest? Have I written myself too far out of the script?
>
> Pat Kidd

"So what you're showing us here is that an outsider can see confusion in a piece of writing more easily than the writer can," says Norma.

"I'm trying to help you see how input from other people can help us attend to clarity and correctness. Here's where writing becomes really collaborative, I think."

"But what about ownership?" Earl wants to know.

"That notion is a very misleading one, I believe. It lures us to conceptualize writing as a solitary activity. I think there is another idea that's more useful—I mean, as author I have a responsibility to make my writing as clear and as conventional as I can but I don't have to do it all by myself. I'm free to call upon anyone I want to help me make decisions about my text. The copy editor, among others, puts in her two cents."

I'm raising a point here that has been fascinating me of late. It's best articulated by Sharon Crowley (1989) in her short but wonderfully concise **A Teacher's Introduction to Deconstruction.** *Crowley contends:*

> ... a deconstructive analysis undermines the notion that the composing process begins with an originating author (p.31).

Crowley is attacking what she refers to as the fiction of authorial sovereignty. *She explains:*

> The fiction of authorial sovereignty is lent enormous force by the power relationship that is inherent in all writing, when

seen from the writer's point of view. The solitude that often accompanies the act of writing seduces writers into believing that they are engaged in individual acts of creation; it is all too easy to forget, while writing, that one's language belongs to a community of speakers and writers, that one has begun writing in order to reach (absent) readers, and that one's 'innovative ideas' have long textual histories behind them, histories which contain many many voices (p. 35)....

...to center a writing pedagogy on authors, rather than on readers and the common language of the community, is to insert an attitude into the composing act that misunderstands its focus (p. 35)....

...writing is communal, that, as Michael Ryan puts it, "writing can belong to anyone; it puts an end to the ownership or self-identical property"...(p.36).

It's precisely the notion of ownership that's keeping teachers from raising clarity and correctness with students. I understand why a number of researchers have argued for children's ownership of their writing—it was to keep us teachers from doing what we've done a lot of: leaving our bleeding red marks all over students' pages. But the notion of ownership undermines the development of students' writing because it leaves it at the level of fluency without helping children, or older writers, tackle the complex business of bringing clarity and correctness to their texts.

"What demonstrations about responsibility rather than ownership am I trying to create for you here?" I ask the group.

"You're trying to make it legitimate for all of us to help each other out with every aspect of the writing," Helen answers. "You're showing how in the real world of publishing other people become involved with an author's text and I suppose you're saying we need to learn how to do that for one another."

"I'm trying to think about how this would come into play with my first graders," reflects Lorna. "I suppose in lots of ways it's happening already but I just didn't see it that way. I mean, the kids are always helping each other spontaneously. If anything, I've been guilty of trying to stop their collaboration sometimes. I know I've insisted they work on their writing alone. I guess I can see how I need to think about this collaboration business some more."

"You've also been trying to help us see that the boundaries between fluency, clarity, and correctness are really quite blurred," Norma says. "I can see as a resource teacher, I might be trying to encourage fluency for a number of the kids, but on specific occasions I might want to nudge a couple of them toward clarity or further. And I could do that by having them help each other out more."

"Yes, I think something you could do that might be quite useful would be to juxtapose the published books the kids are reading with their own writing to raise questions about writing conventions and then to encourage them to work together on making their own writing more conventional," I reply.

"What you're saying is I have to keep the reading connection in mind here as well," Norma returns.

"Yes, published authors are important collaborators. Can we get back to Lorna's opening paragraphs?"

"Well, when I read what was on the page I was aware that I didn't know who Bubba was at first, that she was the grandmother. As I listened it became clear who Bubba was. So I substituted 'grandmother' in the first line," says Diane.

"I didn't make a change there, but I wasn't sure who Bubba was either," Earl agrees.

"We found ourselves overtaken by all the names in the second paragraph. We wondered about introducing all of these people in a lump like that," Helen says.

We share questions, react to specific words, and discuss the opening of Lorna's story. I keep the conversation brief—we're only talking about a couple of paragraphs, after all, and all Lorna really needs is a few queries to get her thinking about the detail of her text.

"Now, let me suggest you get together in pairs and do a careful copy-edit on one another's writing. You might find it helpful to keep Murray's third read list close by; you might not. Just try and see what you learn."

My suggestion is, I know, premature for a number of people, but our deadline is fast approaching and I would like people to make some effort at copy editing their work before we're finished.

I turn to Lorna and ask if she'd like to talk with me about "Bubba's Birthday."

"No," she replies. "I can see some things I want to look at. I want to have a try doing this third read with Norma right now. I'll talk to you after we've had a go, OK?"

"Fine."

There were several important concerns raised in that conversation: the issue of ownership vs responsibility and the role of copy editing were two. I have no way

*of knowing who connected with what, but I could see
faces were attentive and they certainly were asking
significant questions.*

By this time the other groups have disbanded. I notice
people in twos and threes engaged in conversation in the
classroom and the hallway. As I pass, I hear them discussing
one another's writing. Sometimes a comment draws me in.
Other times I listen for a bit, then move on. I track down people
on the **Writing Conversations** list and we chat.

*I look for opportunities to help people attempt a third
read. I encourage the teachers to third read for one
another.*

Lorna finds me about an hour later. She hands me her story;
I place it on the table between us.

"Talk to me about what you've learned," I prompt her.
"How did you feel when I asked the group to work on your
opening paragraphs?"

"I was self-conscious at first, but once I started talking with
Norma I got caught up in our conversation and forgot about
feeling uncomfortable."

"Did your conversation help you?"

"She had some of the same questions people raised—about
Bubba's relationship needing to be made clear at the start, stuff
like that."

"What did you learn when you carried on with her?"

"The questions and suggestions on those two paragraphs got
us going. I was able to stand back from the writing and could
see it better as a detached reader might."

"How do you feel about your story now?"

"It's hard to tell, there's so much writing all over it."

"When I'm at that point I return to the computer, make
changes to the text then print out a clean copy. I find I have to
play between the computer screen and hard copy. I do some of
the third read directly on the computer although I usually lose the
sense of how things fit together after a couple of pages so I have
to work on a printout with a bright colored pen as well. I'd be
glad to read 'Bubba's Birthday' when you're ready."

*I could have asked Lorna what she was going to do
next. Instead, I share my own working strategies with
her. I'm not saying that's how she should continue
herself; I'm simply suggesting an option.*

After lunch, Lorna returns with a fresh printout:

Rachael stopped at her grandmother's house on her way home from school. Bubba lived about half way between the school and her house so Rachael often visited her.

It was Friday today and Bubba was busy baking bread. Rachael usually helped her make bread for Friday night dinner. This week they were taking particular care because it was Rachael's birthday and the whole family was coming to Rachael's to celebrate.

By the time Rachael arrived at Bubba's house, Bubba was just about ready to shape the loaves. This was the part of bread-making Rachael liked best. She always got to makes some small loaves herself.

Rachael pulled up the old wooden step stool beside the kitchen table. Bubba was so short she had to use the stool whenever she wanted to reach for anything higher than the first shelf. The stool had once been painted bright blue but years of use had worn most of the paint off the two steps and all that remained were some faded flower patterns on one side. Rachael used the stool so she could reach the table.

Bubba had sprinkled the top of the table with flour so the dough wouldn't stick. She dumped out the dough from the bowl where it had been rising. She divided it into four large lumps. She took one of the lumps and cut a small piece for Rachael.

Rachael watched as Bubba kneaded the dough. She pushed down on it slowly, spreading the dough thinner. Then she folded the dough in two and pushed again. She pushed and folded, pushed and folded, again and again. Rachael did the same thing with her lump of dough.

"The bread today is special," said Bubba. "It's birthday bread. I can remember when you were born. I came to stay with Marta and David while your Mother went to the hospital. We waited all afternoon to hear from your Dad. I can remember how excited we were when he called late that night with the news."

"What was I like when I was a baby?" asked Rachael....

"That's coming along very well. How do you feel about it?" I ask.

"It feels more together," she replies.

"It definitely reads more smoothly," I affirm. "Have you done the whole piece yet?"

"No, just this much, so far. I wanted to show it to you to see what you thought."

"Have you shown it to some of the others?"

I don't want to be her only source of feedback.

"Yes, Norma said she liked the way it was shaping up."

"I like what you've done, too. Carry on, then. Let's talk about it when you're finished editing."

Lorna departs and I visit with others. The place is populated by people in twos and threes helping one another with a third read, dealing with issues of clarity and correctness; more conversation about theoretical issues; further discussion of learning and teaching.

*Peters and Waterman (1982) in their book **In Search of Excellence** talk about 'management by wandering around.' I teach by wandering around.*

> ..."management by wandering around." That's how you find out whether you're on track and heading at the right speed and in the right direction....By wandering around I literally mean moving around and talking to people. It's all done on a very informal and spontaneous basis, but it's important in the course of time to cover the whole territory. You start out by being accessible and approachable, but the main thing is to realize you're there to listen (p.289).

I spend part of each day wandering—classroom, hall, library, office. My grade 6's spend a fair bit of time out of the classroom and I wander to keep an eye on what's going on.
Linda Swinwood

Not only am I there to listen, I'm there to respond. I'm constantly watching for potential teachable moments. I deal with our writing-on-the-go. I also ask and respond to questions about the politics of learning and teaching in general, to help people make connections between the professional, theoretical reading they're doing and their own teaching.

The end of the day comes before any of us is ready for it. I intend to invite a discussion about 'structure' in an enterprised-based classroom tomorrow, so I suggest the teachers think about the issue this evening. Perhaps they might jot some reflections on what they've perceived about the structure I've tried creating during the Institute and what questions it raises about their own classrooms.

> *We have just two days remaining in the Institute.*
> *Things are coming together nicely. It's now time to*
> *put instruction on the table so the teachers can think*
> *about it explicitly.*

I remind people to begin thinking, as well, about some kind of final reflection.

"We've actually been collecting data on ourselves since we started out. You need to start thinking about what you've experienced and what it's helped you learn. We need to try finishing our short stories, children's books, poems, and professional articles by Friday noon if possible so we can spend the afternoon writing a final reflection.'

Someone asks what a reflection should be like.

"That's up to you," I reply. "I don't have any prescribed form. What I plan to do myself is jot on an index card a few things which have stood out for me and then compose at the computer."

> *Another joint experimentation response: here's how I*
> *plan to proceed, you're free to find your own way of*
> *tackling the problem.*

I notice a number of people return to the computers to work for a while longer. Exhausted, I go home.

Later, after my usual evening walk with Sumitra, I relax and read journals. There are several interesting responses to the fluency—clarity—correctness issue.

Leslie has written:

> This is where so many misconceptions about whole
> language come in—parents, and some teachers, believe
> that the whole process starts and ends with fluency.
> Clarity is of lesser importance, and correctness has gone
> by the by. Keeping these three terms in mind will
> certainly help me offer different types of support and
> direction.

Diane has reflected:

> I have not thought through the role of the teacher in these
> terms. As an inexperienced short story writer, the help
> you've given me at each stage has been significant. Our
> first chat about my story (I think it was after my first
> draft) your questions helped me see what direction my

story might go (several directions, actually). Midway through the process, your suggestion that the story needed a critical issue made me think about what kinds of crisis situations would be appropriate. Finally, when I was ready for some talk on conventions, you were ready with questions as well as expertise.

Norma, too, has made some interesting observations:

Yesterday, we had one conversation about style and another later dealing with fleshing out details. It clearly demonstrated to me that conversations change as the writing progresses. In your journal you asked how what you've done could have interfered with me as a writer. I don't think it has, because by the time I came to you I had exhausted my own resources and both needed and wanted some input. The direction you provided—your suggestion that I should think about describing a couple of incidents to show the reader Robert's struggle—was very helpful. Suddenly I could see how I could pull the whole story together. Had the conversation been at **your** discretion, then the suggestion might have been interfering. This is another very good reason for letting students judge when sign-ups are necessary.

As I read people's response to the fluency—clarity—correctness continuum I make a connection of my own. I write in my reflection/letter:

A connection I made today myself has to do with the relationship between the idea of **fluency—clarity—correctness** and the kind of conversations we're looking for in an author's circle. I think I probably knew that what I wanted from the others in an author's circle was input on clarity but I'd never consciously articulated the connection before. That, then, raises the question of what sorts of conversations are useful for dealing with correctness. It seems to me editorial conversations are likely one-to-one encounters, perhaps done with pencil in hand where people collaborate on a **third read**.

Today I tried to help you set up this kind of situation so you could see how it might work for you. I suppose I want to ask you directly: what have you learned about these various aspects of writing and how do you see yourself applying what you've learned with your students? What kind of support should we offer, how and when? We need to remember there are some first graders who occasionally might be able to deal with correctness matters in particular situations and eleventh graders who are still struggling for fluency.

What else do I want to mention? I guess the issue of curriculum consisting of many interwoven conversations is worth raising here. One of the nice things about this conversation metaphor is how it highlights the fact that books (poems, short stories, films, etc.) can actually talk to each other. It brings a new dimension to the fundamental arguments of a whole language philosophy. That is, it makes it clear that all of these conversations connect (we are dealing with our experiences with language in their entirety). So my journal letter to you may trigger a retrospective look at something you've read, or written, a conversation between you and a particular text creates connections with other texts, a chat about some experience forges new understanding of some previous experience or reading or writing. I guess I've been trying to set things up so that you would be engaging in these many levels of conversation. What surprises have occurred for you in this regard?

Some other thoughts on curriculum. In the teachers' guide to the Maritime Studies textbook: **The Maritimes: Tradition, Challenge & Change** (Peabody, 1987), Gerry Clarke says some interesting things in his introductory essay. He begins by pointing out

Curriculum is controversy;...is problems, issues, questions and felt needs. It is not a book and is very different from an academic discipline, even though books and academic disciplines are often important parts of a curriculum.

Curriculum lives in the political world and is never fixed. ...curriculum has at least **five** levels at which it can be understood: the **ideal,** the **formal,** the **perceived,** the **operational,** and the **experiential**....The experiential curriculum (is) the essential curriculum (p. 10).

While Clarke is talking about social studies, the same is true for language arts curriculum. In Nova Scotia, for example, the **ideal** curriculum consists of the outlines based on current theoretical writings which lead to the **formal** curriculum: the provincial language arts guidelines. The **perceived** curriculum is the one understood by teachers as people talk among themselves, read the provincial guidelines and plan based on the various reading programs in their schools. The **operational** curriculum includes the activities and materials actually used. The **experiential** curriculum is what students come to understand as they engage with the various demonstrations, both intentional and inadvertent, in the classroom. As Clarke says, this experiential curriculum is the essential curriculum. All the rest are merely means to this end.

> Over the last three or four years I have been moving to a holistic approach in my high school classroom. Why? Because I needed change, and I liked the kind of change holistic teaching seemed to signify. But I didn't look any further than that for a reason to implement holistic practices in my classroom. I looked for handy *tips*, the *how-tos*, and then wondered why things didn't always come together. I now realize that under-standing the epistemology is basic to the success of any holistic practice. I have to know why I do what I do if I want to get the maximum out of my teaching.
>
> Patricia Whidden

With the Institute, I start with an ideal curriculum. That is, I identify some theoretical principles to guide me. I ask "What's one thing I'd like people to understand from this experience?" From there I move to an operational curriculum: "How can I help them experience and understand that?" Of course, my operational curriculum is constantly being revised based on what happens in class, on what you write in journals, etc. Other than my Department's general course structure I don't have a formal curriculum to deal with. You have the provincial guidelines as a basis for planning. However, this public document, is only a blueprint; the operational curriculum is still up to each individual teacher.

I'm offering these thoughts on curriculum because I find so many teachers believe they have no power to determine curriculum. What Clarke's scheme makes clear is that students control the curriculum that matters. Ultimately, **it's what happens in students' heads that counts.**

That raises questions about 'holding in' and 'teachable moments' and how these ideas fit together. Holding in doesn't mean not teaching. Choosing to say nothing at a particular moment, to let learners make their own decisions, is a teaching response. The decisions we make at the point of contact with a student, or students, those momentary judgement calls, all represent teachable moments. How does this 'teachable moment' notion help you think about your own teaching differently?

Coming Together 12 ❖

Thursday morning. Two days left. I find it hard to believe we're almost finished. The pace and intensity of this experience has been mind-boggling. I'm exhausted, as is everyone else, but in spite of the fatigue our level of excitement remains very high.

This morning the whole group meets to discuss 'structure.'

The wrap-up is beginning.

"What things have surprised you?" I ask.

Leslie: "That you don't have a day book."

"I do," I reply.

"You don't have the regulation red-covered, spiral-bound plan book," laughs Bruce.

"...made up a week in advance," adds Leslie.

"Why is that?"

"Because you don't know what's going to take place," Leslie answers.

"Now, that's not so; I have a pretty good idea what will happen."

"You don't keep a planbook because you don't want to regulate what's going to happen," Leslie persists.

"You don't know what your focus is going to be until you find out from your learners," says Lorna.

"But I do have a planbook here."

"In your head."

"In your briefcase."

"On the blackboard," I reply.

I hadn't planned this use of the blackboard in advance—it happened quite spontaneously when I initiated the writing sign-up and then used the blackboard later as a notice board to remind people about upcoming conversations. I've been keeping track of what's been happening in my notebook as well, writing reminders about things to remember, critical incidents that have occurred. But Leslie's assertion has made me suddenly realize that the overall evolving plan for the Institute has been happening publicly on the blackboard. Everyone has had a hand in shaping the experience.

"We talked about that yesterday in our group," says Norma. "You wouldn't have had the children's book discussion if you'd written up your lessons ahead of time because there wouldn't have been room for it on your agenda. At first, I didn't realize what you were doing with the blackboard."

"I wasn't aware of it to begin with, either. But I can see there are several kinds of 'lessons' included in my blackboard planbook:

conversations we decided to have as a group,
small group issue-focused discussions,
and individual conversations.

What's interesting for me is how what's on the board represents our evolving agenda. The issues I want discussed are there but your concerns are there, too. What are you laughing about Bruce?"

"But if you fill up your blackboard with things like your planbook and the names of people wanting to conference, where do you put the notes that we're supposed to copy down?"

"You're right, a terrible problem," I shrug and everyone laughs.

Norma continues, "It's also interesting to look at what your use of the blackboard says about you as a teacher. It demonstrates a lot of letting go. The blackboard opens up several invitations to us. It's up to us to decide whether we want to participate or not. The whole sense that there is an ongoing negotiation of curriculum and responsibility to engage is right there on that blackboard. We decide when to put our names down. The fact that our names do get written there sometime is not an option—at some point if you feel some of us are not engaging you may decide to step in—but we have lots of latitude with that responsibility."

"What you've done about the physical environment is very interesting, too," says Leslie. "We spent some time in our group yesterday discussing the fact that the tables invite participation in the small group conversations and yet there is flexibility with the furniture to allow us to form larger groups, like here."

"And we move between large and small group discussions in almost no time at all," comments Lorna.

"Yet it has been important to me that everything has returned to the 'start' arrangement with our four small groups. I can find **my spot** when I arrive in the morning," Barb observes.

"Yes, that predictable orderliness gives me a sense of security," affirms Lorna.

Bruce comments. "Something's just occurred to me. I'm starting to look at the underlying assumptions. When you put people in groups around a table the underlying assumption is that everyone is going to talk. If you seat people separately in rows then the underlying assumption is the teacher is going to talk and everyone else has to be quiet."

"We discussed arranging people in a circle," says Barb, "and how it's important for the teacher to be part of the circle because that way there is no focal point. Even with a semi-circle there's still a focal point. I realize now that when we first walked in we found a particular number of chairs at each table. You put just the right number of chairs around to control the group size, didn't you?"

Interesting. I better comment here. I want people to think about how the physical layout evolves as the experience evolves.

"Um-hmm. Notice, though, that now the number of chairs around each table is flexible."

"But initially," says Barb, "you set the room up a specific way to establish a particular way of working."

"You're right, I did."

"I was struck by your comment the other day," comments Norma, "when I suggested we just pull the chairs around in a circle and you replied 'I think we need the tables because it helps anchor the group.' I hadn't thought about that before."

"'The elbows,' you said," adds Barb, "everyone can get their elbows on the table."

'Elbows on the table' is important. I don't find the same kind of engagement when people are seated in a circle without a table to lean on.

"In a small group, a large table so people can spread out to work; in a large group, tightly packed so engagement is focused," observes Maggie.

"But what about thirty squirmy first graders?" asks Carmina. "I haven't got the furniture to accommodate a single large group, and I can't imagine the kids not poking and nudging one another if they were sitting like this, squished around a single large table."

"I have reservations about high-school students, as well," adds Bruce.

Bruce and Carmina are expressing important 'Yes, but...'s. They're looking to me for some input to help them consider ways of implementing what they've experienced.

"Remember, there's no one magic right way of doing anything in a classroom," I respond. "The issue we're discussing is how the arrangement of furniture can affect interaction and engagement. You have to work with what you have and figure out how to make the most of it."

Here's another opportunity to teach by telling a story.

"I remember one horrendous classroom I used to teach in several years ago. I was just beginning, at that time, to experiment with small group work. The layout of that room and the furniture arrangement presented terrible obstacles. The room had four pillars, strategically located so if we arranged the desks conventionally, aligned in rows parallel with the blackboard wall, people couldn't talk to one another and at least half of them couldn't see the overhead screen because the pillars obstructed their view. With some experimenting I discovered sight lines worked much better if we clustered the desks in groups of four, arranged the clusters diagonally, and positioned the overhead in the corner of the room. That allowed small group conversation and some large group wrap-up. However, the other people who used the room would restore the furniture to its conventional position, so before every class the students and I would have to rearrange it. I learned a lot about the importance of the furniture for establishing a learning context from that experience.

"In any case, you're right, Carmina," I continue. Thirty first grade students might not be able to handle a single large group; if they can't, you have to consider other kinds of groupings that might work better."

"What you're saying is we have to examine our options and think about what we want to have happen," says Bruce. "If things aren't working the way we'd like them to, we have to think about physical arrangements as well as look at what we've asked students to do."

I see here another opportunity to reflect on what's happening here in the Institute.

"Let's talk about the timing of our large group conversation and how that discussion has evolved over the past two weeks."

"In the beginning you used the large group primarily to tie up small group discussion, right?" asks Maggie.

"We didn't actually move from the small group tables," remarks Norma. "I noticed that you led those discussions from different locations in the room, though, so the small groups took on the feel of a single large group."

"That was intentional. My moving around includes everyone in the conversation. When did we first begin meeting in larger groups around one table?" I ask.

"The first time we did it was to discuss the short stories," Maggie answers.

"Talk about the conditions we had in place by then."

"Not everyone attended the discussion," observes Leslie.

"We'd prepared for it by reading some or all of the stories," adds Bruce.

"We chose to be there and had something to contribute," Norma says.

My first-graders have once again pushed me to reappraise some of my expectations. I'd been after them, first thing in the morning, day after day for the first several months of the school year to make their own decisions about what they wanted to read or write about and get on it without further direction from me. Each day I'd tell them time and again that they didn't need me to make these decisions for them. I can hear my myself: 'You know where the paper and pencils are, you don't have to ask to use them.'

However, just after recess, I wanted everyone to gather on the carpet so I could read a story. That worked fine for several months but lately I've been getting resistance from a few children. They've gone straight back to their writing instead of joining the rest of the class on the carpet. I was getting annoyed when I had to wait for them to join us. It took several days before I recognized the inconsistent messages I was sending. That still left me with the problem of what to do when I wanted to read to the whole class. I decided to discuss the problem with the children. They nodded in compliance but the following day some of them still resisted the group gathering. I decided not to make an issue of it. I relinquished power, allowing them to continue writing quietly rather than joining the story group, but I was feeling guilty that they were missing some valuable tidbit from my teacher-led discussion. Kristy proved me wrong.

For the last few days I've been pointing out some of the descriptive language in the books I've been reading. The children have joined in this discussion of what I've been calling picture words. I'd no sooner finished reading to the group when Kristy bounced up to me to share her writing.

"And you turned the talk over to us, you didn't sit at the head of the table and pronounce on what the stories were about, you let us talk," Earl mentions.

"How did that affect your behavior in the group?"

Hanna remarks, "I was interested so my attention didn't wander. I was listening to the conversation and looking for opportunities to contribute. "

"Again, let me kind of reflect here," says Bruce. "You're wanting us to think about a number of things: about timing, about preliminary work, about choice. What you're saying to me is that I have to think about why I want to use a whole class discussion, about my role in the discussion, about work that leads up to the discussion, and so on. I guess I can see how if I had the kids working on stuff that engaged them, they'd be focused on the conversation and contributing to it and disruptive behavior would be less likely to occur."

"Let's come back to some other surprises," I say.

"A lot of the structure here has been very subtle," Penny observes. "Like where you put your reflections on that long table at the back of the room so we could pick them up as we came in the door. Little things you've obviously considered that I've never given a thought to."

> "Look at this word, Ms. Sawyer," Kristy exclaimed, pointing to 'darted' as she read her latest story to me. "The dog darted to the porch." Grinning from ear to ear she continued, "I was trying to use good words like the author of the story you just read to the class!"
>
> Another critical incident!
>
> Lynn Sawyer

"So it all becomes just a part of what we're doing together rather than a big production," says Leslie. In fact, there's so much going on that all of it becomes less of a production and more of an integrated process. We don't have a separate time for doing the professional reading, a block of time for writing, another block of time set aside for conferencing. There's a big agenda with lots of things we know we need to accomplish and large blocks of time in which to accomplish them."

"The thing for me," Penny continues, "is realizing how important the little things are. I did a lot of them intuitively, I never thought about them creating expectations but they're very important, aren't they?"

"You also established a routine," says Maggie. "You opened with small group discussion followed by a brief large group conversation, returning to the small groups, and coming back to the large group. Then on to some independent work."

"Your opening letter established a climate," notes Norma. "It made it clear that this would be a social, collaborative experience."

*We haven't taken the notion of **routine** far enough.*
We need to unpack that one further.

"Come back to routine," I ask. "How did routine evolve?"

"What's interesting is that I'm not sure the same routine evolved for everyone," Hanna says. "For the first couple of days you kept a fairly tight rein on what was going on. Then, once we had some writing underway you stepped back from a lot of whole class routine and let the various writing, reading, talking activities take over. We didn't all have to be engaged in the same thing at the same time. Yet I knew I always had something to do. If I got tired with one thing, with working on my story, I could always stop and read children's books, or look through professional material, respond to your journal or someone else's reflection."

"Even our first day, you were able to launch into a routine because we'd prepared in advance," says Maggie. "I can't do that with my junior highs but I suppose I could begin the second day that way, couldn't I?"

"Let me paraphrase once more," says Bruce. "The situation you've created for us has a number of legitimate activities for us to engage in. You helped get us started with each of them pretty much as a whole group but once we were underway we had lots to do and you kept orchestrating things overall. That means I need to think about my grade 10 English course in a different way. I need to think about what tasks I'd like my students to engage in and how to pace out the week so that we make time both in school and out for working at a number of different things. I wonder if the kids will buy into something like that?"

"They have pretty much with the writing workshop Maggie and I did with the grade 8s last year," says Shelagh. "We set it up so on three days we did reading related things and on three days we did writing."

"But what I've experienced here," Bruce comments, "hasn't been regimented in that way. The whole experience has been highly structured but at the same time much more free flowing. Judith has had close control but I've also had a lot of choice and freedom. What I wonder is if my kids will accept the responsibility to work steadily on their own."

"Have a look at **Through Teachers' Eyes** (Perl & Wilson, 1986). The chapter on Diane Burkhardt's eighth grade class is interesting," I tell him.

> *Once again, an instance of teaching by suggesting resources. I found the chapter useful—given Bruce's concerns, he might, too.*

"This may be a personal question but how do you deal with the administration's regulations about grading? How do you get away with giving us all As?" Carmina asks.

"Nobody has ever questioned me. I send the opening letter I give you to the Dean for her files. Those same letters are in my file in the VP's office. The Department Chair and the Registrar keep seeing my grade lists when I hand them in. No one has ever said anything."

"I'm not joking, I'm asking a serious question...," says Carmina.

"I know you are. It seems I have a reputation as a competent teacher so people let me go my own way. Also, I teach mainly graduate students. Until recently we had only two possible passing grades anyway—A or B, there were no gradations recorded, no B+, for example. (Now we do have a B+ grade, not that that makes much difference.) So my giving all As, or all Bs as I've done on some occasions, hasn't produced a great outcry.

> *This spring an interesting problem did occur: one of the graduating MA students was nominated for an award and was eliminated from the competition because of the B grades she'd received from me*

several winters ago. I wrote to the awards committee
explaining how I'd given Bs to everyone in the class
as a way of creating a pass-fail grade and explained
that this particular student had certainly been an A
student. My letter was dismissed by the Dean—the
student still had Bs on her transcript. The message
was very clear: only A grades count. So it looks as if I
will be awarding A grades from here on in.

"Despite my situation, though, I think my experience can
have relevance for you," I continue. "I believe it's possible to
think about the whole issue of grading and evaluation in a more
open way."

"What you do is fine if everyone engages, but what if you
have people who don't engage?" Shelagh insists.

I notice the tables have turned—they're now asking
the questions.

"That has happened. Not often. I've told you some stories
these past two weeks about non-engagers. I talk with these
students and we try to negotiate a compromise of some kind.
Dealing with non-engagers is never easy but I'd rather err on the
side of expecting the best of people rather than policing
everyone."

"What do you say to those students?" Earl wants to know.

I think the key issue here is finding the
VALUE in evaluation. I'm convinced the
only evaluation of value to students is
self-evaluation. I think it's crucial for
kids to learn to ask themselves: What
have I learned? How have I learned it?
Where do I go from here? and How do I
want to go about it? As far as I'm
concerned answering these questions is
necessary to enhance and guide future
learning.

Linda Swinwood

"I ask people to articulate their
expectations. I explain the situation
I'm trying to create and my
expectations. We discuss what is
usually a clash of theoretical
views. If the behavior is really
obstreperous I have sometimes
resorted to asking 'If you were the
teacher, what would you do with a
student who is behaving the way
you are?' On one occasion, I
actually asked that of a student in
front of the whole class, then invited the class to respond."

"That still begs the question of grades," insists Shelagh. "I
have to hand in numeric grades each term and they have to come
from somewhere, they can't just come from thin air."

This is the issue we've been skirting. I saw no point
in raising the matter of grading until it came up
spontaneously. But we need to think about how to
handle evaluation and grading in a learning-focused,
enterprise-based classroom.

"What would be some ways of negotiating grades with students that would be more in keeping with the philosophical basis of a learning-focused curriculum?" I ask the group.

Grading has to be one of the greatest horrors of the senior high school, especially if your teaching leans toward holistic practices. Everything has to be translated at the end of the school year into that almighty mark which states whether students pass or fail and how they rank in relation to others. And to whom is this so important? Universities, businesses, parents and students who are expecting scholarships. Evaluation ultimately means grading, and in public schools there isn't even the cushion afforded by letter grading. The cold, hard number seems to be all that counts.

Patricia Whidden

"We could have the kids select the two or three best pieces from their writing folder, say, and have them write what they learned from working on them," says Norma.

"I suppose we could then sit down and talk with the kids about what they learned and help them grade themselves," Barb says.

"You mean, I should talk with each first grade child and ask about what she's learned?" Carmina asks. "In math?"

"It's not so far fetched," retorts Hanna. "I find the kids are very aware of what they're learning and there's no reason why they shouldn't have input into what appears on their report cards."

"I think it's very important for students to reflect on, and write about, what they're learning. You might want to read Mike Coughlan's **Language Arts** article from April/88: "Let the Students Show Us What They Know." He describes how he invites his Junior High students to discuss their learning as an integral aspect of his social studies program. Take a look as well at **From Teacher to Teacher: Opening Our Doors** (Halifax County-Bedford District School Board, 1989). Those teachers describe a variety of ways they have tried opening up the grading process. They still face contradictions but they've begun questioning their grading practices."

I have agonized over this issue of grading a great deal. Fundamentally I'm in accord with Frank Smith's contention that grading interferes with learning (Smith, 1988). But I, too, am responsible for submitting grades. I've used a variety of schemes myself to arrive at a grade. I've explored self-evaluation in a way similar to that described by Diane Stephens (in process). She explains how in class, her students work together to establish criteria for evaluating, they then each use those criteria to assess a

grade. If they have been reasonably reflective then Stephens submits the grade they give themselves, otherwise she discusses her perceptions of the student's work and they negotiate a grade.

Stephens also describes how self-evaluation has been used similarly by Jennifer Story a fifth/sixth grade teacher. Story asks her students

> to evaluate their growth at the end of the six-week marking period. Students... address a series of questions, relative to reading, writing and spelling, and then assign a grade. Karen's responses capture the essence of this experience:
>
> 1. How hard have you worked at writing this six weeks?
>   **I think I've done good because I have done a lot of writing. B-**
> 2. Have you been trying new things in your writing?
>   **I done fiction and non-fiction and poems. A+**
> 3. How careful are you about proofreading and editing?
>   **I don't think I do too good on this. C-**
> 4. What was your best piece of writing this six weeks?
>   **Games. It was my first piece of writing and I enjoy it when I read it.**
> 5. What are your goals for the next six weeks?
>   **I'm going to write some more stories. I am also going to look over my writing.**

I had thought about using some kind of self-evaluation process for the Institute. In the end, however, I decided, given the nature of the enterprise I was attempting to get off the ground, to side-step the issue and assign a blanket grade at the outset. I was willing to risk non-engagers and to deal with any problems should they arise. The workshop, I decided, was not about 'grading and evaluation' but writing/reading relationships. If I wasn't going to hand out a ready-made scheme and simply have people apply it, the amount of time we would need to read a range of articles and chapters on evaluation/grading issues in order to establish some basis for thinking about evaluation would be substantial. On this occasion our time, I thought, would be better spent writing, reading, and talking.

My position on grading and evaluation is still highly fluid. For the last many years I've struggled with what to do about grades myself. I'm convinced Smith is right when he contends that enterprises require no

For a long time now my junior high students have had to set criteria and grade their assignments. These long- and short-term evaluations have taken many forms: charts, letters, correspondence, freewrites. All have required much writing and have stressed strengths and goals and yet, I know, with parents and students a numerical mark has overshadowed and consequently devalued the students marvellous written insights. I hope this term I can be brave enough to do as you do—to begin with an B+ or an A and challenge the kids to earn it by devising their own curriculum and showing me and themselves what they've learned.

Pat Kidd

grades. But like the teachers I work with I, too, am responsible for submitting marks. I have no simple solution to the predicament.

It seems to me we need to ask ourselves:

Why are we evaluating?
Who is the feedback for?
What purposes does it serve?

The more I think about it the more I see myself engaged in three different activities all of which educators loosely call evaluation: **responding**, **evaluating**, and **grading**. The first, **responding**, is intended to offer specific feedback to the learners; the second, **evaluating**, helps me as teacher keep track of students' experimentation and progress so I have some sense of what I might offer next; the third, **grading**, is for institutional record-keeping purposes.

A large part of what I do under the evaluation umbrella is respond to students as they're working. **Responding** has a heavy evaluating component—it does inform me as teacher; but the purpose of that kind of information is primarily to provide feedback to students about what and how they're doing. It can take the form of conversation about work in progress and/or work that has been completed. It might involve discussion of tactics for going about specific tasks. It might involve written responses to all sorts of things like journals, reading, writing, science, and/or math logs, and to finished endeavors as well. This responding is not just one way; I make a point of giving students opportunities to respond to me as a learner, as well.

What I want to call **evaluating** is feedback intended for me—the teacher—to help me determine how I might best sustain and support individual learners. I am evaluating while I'm responding. In that context I'm making judgements about what kinds of activities to initiate, what sorts of feedback might *prove helpful, what suggestions I might offer based on what I've read, seen, heard, or overheard. I make notes for myself on index cards, on post-it notes, and directly in my notebook. There's also keeping track of what students do over time—a record of progress which won't, and shouldn't, have any quantification attached to it—based on the notes to myself which are a synopsis of the exchanges which have taken place between me and students, brief descriptions of changes I have perceived in the work they're doing, within individual pieces of writing, across pieces, and so on.*

I have been using several different forms of evaluating. Now I have to learn how to use the information I've been collecting to help my fifth grade students. I keep a writing file for each student which lets me look at their progress over time. What I have to learn is how to use that information to plan my daily lessons. If I see a number of students who could use some attention to paragraphing, then I should form a small group to help them work on it. I think I have known this for a long time but was unable to follow through. I now realize that I have to free myself and the students from my rigid schedule to give them and me room to grow.

Marilyn Hourihan

This keeping track is where devices such as writing folders are handy because with them I can peruse students' work over time and make some hypotheses about their growth as writers, readers, and learners. More important, students can use them themselves to document their own development.

*Finally there is institutional record-keeping—**grading**. Data on students ongoing work can also serve as the basis for some sort of institutional record-keeping. That is, I might take the information that has helped me make instructional decisions and recast it in some way to meet the institution's requirement for a grade. I can use those data for quantifying final student performance in some arbitrary way. But there is no reason why I should be sole arbiter of students' final grades. Students themselves have a right to participate in determining the institutional record.*

If there's been one single positive influence of holistic education it's been the emphasis on what learners CAN do. I find this very hard to translate into grades. My 'A' could be someone else's 'B.' Some teachers in my school swear they never give 'E's, certainly not first term. Others hand them out like 'M & M's. What mixed messages are we sending kids if we spend all term 'process-oriented' and then award letter or numeric grades?

Lynn Moody

Responding, evaluating, and grading—each serves a different audience and purpose; each takes a different form. The real contradiction for me concerns the problem of institutional record-keeping and still retaining some vestige of a transactional, uncommon sense theory of learning. There is, for me, no easy way of grading within a transactional model, since as we begin to understand the complexity of learning, of writing and reading in particular, and their essentially collaborative nature, we recognize the meaninglessness of putting arbitrary numbers on what are fundamentally collaborative efforts.

What intrigues me is how the least important of these evaluative functions, institutional record-keeping, drives so much of what happens in classrooms. So many people find it very difficult to move beyond formal testing as the sole vehicle for serving all three evaluation purposes. But the range of possibilities is limited only by our imaginations. I think it's entirely possible to back away from all formal testing and still meet institutional record keeping requirements. And certainly there should be room for student input into the process as well. Seems to me students have to learn how to judge their own work, to put into words what they've done well and where they might go next. In the end, this is the evaluation that matters most.

> We continue to ask questions about the text, not about the transaction.... We still refuse to understand and accept [the] writing process as a highly idiosyncratic recursive mess of judgements because grading such a mess is impossible and grades, after all, is what school is all about. (John Picone, 1991, p.1.)

We move on to a related issue.

"At first I was uncomfortable with the questions you were asking us," Lorna comments. "When the teacher asks you a question, there's supposed to be a right answer and I felt that moment of panic—I didn't know what answer you wanted."

"You're right," agrees Theresa.

"When I ask you about what you're learning, I'm trying to find out what connections you're making."

"I've also heard you respond 'I don't know, let's find out,' or 'let's talk about it' when someone asks you something. That's a new experience for most of us as learners. Most of the time the teacher knows the answer she wants. As teachers we need to see ourselves as learners, too," says Hanna.

"Your comment brings us back to my agenda in a situation like this. There is content to be learned in this workshop—we're trying to identify the major researchers in the field and what their positions are—but content isn't our sole focus. I'm not interested in you simply knowing that specific content; I'm not grading you on the facts you learn. Instead I'm trying to help you develop an awareness within the context of these various theoretical arguments of how you're learning and what that means for your teaching, and so when I ask you what sense you're making, what I'm trying to find out is what's affecting you so I can make a stab at helping you take the learning further. Until you share what you're learning with me, I don't know where to go next."

A hall of mirrors moment. I'm trying to share the
dilemmas which concern me in my own teaching.

"You mean you try to bring learners into the process more," says Bruce.

"It's not that I try to. It's that I **have** to. Without your contribution to what's going on, I can't teach. Let me tell you about an interesting experience I had in Hawaii. I was doing some extended inservice there and the teachers, predominantly second-generation Japanese women, would talk to one another in small groups but they wouldn't talk to me much, either when I joined a small group or in the group as a whole. It was very frustrating, because without feedback from them I didn't know where to go next. I explained that to the teachers, but their cultural background made it very difficult for them to talk to me—an 'expert' with authority. I was thrown and found it unsettling to teach in that situation. That experience made me think about cultural differences and how they affect our teaching. It forced me to examine my interaction style."

"Something our group discussed," says Leslie, "is how you know where you want us to be. You knew at the beginning what we were capable of doing long before we ever dreamed we were capable of doing it ourselves."

"That has to do with the amount of experience I've had working with teachers. I've learned over the years just how much more people can do than they believe they can. I've been learning how to set up situations so people can push beyond the boundaries they think limit them."

"Well, if you'd told me I was going to write a short story," laughs Earl, "I'd have said you were nuts; but I have to admit I've done it and it was fun too."

*An important issue to comment on. Mayher (1990)
discusses a prevalent myth about learning. Most
people seem to believe*

A real issue for ESL parents, and others, too, who see standard English as the language of power. Most also want the kids to 'work'—to see learning as work.

Linda Swinwood

It may be pleasant once we've learned something...but doing so is likely to be quite tedious, boring, and painful. The commonsense equation seems to be that if it's painful, it's productive; if it's fun, it's trivial and a waste of time (p. 52).

"I should point out that fun isn't a focal aspect of my curriculum. I mean, I'm not going out of my way to make the Institute fun, although you all seem to be enjoying yourselves. Where does the fun emanate from?"

"From ourselves," replies Theresa.

"What's happening that makes you feel a sense of fun?"

"We're doing things we want to be doing, and we're enjoying ourselves doing them," asserts Earl.

"We're also making connections for ourselves. That personal 'ah-ha' is exciting. It's wonderful," says Hanna.

"The interesting thing, I think," reflects Norma, "is learning on my own has never generated this kind of excitement. Working with other people, knowing I can ask for help, share my 'ah-ha's makes me high. The sense of fun comes from the social learning context."

"Let me try and sum up the discussion we've been having," I say. "Seems to me we've been talking our way around a number of myths about whole language, that in whole language you don't evaluate, a whole language classroom is unstructured, in whole language there are no standards, you just deal with process (products don't matter), there's one right way to do whole language, and so on. Are there any others?"

"It's clearer to me now just how structured a whole language classroom has to be," says Diane. "I have to think about the furniture, the activities I initiate, the books and other materials available and where they're located. I have to think about timing and juggling. It's a lot to keep in mind at one time."

"You haven't just been dealing with the process either. It's very clear we've reached the stage where the products matter. Now I'm really learning about conventions and using the computer. I feel a lot of pressure to have a well-written, neatly presented story for the book," says Norma. "I'm also intrigued by how you're helping us meet those challenges."

"I have a better idea how clarity and correctness come into play," says Bruce. "Now I have to think about some possible projects (not too many though, I guess) that would interest my Grade 10s and still fit in with what the other teachers will be doing. We're talking superteacher, here, aren't we?"

"I think superteacher is another myth," I respond. "I agree, trying to implement enterprise-based teaching is difficult in a junior or senior high school. You have to fight against a lot of constraints, like the large number of students, the short duration of classes, the assumptions of the administration and other teachers. It's not impossible if a number of teachers are working together, it becomes more and more of a compromise when fewer teachers are engaged in the process. Although many people think you've got to be a special, intelligent, well-read, ambitious, sensitive, brilliant person to teach from a whole language perspective, the truth is anyone willing to take some risks can begin the exploration. It's much easier for elementary teachers to begin examining their assumptions and questioning their practices, but it's not a pipe-dream for the rest of us."

There's one further myth I want to put on the table. I think it's time to say something here again about it depends.

"I overhear lots of people saying things like: 'In whole language you only work in small groups.' 'You never spell a word for a child.' 'You never tell them what a word is.' 'You never do any grading.' And on and on. Statements like these are what Don Graves calls 'orthodoxies' (Graves, 1984). They embody the belief that there is some magic correct way of delivering instruction. But the reality is there is no one magically right answer to any question about teaching. We've got to remember the answer is always 'It depends.'

"I think I'm really beginning to understand that," says Maggie. "I've been watching how you offer one kind of support to one person and something quite different to another. I thought yesterday when you mentioned in our author's circle about how you saw Debra, Shelagh, and I at different places with regard to fluency, clarity, and correctness that writing is not a neat tidy lock-step activity in the classroom. I have to be able to gauge where students are and to respond to what they're doing on an individual basis."

"I guess I feel insecure in two ways," Bruce comments. "First, I'm not sure I can determine just where a student is functioning, and second I don't feel I know enough to be able to decide what questions to ask."

"Your concerns are legitimate," I respond. "But there's a hidden assumption in what you've said. You're implying that first you have to learn what you need to know before you will be able to work with your students. That's our commonsense transmission view of learning rearing its head. The reality is your understanding will grow as you learn along with your students. It's the questions raised by the teaching itself that will push you to explore the research literature in greater depth; that is, if you can let yourself be a reflective practitioner. That's where the discomfort comes in. As a reflective teacher I know I'll never know enough to deal with the many complex situations in which I'll find myself but I have no option but to carry on. I can't say to you 'Stop a minute, I need to study for a week' when something happens that I don't feel comfortable handling.

Everything carries on and I have to just try. The vital thing I've learned is that mistakes are an integral part of learning. I've become reasonably comfortable with making mistakes because I understand mistakes are what help me learn about teaching."

> It would have been helpful to see you taking risks all along. You always looked confident. But maybe that's not possible. I mean, if you aren't worried about mistakes, if you see them as learning opportunities, then even risk-taking is done with confidence!
>
> Diane Stephens

I'm not afraid of my own mistakes or those of my students. In fact, I welcome mistakes as opportunities for allowing us to learn. I don't purposely set up situations to force mistakes—what happens is that we jump into some kind of enterprise and deal with mistakes or problems as they surface naturally. One thing I am certain about is that the unexpected, the unpredictable, will definitely occur in any learning/ teaching situation. It's learning to deal with the unexpected that allows me to meet the needs of individuals and of groups.

"But you've been teaching this way for a long time," says Shelagh. "You have a lot of knowledge you're bringing to this classroom."

"Yes, I have. But, just as each situation is new for you, I, too, have to make on-the-spot judgements based on whatever limited information I have about you as learners. If I see engagement, then I assume what I offered was supportive; if I see you pulling away, I know I have to think about the situation some more. The critical thing is allowing myself to observe so I can learn from you. It's very easy to forget to watch for learners' responses but it's only by watching how you respond that I can learn how to teach you."

"That brings us back to critical incidents, doesn't it?" asks Leslie.

"You're right, it does."

A glance at the clock reminds me it's time to bring our discussion to a close. We've explored a number of interesting issues. I suggest they may want to consider some of them again in their final reflections tomorrow.

Since I have the entire group around the table I ask if there is anything we want to attend to before tomorrow. Earl looks at our agenda on the blackboard and comments, "I can't believe it, but we've talked about everything we've put up there."

"Well we still haven't pulled together the **Issues** groups," remarks Connie.

"I think tomorrow morning we can do a wrap-up by sharing the conversation that has taken place in the **Issues** groups, OK? We have talked around those three issues: responding to writing, revising and editing, and reading/writing relationships, in a variety of ways. I suspect, though, it would be useful to bring closure on those discussions in the large group. We'll do that in the morning."

The rest of Thursday is taken up with more sharing of writing, revising, reading, and responding to professional material. Again, I wander around, keeping tabs on what's happening. I have my notebook on hand and begin jotting notes to myself about things I want to reflect on. I scribble in my notebook

    authentic / inauthentic
    transaction
    research / reflective practice
    metaphors

I know other things will come to mind later, particularly when I read the teachers' reflections.

Today, I've constantly been on the look-out for opportunities to raise instructional concerns for the teachers to consider. There was that moment, for example, when I saw we could use Lorna's writing to explore Murray's third read. There were lots of more subtle moments as well, points when I felt a need to state my position on some issue or other, like mentioning the myths. The thing about teaching is I can't control who engages with which lessons. I have to keep as many topics on the table as I can so people have an opportunity to connect with those issues that are important to them.

One thing I've learned: there is no particular order in which these discussions must take place. The teachers need only find an entry point. Their willingness to become reflective practitioners will look after the rest. They'll consider the important issues when it matters to them.

Making Connections 13 ❖

Friday morning. We quickly arrange five small tables into a single rectangular area large enough to accommodate the twenty-one of us. Everyone pulls up a chair and discussion begins.

"Where do you want to start? What were some things that surprised you about responding to writing, about revising /editing, and about writing/reading relationships?" I ask.

"I jotted some notes last evening about conferencing," begins Barb. "Here let me read a bit."

> I was nervous the first few times I conferenced with someone about their writing. What would I say? I discovered that if I listened carefully and took my lead from the writer, it all fell into place. Basically, I realized that I needed to respond to the writing in the same way I would respond to something I'd read—How did it make me feel? What did I think the author was trying to say?

"I discovered the same thing," Leslie adds. "I used to think conferencing was something you did only after the kids were finished writing. I saw it as a time to point out mistakes. Your comments, Judith, about having conversations rather than conferences really helped me see responding to writing differently."

That 'conversation' metaphor has turned out to be very useful. It's allowed us to abandon a lot of the traditional formality of classroom interaction.

Hanna continues, "Our talking about our writing definitely became conversations. I stopped trying to remember what questions I was supposed to ask and started listening to what the writing was saying. I began giving movies of my mind, trying to let the writer know how the writing was affecting me. I found it hard at first but after our poetry and short story discussions it came more easily. Like Barb, I realized that I wanted to respond to someone else's writing in the same way as I would respond to something published."

"Something that surprised me was how my writing ended up in a totally different place from where it began," says Diane. "The fact that I started out with the intention of writing a children's story and have ended up with something else (I'm still not sure if my story is for children, early teens, adults, or perhaps all three) tells me a couple of things: first, I don't always end up where I think I am going; and second, a story can take on a life of its own. I must remember that when I'm working with my students."

Understanding how 'writing finds its own meaning' is so important for developing proficient writing. It allows people to stop worrying about clarity until some fluency with a particular piece of writing has been attained.

"How do you see those insights affecting your teaching?" I ask Diane.

"In two ways, I think. First I realize I have to be a writer myself in the classroom so I can talk about my own writing strategies as they come into play, as you did. I think I can probably affect students' writing a great deal through my own writing. I can also see I need to help my third graders just write to get their ideas on paper and to talk about the surprises that happen for them."

"The thing that had an impact on me," Connie comments, "was the comparison between writing and making a film. It made me understand that writing doesn't always start at the beginning. It's more a matter of creating pieces and fitting them together the way a film is done. That really helped me with my story. I could work on parts as ideas occurred to me and then think about how to weave them together. I've never written anything that way before but doing it like that sure kept my anxiety under control. Judith, you were also right about sharing writing all along the way instead of at the end of a completed draft. I found it much easier to change things when I knew the story was still incomplete. By listening to people's reactions and questions I learned to think about things from someone else's point of view and it helped me make decisions about shaping the story."

"On the first day when we talked about issues we wanted to investigate," says Debra, "I wanted to know more about how people came to see themselves as writers. I was thinking about helping my first-grade students but it turns out I was really needing to deal with my own anxiety. I could glibly say 'You learn to see yourself as a writer by writing.' But it certainly wasn't easy for me. I had to overcome a lot of anxiety. I didn't find it difficult to come up with a story but believing and trusting my choice was very hard."

As Debra now understands, it's easy to say 'you learn to write by writing' but to feel it is another matter. That's why I devote so much energy to helping people actually engage in various kinds of writing—so they can find out first hand how writing, itself, teaches them.

"I want to come back to conferencing as conversation," says Hanna. "I think conversation is a much less threatening word and it really does epitomize the process. I also learned I could conference by eavesdropping on conversations. You did that all the time, Judith. You'd listen on the edge for a few minutes and if you saw us engaged and moving along you made an affirming comment, something like 'Have a go,' or 'Sounds reasonable,' or 'Keep at it,' and left us alone. However, if you felt we were trying to handle too much on our own, or going too far without talking about our work, then you intervened more directly to help us stay on track."

I'm not surprised Hanna's been watching me that closely. She's been working seriously at changing her classroom this past year.

"Two things really surprised me," Cathy remarks. "One is that having written a couple of poems I now see so many potential poems in everything going on around me. There are topics everywhere. The second thing is how important it is to have sustained time to write, talk, and reflect on the writing. I'm really going to have to think about how that affects the school timetable. As principal I'm going to have to help the teachers create blocks of time so kids can really work on something."

"I think," says Janice, "I have a much better idea about the whole responding process. When I look back on the way you dealt with our writing as it evolved, I see how a classroom of writers needs to be handled—not as a homogeneous group who have all reached the same spot at the same time, but as individuals who all have their own pace and strategies."

"The thing I've learned here is how to draw on others in the process of writing," says Norma. "By 'others' I mean my peers. Our talking about our writing with each other helped sustain me over the rough spots in my own writing. I mean you, too, Judith. Your conversations and reading and talking about your own writing affected how I wrote. And I mean published authors. I think I started reading like a writer. I started noticing how writers did certain things. When I had a specific problem you suggested we look at some short stories and that really helped me out.

A reflection point. I don't want to leave the teachers just with their experiences; I think they have to be helped to see implications of these experiences for their students' learning.

"What are some questions about teaching these insights raise for you?" I ask.

"Well," answers Leslie, "I know I have to encourage a lot more talking and sharing, not just for writing but for everything—for science, math, social studies. I've never learned as much as I did in these past two weeks and I'm convinced it was because we were working on everything together."

"I was surprised how little content we had to learn," says Michael. "I thought we were mainly focusing on process."

"You're saying we didn't deal with content," I reflect back to him.

It's easy to lose sight of content in an enterprise-based curriculum. Our attention is focused on what's happening and I sometimes forget to make sure people see how their knowledge of the theoretical issues and various researchers' arguments is developing.

"I disagree," replies Norma. "We actually were dealing with a content here. I mean, we were trying to make sense of what research has to say about writing and about reading and how the two are interconnected. It was interesting how we became familiar with who argues what even though you didn't have us memorize the stuff."

"How did that come about Norma?"

"We were discussing the articles so much and referring back to them, and writing about them, the ideas just became familiar."

"That's right," adds Bruce. "You had us reread a number of the articles. We even discussed them again. I found the arguments much easier to follow the second time around and I found I could remember who said what."

"Something I noticed," Hanna comments, "was how you always suggested we read and respond to more than one reading. I can see now how that shifted my attention from trying to remember what each author was saying to comparing people's arguments. Ironically, doing that helped me retain the details better."

I'm always trying to help people read comparatively rather than reading to memorize 'facts.' Reading critically, seeing relationships and contradictions, really only occurs when we're reading a lot of material quickly and discussing it as a group.

"So this course has dealt with content as well as process, then," I restate.

"Yes, you kept having us compare various authors' ideas on conferencing, for example. You wanted us to know how different people viewed responding to writing," says Maggie.

"Can we get back to questions these insights raise about your teaching?"

"Let me reflect here," says Bruce.

He's done this a lot this past week.

"We've just raised two insights; no, it was three: first, we were dealing with a content, partly determined by you—you assigned us some readings—and partly by us—we were reading things we selected ourselves that connected to what we were interested in learning; second, we always read more than a single thing which pushed us into reading and responding comparatively; and third, you had us reread and discuss again some of the same material we'd talked about the first day. Now, what questions does that raise about my teaching? It certainly would make for a very different grade 10 English class. It wouldn't any longer be a matter of everyone plodding through the same novel at the same pace, answering set questions. How can I take the same curriculum the other teachers are using, but use it in an entirely different way? I really have to think about that a lot more."

Some people have difficulty recognizing that the learning, writing, and reading strategies we're using are also useful for younger students.

"How do you see those three insights affecting a grade 4 or grade 5 class?" I ask.

"It's interesting," says Cathy, "I can see I need to help my staff think about how science and math provide opportunities for learning about writing and reading. So much of what we did to develop fluency—the freewriting, for example—would work very well in a hands-on science or math situation."

"I have never asked my third graders to read more than one thing at the same time," Diane remarks. "I can see how if they all read a couple of things we could compare how authors do things. I can see that kind of discussion would open writing doors I hadn't been aware of."

"They don't even all have to be reading the same thing," adds Hanna. "If the kids read something in common and then each looked for stories or poems or whatever that connected in some way, that would lead to an interesting conversation as well. We could still end up with a similar discussion about writing."

"And of course," Barb says, "if some of them happen to be writing in the same genre the reading would help them think about what they were trying to do themselves."

"You might find it interesting to have a look at Chapter 24 in Lucy Calkins's **The Art of Teaching Writing** (Calkins,

1986)," I suggest. "In it she describes how Rose Napoli figures out ways of helping her students explore reading/writing connections. I have some reservations about how prescriptive the rest of the book is but Chapter 24 I found very helpful. I learned a lot from it."

"I want to change the topic a bit," says Bruce. "I've been thinking about how you operate from a set of beliefs that are quite different from what students expect. That could create a lot of chaos and confusion, couldn't it? I wonder what would be the effect of having a list of beliefs posted in the classroom so students are aware of the context I'm trying to establish?"

"I don't think you have to do that," I reply. "I'm sure you could have described my beliefs within a day or two and we have been talking about these beliefs openly anyway."

"I'm not talking about putting them there for the kids to memorize," Bruce says, "I want it there so students can say 'OK—now how does what we've just done relate back to that list?'"

"I actually gave you a 'list' of my assumptions before you arrived, didn't I?"

"Yes," answers Barb, "in your opening letter you gave us some idea of what to expect."

"Why didn't I post a list of my beliefs on the wall?"

Silence. I wait but no one ventures a reply.

"The only lists I want on the wall are lists we've generated together; not my lists, but our collaborative lists. Then the list serves as a confirmation of what you've been experiencing because the ideas are already your own. Do you see the difference?"

Bruce nods.

"The problem with posting teachers' lists is that it absolves students of the responsibility of having to sort out the problem or issues themselves. We've got to solve problems together; that's the crucial part of learning in a collaborative situation. It isn't **my** agenda; it has to be **our** agenda."

"That's one of the hardest things I'm trying to come to terms with," says Maggie.

"I agree, it isn't easy," I respond. "I'm always fighting the impulse to make decisions unilaterally. I'm getting better, but I still don't always manage to negotiate the curriculum as well as I'd like."

This Institute has been the most open, enterprise-based learning situation I've ever managed to establish and it's raised lots of questions about my winter on-campus teaching. It's forced me to think about how to structure the kind of continuity we've been able to build here in our day-long sessions in two and a half hour classes held once a week.

I have my eye on the clock again. There's still a lot of finishing up to do—the short stories, children's books, and poems need to be formatted and printed out and there are final reflections to write.

When I arrived this morning, I randomly picked up a pile of books so we could take a quick look at formatting.

Since the writing is going to be published as a class collection we need to think about consistency of presentation. I pass around the books. Time for a bit of joint experimentation.

"What do we want our book to look like? Any ideas for a title?"

"I think we should call it **Coming Together**," says Leslie. "We came together as a group, this Institute has come together, the writing has come together."

"I like that," says Maggie.

"Me, too," agrees Diane.

"**Coming Together** it is. How should I format the cover?"

"What options do we have?" laughs Earl.

"Look at the books, what options do we have?"

"Are we going to have a picture?" inquires Carmina.

"I think it will have to be a text-only cover unless one of you wants to design something."

No one takes me up on the suggestion.

"What choices do we have, then?"

"I haven't looked at covers with that question in mind," observes Norma. "The one I have here has the words on the cover all centred. But on Michael's they're right justified."

"What about the relative sizes of the title and author's name?"

"On this one," observes Michael, "the title is very large but the author's name is near the bottom and quite a bit smaller."

"Mine has them both about the same size."

"Is the title always first?"

"No!" says Cathy. "This collection of short stories has the author's name at the very top. I never noticed that before."

"So what should we do?"

"Why don't we do something simple—put the title first, centred near the top, in large letters with 'by The Teachers at the Mount Saint Vincent University Summer Institute, 1989' in smaller letters near the bottom," suggests Michael.

"What do you think?"

"That's fine," says Penny. Comments of agreement from the others.

"OK. I'll look after the cover. What else are we going to need?"

"A preface and an index," says Hanna.

"I'm happy to look after those as well, if you like. They can't be done until after we've compiled the entire collection anyway so I'll do that tomorrow," I offer, "but I need some suggestions for how to order the pieces."

"Again, why don't we keep this simple," says Bruce. "Let's just put the pieces alphabetically by author."

"Is that OK?"

Again nods of assent.

"What's happening here?" I ask.

"You're having us consider the final production stuff—how the book should look, sizes of print, positioning of titles, and so on," replies Leslie.

"Now, how are we going to set up each individual piece. How is that handled in anthologies?"

"They're all laid out the same," says Michael.

"How shall we do it here?"

"Let's put the titles in capital letters and centre them," suggests Barb.

"Then a couple of lines below that the author's name centred," Connie says.

"How many lines below the title should we place the author's name?"

"How about three?" says Earl.

"I think we better write this down so we'll remember," I comment. I go to the blackboard, clear a space and write

FORMATTING CONVENTIONS
TITLE (upper case, centred)
—three blank lines
Author's Name (lower case, centred)
—two blank lines
body of writing

I turn around. "Now here's something I want you to notice. Look at the opening paragraph of a chapter. What do you discover?"

"That first paragraph isn't indented," says Maggie with some surprise.

"Mine's like that, too," Cathy affirms.

"Are there any that are indented?" I ask.

"I have one here," answers Connie.

"Who's the publisher?"

"Boynton/Cook."

"Any other Boynton/Cook books around?"

Michael goes to the table, selects a few volumes and hands them around.

"Looks as if Boynton/Cook has decided to indent," observes Bruce, "but it looks as if most other publishers don't. The journals don't seem to indent that first paragraph either."

"What shall we do?"

"I think we shouldn't indent," says Leslie. "It looks as if most publishers don't do it."

"OK, we better make a note of that.

First paragraph—NO INDENT

And you should also make a note of the fact that you should have two spaces after every end-of-sentence punctuation mark.

TWO spaces after end of sentence punctuation

That is you should type period, space, space or question mark, space, space. Within sentence punctuation, commas and semicolons are followed by a single space. To save paper I think we should single space within the body of the text and between paragraphs; double space between sections."

I add those formatting conventions to the list on the blackboard.

SINGLE space within body of text
SINGLE space between paragraphs
DOUBLE space between sections

Seems like a lot to remember but it won't take long to do the title/author formatting. It'll take a bit more work getting the spacing after punctuation correct. Quite likely they'll need to proofread for one another to catch those and other typographical errors.

"Let's get on with finishing up. There are new ribbons on the printers so we'll get clear, dark printouts. I'll be handy if you need any help."

We spend the rest of the morning finishing up the writing.

We return early from lunch. I want to conduct a sharing session to celebrate everyone's writing. Although the teachers will all receive a copy of the class publication

> *and I intend to include names and addresses so people*
> *can write and respond to one another*

it's likely some people may not receive reactions to what they've written. The purpose of this sharing, then, is to celebrate our anthology.

This time we move the tables aside, arrange chairs in a circle, and begin reading to one another.

Earl begins:

The black wall phone rang at the most inopportune time. The children were just returning from Bill Moore's art class pumped up as high as robins on a spring breeze— the persistent ring calling me to rescue the party-line customer from that irritating sound. Torn between settling down a classroom full of energy and leaving abruptly to answer the telephone, breathlessly I answer.

"Hello."

"Earl?"

It was my wife Marg; she rarely calls me at school. I gave her my full attention. Marg has been having a long winter. A non-driver living in a remote area miles from any source of human companionship outside of her immediate family.

"Earl, I can hardly hear you. The lines are bad today. Listen carefully...your mother called, she wants you to call home. Your Dad is not feeling well."

"OK. Thanks Marg, I'll get back to you. Don't go far." A muffled "Humph, yeah, you know how far, call me back. Bye." The dial tone buzzed in my ear.

Slowly, ever so slowly, I hung up the phone.

Dad?

Many images flashed through my mind. Images of smiling blue eyes with laugh wrinkles and silver-grey hair; of situations that I thought I had forgotten. I sat back oblivious to the mounting free-for-all developing in my classroom....

The wind was blowing through the open windows. Boy, it's cold this morning, I thought.

"Roll up your window Billie. Dad, tell him to roll up his window." The smell of day old fish drifted throughout the car as the windows went up. I took a quick look around and sized up my surroundings. A 1962 Dodge Dart with a stick shift, black bucket seats

and a red exterior. I can hardly wait till I get my
licence....

Earl finishes his story. Faces around the circle are sombre.
Death is sobering. Although we laughed when Earl read the bit
about his father's only foray into sex education, we all feel the
sadness of his loss.

"I really like the way you weave between past and present,"
says Bruce. "The way you used small things to tie the piece
together: the open window in the classroom now and the open
window in the car then. You did that each time, didn't you?"

"Yes. It wasn't easy though," said Earl. "I had to work at
that but I thought I needed some particular trigger in the present
to connect with each memory."

"I like how some parts were funny and other parts were
quite sad," says Norma. "As you were reading I remembered
things about my mother."

"Yes, while I was laughing at your memories, I was
connecting with memories of my own," Maggie adds.

"Talk about what you've learned from writing this piece," I
ask Earl.

"I've never written a story before. I guess the thing that
surprised me was how it was done in segments and then assem-
bled. I think I always thought writers started at the beginning,
worked through the middle, and finished at the end. That
certainly didn't happen here."

"That happened to a lot of us, didn't it?" Diane says to me.

"Yes, it did. How was the situation set up so that could
happen?"

"Well, all the talking we did while we were writing, getting
people's reactions, seeing how people were working out their
stories, reading various published authors, it all kept the writing
fluid," says Diane. "You kept encouraging us to shift segments
around."

"What does this mean for helping kids write?" I ask.

"I guess it means we have to make sure there's time to do the
messing around that writing needs," says Bruce.

"And we have to encourage kids to help one another out,"
adds Maggie.

A few more comments, then I move us on.

*If we're going to get reflections written, and I feel we
need to, we can't take the whole afternoon to share
our writing. Have to move a bit more quickly.*

Bruce offers to share next.

"I'm not going to read my short story—it's too, too long. You can read it in the class book," he laughs. "I'd like to read a poem instead:

Low Mileage

For some years now
my mind has only been driven
for running errands about town
or taking a leisurely drive with the kids
it has stopped at all the stop signs
has never run more than fifteen minutes at a time
and some days never left the driveway

But now
through writing
it is out on the open highway
cruising at 120 klicks
(beyond the conventional limits)
the engine is purring smoothly

And I am surprised by its power

There's a round of applause and exclamations of admiration.
"Mind as motor car," says Maggie, "what a nice metaphor."
"I had this image of a sleek-shaped mind with wheels roaring along the road," says Janice, "like in the cartoons—very effective."
"You captured just what I'm feeling, too," says Barb. "When I arrived my mind was in slow gear but it sure speeded up in a hurry. Now I feel like I'm zooming along; almost, but not quite, out of control."
Connie shares next.
"You remember how I started writing about my nephew at his T-ball practice. That's still in the story but it ended up in a letter near the end of the piece. Here let me read it:

As a gigantic sob escaped, James thought with despair
that this was the worst summer of his life. He lay on his
bed, face pressed into his pillow. He didn't want anyone
to hear him crying, especially not his mother. Both of
them had come to live with his father's sister, Aunt Joan,
exactly one month ago. It had been rough going for the
past two years since the accident and his father's death
but a very strong relationship had grown between him
and his mother as a result. They had stayed in their home
town as long as possible but the bills and expenses had

begun piling up. When a better job offer came from
Toronto, his mother had sold most of their possessions
and packed the rest into their old stationwagon and a U-
haul trailer. Aunt Joan was thrilled to have them at her
home and had overwhelmed them with her welcome
when their tiny caravan clattered into her driveway....

Aunt Joan masked a smile as she dug through the
pile of old letters on the bed. She located a particular
one, pulled it from the pile and opened it up. It looked as
though it had been read often.

Dear Sis,
It's been a while since I wrote. Everyone is fine and
little Jimmy is really sprouting up. I guess it's true about
bad weeds growing fast! Sarah and I signed him up for
T-ball this summer. He got his uniform last week. It was
all I could do not to laugh. KENTVILLE FIRE DEPT. is
stencilled on shirt front but when he puts on the whole
uniform only KENTVILLE shows. The rest is tucked
inside the long white pants that make his skinny legs
look like picket fence posts. The way he sticks out his
six-year old chest you'd think he was a real player in the
majors—just like big Jimmy....

Again applause when Connie finishes reading. We
congratulate her on the story and share our reactions to various
parts that have caught our attention.

*The reason for sharing at this point is to celebrate the
writing. The pieces have come to closure; now is not
the time for critical input—it's time for praise. This
was brought home to me forcefully on one occasion
last winter when a teacher wrote the following in her
journal:*

> I want to say something about vulnerability,
> sensitivity and all of those things that are exposed
> when we write and then share with others. I was
> really beginning to feel as though I could now
> write, maybe not as well as I wanted to but I could
> feel growth in my own confidence. This
> confidence was shattered when I received a
> reaction to my story in the class collection. Maxine
> wrote a candid reaction—it resembled a critical
> analysis, one I thought I might have appreciated
> earlier in the writing. I felt it was too late, now, to
> say what I should have done, or that parts were

confusing. I needed this feedback before the story was in final form. What her reaction did was make me ashamed to read my story again or to share the book with my family. The thing that upset me most was that it was too late to change anything and maybe everyone that read it thought the same things but were too polite to say them, so just didn't react at all.

I didn't handle it well. After a week of feeling sorry for myself, however, I began asking myself, now what would Judith say about this? Without even asking you, I knew what your answer would be. You'd ask a question, or two questions, actually: What have you learned from this experience? What implications does this have for you as a teacher?

I think it has many implications for me as a teacher and it all comes back to this sensitivity and vulnerability thing. For me as a writer, I think I must be careful not to transfer my sensitivity to a defensiveness about my writing. However, it could easily happen with children if we don't handle their feelings with extreme care. How do I help students detach their feelings from their writing? What about the timing of critical feedback? I can see I have a lot of questions to think about in the coming weeks.

> I'm not always great at backing off. Sometimes it takes a while for the message to sink in. Nick's reading of his story about learning to swim jumps to mind. He read with an obvious feeling of pride to a group of fellow first graders and me. I thought it was wonderful. I could see lots of important detail that he revealed in the ensuing discussion that I thought would make it even better. I asked my barrage of questions and Nick answered them with authority. When I asked if he thought including any of that information would make his story better, he replied 'Maybe.' I pushed further, 'Are you going to put any of it in?' His flat 'No.' forced me to shove my scarf in my mouth and back away.
>
> Lynn Sawyer

The time for critical feedback is while the writing is incomplete and the writer is still struggling to make decisions. Once a piece is done it's time to back away. The difficult thing about working with novice writers (child or adult) is dealing with their premature sense of closure. A finished draft and they're done—no going at the writing again. I've made lots of blunders trying to help people rework a piece of writing they considered finished. I've learned the most useful thing I can do is demonstrate how I rework my own writing. Showing people how I recast a story or poem allows me to ask whether it might not be something they could try as well. However, once we've published the class book, nothing but praise is in order. If I haven't been able to help someone rework a piece earlier on, my suggestions at this point will only serve to undermine confidence. That's of no use whatsoever.

Hanna reads her story next:

Hubert was a silky haired, wheat-colored terrier named after his owner's uncle in Ireland. He lived with the Gingles in a big, brown house which backed on a lake. Mr Gingles had spent long hours building a picket fence to keep Hubert from wandering off or to stop him from plunging into the muddy waters and disturbing the ducks.

Hubert spend his days romping among the tall grasses in the backyard and thundering from one side of the fence to the other, following anyone who happened to pass by.

Jon, the Gingles' son, loved Hubert. He and Hubert would go for long walks through the park and play ball until dusk. Life with Hubert would have been perfect except for one thing.

Hubert would not stop barking.

In fact, Hubert barked at just about everything.

When Mrs. Blackburn, the next door neighbor, hung her washing on the line, Hubert barked. "What's your problem, dog?" she would ask him.

Mr Blackburn was less polite. He got very annoyed when Hubert barked and jumped against the fence while he was working in his garden. He would yell, "One of these days I'll load my gun and BOOM!" Hubert didn't seem to care.

The Connolly children down the street shouted, "Shut up, Hubert!" as they flew by on their skateboards.

On her way to school, Tina Caravecchio hated to pass by Hubert's house. As he stood guard on the sundeck, Hubert would see her coming and bark his head off. She had already complained to the Gingles that they should do something about Hubert and that she was going to tell her parents.

One day when Mr Mack, the postman, was delivering a parcel, Hubert went into a frenzy of barking. The doorbell was what bothered him most and unless the Gingles managed to get to the front door before it was rung, Hubert barked. No one could quiet him down. Not Mrs Gingles. Not Mr Gingles. Not Jon.

"Get something done about that dog, or else I'll stop bringing your mail!" the postman warned then, stomping off.

The Gingles agreed something definitely had to be done about Hubert....

Hanna's story evokes gales of laughter. When she finishes reading we all clap loudly and offer our congratulations.

After Hanna, Leslie, then Penny, followed by Norma. Everyone takes a turn reading something aloud.

There's a powerful feeling of accomplishment as our sharing draws to a close. Everyone has had to overcome feelings of panic but now having read their writing aloud to the group I can sense their strengthened confidence.

Time now for final reflections. The rest of the afternoon is spent freewriting at the computers. The computer lab is a hive of quiet activity. The clatter of keyboards fills the room. Not much conversing going on right now.

At three-thirty we reconvene in Room 431 for the last time. We chatter as we gather up our belongings. People help me box up the class library and take it to my car. We return the periodicals we borrowed to the University library. We replace furniture, leaving the room as I initially found it.

Although tired, we have decided to celebrate the end of the Institute by going out together for dinner. People are reluctant to have this experience end. We've all been powerfully engaged. The teachers have learned a great deal—I have, too.

Later that evening, after dinner and good-byes, I have a chance to sit quietly and read the teacher's reflections. This final freewrite has provided people with an opportunity to examine their personal learning during the Institute and consider questions it raises about their teaching. The conflicting views about conferencing, for example, that we discussed, the responding to various kinds of literature and film, the informal as well as formal writing, the sharing and the responding are all data for them to consider as they look at their assumptions about learning, writing, reading, and teaching.

As I browse through the teachers' writing I see several important issues discussed. They have written about their insights into writing and reading. They explore the implications of describing writing as moving from fluency—clarity—correctness rather than the other way around. They discuss their anxieties about writing conferences and what they've learned about responding to literature. There are reflections on writing /reading relationships and writing to learn. A number of people mention writing and learning as collaborative activities. Responsibility is discussed, as is the teacher's role in a collaborative classroom. Some of the teachers reflect on what I did as a teacher and how it affected them. They each share interesting insights.

Hanna, for example, sums up what she's learned about writing in the following way:

> Writing the children's story has been such a great experience for me. Having gone through the process I understand its dimensions, its frustrations, and its rewards. I know how hard it is to brainstorm for ideas when the old pump goes dry and what you can do to get back its prime. I know how many authors you need to read to develop a sense of how people write. Then there are the freewrites to get the juices flowing, the conversations in between to keep them going, the many drafts to revise for clarity and the final editing reads, where people help you with conventions. I finally can empathize with students who feel so vulnerable that they refuse to read their writing to classmates. I, too, ache with caring like the bat who wants his story to be understood. And I'm desperately wanting my readers to like what I write. I now know the thrill of having a reader say "I like it!"

Hanna now sees herself as a writer. She has a stronger sense of how to orchestrate writing for herself and her experiences have given her some insight into how students may feel about writing.

Fluency—clarity—correctness comes up again and again in the reflections. Maggie says, for example:

> You really helped to put the developmental progression in perspective. I wonder if I give enough thought to the fact that in any given class different kids can be experiencing different aspects of the process. When you said a grade 11 student might still be struggling for

fluency, I thought I'd better give this idea of fluency—
clarity—correctness more thought and also pay attention
to the different kinds of support that is called for in
different circumstances.

This was certainly an issue I was trying to raise. Mayher's discussion has had a powerful impact on how I see my writing teacher role. Like the teachers, the questions raised by this continuum have forced me to think about what kinds of support and input different writers need at different times.

Conferencing has been an up-front, common concern from the outset. On the first day several of the teachers identified writing conferences as a topic of special interest. Now at the end Barb reflects:

I am going home with a new appreciation of
conferencing. When I started out I didn't realize
conferencing could also include things other than people.
I could dialogue with myself in my log book. I might
draw on books that I have read long ago, stories I've
heard or films I've seen, a piece of music that evokes
memories, etc. In fact, these are all aspects of **one big**
conversation.

Bruce writes:

The first conference I had with you about my story was a
critical incident for me. I went to the table, sat down
beside you, and expected to be told what to do. So when
you asked me what help I wanted, I really had to think.
What **did** I want? What did I need? I didn't want
suggestions about what to do, I didn't need help with
editing (eventually I would but not at that point). I
needed to hear your perceptions of the relationship I was
portraying. So that's what I asked about. Before this
experience, I would have followed Calkins's step-by-
step procedure for conferences and the kids would have
got the idea that conferences are not what they really are:
natural spontaneous conversations that arise out of a
writer's desire for collaboration and response.

The fact that there wasn't a single format for a conversation about writing became apparent to many. Norma observes:

You never **told** us what a good conference was or how
to go about it. We just did it naturally as writers who
needed help. As we went along our writing
conversations changed in nature. Initially conferences

were informal and focused on content and intent with some discussion of process. As we neared publication, we began to look more closely at organization, editing, form and style. The main focus, however, at all times was on meaning.

Diane considers how she might implement what she's learned:

Conferencing took on a whole new meaning for me. I can see how easily these brief conversations could take place in my classroom, too. I could just move about and talk with the kids about their writing. Asking my third-graders about what they've written might lead them to write more.

Thinking about responding to literature in personal ways was another aspect of our agenda. I put the issue on the table by inviting people to give movies of their minds and carried it through the reading of various kinds of textual material. I wanted people to experience how a literary work can allow us to learn about ourselves. Penny writes:

Learning to give a personal response to literature has been such a liberating experience. My awful fear of having the incorrect interpretation has vanished.

Debra, too, has been affected by our responding to literature:

I can see how I would get so much more from a story if I would allow myself to feel. I know that when the kids and I read stories together in the fall my question won't always be "What was your favorite part?" but "How did it make you feel?"

Intertextuality is a complex concept. In our discussions I tried to avoid as much jargon as I could. The metaphor of poems or stories talking to each other just slipped out as we were talking ourselves. It connected for Maggie.

I can still hear your question "How do the poems on this page talk to each other?" Such an interesting metaphor. There's something fundamental in that question—that language is what we connect with. Poems talking to each other is a way of showing how we connect our experiences. I can't wait to hear the responses when I pose that question to my junior high students.

I began this Institute with the intention of helping the teachers explore the many interconnections between reading and writing. I had realized that in spite of the interweaving I had tried in the past, many people still missed their essential interplay. Consequently, I tried to make the intricacy of what we were doing in the Institute more explicit. It seems as if our discussions paid off. Hanna discusses how the fact that she was engaged in writing affected her reading:

> The idea of 'showing' not 'telling' caused me to see books differently. When reading for relaxation I found myself looking at how various authors wrote. During our discussion about the short stories I found myself becoming more aware of specific instances of authors showing not telling. Writing to 'show' myself, however, was hard work.

In addition to helping the teachers consider how writing feeds reading and reading affects writing, helping them to experience collaboration—learning as social engagement—was an important aspect of my initial agenda. That message clearly did get through. Cathy, for example, writes:

> In the past I thought learning was something you did on your own. I now realize learning isn't solitary but a social process. Without the help of our poetry writing group I would never have been able to produce the writing I did. There were times I couldn't distance myself, I needed an outside response and it was there waiting for me.

Bruce considers what a collaborative learning context means for his teaching:

> In my English classes, I certainly have had group discussion, and opportunities for collaboration on projects, but I didn't really believe that the students learned anything of significance from each other. I 'allowed' them time to talk and work together but I didn't structure things so they were responsible to each other in any way and I certainly haven't maximized opportunities for learning together. During this Institute, I discovered how collaborative learning can really be used. I felt that the group time was different from any other I had experienced. While we all had individual goals, independent work, personal constructs and understandings, we were all working in a common direction, with some common goals, and we grew to

depend on each other for support, feedback, jokes, and sympathy.

The issue of control is a difficult one for most of the teachers to deal with. Who's responsibility is it to do what? Taking charge of your own learning is scary, you might make mistakes, go in unproductive directions, waste time. Cathy writes:

I had trouble at the beginning making choices and decisions about my own learning. I didn't want the responsibility—it was too hard. I really had to come to grips with that. Initially, I wanted the security that goes hand in hand with you, the teacher, controlling, and me, the student, fulfilling your mapped-out agenda. However, it was very clear that you weren't going to take that role; I had to become a risk-taker!

Maggie writes of letting go:

I think I'm beginning to understand the idea of learner responsibility; however, the whole concept of letting go leaves me in a panic. This is where I'm going to need help. I know where I want to head but letting go will require continual personal reflection on my part and constant encouragement from other people.

I repeatedly invited the teachers into our hall of mirrors. "What's going on here?" I asked again and again. People began watching and thinking about what was happening. Penny observes:

All along I had the distinct impression you never **told** us anything, but you really did explicitly reveal a lot in your reflection/letters to us, during your class involvement, and in your responses to each of us personally. Your 'mini-lessons' did not provide **the** answer. Your emphasis, instead, was on getting us to question and only now can I see how you explicitly and sometimes subtly nudged us to try many of your suggestions.

Bruce's observations are interesting as well:

So how did you do it? Obviously you did set a structure from the beginning. The reading you sent us before we even met, the small and large group discussions, the **Issues** questions, and so on, all established a way of going about things. And then, perhaps most important, you weaned us away from you and left us to each other. Gradually, we heard less and less from you in terms of what to do, what to talk about, and because it was gradual, we were ready to assume responsibility for carrying on. The agenda ceased to be set by you, at least in a moment-to-moment sense. It took all of us a while to really value what we were doing without you.

Although the Institute began with my opening agenda, once underway, the curriculum became a joint responsibility—the teachers directed their efforts toward their own questions. Norma reflects on negotiating the curriculum:

No "one-size-fits-all" pantihose curriculum here! You allowed me to see that as long as I became engaged in the learning by accepting some of the invitations extended to me, then your agenda could be negotiated. That is, there were many activities from which to choose and many resources on which to draw. However, I was responsible for my own involvement.

The foreshadowing I was doing worked quite well, in some instances much better than I could have planned for; however, I didn't think it was receiving much notice. Yet it caught Maggie's attention:

I now realize how you foreshadowed 'conferencing' by having us respond to the short stories by giving movies of our minds. You were giving us the opportunity to participate unknowingly before we were intentionally encouraged to try conferencing. It allowed us time to think about the experience and say 'ah-ha' when we realized our ordinary conversations within the small groups, or with you, were precisely what we needed to do when talking about our own writing.

Evaluation and grading are, of course, crucial issues. Unless we can work out ways of making our evaluating and grading practices more consistent with our beliefs we're in for trouble. Janice comments:

As far as evaluation goes, I think we teachers need to ask ourselves why we're evaluating. Everything that is done can be a part of evaluation. The most difficult part to assess is the unconscious learning that is taking place. Now I see why you relentlessly bombarded us with 'why's and 'what is going on here?' As well as helping us to uncover what we were learning, it let you see where we were as learners. In this way you were able to set up new learning situations to guide us. I also realize how valuable the kids' attempts are and how evaluation must be done in context since each student and situation differs.

The journals and logs function as mirrors for reflecting our beliefs back to us. Through our freewriting we find ways of examining our strategies, our assumptions, our tentative understandings. Journal or log writing creates opportunities for the unexpected to emerge. Our comments, assertions, questions can make us aware of new ways of seeing things as Diane explains:

> My log became indispensable. In it I had conversations
> with myself, jotted down random ideas and those flashes
> of insight that occur when connections are made.
> Through it I was able to discover what I was thinking as
> a writer, a reader and as a learner and teacher.

Barb compares her log with the one she's been asking her students to keep:

> I've had my students keep a reading log but it was much
> less flexible than the one I've been keeping. I think the
> little detail of it being notebook-size is important. It's
> more manageable to carry around than the regular
> scribbler I've had them write in.

What impressions, then, are the teachers taking away from this Institute? Norma explains:

> I now understand my main responsibility is to set up the
> **conditions** for learning to occur, situations which let
> students try out different ways of accomplishing their
> intentions and then letting them talk about what they've
> done so they can reflect on what's gone on. I need to
> teach not by telling but by doing, thinking about the
> things I want students to experience.

Janice shares an important insight:

> When I first started reading professional articles and
> books I was looking for tips, practical applications to
> help me with my students. I realize now I have to read
> from the perspective of 'does this match what I believe
> are my assumptions about learning?' This ability to read
> critically becomes easier when you understand what you
> believe about learning.

Looks as if Helen has understood 'it depends':

I came to a better understanding of the fact that there are no answers. We all seem to be looking for answers but I learned we need to be looking for questions. The more questions we come up with, the more we reflect, and the more connections we can make to our own experiences.

Cathy has been reflecting as an administrator:

As a school administrator I feel I have gained some valuable insights but I have this feeling of being just on the brink. I need to establish a climate that will invite the teachers on my staff to grow with me as readers and writers. I know I can't be evangelistic; I must find a balance that will communicate my intentions clearly but without alienating them. I have to keep my eye out for people who will be willing to join me in this adventure.

Hanna:

I want to comment on our conversation yesterday that in your classroom fun is not the focus of learning but that it comes as a natural offshoot when students become engaged. How many times have I felt the need to provide entertainment so that the students would enjoy learning? I can see this so plainly now because I have experienced being a part of a community of writers and readers who supported each other and were sincerely interested in one another's work. We have had a lot of fun learning but it's been a by-product of the whole experience.

Bruce:

More important than everything else, I have experienced the validity of Frank Smith's contention that learning is natural, incidental, and happens virtually automatically. A lot of learning happens when you're doing something else. The computer is a perfect case in point. I no longer need to check the cribsheet to find out how to print, save or exit. I have learned those skills. But this wasn't a course on computers. The learning of computer operations was incidental. It happened because it was useful for us to know. I can see I've been guilty of teaching both writing and literature in a disconnected way—disconnected from any useful purpose. So one of the things I'm going to be doing in the fall is having the students write for a much wider variety of purposes....

❖

One reflection has left me wondering. What is striking about Shelagh's brief freewrite, in comparison to the others, is how she still holds the mirror turned away from herself. Although present during the morning discussion, Shelagh offered no comments. Here, too, she plays safe. While she remarks on what she's learned, she doesn't consider what questions this experience raises about her own teaching. She's still not willing to examine contradictions within her own practice. I haven't, it seems, been able to help her look at herself reflectively.

Having done the writing workshop for only a year, I wasn't sure my methods and approach were on the 'right track.' I had read a lot about writing and about whole language but I hadn't had much demonstration of the reading/writing workshop in action. The institute has helped me feel more secure about what I'm doing. In my classroom, I think I exercised good judgement about the formal and conventional aspects of writing. I think I knew when to intervene and when to leave the students alone. Having had this opportunity to write myself, I think I will be better able to make effective teaching decisions. I think I have always been quite sensitive to the students' needs. I am there to support their efforts and to sustain their engagement. It is important that I assist them with examining their own strategies when the time is right.

I feel I could probably write a book on what I learned. I accepted your invitations to write, to read, to participate, to discuss, to take risks, to collaborate, to dialogue, and to connect with my teaching. I was encouraged to find my own area of interest so that I soon assumed control yet I was invited to be part of other people's interests as well. I was given support when I needed it. I shared, I was given feedback on my ideas and was expected to respond to others. I was pushed to go beyond what I might have done on my own. I laughed a lot. I have a better appreciation now of writing for learning. I see much personal growth as a result of what I have been engaging in and the risks I have taken as a learner have helped me get there. It has not been easy. At times, down right frustrating—but nevertheless, I have enjoyed learning and feel I have stretched.

Evaluation was the issue that interested me. I read as much as I could on the topic trying to find ways of dealing with the incredible marking load I seem to face. I

found a number of resources on working with
elementary age students. However the elementary and
junior high contexts are so different that not a lot
transfers to the secondary situation. The pressure for
grades is much more intense in the junior high and there
is really so little written which helps with the problem. I
still don't know how to handle the volume of journals,
reading logs, and writing in progress that I have to mark
regularly.

In my reply to Shelagh I take a last stab at nudging her
toward a more reflective stance:

I, too, have seen you grow in various ways—as a
reader, a writer, and a learner. In discussion I heard you
ask questions about your own teaching. What I sense
here in this freewrite, however, is a return to complacency, a lack of critical appraisal of your teaching. In the
long run, looking at only what's comfortable won't
serve you well. Even when we're managing the surface
aspects of writing instruction comfortably, it's quite
likely we're missing the boat for individual students. No
one way of conducting a reading/writing workshop is
going to work for every student. That means we can't
become self-satisfied—we can never really say "I think I
have always been quite sensitive to students' needs" as
you have because there will always be students whose
needs we've inadvertently overlooked, as I inadvertently
overlook yours. I felt a lack of specific learning incidents
in what you've written here. You share a general sense
of how this experience has had an impact on you, but
with an impersonal distance. What's missing in this
reflection is YOU. How did the experience affect you
and help you think differently about your teaching?

And how did this experience affect me and help me think
differently about my teaching?

Reflecting 14 ❖

I write this reflection many months after the Institute and as I write I discover new insights which the experience offers me. Writing about what happened each day, thinking about why I made specific decisions and responded as I did, has allowed me to reflect anew.

So what did I learn from the Institute experience?

One thing that stands out for me at this distance is the number of times our agenda evolved in unexpected yet productive directions. I had used Peter Elbow's advice with a number of previous classes as a way of helping teachers respond to one another's writing. When I introduced his ideas during the Institute I did so primarily with that same intention of facilitating responding to writing. What I didn't anticipate, and didn't see until the Institute had come to an end, was how giving movies of our mind had, on this occasion, become our principle way of responding to literary works as well. Sharing our responses to literature and film in this personal way had unexpected benefits for learning to talk about our writing. As we all became more comfortable and adept at discussing short stories, poems, films, and children's books we found ourselves talking about one another's writing more naturally.

There was also the moment when I saw our learning/teaching exchanges as conversations. There were many different, interconnected conversations: between me and individual teachers, between and among the teachers, with published authors, with researchers, with one another's writing. There were potential conversations between the film **Dead Poet's Society** and with our past experiences both as learners and teachers. I was surprised, and intrigued, by the metaphor of poems or short stories talking to each other which slipped out spontaneously during our short story discussion. Later, after I had reread Margaret Meek's article on what texts teach, I saw how we had constructed another way of describing intertextuality.

By referring to what was going on as conversation I can now see I was foregrounding listening and responding as natural aspects of the learning context. This metaphor let me openly build new connections among the various strands of the Institute experience by asking questions like: How do these short stories talk to one another? How does the poetry talk to the short stories? How does what you're reading talk to your writing? These proved to be very important and powerful questions.

The spontaneous emergence of the blackboard plan book was another unexpected instructional strategy. In previous classes I had gone as far as creating a writing conversation sign-up list. I had, however, never negotiated curriculum publicly in this way before. The plan book emerged when I inadvertently wrote a reminder about some upcoming discussions beside the **Writing Conversations** list. The way the blackboard plan book took on a life of its own from that point on amazed me. It made it possible, and legitimate, for everyone to contribute to our unfolding agenda.

What's important about each of these aspects of the Institute experience—giving movies of our minds, exploring how texts talk to one another, and our keeping track of our agenda publicly—was that none of them had been preplanned. I hadn't thought in advance 'Oh, we must do this!' These ideas were generated on the spot, out of our collaborative situation. They helped me see that when teachers have some overall sense of what it is we would like students to be able to do and to understand, when our pedagogical intentions have a fairly clearly articulated theoretical framework, then we may be able to improvise on chance comments, a timely film, or an unusual piece of text.

Learning to build on teachable moments is what a transactional theoretical perspective is all about. There is, however, no way opportunities like these can be specified in advance. Being able to do something with these teachable moments depends on two factors: first, we have to have a global sense of where we're heading and why; and second, we have to learn to recognize a learning moment when it presents itself.

What else did I learn? I used to believe teachers had to have a solid theoretical grounding before we could deal with practical matters. I no longer believe that. I now recognize, both individually and collectively, we build theory out of practice. New understanding develops as we teach. It can come from a variety of sources—from critical reflection on instruction, by reflecting on learning, as well as from questions raised through reading and discussion. There is no single source for change. I can initiate a learning context, but each teacher must forge her own connections.

In the Institute I set out wanting to weave practice and theory more closely together. I tried to launch activities which would let the teachers discuss what they were experiencing and infer some of the theoretical principles I was trying to put into operation. I used various readings to help the teachers identify and understand what those theoretical principles were. I was also trying to help the teachers experience the power of a collaborative learning context. I wanted them to understand the importance of making it legitimate for students to learn with and from one another.

Everything we did in this Institute was directed toward that end. I wanted people to discover that we learn something like writing not by being taught about it, but by engaging in writing that we care about and by helping one another toward more coherent, proficient, compelling stories, poems, and expositions. By working together we discovered what sort of strategies can sustain writing, what to do when we're stuck; by sharing our writing we discovered what sorts of questions and comments are useful in what sorts of situations and for which writers. And yet, within this communal endeavor, the teachers were learning as individuals. Each of them wrote by himself, read on her own, did individual 'homework.' Not everyone learned exactly the same thing, nor did I expect they should. As teacher, I was trying to meet individual needs and interests through our collective efforts.

Here in the Institute, more clearly than in any previous teaching/learning situation, I was able to see the connection between the physical structures of a situation and the social relationships that evolve. I devoted a great deal of time and energy both before and during the Institute to organizing a setting which would foster a particular kind of engagement. The furniture was set up to facilitate talking in small groups. We moved it when we wanted to work in a larger group. By using the furniture in a variety of ways I was able to create and sustain an engagement among the teachers in a way I'd never quite managed to achieve before. By talking to one another in pairs, in a variety of small group settings, in the classroom, in the hallway, in the computer lab, during lunch and in the evenings, the teachers forged trusting relationships with one another which allowed them to share their uncertainties and their insights.

Placing the class library where I did was another important organizational tactic that affected the social dynamics of the class. Because professional books, children's books, literary works and articles were at hand, people were drawn to them. They browsed through the material. They contributed material of their own. Published authors became participants in our conversations and people turned to them for help.

The evolving of a fluid daily agenda and the **Writing Conversations** list were other organizational structures that furthered the building of a trusting collaborative relationship. In previous classes I still held the reins and while people worked in an engaged way I felt a dependence on my control that I wanted to diminish. The Institute experience affirmed for me the benefits of letting go. By letting go I was able to allow the teachers to show me how to teach them. Giving them the latitude to find their own way into the communal learning enterprise allowed problems and issues to surface naturally and together the teachers and I were able to explore them. People took more risks, allowed themselves to be more vulnerable than I've ever experienced before.

Having completed the Institute are there things I would now do differently? My answer is 'Of course!' Although Elbow's giving movies of our minds went much further than I had planned, the reading/talking with a pencil in hand strategy didn't really succeed. A few people began keeping track of ideas as they read and talked but, on the whole, my attempts to create a need for personal data-collecting didn't work. The idea of interviewing ourselves and others simply didn't catch on. That was due, in part, because the lesson I was trying to teach didn't make it into the conversation. Had I asked people to talk about the strategy and what they were learning from it, I suspect it would have had a greater impact.

In the beginning of the Institute I had to bring a lot of activities into play quickly; some were bound to fall by the way. Initiating more than we could possibly sustain was necessary on my part, though. In an enterprise-based curriculum I need to offer as many potential invitations as possible so people can find some way of becoming engaged. I can't know in advance which experiences will capture people's attention; I simply have to just try and then let drop those invitations and activities which don't fly. During the Institute, reading/talking with pencil in hand was one of those invitations.

Although I was foreshadowing in various ways, instigating strategies and ways of working before making them part of the overt agenda, the metaphor "wax on,'wax off," as well, failed to become part of our conversation. I mentioned the film **Karate Kid** in passing but I neglected to ask the teachers to think about the indirect teaching I was doing.

In hindsight, it might have been possible to have had the two films, **Karate Kid** and **Dead Poet's Society**, talk to one another. Had I asked Margaret Meek's question 'What lessons do these particular films teach about learning and teaching?' I suspect the idea of 'wax on, wax off' would have arisen. I might also simply have asked the teachers to think about how I was anticipating certain strategies directly, as I did recently during a three-day inservice session. On that occasion the 'wax on,wax off' metaphor became part of our conversation. The teachers on their own discussed ways of invoking learning indirectly.

The read fast strategy, too, didn't gain much currency. I now see why that happened. Our attention became focused on writing and learning about writing and as we pushed toward clarity a 'read slow' process developed, instead, as people began actively reading like writers.

Our written dialogues also took a back seat. It quickly became apparent that trying to write a short story, a few poems, or a children's book would consume a large part of people's energy and that their pieces of writing weren't going to develop quickly. That meant I had to back off from requiring, as I usually do, daily written logs or reflections as a way of conversing with each teacher personally. Instead, I shifted my responding to our conversations about our writing and to the small group discussions.

With such a circumscribed period of time in which to produce a 'finished' piece of writing we had to make choices. Because of the teachers' involvement in writing I also had to back away from many important controversial issues. We didn't read and discuss the implications of Mark Clark's "Negotiating Agenda: Preliminary Considerations" (1989) or Nancy Lester and John Mayher's "Critical Professional Inquiry" (1987), both on factors affecting teacher change. We didn't discuss Pat Shannon's "The Struggle for Control of Literacy Lessons" (1989) or Garth Boomer's "The Helping Hand Strikes Again? An Exploration of Language, Learning, and Teaching" (1989) which deal with control of curriculum and direct vs indirect instruction. Although those political issues surfaced during our conversation, we missed the critical reflection these and other articles and books might have elicited.

I return to the classroom again in a few weeks. What do I bring from the Institute to these future teaching experiences? There's the temptation to think the differences between a two-week Institute and teaching in a classroom are so great the lessons aren't transferrable. However, the questions I ask myself whether I'm conducting a two-day workshop or a year-long on-campus course are the same. The scope of the enterprise is clearly different, but the teaching strategies I employ are common. What I learn about teaching in one instructional situation carries over to others.

And yet there clearly are differences between an Institute and other teaching situations. During the Institute we met all day for several consecutive days. In some ways that was an advantage. People came expecting to be engrossed full time and had set aside other responsibilities. The major disadvantage of an Institute learning situation, however, is that the teachers don't have an opportunity to return to their own classrooms after each session to observe and reflect on what's happening there. The learning from and with their students is absent.

Clearly there are trade offs. The challenge I see myself facing is finding ways of establishing a community of learners with the same intensity of purpose as the Institute format fostered. Meeting once a week for seven or eight months can't carry the same kind of sustained engagement as a two-week learning experience can. But I learned a number of things from the Institute which should have an impact on my regular on-campus teaching.

Something I want to take from the Institute is the classroom library. During the Institute I was forced, because of recent copyright legislation, to initiate the classroom library in lieu of using a common set of collected readings. The class library worked much better than I might have hoped for. What I discovered was that people read a great deal more than if I had assigned readings, and they read material that answered some personal need. Having a broad range of books, periodicals, and articles on hand also gave me a chance to respond directly to people's concerns—when someone espoused a closed position on some issue, I was able to suggest something else to read that might let her consider another side of the argument. That was an unexpected benefit, from my perspective, of this more open access to reading material.

The teachers found it difficult both to select material that challenged them and to perceive common concerns when everyone was reading something different. What I still have to work out is how to help people initiate and sustain discussion in these circumstances. I suspect I could focus the conversation on issues common to the various readings with a question or two. After a few sessions I could then encourage people to come up with questions of their own. Anyway, I'm planning to give it a try and see how it works. I'm sure the whole process will need refining, but at least I have somewhere for us to begin.

In the past I've had the teachers in the writing class explore a common genre—we have all attempted to write personal narrative or postcard stories or poetry as a group. The Institute was the first occasion where I threw the writing curriculum wide open and I learned chaos didn't ensue. Quite the opposite, in fact. The teachers formed working groups with a purposeful focus. They had important issues to discuss, problems to solve, and opportunities for offering one another support. The coherence of their writing extended further than in any previous class. Certainly, the intensity of the experience had something to do with that, but the fact that the teachers were working together on something they had chosen to do also contributed to our high level of engagement. I intend opening the writing invitation with the next classes I teach.

One terrific advantage I had with the Institute was knowing ahead of time who would be attending. Because of that, I was able to establish a sense of common purpose several weeks in advance by sending a letter and a few readings for people to respond to. I don't have that opportunity with regular on-campus courses. I rarely know who will be attending until we actually meet. So I have to think about other ways of establishing a common purpose within the first session or two. I'm not sure what initiating activity will work as well as the reading and responding in advance did. That's something I expect I'll be thinking about as I walk into class.

I also have to think of some way of operating the equivalent of the blackboard plan book. I teach many of my classes in the Curriculum Resources Centre. There is no blackboard in the room. I have access to chart paper, though; that might work equally well. The problem will be that other people teach there, too, so I'm not going to be able to keep our plan book posted from week to week. I'll have to keep taking it down and putting it up, I guess.

I can see once again I'm preparing an environment. From the Institute experience I have learned more about which aspects of procedure draw people out and which may not. What I can't take from the Institute, however, is the curriculum we generated. With a negotiated curriculum I can't write a syllabus or lesson plans in advance because I don't know where the teachers and I will be travelling. I may be responsible for getting the enterprise off the ground but once begun each class takes a journey of its own and I have to be ready to be tour guide over territory both familiar and unexplored.

Shortly after the Institute was over I happened to read Sharon Crowley's **A Teacher's Introduction to Deconstruction** (1989). Her third chapter 'Deconstructing Writing Pedagogy,' coming so immediately on the heels of the Institute, resonated with the learning/teaching experience I'd just had. Crowley offered me another theoretical perspective with which to examine my pedagogical beliefs.

Crowley discusses the implications of a deconstructive stance on teaching in the following way:

> I am not sure that a deconstructive pedagogy can be realized—the term is itself an oxymoron. Nevertheless, I can guess about some things a deconstructive pedagogy might be up to if it were thought of as a set of strategies for teaching.
>
> First of all, it would reject the traditional model of authority that obtains in most...classrooms, where the teacher is both receptacle and translator of received knowledge. At the very least a deconstructive pedagogy would adopt the positions that knowledge is a highly contextualized activity which is constructed within groups, communities, or societies; that knowledge itself is a volatile construct, subject to alteration when contexts for knowing are altered; and that so-called "received" knowledge is just that—received. That is, the knowledge which is preferred and privileged at any given moment is so, simply because influential members of the concerned community have subscribed to it (pp. 45-46).

During the Institute I struggled to embrace what Crowley identifies as a deconstructive stance on knowing: that it is a highly contextualized activity, a volatile, social construction. I tried to downplay my privileged expert position by letting the texts and the conversation do the teaching. I accept, of course, that many of the professional texts we discussed were ones I had selected. On the other hand, these texts were being read in conjunction with books and articles chosen by the teachers themselves. So while people's choices here weren't completely open ('complete openness' is a fiction—a mirage—in any case) there was a large element of choice in the situation.

I find setting aside the traditional model of authority difficult. Graduate students come with firmly established expectations both for themselves and for me. Even teachers who have studied with me previously haven't shed their expectations of an authoritarian teacher completely. In most of my classes, the teachers find it hard to determine their own agenda; at first, they hold back expecting me to assign a direction.

Is there any way of removing myself completely from a position of authority? The reality is that I have read widely and thought a great deal about the issues being discussed. Do I want to back out of the classroom? Definitely not. I think my voice has a legitimate place in the conversation. I know, though, I'm not yet comfortable with how I position my contribution. Perhaps I never will be.

> A deconstructive pedagogy would reinforce the notion, as composition specialists would have it, that writing is a process. But it would interpret this slogan more profoundly to mean that the process that is writing is differentiation and not repetition of the same[1]. The writing process differs to some extent with every situation or task; which also implies that no universally useful model or tactics for generating writing will ever be found....This does not mean that the writing process cannot be generalized about, of course. It simply means that writers must always take into account the constraints of the rhetorical situation in which they find themselves (Crowley, p.46).

The phrase 'writing is a process' bothers me—writing isn't constituted by a single process; there are many interwoven processes just as there are with reading. These days, I'm unable to separate what I'm learning about writing while I'm reading from what I'm learning about reading while I'm writing. The boundaries of both aspects of literate behavior have become blurred. Talking and listening, too, play crucial roles.

In the Institute, I tried establishing a context which legitimized many ways of writing (and reading and talking and listening) so that the teachers could reflect on how inextricably linked are the various aspects of language. I sensed that the experiences we negotiated were reasonably successful in raising the teachers' awareness of how interwoven and context dependent writing, reading, and talking are, but I can't judge the extent to which they perceived the inherent contradictions between the uncommonsense view of language which undergirded their experiences in the Institute and traditional instructional assumptions.

> That writing is a process of differentiation also means that a syllabus for a writing class would always be in revision, would always be

---

1 Crowley (1989) means these terms in the sense used by Derrida. From a deconstructive perspective written texts are not synopses of previously worked out thought (repetition) but are representations of thought in action (differentiation). (See Crowley's elaboration of Derrida's arguments in her Chapter 1 "Reading/ Writing Derrida.")

available for alteration as class members' writing changed the focus of the class.... Freewritings, journals, essays, papers, are all part of a differentiating process that they only seem to halt by being put down on paper. They are all susceptible to revision, to incorporation into other texts, whether those texts are written by the same or another or several writers at once. It may (should?) be that no "pieces" of writing are ever completed in such a class. The feeling that a writer can "finish" a piece of writing may simply disguise her exhaustion, her inability to go on, her lack of resources like time or money (Crowley, pp. 46-47).

I certainly tried to hold the Institute agenda open to revision. I saw the activities I initiated as simply a jump-off. While I had a sense of the issues I wished to bring to the fore, how we reached them required input from the teachers. They had to show me how to teach them.

One of the things I find difficult as a teacher is handling the inherent closure of a situation which is bound by a specific time frame the way the Institute was. I constantly felt pressure to keep uncertainty at a tolerable level. I knew from previous experiences that the first few days would seem a jumble for many of the teachers, especially those new to the graduate program at MSVU—I didn't wish them to become overwhelmed. That meant trying to make order apparent from what is essentially an unpredictable and messy enterprise. Talking about 'what's happening here?' certainly helped.

The pressure for closure became more intense as the second week progressed. I felt a strong need to help each person complete a piece of writing for the class publication; in part, because I wanted the teachers to experience the feeling of satisfaction which accompanies a deadline met; in part, because we couldn't discuss a variety of instructional and political issues until they had arisen from the experience. At the end I felt, as I generally do when a course finishes, that we had reached the point where we were now really ready to begin learning together.

A deconstructive pedagogy would devise ways to engage students as active readers—that is, as re-writers—of the teachers' writing—her course. It would encourage students to revise assignments and syllabi, to reject an assigned text and choose new ones. Such procedures would acknowledge the...changing relations that develop between teacher and students—and among students—as the writing class evolves, would mimic the changing relations that occur between words and sentences in a discourse as it is revised. Any readings that were undertaken in connection with such a class, literary or not, would also be seen as texts to be rewritten, to be incorporated into students' writing processes (Crowley, p.47).

One intention I had in setting up the Institute as I did was to make the roles of reader/writer, learner/teacher less distinct. I wanted to help the teachers experience the movement from one stance to another and to think about the questions their shifting from writer/reader, reader/writer, learner/teacher, and teacher/learner raised about their own classrooms. During the Institute I tried, more deliberately than ever before, to open up my own learning and teaching for discussion.

> In a writing class governed by deconstructive attitudes... teachers would sensitize their students to the institutional realities in which they write, and they would treat the institutional situation as a "real-world" one where students are expected to learn a special brand of writing—academic discourse. And since knowledge itself is always in flux, and since preferred knowledge is always inscribed by a culture in its institutions, students and teachers would examine the institutional ideology that governs their work: why "academic discourse" is preferred in school to whatever discourse(s) the students bring to school with them; why students might want to learn it (or not); why teachers are invested with institutional authority; why they are expected to give grades; how this constraint both interferes with, and encouraged, the writing process (Crowley, p.47).

Given the nature of the Institute, the fact that the learners were teachers interested in exploring writing, I was able to set aside academic discourse as the instructional genre. I used our learning situation, instead, to allow us all to explore a variety of non-academic writing possibilities. We used our learning, reading, and writing experiences to discuss the various political issues Crowley mentions.

"Perhaps," Crowley concludes,

> the best to be hoped for is that a deconstructive critique demonstrates the necessity of continued interrogation of the strategies used to teach reading and writing (p. 48).

Toward the end of the Institute I tried to help the teachers understand that the enemy is complacency. The moment we think we've got the situation in hand, when we stop questioning, that's the moment to beware. Assumptions. They're at the heart of any teaching enterprise. Uncovering our tacit beliefs is no easy task but it's essential for becoming a transactional, uncommon sense teacher.

Our classrooms, mine as well as other teachers, abound with orthodoxies—things we do without thinking because we've always done them that way. Trying to work from a transactional perspective means actively trying to see with new eyes, asking ourselves 'What if it's otherwise?' It's only when we're able to acknowledge 'That didn't work!' and then try to understand what we might have done differently that we can begin changing and grow. Neither an easy nor comfortable exercise; but a necessary one.

The issue I was grappling with during the Institute, and which always concerns me as a teacher, is that of control. I am aware there are contradictions between my avowed philosophy of collaboration and transaction and my practice in the classroom. Frequently I appear to be in charge and transmitting what I know. But I know my control is illusory. I know as well as anyone that ultimately my students determine their own learning.

> In every classroom there is a power relation such that the teacher has power over students. I think this is an inescapable fact of the classroom contract. The issue is not whether the teacher is in power, whether she controls, but how she uses that power and negotiates that control. You are still 'in control' as students who attempt to make you responsible for their decisions quickly discover. You use your power in a very different way, and you don't give it away—you simply require your students to take responsibility for themselves.
>
> Ann Vibert

Certainly, I attempt to keep the teachers' focus on our central agenda and on the issues which arise from it. I believe it is my responsibility as teacher to offer some shape to the learning enterprise. But, in reality, my control is much lighter than may come through in these pages, simply because I am not a participant in the majority of conversations which take place in my classroom. Since we spend most of our class time working in small groups, people are on their own a great deal. I attempt to touch base regularly, but the amount of time I can spend in conversation with any one group or individual person is limited, the sense-making that goes on is of necessity in the hands of the learning community.

This issue of control is a complex one. Classrooms generally don't function well if the majority of learners have no sense of what to do and how to do it. Nor are they conducive to learning when the constraints are so limiting that students can make no personal commitment to the various required tasks.

Chaos or compliance, are these the only choices? I believe there's another workable position: a negotiated curriculum. Dewey (1939) explains

> Because the kind of advance planning heretofore engaged in has been so routine as to leave little room for the free play of individual thinking or for the contributions to the distinctive individual experience, it does not follow that all planning must be rejected. On the contrary, there is

incumbent upon the educator the duty of instituting a much more intelligent, and consequently móre difficult, kind of planning. He must survey the capacities and needs of the particular set of individuals with whom he is dealing and must at the same time arrange the conditions which provide the subject-matter or content for experiences that satisfy these needs and develop these capacities. The planning must be flexible enough to permit free play for individuality of experience and yet firm enough to give direction towards continuous development of power.

...The principle that development of experience comes about through interaction means that education is essentially a social process. This quality is realized in the degree in which individuals form a community group. It is absurd to exclude the teacher from membership in the group. As the most mature [I would say experienced] member of the group he has a peculiar responsibility for the conduct of the interactions and intercommunications which are the very life of the group as a community (p. 58).

At the centre of the current debate between transmission and transactional views of education rests this issue of control. Are teachers in control or should students be? Commonsense transmission classrooms operate on the fiction of teachers in control. However, whether we believe it or not, the reality is learners control the decision to engage or not to engage. As a consequence, many teachers attempting to implement a transactional perspective have adopted the myth of students in control and they have backed away from any teacher direction. But that hasn't worked either. In our local region, a new breed of reading and writing 'disabilities' has begun to emerge precisely because many teachers have provided inadequate focus and direction. We are now seeing children, for example, who are having difficulty reading because they have no idea how to orchestrate graphophonic cues. They guess at meaning reasonably proficiently but are stuck when the semantic or pictorial information isn't sufficient for carrying on. There are also now many more students with a limited control of spelling and other writing conventions.

It isn't their teachers' fault entirely. I'm as responsible as anyone for these students' lack of proficiency. In my efforts to help teachers broaden their own and their students' understanding of the many sources of information used for reading and writing, I've de-emphasized the role of conventions. In my attempts to help people develop fluency I offered, until recently, little assistance with clarity and correctness. In my efforts to help teachers provide their students broader opportunities for choice I've neglected an exploration of teacher responsibilities in negotiating curriculum.

Only recently have I begun making my own teaching open to inquiry. By asking the teachers 'What's going on here?', I've allowed us to explore the fine line between guiding and control. For the kind of teaching that Sondra Perl and Nancy Wilson (1986) call 'enabling,' each teacher

> must find his or her own balance between imposing judgement and allowing for students' spontaneity, between controlling students' actions and offering free rein (p. 256).

As teachers we will always have to struggle with this dilemma. As friend and former student, Ann Vibert, writes:

> Your classroom is not really learner-centered any more than a 'traditional' classroom is really teacher-centered: both only appear that way. The difference is everybody—teacher as well as student—is more honest about what is actually going on, and what is actually going on is the curriculum. For instance, in your class if a student draws a caricature of the teacher she'll probably be published rather than punished. The class will go the way you intend it to, though, or you'll fiddle until it does.
>
> But part of your intention is a definite openness, a certain wait and see about what might occur. There are, nonetheless, quite a range of things that will not be in your class, or at least they won't be for long after you discover them, which is the problem with this student-centered jargon. The whole project of education—the great difficulty, the dilemma, the mess as you call it—lies in the fact that it happens in the meeting of learner, curriculum, and teacher. You just can't leave any of the terms out and keep your integrity, as far as I'm concerned.
>
> Of course there's considerable blurring and switching of roles, so that the teacher is a learner and the learner is a teacher and together they create the curriculum. But all the elements must be there and must be accounted for if we are to avoid the charge of manipulation.
>
> Your classroom is not learner-centered; my fellow students and I were intensely aware of you and of the central role you played in what was going on. It was different, though, because what was going on, the process itself, was right out there on the table, open for negotiation. (Vibert, 1989).'

Ann raises the question of manipulation. Is that a concern? Manipulation implies the teacher has everything worked out in advance and sets up the situation to ensure various prescribed outcomes. Although I quite openly employ all kinds of structure—I prepare materials, set up activities, frame discussions, arrange furniture, ask questions, and respond regularly to writing—I try leaving the agenda as open as possible. I do worry about pacing, about keeping activities moving, about the level of engagement, about generating and sustaining interest. I always have to be on the alert for opportunities to step in and offer direction and support. However, no outcome is guaranteed. While I've tried to arrange activities to help people reflect on particular learning and instructional concerns, each learner has to evolve his or her own understanding. I cannot make sense for people; they have to do that for themselves.

My experiences during the Institute have also made me think about the current push for teachers to become researchers. A lot of academics present what teachers know as a "muddled combination of half-truths, myths, and superstitions" (North, 1987). A remedy, people argue, is to teach teachers how to make a more coherent kind of knowledge of practice by adopting the investigative strategies of scholars and researchers. However, as I have learned from personal experience, it is very difficult to maintain a researcher's stance and keep a class going at the same time. Again, during the Institute, I experienced how hard it is to be a 'teacher-researcher' (Goswami and Stillman, 1987). Expecting classroom teachers to be researchers in any formal way is not only misleading, I think it's wrong. Calling for teacher-research shifts our gaze from what I think is the essential aspect of teaching: reflective practice.

> I have been bothered by the teacher researcher stuff more and more lately. I just think its another instance of the university deciding what the classroom teacher should do. It seems to me that we're trying to sell something to others in spite of the fact that many of us have decided it's neither viable nor useful for us to do ourselves.
>
> Diane Stephens

I have come to believe there are two reasons for engaging in reflection: to get to know my students better, to understand what they are doing and experiencing; and to learn more about myself as a teacher. As a reflective practitioner the primary audience for my classroom inquiry is **me**. I may choose at some point to share my reflections and insights with other teachers, as I have done here, but I undertake to teach from a reflective stance as a way of

coming to understand what's happening in the classroom so I
can refine my teaching.

I have done teacher-research on and with my students
(Newman, 1987, 1988). A small focused study of some aspect
of what students might be learning is certainly manageable. But
trying to capture aspects of the multiple conversations I hold
with students, documenting them, trying to show the mess of
teaching, the moment-to-moment decision making has proved
far more difficult than I could have imagined. The teaching, not
the research, has had to come first. And that's the case for most
teachers.

Why should we bother undertaking "reflection-in-action" as
Donald Schön (1983) calls it? Schön himself explains:

> The new satisfactions open to [us] are largely those of discovery—about
> the meanings of [our] advice to our clients [both students and the
> public, including parents], about [our] knowledge-in-practice, and about
> [ourselves]. When a practitioner becomes a researcher into his own
> practice, he engages in a continuing process of self-education....When
> she functions as a researcher-in-practice, the practice itself is a source of
> renewal. The recognition of error, with its resulting uncertainty, can
> become a source of discovery rather than an occasion for self defence (p.
> 299).

What Schön is saying, I think, is that becoming a reflective
practitioner makes it both possible and legitimate for me to
acknowledge the mistakes I make. By exploring teaching
enterprises that seem not to be working I am in a position to
discuss what has happened, or is happening, with my students,
so we can renegotiate the experience to allow more effective
learning to occur.

But there are costs to taking a reflective stance. As Schön
points out, it means we must give up

> the rewards of unquestioned authority, the freedom to practice without
> challenge to our competence, the comfort of relative invulnerability, the
> gratification of deference (p.299).

As a teacher I'm not sure I ever had unquestioned authority or a
sense of invulnerability. I think I have always felt a sense of
uncertainty about how effective my teaching really was. As I
struggle to be a more reflective practitioner I find the freedom to
admit I'm sometimes wrong strengthens my relationship with
my students. They welcome me more readily into their learning
club.

Says Schön:

When we reject the traditional view of professional knowledge, recognizing that practitioners may **become** reflective researchers in situations of uncertainty, instability, uniqueness, and conflict, we have recast the relationship between research and practice. For on this perspective, research is an activity of practitioners. It is triggered by features of the practice situation, undertaken on the spot, and immediately linked to action. There is no question of an "exchange" between research and practice or of the "implementation" of research results, when the frame- or theory-testing experiments of the practitioner at the same time transform the practice situation. Here the exchange between research and practice is immediate, and reflection-in-action is its own implementation (pp. 308-309).

I'm not saying no other kind of research is of any value to us as teachers, only that the research which has the greatest immediate impact on my teaching is the ongoing personal inquiry into my own practice.

Becoming a reflective teacher isn't an easy undertaking. It involves being receptive to the unexpected. I have to be willing, just like my students, to take risks. I have to be prepared to make mistakes and to deal with problems as they occur.

As a teacher I always have this nagging question 'Am I doing this right?' The answer, I have discovered, comes from my students. In order to learn from my students I have to let them teach me.

My teaching as a reflective practitioner, however, has serious repercussions for all of my students. The experiences I initiate force a comparison with the teachers' own beliefs and practices; they evoke both self and social reflection. Most teachers arrive in my classes with a tacit commonsense view of teaching. Confronting those beliefs causes most people considerable discomfort.

First, people have to confront their expectations about being students. They have to overcome their bewilderment with my not telling them what they're supposed to do and how to do it. They have to learn to 'just try' and see what happens. They also have to learn how to react to my feedback and probing questions, not as criticism of their efforts, but as a nudge to look beyond present assumptions. They have to learn to trust that I really mean it when I say helping one another isn't cheating.

Then they have to learn to work together. They have to learn how to initiate and sustain a focused discussion, to venture candid reactions to one another's ideas and experiences, and to respond openly to the feedback that's offered. It all requires trust and developing trust takes time.

As the teachers begin to build a learning community a new level of discomfort emerges. People suddenly become aware that we're not play-acting, we're engaged in serious business. As one teacher wrote last winter

> I've just realized that we aren't play-acting in your class. You really are engaging with us and learning alongside us. You aren't just getting us to write in order to evaluate us. I didn't realize that I have been doubting you until now.
>
> Through all these years of formal schooling I've been thinking of myself and the teachers/professors as play-acting. We all 'act' as if the roles we're playing are for real. We adopt the role of 'learner /student', just present our 'work' and 'act' as if we've learned something of value and the teacher...well, she'll just 'act' as if she's really interested and is learning something from all of this. (Of course we all know she's not because she has all the 'right' answers anyway and this will be reflected in the mark we receive.)
>
> I can see now that this play-acting ritual is just what we subject children to. We expect them to read, write, study science, do mathematics and a host of other subjects and yet they see us doing very little except grading. Of course, there are the 'good' teachers, the good 'role models,' who write when the children write or 'act' interested in the students' work but most often the situations are so contrived that the whole thing is really just play-acting. The students (and teachers) learn to become very good 'actors.' The only problem with this whole set-up is that the 'top' students waste their talent because they spend most of their time trying to figure out just what it is the teacher wants; the 'weaker' students have no acting skills whatsoever, and the vast majority who fall somewhere in the middle just mosey along, churning out one meaningless piece of work after another.
>
> Do I do this to my students? You bet I do! But not as often as I once did and after tonight hopefully less often still.

Play-acting is safe—beliefs aren't on the line. You go through the motions, receive a grade, and it's business as usual back in the classroom. But as the teachers begin trusting our evolving learning community they meet **fear**—fear of silence, fear of losing control, fear of being accountable, fear of exposure, fear of confrontation, fear of uncertainty—the list of fears is long.

At this point, many people attempt some fence-sitting: 'Yes, but...' they say, 'that won't work with my students.' 'Yes, but I don't have the resources, the furniture, the know-how to make it work.' 'The principal won't let me.' 'What would I say to parents?' They identify an extensive list of barriers. People are afraid to admit that we created the present situation and have both the responsibility as well as the right to examine and even change it. Their 'Yes, but...'s serve to protect the status quo. However, the collaborative context allows us to deal with these evasions. Some of the teachers begin to just try with their students and return to class eager to report on what happened. Nevertheless, there are times when I am pushed to decree "No more 'yes, but...'s! Let's consider 'what if?' instead."

As people begin looking at themselves and their assumptions, as they alter some instructional practices, the community around them starts pushing back. These teachers are no longer comfortable with their colleagues who feel threatened by the changes they are attempting. Some parents respond with hostility and demand a return to familiar transmission teaching. Principals react to what appears to be lack of control and students who now question rules. And students, particularly older students, balk at what looks like a lot more work and unnecessary investment.

The kind of learning I'm trying to foster develops a democratic, critical, analytic discourse. As David Dillon (1990) puts it:

> This kind of learning values and fosters diversity, complexity, ambiguity, and multiple perspectives—the very messiness and mystery and magic and myth of life which schooling seems too ill-equipped to deal with. This kind of learning...is what frees or liberates us from seeing things as they are to reseeing them as they might be. It's what critical thinking really implies, what our imaginations are for—to remake the world by renaming it with our **language** and thus living differently in the world, and doing that over and over again in an endless journey (p. 334).

My assuming a reflective stance pushes my students to become reflective practitioners themselves—to become critical of their own experience, to question the way schools are run, the way classrooms are conducted, the way students relate to one another. And as these teachers become more openly reflective, they open the way for their students to move beyond doing what they're told to do, to learning to reflect and question for themselves.

This kind of learning, as Harman and Edelsky point out, is both empowering and alienating. It has the potential to produce both personal and political change—and while change can be empowering, it can also provoke estrangement. If I'm successful as a teacher, I push people into a very vulnerable position. Not only are their professional lives affected. Personal relationships are open to new scrutiny as well. These people now question assumptions. They are no longer satisfied to accept directives blindly. They expect and want to have some input into what's going on, to participate in decision-making.

Can I avert the alienation that change produces? Not easily. But I can help people understand it. I can help them examine what they are experiencing, supporting them as they explore their responsibilities in new ways. I can raise questions, share my own decision-making as a classroom teacher and professional educator, show myself still learning, offer evidence that changing is a slow process and that no one ever arrives. I can help people sort out the inconsistencies, the incongruities, the conflicts of teaching. I can help them cope with the strain of trying to maintain a professional stance when their judgement is challenged. I can help them develop the confidence to question what they're doing and affirm that it's OK to make mistakes. I can help them discover a new sense of themselves as learners.

> My grade 11 and 12 students have had no experience with open-ended teaching practices. I can tell because when I offer a new strategy or task I get dead silence, sort of a 'let's-wait-and-see-what-she's-up-to-now' attitude. They expect me to lecture and give notes. I'm supposed to put red marks on essays they can throw in the garbage can. I'm suppose to chastise them for talking. 'Your expect us to do all the work,' they complain, and I say, 'Yes, I do.' Many are there for the mark and not the learning. Once in a while, though, I'm pleasantly surprised by a student who gets into a book or a piece of writing for something othen than the mark. Like Darrell last year—a bright yet lazy twelve general student, who read a novel because he had to and then went looking for more by the same author because 'I like the way he writes description.'
>
> Patricia Whidden

As I see it, my job is to help people engage in an ongoing conversation which allows them understand the theoretical debates, to entertain conflicting points of view, to examine and question and restructure the world as we currently perceive it. My responsibility is to help people struggle actively with the issues of literacy, community, identity, and social change.

And are you still wondering about Gerry? Occasionally I wonder about him, myself. I can't tell you what happened to him, or to the other children, in the special education class because I do not know. When I took off that November day in 1971 I had no further direct contact either with those children or that school.

At one point I was tempted to end this narrative by rewriting the opening scenario. I thought about presenting that class as I might teach those children today. But I have chosen not to do that. The story of Gerry didn't have a happy ending. To create one here would be to undermine the lesson I learned. My experience with Gerry was a failure I had to accept and grow from. I nearly didn't learn it. Having hardly begun, I almost walked away from teaching as a result of that experience. Now I'm thankful I didn't.

Teaching as a profession demands of its practitioners an ability to live with a great deal of ambiguity and uncertainty. While I am continually building a body of experience which I can draw upon, each new encounter with a student or group of students is unique. I will need to make most instructional judgements on the spur of the moment. And quite likely, whatever my response, it will be useful for some and interfering for others. I have come to accept that all I can do is just try and to learn from how my students respond.

In a few weeks I'll be engaging in conversation with new students. One of the joys of teaching is being able to use the teaching situation itself to explore ideas. I know that what I currently believe about teaching will be affected by our many conversations and by what I read next. In a year's time, who knows what new insights I will have gained about myself as a learner and as a teacher.

Teaching is a puzzle. Unlike conventional jigsaws, however, there is no solution; each class creates an intriguing picture of its own. And as a teacher I must become an adventurer because "The Road goes ever on and on..."

APPENDIX READINGS
Reading Like a Writer

Frank Smith

The first time I explored learning to write in detail, I was tempted to conclude that it was, like the flight of bumblebees, a theoretical impossibility. I examined the trivializing oversimplifications that writing was basically a matter of handwriting and a few spelling and punctuation rules. I questioned the myth that one could learn to write by diligent attention to instruction and practice. And 1 was left with the shattering conundrum that writing requires an enormous fund of specialized knowledge which cannot be acquired from lectures, textbooks, drill, trial and error, or even from the exercise of writing itself. A teacher may set for children tasks that result in the production of a small but acceptable range of sentences, but much more is required to become a competent and adaptable author of letters, reports, memoranda, journals, term papers, and perhaps occasional poems or pieces of fiction suitable to the demands and opportunities of out-of-school situations. Where do people who write acquire all the knowledge that they need?

The conclusion I reached was as problematical as the riddle it was supposed to resolve, because I decided that it could only be through reading that writers learn all the intangibles that they know. And not only is there an unfortunate abundance of evidence that people who read do not necessarily become competent writers, but I had myself argued that fluent readers need not pay attention to matters like spelling and punctuation which must be the writers concern. To learn to write, children must read in a special kind of way.

This article will follow the sequence of my reasoning. First I shall try to show that writing demands far more specialized knowledge than is usually realized, very little of which can be contained within formal instruction. Next I shall argue why this knowledge can only be acquired from a particular kind of reading. I shall then try to illustrate how this kind of reading occurs, and show that children are very experienced at learning in this way. Finally I shall consider how teachers can facilitate such learning. I shall be concerned throughout with what might go wrong, so that even people who read extensively may fail to learn about writing.

The Complexity of Writing

Even the most mundane kinds of text involve a vast number of conventions of a complexity which could never be organized into formal instructional procedures. The scope and scale of such conventions are generally unsuspected by teachers and learners alike. Spelling, for example, demands the memorization of every word we are ever likely to write.[1] The "rules" of spelling can be numbered in the hundreds and still carry only a fifty percent probability of being correct for any particular word. There are so many alternatives and exceptions that we must confirm and memorize the correct spelling of every word we hope to write with confidence in the future, even if it does happen to be "regular." When does anyone check the spelling of all the words that are routinely spelled correctly, let alone commit them to memory?

Punctuation, capitalization and other "rules" of grammar are essentially circular and meaningless to anyone who cannot already do what is being "explained." Children are instructed to begin sentences with a capital letter and to end them with a period, but if they ask what a sentence is they will sooner or later be told that it is something which begins with a capital letter and ends with a period. The statement that a sentence is "a complete thought" is as inaccurate and useless as the assertion that a word is "a unit of meaning" or that a paragraph is organized around a single topic. How would anyone recognize a unit of meaning, a complete thought, or a topic in isolation? Linguists are unable to make any constructive use of such statements, which are definitions, not rules of application. They are meaningless to anyone without an implicit understanding of the conventions that determine what shall constitute a word, sentence, or paragraph, conventions which differ from one language to another. Unfortunately, those in possession of such implicit understanding tend to find the definitions transparently obvious and to regard them as the basis of learning rather than the consequence of having learned. Obviously anyone who can write must have knowledge of these conventions, but this knowledge cannot be made explicit and taught to others.

Even arbitrary "rules," descriptions, and definitions evade us when it comes to such subtle matters as style, the intricate registers that depend upon the topic of discussion and the

---

[1] The arguments in this section concerning the inadequacy of the "mechanics" which are the grist of writing instruction are condensed from Chapter 10 of Smith (1982).

audience addressed, and the "schemas" appropriate to the particular medium being employed. Not only must letters, telegrams, formal and informal notes, newspaper reports, magazine articles, short stories, and poems be composed differently, the format of the genre itself varies depending upon its specific purpose. Letters to close friends and to the bank manager have no more in common than news items in the *National Enquirer* and in the *Wall Street Journal.* These conventions remain to be fully investigated by linguists, who have only recently begun to analyze many critical aspects of language which everyone observes and expects, in speech and in competent writing, without awareness of their existence. There are, for example, the complex rules of "cohesion" which link sentences to each other and to the non-language context (Halliday and Hasan 1976). How could any of this be reduced to prescriptions, formulas, or drills? Even if we could and do learn a few hundred spellings, some useful grammatical constructions and some precepts of punctuation through diligent study at school, these would be only a fraction of the expertise a competent journeyman writer requires.

What about learning by trial and error or "hypothesis-testing"? I thought the answer must be that we learn to write by writing until I reflected upon how little anyone writes in school, even the eager students, and how little feedback is provided. Errors may be corrected but how often are correct models provided, especially beyond the level of words? How often is such feedback consulted, and acted upon, especially by those who need correction most? No one writes enough to learn more than a small part of what writers have to know. Most experienced writers can produce text that is right the first time, or at least they can edit or rewrite into conventional form, without extensive feedback, what they more hurriedly produce. Besides, if we learn to write by testing hypotheses in writing, where do the hypotheses come from? Practice and feedback may help to polish writing skills, but cannot account for their acquisition in the first place.

Learners need to find and assimilate a multitude of facts and examples, ranging from individual spellings to the appropriate organization of complex texts. Where can all these facts and examples be found, when they are not available in the lectures, textbooks, and exercises to which children are exposed in classrooms? The only possible answer seemed as obvious to me as I hope it now is to the reader— they must be found in what other people have written, in existing texts. To learn how to write for newspapers you must read newspapers; textbooks about them will not suffice. For magazines, browse through magazines rather than through correspondence courses on magazine writing. To write poetry, read it. For the conventional style of memoranda in your school, consult your school files.

All this seemed so self-evident, once I dispelled my own illusion that prescriptive instruction could and had to suffice for conveying even a modicum of what writers need to know. All examples of written language in use display their own relevant conventions. All demonstrate their own appropriate grammar, punctuation, and manifold stylistic devices. All are showcases for the spelling of words. So now I know where the knowledge resides that writers require. It is in existing texts; it is there for the reading. The question is how does such knowledge get into readers' heads so that they become writers themselves?

The answer cannot be that all this specialized knowledge is acquired through deliberate formal analyses, by sitting down with the particular texts and making extensive notes, memorizing data and examples. What is learned is too intricate and subtle for that, and there is too much of it. There is not enough time. Instead it must be that the learning takes place without deliberate effort, even without awareness. We learn to write without knowing we are learning or what we learn. Everything points to the necessity of learning to write from what we read. This is the trick to be explained.

Learning as a Collaborative Activity

The alternative I have to propose is that knowledge of all the conventions of writing gets into our head like much of our knowledge of spoken language and indeed of the world in general, without awareness of the learning that is taking place. The learning is unconscious, effortless, incidental, vicarious, and essentially collaborative. It is incidental because we learn when learning is not our primary intention, vicarious because we learn from what someone else does, and collaborative because we learn through others helping us to achieve our own ends.

Consider the range and extent of spoken language children learn during the first four or five years of their lives. Miller (1977) estimated that infants must add words to their vocabulary at an average rate of one every hour they are awake, a total of several thousands a year. Young children learn grammars (in order to talk and to understand) with a complexity which defies linguistic analysis. They master a multitude of idiomatic expressions and intricate nuances of cohesion and register which most adults do not suspect that they themselves observe, let alone their children. They learn complex subtleties of intonation and gesture. All of this is done without formal instruction, with very little evident trial and error, and with no deliberate diagnostic or remedial intervention at all.

There is an exquisite selectivity. Children first begin talking like their parents, then like their peers, and later, perhaps, like their favored entertainment or sporting personalities. They do not learn to talk like everyone they hear speaking, even those they may hear most. They learn the language of the groups to which they belong (or expect to belong) and resist the language of the groups that they reject or from which they are rejected. They learn, I want to say, from the clubs to which they belong.

This pervasive learning extends far beyond the structures and customs of language to mannerisms, dress, ornamentation, and larger patterns of behavior in general. It takes place in the absence of overt motivation or deliberate intention (as all of us know who come away from a film or a book acting the part of one of the characters). Engagement is the term I have used to characterize such learning (Smith 1981a). It is not learning that takes place as a consequence of someone else doing something, but rather learning that occurs concurrently with the original act—provided it is our act too. The other person's behavior is our own learning trial. We learn when the other person does something on our behalf, something which we would like to do, which we take for granted.

Adults have neither the time nor the expertise to teach spoken language to children. Instead, they act as a source of information for children and as unwitting collaborators. They are overheard as they talk to each other, and thereby show children why and how speech can be used. They demonstrate language being used for purposes which children would expect to accomplish themselves. Often the explanation of the language is embedded in the situation in which it is used—someone says "Pass the salt" and someone else passes it. Television is replete with such examples, especially in the commercial announcements. Sometimes the explanation is explicit, as adults or peers elaborate upon a meaning for a child, though the intention is no more deliberately pedagogical than it is when a child is told "Look, there's a McDonalds." And when a child wants to say something, an adult or a friend helps the child to say it. No one gives a child struggling to be understood a low grade and a kit of instructions. But children do not need to be personally involved to learn to say what they would like to be able to say. They learn when others do the talking for a purpose they want or expect to share. In effect, adults and peers admit children to the club of people who talk as they do. They do not expect children to be experts in advance, nor do they anticipate failure. There are no admission requirements.

In such circumstances, children learn from what they overhear by "listening like a talker." They do not regard the language they learn from as something remote, an attribute of others, but rather as something they themselves would want and expect to do. They become "spontaneous apprentices" as Miller (1977) felicitously puts it, engaging in the enterprises of the adults or peers who are their unsuspecting surrogates for the trial and error of learning (and who since they are experienced tend to have a variety of trials and very few errors, a most efficient form of learning). The only source of the complex and subtle language that children learn for their own social groups must be speech they hear in use, to which they can listen like a talker. And clearly, all children who can talk like their family and friends must be very good at listening and learning in this way. They must have been doing it since before the time they could say a word for themselves.

Obviously children do not learn about spoken language from everything they hear spoken. Sometimes they do not understand and sometimes they are not interested, two circumstances which all teachers know are not conducive to learning (except that something is confusing or boring). Obviously also, children (and adults) can pay attention and understand what is said without coming to talk like a particular speaker. We frequently "listen like a listener" when we attend to what is said but have no desire or expectation that we should come away talking like the speaker. We do not see ourselves belonging to that particular club; we are not that kind of a person, and the vicarious engagement does not take place.

The consequence of not being a member of the club is dramatic, for children and for adults. We do not learn. In effect, the brain learns not to learn, it shuts down its own sensitivity (Smith 1981a). Exclusion from any club of learners is a condition difficult to reverse, whether we impose it upon ourselves or have it imposed on us.

Collaboration with Authors

I have discussed how adults and more competent peers act as unwitting collaborators as children learn about spoken language. Children learn vicariously, provided they can "listen like a talker" by virtue of their implicit membership in the particular club to which the practitioners they hear speaking belong. My argument now is that everyone who becomes a competent writer uses authors in exactly the same way, even children who may not yet be able to write a word. They must read like a writer, in order to learn how to write like a writer. There is no other way in which the intricate complexity of a writer's knowledge can be acquired.

Most literate adults are familiar with the experience of pausing unexpectedly while reading a newspaper, magazine, or book in order to go back and look at the spelling of a word that has caught their attention. We say to ourselves, "Ah, so that's how that word is spelled," especially if the word is a familiar one that we have only previously heard, like a name on radio or television. The word may or may not be spelled the way we would expect it to be spelled. It just looks new. We did not begin reading in order to have a spelling lesson, and we are not aware of paying attention to spelling (and to every other technical aspect of the writing) as we read. But we notice the unfamiliar spelling—in the same way that we would notice an incorrect one—because we are writing the text as we read it. We are reading like a writer, or at least like a speller. This is a word whose spelling we ought to know, that we expect to know, because we are the kind of person who knows spellings like this.

Here is a second example. Once more we are casually reading, and once more we find ourselves pausing to reread a passage. Not because of the spelling this time, nor because we did not understand the passage. In fact we understood it very well. We go back because something in the passage was particularly well put, because we respond to the craftsman's touch. This is something we would like to be able to do ourselves, but also something that we think is not beyond our reach. We have been reading like a writer, like a member of the club.

On neither of these two occasions would I want to say that we learn as a consequence of what we read. We do not turn aside from our reading to study the spelling or the stylistic device that we have noticed. If we learn at all, we learn at the first encounter, vicariously, concurrently. If we can write at all we must have learned much more than we are aware of on these occasions. In fact I am inclined to think that the new spelling or style attracts our adult attention because it is an exception, because we know the spellings of most of the words that we read. We must have been adding to our repertoire of spellings at a rate approaching that of children's learning spoken words, namely hundreds, if not thousands, a year. We were no more aware of the individual learning occasions than we were conscious of learning the meaning of all the words we know. It is only after the event, sometimes, that we realize that we have vicariously learned, when we find ourselves using words, phrases, and stylistic idiosyncrasies of the particular author we have read.

I also do not want to say that even accomplished writers read like a writer every time they read. It does not happen when the attention is overloaded, when we have trouble trying to understand what we are reading. (How can one read like the writer of something one cannot understand?) There is not much opportunity to read like a writer when we are totally concerned with the act of reading, with getting every word right, or with trying to memorize all the facts. It does not happen when we have no interest in writing what we read. We do not come away talking like a telephone directory after looking up a few numbers. And it does not occur when we have no expectation of writing the kind of written language we read. The latter illustrates my essential point again, the learning occurs only when we perceive ourselves as members of the club. We can and often do read simply like a reader, for whatever purpose we are reading. But to learn to write we must read like a writer. This need not interfere with comprehension, in fact it will promote comprehension because it is based upon prediction.

To read like a writer we engage with the author in what the author is writing. We anticipate what the author will say, so that the author is in effect writing on our behalf, not showing how something is done but doing it with us. This is identical to the spoken language situation where adults help children say what they want to say or would like and expect to be able to say. The author becomes an unwitting collaborator. Everything the learner would want to spell the author spells. Everything the learner would want to punctuate the author punctuates. Every nuance of expression, every relevant syntactic device, every turn of phrase, the author and learner write together. Bit by bit, one thing at a time, but enormous numbers of things over the passage of time, the learner learns through *reading* like a writer to *write* like a writer.

Of course, there is also a need to write, especially for beginners. Writing enables one to perceive oneself as a writer, as a member of the club, and thus to learn to write by reading.

There is also a need for a teacher or other practitioner to be an immediate collaborator with the learning writer, for support and encouragement and also to provide knowledge of technicalities which a text cannot offer. Such technicalities range from the use of paper clips, index cards, and wastepaper baskets to the nature and utility of drafts and of editing, none of which is apparent in published texts and none of which, therefore, the author can demonstrate. One might add to the preceding list all the emotional concomitants of writing and its blocks, which people who are not experienced members of the club rarely seem to appreciate and which are frequently not dominant considerations in classrooms.

The Teacher's Role

Teachers have two critically important functions in guiding children towards literacy: to demonstrate uses for writing and to help children use writing themselves. Put in other words, teachers must show the advantages that membership in the club of writers offers, and ensure that children can join.

Teachers do not have to teach children to read like writers, though they may indeed for a while have to see that beginners get help to read. And of course, teachers must help children to write—not teach them about writing—so that they can perceive themselves as members of the club. Teachers must also ensure that children have access to reading materials that are relevant to the kinds of writer they are interested in becoming at a particular moment; teachers must recruit the authors who will become the unwitting collaborators.

In particular, teachers must help children to perceive themselves as readers and writers before the children are able to read and write for themselves.

It is not difficult to imagine how children can be helped to read before they can read a word for themselves. Someone must do the reading for them. Teachers should not be afraid that a child who is read to will become dependent or lazy. Children able to read something they want to read will not have the patience to wait for someone else to read for them, any more than they will wait for someone to say something on their behalf if they can say it for themselves.

It is instructive to observe what happens as young children are read to. First someone reads *to* them (they listen like a listener). Then the other person reads with them (they listen like a reader). Finally, that most annoying thing happens—the child wants to turn the page before the collaborator gets to the end of it (the child is reading). Of course, a teacher may not always have the time to read with an individual child, but it is not necessary for the teacher to take this collaborative role. Other children can do this, or children can read in groups, or other adults can be recruited. The important thing is to make the reading a natural activity, preferably one initiated by the child for the child's own purposes, whether that is to enjoy a story, to share a newspaper report, or to find out what is on the lunch menu or the television program for the day.

It may not be so easy to imagine how children can be helped to see themselves as authors before they can write a word. For a teacher (or some other collaborator) to act as secretary for the child, taking care of handwriting, spelling, punctuation, and so forth, is not enough. There are many other decisions and conventions with which a neophyte needs help, as the following illustration will show.

The aim must be a collaboration so close that a child feels personally responsible for every word in a story (or poem or letter), even though the child did not think of a single word in the first place. First the teacher and child have to establish that the child will write a story, that the child is to be an author. The following dialog ensues:

> Teacher: What do you want to write a story about?
> Child: I don't know. (The child's problem is identical to that of a university student confronted with writing a dissertation, not that there is nothing to be written about, but that the number of alternatives is overwhelming.)
> Teacher: Do you want to write about an astronaut, an alligator, a wicked witch, a baseball star, or yourself?
> Child: An astronaut.
> Teacher: (writes down the title): How does the story start?
> Child: I don't know.
> Teacher offers some alternatives, the child decides, the teacher writes.
> Teacher: What happens next?
> Child: I don't know.

And so on. Always the teacher offers some alternatives, and the child decides. This is especially important at the end. There is a myth that children (and many university students) can produce only very short texts. But with appropriate incentive they can write on and on, until in principle I suppose the entire contents of their heads is unravelled. The child's problem (and that of the university student) is most likely to be lack of an appropriate convention for ending. If you do not know how to stop you might just as well stop now. So the teacher must offer a choice of exits.

And when they are done the child feels responsible for the entire story, as indeed the child was. This was a collaboration, and the story would not have been written as it was without the two parties who were involved. It makes no more sense to talk about who did what than to ask who carried which part if teacher and child carry a table together which neither could carry alone.

To become writers children must read like writers. To read like writers they must see themselves as writers. Children will read stories, poems, and letters differently when they see these texts as things they themselves could produce; they will write vicariously with the authors. But to see themselves as writers they need collaboration from an interested practitioner.

There is no way of helping children to see themselves as writers if they themselves are not interested. That is why the first responsibility of teachers is to show children that writing is interesting, possible, and worthwhile. But there is also no way of helping children to write if the teacher does not think writing is interesting, possible, and worthwhile. Teachers who are not members of the club cannot admit children to the club.

How can teachers learn to see themselves as writers? They must learn to read like writers themselves, and to do that they must, like children, collaborate with people who are also engaged in the enterprise of writing. For most teachers this should be easy—they can write with their own students, in a collaboration so close that no one can say to whom the successes and failures belong. What matters is not how well teachers or students may write when they write together but the manner in which they will read when they regard themselves as writers. Teachers who write poetry with children will find themselves reading poetry differently; they will be reading like members of the club of poets. And as members of the club, they will learn.

Overcoming the Constraints of School

Unfortunately schools are not always good places for children to see themselves as members of the club of writers. The membership fees may be beyond many of them. The way in which schools are organized does not encourage collaboration; it favors instruction over demonstration, and evaluation over purpose. A "programmed" approach can reduce literacy to ritual and triviality for many children (Smith 1981b) and leave little time for engagement in meaningful written language. Teachers can never be collaborators with children who regard them as taskmasters and antagonists.

The pervasiveness of the drills, exercises, and rote learning of programmatic literacy activities is such that some teachers tend to lose touch with what writing is really for. I can offer a short and incomplete list that will encompass more writing and reading than is possible in any school day.

Writing is for stories to be read, books to be published, poems to be recited, plays to be acted, songs to be sung, newspapers to be shared, letters to be mailed, jokes to be told, notes to be passed, cards to be sent, cartons to be labelled, instructions to be followed, designs to be made, recipes to be cooked, messages to be exchanged, programs to be organized, excursions to be planned, catalogs to be compared, entertainment guides to be consulted, memos to be circulated, announcements to be posted, bills to be collected, posters to be displayed, cribs to be hidden, and diaries to be concealed. Writing is for ideas, action, reflection, and experience. It is not for having your ignorance exposed, your sensitivity destroyed, or your ability assessed.

So how can teachers help children see the advantages and possibilities of the club of writers, despite all the constraints of school? As I have argued before (Smith 1981b), teachers must engage children in purposeful written language enterprises as often as they can and protect them from the destructive effects of meaningless activities which cannot otherwise be avoided. The first step is for teachers themselves to be able to distinguish meaningful writing and senseless ritual, and the second is to discuss the difference with the children.

In particular, teachers should try to protect themselves and children from the effects of evaluation. Where evaluation and grading are unavoidable, as they so often are, it should be made clear to children that they are done for administrative, bureaucratic, or political purposes and have nothing to do with "real world" writing. Grading never taught a writer anything (except that he or she was not a member of the club). Writers learn by learning about writing, not by getting numbers put on their efforts or their abilities. Children (and university students) who will write only for a grade have learned a very odd notion of what constitutes the advantages of the club of writers.

This is not a matter of "correction," which in any case does not make anyone a better writer. Correction merely highlights what learners almost certainly know they cannot do in the first place. Correction is worthwhile only if the learner would seek it in any case, and to seek correction for what you do you must regard yourself as a professional, you must be a member of the club. I am not saying there should not be standards, but that the standards have to come from what the learner wants to achieve. Emphasis on the elimination of mistakes results in the elimination of writing.

It is difficult for many teachers not to see evaluation as a necessity. It probably pervades the atmosphere in which they work. They may not have been told of its devastating effect on sensitivity or of its inevitable relationship with meaningless activity. Writing done for a purpose requires and permits no evaluation beyond fitness for that purpose, which can only be assessed by the learner by comparison with how the same purpose is achieved by more experienced members of the club. But that is always how children learn; they need not be told to find the better way for doing what they want to do; they look for it. Children never want to speak an inadequate version of the language of the groups to which they adhere, any more than they want to dress in a less than conventional way. If they are members of a club they want to live to its standards. A child who does not want to learn is clearly demonstrating exclusion from the group, voluntary or imposed.

School should be the place where children are initiated into the club of writers as soon as possible, with full rights and privileges even as apprentices. They will read like writers, and acquire full status in the club, if they are not denied admission at the threshold.

References

Halliday, Michael A. K. and Hasan, Ruqaya. *Cohesion in English.* London: Longman, 1976.

Miller, George A. *Spontaneous Apprentices: Children and Language.* New York: Seabury, 1977.

Smith, Frank. "Demonstrations, Engagement and Sensitivity: A Revised Approach to Language Learning." *Language Arts* 58 (1981): 103-122.(a)

_____. "Demonstrations, Engagement and Sensitivity: The Choice between People and Programs." *Language Arts* 58 (1981): 634-642.(b)

_____. *Writing and the Writer.* New York: Holt, Rinehart & Winston, 1982.

A Writer and an Author Collaborate

Wayne Serebrin

"I'm still pretty frisky," puffed Doris from the exercise wheel."Humph!" snorted Olga, munching on the only food pellet Boris had missed. (From *Olga and Boris,* a story by Kristen Matthews.)

Kristen, a seven-year-old first-grader, liked to write about her guinea pigs, Olga and Boris. A week prior to writing the above lines she had written a piece on how to care for pet guinea pigs. Encouraged by the responses she had received from other authors in the class, Kristen decided that she would like to have her account "published." By the time her publication was ready, a number of writers in the class had begun to work on their own "pet care" manuals.

But on this day, her writing was not coming easily. Kristen wanted to "make a funny story about Olga and Boris" but was having trouble getting started. She squirmed uneasily in her seat. Shrugging her shoulders, she looked up at me from her heavily erased page. "Well," I ventured, "how would one of your favorite authors make Olga and Boris seem funny?" For a brief moment she puzzled over the "help" I had offered. Then, with a confident "I know" she stood up and pushed passed me on her way to the book corner. She emerged clutching a well-worn copy of one of James Marshall's *George and Martha* stories. I was no longer needed. I returned to the table where I had been writing and watched her.

While I had hoped Kristen would be able to recall instances of humorous writing which she had enjoyed as a reader, I had no idea how she would proceed from reading to writing. In fact, the ease with which she began writing surprised me. She selected and read only certain passages of Marshall's book, closed the cover, and began her own Olga and Boris episode.

What did not surprise me was her choice of author. Kristen had, after all, introduced our class to James Marshall's stories. After our first read aloud, I, too, had become a devoted fan of these personable hippos. As a class we had talked and laughed about George and Martha—as if they were real—and our dramatic show of affection for them had become part of the ritual we shared with each rereading.

When I checked back with Kristen a short time later, she expressed delight with how well her "funny" piece was going.

At this point I realized that my question had served a functional need for Kristen; it had given her a new perspective of how she could help herself out of her writing problems. I was glad that earlier I had not tried to show her how to make her story "funny"—she had maintained control. And while 1 believed that humorous stories would provide Kristen with the best insights into comic writing, 1 also believed that those insights would have to come from her own current sense of what comic writing was all about. She could only write from what she knew and when it came to humorous writing for Kristen, as a member of our class, that meant George and Martha.

Because these stories were such an intimate part of Kristen's social and literary experience, she knew exactly where to look for what she needed. She was not going back to see how James Marshall had handled humor here or there; her comments during class discussions had already demonstrated that she had insights into his craftsmanship. Instead, she returned to Marshall's story with the intention of writing an Olga and Boris story—"trying out" Olga and Boris in places where they might "work" in Marshall's text. Frank Smith (1983) would argue that Kristen was "reading like a writer;" using Marshall's "nuance of expression, relevant syntactic devices," and "turn of phrase" to support the creation of her own story. And Kristen's story truly was a creative act. She had not just deleted George and Martha and inserted Olga and Boris in their place. Rather, without a formal analysis of Marshall's text, she had captured the essence of his humor "vicariously" and had woven it into her own understanding of Olga and Boris. Marshall had become an "unwitting collaborator" and the children in the class were about to hear a unique variation of an old, well-loved theme.

In deciding to write humor for the first time, Kristen had set herself a difficult task. She had placed herself in what Harste, Woodward, and Burke (1984) call a "position of vulnerability." She was clearly at risk—maybe she wouldn't be able to make Olga and Boris seem funny. But what an opportunity for learning. Here was a chance to develop a new notion of who she was and what she was capable of doing.

As a teacher, how did I set up the learning environment so that Kristen's risk- taking was encouraged and supported? In the first place, I wrote with the children every day and shared my efforts with them. I encouraged them to do the same with me and with one another. We discussed language strategies which had been useful for us; for example, we talked about Kristen's strategy of "reading like a writer" and thereby legitimized its use and invited others to give it a try. We read and wrote as a necessary part of whatever we were doing; literacy was not confined to isolated "language arts" periods. We exchanged ideas for writing. We collaborated on parts of whole pieces. We found an audience or reader who could tell us when our writing made sense and where it was unclear or disjointed. Sometimes, we asked for suggestions on how to proceed with a text. Much later we found writers who could give us editing advice, on such technical matters as choice of words, sentence structure, spelling, and punctuation. We "published" works which writers had selected. Finally, when we were all finished, we celebrated our accomplishments.

In a few days there would be another new book in the book corner. From the excited murmurings which surrounded Kristen's venture into comic writing, I suspected that *Olga and Boris,* like the *George and Martha* stories, was headed for the top of the classroom's "bestseller" list.

Across the room Molly, another first grader, was telling her best friend that she was going to write a "funny" story about her stuffed animals, Hoppy and Mousie.

References

Harste, J. C., Woodward, V. A., & Burke, C. L. *Language Stories and Literacy Lessons.* Exeter, N.H.: Heinemann Educational Books, 1984.

Marshall, J. *George and Martha Rise and Shine.* Boston: Houghton Mifflin, 1976.

Smith, F. "Reading like a Writer." *Language Arts,* 60 (1983): 558–567.

"Could you put in lots of holes?"
Modes of Response to Writing

Russell A. Hunt

The idea that reading, writing, and thinking are essentially and radically social in nature has in recent years gained increasing acceptance among English and language arts teachers and researchers. Accordingly, we have begun to hear a good deal more about the necessity for apprentice writers to acquire a sense of audience by actually having other people respond to their writing. Regularly, it is suggested that writers can begin this process through the help of others—either the thoughtful, expert assistance of the teacher, or the less expert assistance of "peer editors." Peers, it is often said, need to be "trained," but are more likely to be helpful, partly because they *are* peers, and partly because there are more of them—as a writer, you're more likely to be able to get the attention of another member of the class than that of the overworked teacher.

It's not often acknowledged by those who make these suggestions, however, that there are a number of entirely different *modes* of response to writing, some of which are of a good deal less assistance to writers than others. One of the things that our growing sensitivity to the social dimensions of the language-learning process has begun to make clearest is that some kinds of linguistic transactions have much more power to foster learning than others. Unfortunately, the concrete implications of those distinctions are rarely taken into account as we consider what happens in classrooms and outside, as student writing is read by teachers and peers and their responses are read or listened to by writers.

Randall Jarrell's children's book, *The Bat-Poet* (1963), contains the most powerful dramatization I've seen of what seem to me two entirely different modes of responding to writing. In it, a bat (because he can't sleep during the day and because he's inspired by what seems to a bat the mockingbird's "deep bass voice") becomes a poet by beginning to compose texts about the strange new daylight world. The poem that is his first "keeper," though, is about his own night world—a terrifying twelve-line portrait of the owl ("The ear that listens to the owl believes/In death") which he finally works up courage to recite to the mockingbird himself.

The poem ends. "The owl goes back and forth inside the night./And the night holds its breath." Here's how Jarrell describes the response of the mockingbird (a professional):

> When he'd finished his poem the bat waited for the mockingbird to say something; he didn't know it, but he was holding his breath.
>
> "Why, I like it," said the mockingbird. "Technically it's quite accomplished. The way you change the rhyme-scheme's particularly effective."
>
> The bat said: "It is?"
>
> "Oh yes," said the mockingbird. "And it was clever of you to have that last line two feet short."
>
> The bat said blankly: "Two feet short?"
>
> "It's two feet short," said the mockingbird a little impatiently. "The next-to-the-last line's iambic pentameter, and the last line's iambic trimeter."
>
> The bat looked so bewildered that the mockingbird said in a kind voice: "An iambic foot has one weak syllable and one strong syllable; the weak one comes first. The last line of yours has six syllables and the one before it has ten: when you shorten the last line like that it gets the effect of the night holding its breath."
>
> "I didn't know that," the bat said. "I just made it like holding your breath."
>
> "To be sure, to be sure!" said the mockingbird. "I enjoyed your poem very much. When you've made up some more do come round and say me another." The bat said he would, and fluttered home to his rafter. Partly he felt very good—the mockingbird had liked his poem—and partly he felt just terrible. He thought: "Why, I might just as well have said it to the bats. What do I care how many feet it has? The owl nearly kills me, and he says he likes the rhyme- scheme!" (pp. 14-15)

Not long afterwards, the bat makes contact with a chipmunk, and says him the owl poem to show him what a poem is, as part of his offer to "do the chipmunk's portrait in verse." The chipmunk's response is rather different.

> He said his poem and the chipmunk listened intently; when the poem was over the chipmunk gave a big shiver and said, "It's terrible, just terrible! Is there really something like that at night?"
>
> The bat said: "If it weren't for that home in the oak he'd have got me."
>
> The chipmunk said in a determined voice: "I'm going to bed earlier. Sometimes when there're lots of nuts I stay out till it's pretty dark; but believe me, I'm never going to again."
>
> The bat said: "It's a pleasure to say a poem to—to such a responsive audience. Do you want me to start on the poem about you?"
>
> The chipmunk said thoughtfully: "I don't have enough holes. It'd be awfully easy to dig some more holes."
>
> "Shall I start on the poem about you?" asked the bat.

"All right," said the chipmunk. "But could you put in lots of holes? The first thing in the morning I'm going to dig myself another."

When most of us think about responding to the writing of others, what we have in mind is what I suspect Jarrell would have called "mockingbird responses." The mockingbird is positive, supportive, educational, and "kind": he refrains from actually suggesting ways to improve the writing, but he does take the opportunity to help the bat toward more conscious awareness of his skills as a writer. What Jarrell foregrounds, however, is the fact that his response is condescending, judgmental, and of no use to the aspiring bat poet—just as that of a teacher, or a "peer" who has been trained to be helpful, might. ("Why, I might just as well have said it to the bats," thinks the bat.)

On the other hand, the chipmunk responds almost entirely unreflectively. He *responds*. The poem is scary; he's scared. He's not entirely unselfconscious, as we see later on, when after another recital he comments, "It makes me shiver. Why do I like it if it makes me shiver?" (The bat responds, "I don't know. I see why the owl would like it, but I don't see why we like it.") What's important, however, is that through the chipmunk's fear, the bat sees that the poem *works*, that it does what he thought it ought to do. (In fact, it's clearly the chipmunk's response, not the mockingbird's, that encourages the bat to continue his career as a bard.) Whether he's analytically aware of the techniques (how he "gets the effect of the night holding its breath") or not, he's made a better writer by the chipmunk's response, because (among other things) he has more confidence in the communicative and affective power of his writing. Without that—as we all know—technical sophistication about metrics and poetic devices is worse than useless. The technique is a *function* of the poetry, not a *cause*.

Many teachers to whom I've read these passages respond by saying that the bat's situation isn't analogous to that of their students. The bat's text, they say, is a powerful piece of poetry and their students' texts are, usually, profoundly imperfect pieces of exposition. It seems to me this misses an important fact about the nature of reading and writing: what texts *are* is a function of their situation and their reader as much as of the writer and of the presumed "features" of the text itself. For the mockingbird, clearly, the bat's text is an imperfect example of the *genre* "poem," an artifact which needs assessment and whose creator needs gentle encouragement and assistance. For the chipmunk, on the other hand, it's meaningful, socially embedded discourse which doesn't "need" anything at all.

As long as our model of the writing situation is the mockingbird's, we create, because we expect it, a situation in which any student's writing can never be more than an artificial example of text to be dealt with condescendingly, helpfully, and kindly. If, however—and only if—we can begin creating situations in which students' writing serves the real purposes of writers and readers, we can respond to students' writing as though it were real, as though we were its readers serving our own purposes. It will *be* real. We will *be* its readers. We won't have to pretend, to imagine how it might be for someone to read it in a real situation. We won't have to be mockingbirds, basing the construction of our artificial responses on a theory of how language might work (do metrically truncated last lines actually work? Only the chipmunk can know).

And only in use (as, forty years and more ago, John Dewey made so clear that it seems hard to believe we're still discovering it) do we learn to use our tools; only use polishes and refines the tools themselves. "Sheer plod," says Gerard Manly Hopkins, "makes plough down sillion shine."

Once we've decided that it's what we want to do, it's not difficult to begin creating situations in which students' writing works to do what the students want to have done, situations in which their writing is useful to its readers. What we need is to find ways to make students each other's teachers, to help them find things to say which are of genuine interest to their peers, and which they know to be of genuine interest to their peers. We need to use collaboration not to attend to the form of discourse, but to the substance. We need to convert our classes into collaborative learning experiences in which students write *to* and *for* each other, to share what they've learned rather than to demonstrate that they've learned it.

Let me offer one example of how this can be done. In my university course in children's literature I regularly divide the class into groups and send them out to libraries or bookstores to explore different parts of what is obviously too vast a field for any one person to survey (for instance, each group might look at the work of a different writer) and report back to the class as a whole. The reports are photocopied, distributed and read. They are *not* evaluated, edited or corrected; they become the basis for further exploration (for instance, the class might decide that everyone should read a work recommended by a survey group). Such writing is not commented on or "helped"; it is used. If it fails to be usable, it's not used. If (like the bat's poem) it serves its purpose, the evidence isn't the mockingbird's approval but the chipmunk's delicious fear.

In *The Art of Teaching Writing,* Lucy McCormick Calkins recounts the story of Maria, who was miserably homesick and lonely the first day of kindergarten, and the way she found a chipmunk reader who understood what she was saying. On her second day she drew a picture and some letters, and was invited to read her story to the class. Her story was simple:

> The girl is sad.
> She has no friends.

As Calkins recounts its, several children raised their hands with comments like, "I like your picture," and "I like your writing." But one small boy understood: he looked up and said simply, "I'll be your friend."

Calkins points out that "we need to write, but we also need to be heard." I'd go a step further: unless we *are* heard, we'll never need to write, except in the sense that we need to please and placate all the waiting, condescending, kindly mockingbirds.

Teacher as Partner in the Writing Process

Nina Mikkelsen

Last summer I enrolled in a writing institute for teachers. I was enthusiastic about the process approach, and I wanted to learn more. At the institute, however, I soon found we were going to do more than talk about writing. Lucy Calkins, the director, wanted us to test the waters ourselves. Every morning we were going to write and then share our work.

Mornings weren't going to be easy, I decided. I had never written what Calkins wanted us to try—narratives of personal experience. By the second day, when all the others seemed to have a firm grip on the matter and were plunging right in, I was sitting trembling on the brink of hives.

"I have nothing to write about!" I wailed each night to my husband, who was also attending the institute. "Nothing exciting, nothing dramatic. I've never lived dangerously enough!" He was in much better shape. Remembering how he burned his spelling book in third grade, he was always on the trail of a hot topic. If only I could steal it, I thought.

Half the first week passed as I tried to dredge up experiences I could only half remember or simply wanted to forget. Everyone in my section was forging ahead rapidly. And what topics! Death, sex, teaching the Turtle—our group had everything. Or almost everything. It still didn't have whatever I was going to write about. (I didn't have it either.) And I was getting desperate.

Process

My ten-year-old son was constantly creating stories of fantasy creatures. His latest was a blue mouse. I ransacked his head for details; even paid him a dollar to tell me more. But the rewards weren't in it—for me. He had been turning himself into a mouse for weeks now. I had only one night, at best.

My mother-in-law kept a writing journal, I discovered next. And she was delighted to share it with me. What personal narratives she had! I took pages of notes, enough for a novel, only to find myself sinking into fiction quicksand— plots, sub-plots, characters, conflicts that weren't even mine. I jumped out just in time.

Riding the subway next day, I lost my way, ended up collecting images of a dozen trains on as many tracks. Maybe an essay, I thought, staring hard at graffiti walls. But was I looking at deterioration or decoration? I couldn't decide, and time (and the cars) were speeding on. Perhaps a poem, I decided next, the rhythm of the train roaring through my head, wheels turning in my memory back to childhood and the fear of being lost in a rush hour squeeze. But I had never written a poem before. How to arrange words, lines, phrases, spaces. And should it rhyme? The clock was ticking faster now. I needed more time.

I climbed into the car next day, reciting my usual litany of complaints why I couldn't write this, shouldn't write that, fussing, fretting, when suddenly I saw myself—a big game hunter of writing topics, stalking stories everywhere. It was a funny picture, me on the prowl, and I stopped to laugh. But not for long. Progress reports were due first thing that morning and I had nothing to say!

All the other papers were cranking along, greased and oiled, some by now even in the fine-tuning stage. None had broken down as many times as mine. And so, when at last it was my turn to talk, what came spilling out of me was the terrible story of my week—all the misery, the frustration, the struggle of trying to find something to write about. "I've never hated writing as much as I do now!" I nearly screamed. But the more I raged, the more they laughed—and nodded. Lucy, in fact, seemed delighted.

If what I was saying was funny, however, it wasn't too funny for words. For talking was breaking the spell for me, of blank pages and nothing to say. Maybe you could write about real things I began to think, because at long last I was doing it. I was writing all the time now—in the classroom, in the car, in restaurants, in the middle of the night, writing when I was writing, writing when I wasn't writing, writing about me and my struggle to write. My mind was now like the magic pot in the old tales, with ideas bubbling out faster than I could even write them down.

Eric, Lucy's assistant, heard "voice" in my introduction. And I began to recognize it too. (After wailing so long about my predicament, I had developed great strength of conviction about it.) Also he saw what was happening to my focus. "Don't try to tell everything or you'll lose sight of your major idea," he warned me. I had already lost sight of it though. I was spinning too many threads and the weight of them was making the whole web of my story sag. I needed to cut and reshape to highlight my theme, my struggle to write. But eliminating words, I soon discovered, could be as difficult as conceiving them. Knowing we would all be sharing our writing in a few days was strong motivation, however. (There wouldn't be time to read a novel to the class.)

Cutting back took several drafts, but soon I was discovering that a sentence or two could set a scene as well as a page if I selected the right words. Instead of a long story about getting lost on the subway, I could simply picture myself watching people on the train, wishing I had their stories to tell. This wasn't exactly the way it happened, but telling it this way kept all the threads running to a common center—my attempt to produce a story. And the people were still so vivid to me, I could write about them easily. The pictures were still running through my mind. As British writer David Rees (1983) says,

> writing molds thoughts and feelings, imposes structures, strikes from us new thoughts and feelings we would not have if we were not writing. That is why most of the author's work is done at the typewriter, not in preparation beforehand. (p. 167)

Also I could compress the time frame of the piece if I showed myself discovering I had a story as I was driving into the institute one morning. This would be better for the structure, better for the pacing. I was learning what storytellers know; you could hang a story on a skeleton of truth, then embellish to shape and entertain. In fact, I was beginning to see personal narrative as the hub of a great writing wheel, with rays of all writing modes emanating from it. The writer experienced something, then retold it as narrative, pictured it as description or poetry, analyzed it as essay, or reshaped it as fiction; but any comparison, it seemed, was rooted in some aspect of the writer's experience.

My last major change was fundamental. I needed a better opening. "I have no writing topic!" was the way I had begun every draft. This did express something of my anxiety the first week of the institute, but it didn't really express what I had discovered as the piece evolved. What I was searching for in the beginning was something to write about (a topic). But topics, I knew now, were really just words on a page. What brought them to life was stories.

In the preface to her book, *Lessons From A Child* (1983), Calkins says she remembers Donald Graves often quoting the words of Harold Rosen, "every child has a story to tell." At the institute, my own biggest discovery had been that I, like children, had a story to tell. I decided to make Rosen's phrase my opening statement. It led to my title, borrowed in part from

Sendak and to the closing words. It also led to my putting the piece through one last draft to highlight this concept I now had of stories. The idea was already there, had been there all the time. It just took matching words to ideas now. Then with opening and closing in hand and the middle somewhat in shape, it was time for the sharing of products.

I didn't volunteer to go first.

Product

Where the Stories Are

Everyone has a story to tell. Harold Rosen said it. Donald Graves spread the word. Lucy Calkins wrote it down. Have I got news for them. A STORY TO TELL I HAVE NOT GOT! I'm indignant, impatient, disgusted, and outraged. I've never been so angry in my life.

I am a teacher of writing. I encourage others to choose their own topics, take risks, share, respond, revise. But here I am at a Writing Institute, where I am supposed to be writing, and I am sitting with nothing to say. And feeling very uncomfortable.

Every day when others are accumulating line after line of powerful prose, I sit hovering over my paper or peeping over my shoulder. Is there anyone as miserable as I?

The first day I thought there was. Everyone seemed itching to escape. But the second day words began to flow—for them. The third day everybody was writing while I was poking around—pretending to write. Today the fourth day was the worst. I spent lots of time in the bathroom. I could have jumped out the window. It was open. No screen. I'm saving that for tomorrow, if I don't come up with something tonight.

Every night I ride back to Connecticut, gnashing my terrible teeth, roaring my terrible roars. I am a Wild Thing, looking for a story. And I can't find one anywhere. There has to be a story somewhere in my head. Others have stories to tell.

My son greets me with a new story each day. "There is this big white mouse," he is telling me today. "A stuffed mouse, with special powers. He shrinks down into a little blue mouse with wings. He's a bat mouse," he whispers confidentially. "And then he changes me into real small too, so I can see into mouseholes and fly up to the trees. Well, do you like it?"

Do I like it? I want to steal it. Such a wonderful story starter. Will he tell me more? I'll pay him a dollar, no, whatever he asks. It's worth the price.

But he goes on easily. *He* has a story to tell.

"The bat-mouse is going to take me to the Dark Island, where I will meet the Firechubs and the Tar Monsters. The Tar Monsters are cousins to the Whooshkabobs, remember?"

Whooosh! I sink down exhausted, as he flies out the door. Someone has unzipped me and all my stuffing is spilling out. My son is a mouse today, not I.

Staring hard at the ceiling, I am looking for a story, but only pictures keep running through my mind. Pictures of my week going by. Two days ago, an oak carved room, women in silk, men in gray at the end of the day. I watch waiters' faces, pale silent masks. But their eyes, centuries old, what stories they told.

Yesterday a subway ride. I see it now. How I love subways! Dark sooty places. I love the noise, the roar of the wild cars, the lurching about. Lights blinking. Doors banging. Watching the people.

Here a young boy thin as a pipe, curled up fetal style, sleeping. What is his story? There an orange-haired girl, porcelain skin, blue-rimmed eyes. She comes ramming, snarling into the car. Stamps on my foot. Then settles down to bob along, zombielike into the city. I need her story.

Ten little girls clustered in a row, drooping butterflies in the heat, one fast asleep. But when the time comes, she too flits away, nearly sliced in two by the slamming door. Where is she going? If only I could follow her. I might just find a story.

But I go zooming on, encased within graffiti walls. Ancient steel cage. Who draws on subway walls? Someone with a story to tell? Not me. I don't have a story. Has anyone noticed?

"I'm writing all the time myself," my mother-in-law suddenly announces at dinner. "In my journal. I call it 'Live, Learn, and Love.' The 'Love' part is new. It used to be just 'Live and Learn.'"

"What did you write about today?" I ask. (Maybe I'll borrow this journal for tomorrow, I'm thinking.)

"About your visit," she says. "I feel good that you're visiting me, so I put it down in black and white."

"You really write too!" I cry. "This is amazing. Everybody's writing now but me."

"What can I tell you?" she pauses to advise, tiny ring-covered fingers waving in the air. "They used to call me a born philosopher. Fear! There's a topic. Write about fear!"

"Even your mother has a story," I wail that night to my husband, who also is attending the institute. "And right this minute she's probably downstairs writing it, while I'm still stuck!"

"I don't know why you're having so much trouble," he sighs. "You just have to sit down and write your way into something. Now I started out writing about burning my spelling book in third grade—"

"I never burned a book!"

"Then I ended up thinking of a job interview I once had, how hard I worked getting a stain out of my jacket. And that turned out to be my topic—Stains and Clothing. I see it as a major issue of my life—how I hate conforming. Still I do it. I don't know why. I can't wait to get there tomorrow to write more about it."

"Oh," I moan, "I want your story! I want a major issue." (I want some stains, I decide, stopping to examine all my clothing. But there's nothing there, not even a smudge.)

Where are the stories? I fall asleep wondering. There ought to be stories.

Soon light is seeping through the window. There's thunder in my head. We're bumping down the parkway. Two hours to go. Someone help! What am I going to write about?

"If only I had a daughter," I begin. Eileen is writing about her daughter growing up, looking spiffy in a bathing suit. `There are two women in my house now,' she says. It's a nice phrase, isn't it?

"Or if I could just remember kindergarten. Eric wrote a great piece about his first teacher. Rose is writing about her students."

"Do that!" my husband offers eagerly. "Write about your students."

"I can't. I left all my notes at home."

"Write about this traffic," he says, gritting his teeth.

"Can't. Joe already has that one. He has a real system. He watches the cars and takes notes while he drives. He's been doing it for a week now. A week. Everybody's been writing for a week now! They write when they're driving. I just sit and think about writing. Give me a topic!" I suddenly scream, "Hand me a topic! Now!" I slam my fist into the dashboard.

"Well have an accident!"

"An accident?" I murmur. An accident? Did he say an accident? I'm seeing something now—my big moment. A story! A story! Ambulances roaring. Blood everywhere. I may have to sacrifice myself. Should I go for it? Yes! Why not? "Why not?" I cry. "Let the Wild Rumpus begin!"

He is ignoring me. The cars are whizzing by. I pick up a book and try to read. But I don't see the words. I feel panic creeping through my body. Sick. Sick. I am sick. What's the name of those people that can't come out of their houses? Don't come outside for years. It's happening to me. I'll have to hide in this car all day. Won't be able to open the door.

Crouched safe inside that dark, cavernous parking lot all day. Trying so hard to find a story. Pictures of my week spraying like bullets through my mind. Blue mice. Subways. Fears. Stories to tell. My stories. All my stories. Deep down in a dark place. Where the stories are. There I am. I see myself. All day long, trying so hard. And the car still bumping along.

But I don't see the traffic. Don't see Columbia looming up ahead. I'm seeing something else now. The shape of something. The shape of a story. My struggle for a story. How it will begin, how it will end, how I will design it and shape it and tell it.

I'm telling it to him now. He listens. Then he laughs. And I'm laughing too. It's the right story now, all mine, and I didn't have to buy it or steal it. Didn't even have to kill for it. There it was all the time, growing, bouncing along with me. While I was looking so hard for it, I was living right through it.

We bump along. Closer we come. There it is—125th Street.
Subway tracks, graffiti cars, Spumoni colored, roaring over my head.
The cathedral in full view now, gleaming in the hot air.

Lovely. I cant wait to get there. Running through my head now.
Running through my head now.

Stories.

Reflection

I enrolled in a writing institute to learn how to teach, but in the
process I learned about how I write—about what works for me,
what strengths to build on, what lapses to avoid. Most of all I
learned what fun it is to be a storyteller and how important the
storytelling impulse is for writing. For no matter what we write,
whether it is autobiography, fantasy, news report, even poetry,
we are somehow beginning with narrative, a sequence of events
in time and memory. We are sharing stories with others—
bringing the news, spreading ideas, reaching for feelings,
remembering experiences. And we are receiving stories,
messages, responses, in return. If others like what we have to
say, they respond, and the result is dialogue. They tell us how
they feel. We want to tell them more, and each time we try to
make the writing clearer, more cohesive, more intelligible—for
them.

But what do my discoveries about writing have to do with
children? As a teacher, do I really have to be a writer? Is it
crucial? Haven't nonwriting writing teachers been able to elicit
well-crafted, memorable products from children? Yes, but how
much easier if I can be a partner in writing, write to show
children what writing is, rather than merely tell them.

Always before when I taught writing, I taught it as a reader,
either as critical reader or as proofreader, rather than as a writer.
I gave students topics I wanted to read about. Then I complained
when their papers were dull and lifeless and they continued to be
dependent on me for ideas. I hadn't thought much about what
brings writing to life, namely the writer's voice, because I
hadn't really discovered my own voice in writing. No one had
ever encouraged me to seek out a story for myself, or for that
matter, about myself. No one had warned me how difficult it
could be either, but that it could still be done. It's one thing to
ask children to voice their own feelings, to write about what they
care about in personal narratives; it's another to strip off our
own protective shields and write one too.

I also complained when I had to read papers that didn't make
sense to me as a reader. I was a good diagnostician, however. I

could tell students exactly what was wrong with a piece of writing. I just didn't know much about writers themselves, why they wrote unclearly in the first place. And I hadn't analyzed my own writing process enough to find out. It's one thing to plunge children into writing and see them anxious, careless, even outrageous writers; it's another to have plunged in before them, to struggle with focus, length, pacing, gaps, openings, closings, even spelling, and punctuation, so that we can offer them better help in the recovery room of writing.

Finally as a reader, I wanted students to feel that they were writing for an audience. I thought this would help them to revise. But I was their only audience and the only sense of approval they could earn was a grade. So they went on trying to find out what I wanted, and I went on telling them. It's one thing to share writing with a teacher (and receive a grade); it's another to share writing with peers, to hear their responses, consider their suggestions, and finally win their applause.

During the second week of the institute, all twenty-four members of my section were asked to share our completed pieces and to respond to one another's writing with notes of celebration. Throughout the previous week, in groups of four we had listened to one another's stories, receiving and responding and urging the writing process along. Now like relatives at the christening, we could celebrate. As Helen, one member of my response group wrote me, "I felt as I listened that I was lucky to have had you in my group, so that I was able, in a very small way, to watch your story emerge. It's wonderful."

There were no jealousies here as occur when students are pitted against one another in order to promote one way of doing things, one process, or one type of product. We had each been urged to find our own way, to discover what worked for us, and then to share this knowledge with one another. Hopefully we would also find ways to share it with children, to be able to say as Rose wrote me six months later,

> What a trip this has been! Getting the reading and writing connection going in my classroom. All in all it's been a term of growth for me as well as the kids and I see us *both* reaching for the stars. I'm having a great time and the kids are so responsive!

These days I'm also finding out what it is like to become a writing partner. Now if I want students to learn to create word pictures, I create word pictures too. Then when it is sharing time, I can show what I mean rather than just talk about it. If I want students to write about what really matters to them, I write about what really matters to me. Then as I show what works for me in my writing, they can begin to see what might work for them in theirs. I can teach more than rules now. I can teach writers. I've become one too.

Becoming a writing partner is also helping me to become a better reading partner. As I create word pictures and shape narratives of my own, I have more interest in discovering how other writers, both professional and student writers, solve composing problems. Writing thus sends me to books which I can share with children. Books bring us back to writing too, for children reading fiction and poetry want to work in these modes. And when they do, I have learned I must meet them halfway.

Fiction, especially fantasy, is too difficult to execute, let alone teach, for me not to become involved. If I am to help children avoid the pitfalls of ready-made plots and characters, I must learn to avoid them too. I must explore plot patterns with my own pen, develop characters out of my own experience. And if children are to write poetry, I must also come face-to-face with my own word patterns on the page. I must explore my emotions, find my own feelings. Then I will have more to. teach.

But no matter what mode children are exploring, they will need to open themselves up to experience, see the world with a writer's eye, in order to recreate experience on paper. And if I am not writing with them, how can I show them how important it is? How will I know it myself?

"Painting teachers should paint," says Newkirk (1980):

> acting teachers should act, carpentry teachers should saw, and writing teachers should write. No component of a writing institute will provoke as much anxiety among participants as the writing workshops, and at the end of the program no other component will have done as much to generate enthusiasm in the writing process.(Pp. 11-12)

It is true, I can say now. I've been there and I know.

References

Calkins. L. *Lessons from a Child.* Exeter. NH: Heinemann, 1983.

Newkirk. T. NIE Grant Proposal for Summer Writing Workshops, University of New Hampshire, Durham, N.H., 1980.

Rees, D. "On Katherine Patterson, Alexander Pope, Myself, and Some Others," *Children's Literature in Education,* 14(1983): 160-169.

The Risks of Whole Language Literacy: Alienation and Connection

Susan Harman
Carole Edelsky

Explanation at the start of *The Adventures of Huckleberry Finn*::

> In this book a number of dialects are used, to wit: the Missouri negro dialect; the extremest form of the backwoods Southwestern dialect: the ordinary "Pike County" dialect; and four modified varieties of this last. The shadings have not been done in a haphazard fashion, or by guess-work; but painstakingly, and with the trustworthy guidance and support of personal familiarity with these several forms of speech.

> I make this explanation for the reason that without it many readers would suppose that all these characters were trying to talk alike and not succeeding. (Twain 1884)

Literacy as Liberation

There is a long, honorable, and articulate literary and political testimony to the mixed blessings of "the immigrant experience." Abandoning one's social class roots and moving "up" into the American Dream—leaving home—has always been risky business. And whether the journey is from the old neighborhood to the suburbs or condo; from the father-son union to a desk and white collar; from kinder, kuche, and kirche to the schoolroom or real estate office; or from church picnics to dinner parties, the distance is rarely covered without leaving someone or something behind.

The achievement of literacy, however, unlike changes in class, is recently and universally seen as politically neutral, a tool, unambiguously positive, and very powerful. Just as language lifts one's dreams out of the inchoate and makes them articulate, so literacy can multiply those dreams by the factor of each that has ever been written down; it can allow the reader to borrow, steal, and adapt as her own every dream ever inscribed. Literacy potentially provides the ability to enter others' worlds, whether through novels or through political analyses, and that entrance immediately presents contrasts, alternatives, and choices; and hence, the possibility of change. There is, of course, no guarantee that the mere presentation of choices will result in a reader choosing something new and better, but without the data—the images of possibility—which literacy gives a reader, the likelihood is small of her inventing new worlds out of whole cloth.

One needs only look at whom schooling has traditionally been denied (blacks, women, the underclasses of every culture) to recognize the awe in which literacy has been held and the frugal and discriminatory way in which it has been allocated. The legends of stolen literacy speak for its magic: Lincoln studying law in the flickering kerosene light of his log cabin, Douglass teasing white boys into spelling words out for him, Hassidic girls shearing their hair and binding their breasts to sit as disguised boys in yeshivas, George Eliot creeping out of bed before dawn to write and then hide away what she had written before she lit the kitchen stove for the day, the Hispanic cigarworkers in New York at the beginning of this century listening rapt as the professional "readers" read aloud the news and the classics.

But literacy is not necessarily liberating. *First, merely knowing how to read and write guarantees neither membership in the dominant culture nor the concomitant political, economic, cognitive, or social rewards of that membership* (see Graff 1986 and 1987; Street 1984). The consequences of literacy have always been related to what it is used for, what value is placed on it, and who is permitted to become literate. Although one of the powerful meanings surrounding literacy in the Western World today is a belief in its liberating potential, in fact, literacy is a necessary, but hardly sufficient, passport to the mainstream. If other stigmata—such as color, sex, or class—betray one's membership in a subordinate culture, one may not be able to talk (or read or write) one's way across the frontier.

Second, the traditional approaches to literacy instruction can fetter students, not liberate them. Mastery of traditional literacy instruction sometimes permits access to certain societal resources. But these traditional curricula depend on: one single interpretation of one prescribed text; the use of conventional Standard English as the only criterion for evaluation of writing; and the standardized, multiple-choice reading tests, which have only one right answer per item, as the passport to the next grade. Therefore these literacy curricula inordinately favor speakers from middle and upper-middle classes; from those dominant groups who simply "acquire" Standard English at home, as contrasted with those who have to "learn" it consciously in school (Gee 1987). The prescribed texts tend to be seen as the only texts, as "natural" rather than constructed or chosen. And these curricula tend to maintain, rather than improve, the status of subordinant groups.

Members of such groups are held behind "gates" in elementary grades, kept from graduating high school by "competency" tests, and reminded one last time (if they didn't understand before) when they score poorly on the standardized tests in adult basic education (ABE) classes, that they do not belong in the mainstream. As Villanueva (1988) describes his experience:

> I do not believe I had a problem with English after kindergarten. I could switch from Spanglish to Street to Standard at will. I read. I didn't fear writing. I could mimic the prestige dialect—both the spoken and the written. I could even add "however" to essays on the basis of sound, although not often on the basis of sense. I was, however, apparently unable to mimic the school's way of viewing the world, the ways reflected in rhetorical patterns. The literacy we [Puerto Ricans] acquire tends to be of the wrong sort, even when the dialect is right. Basic literacy yields little power.

Despite progressives' unreflective faith in the benefits of literacy, neither the ability per se, the method by which it is acquired, nor the materials used to teach it, is neutral. Both the methodology and the content of the traditional curricula center on obedience and acceptance: there is only one English that is Standard and only one right answer for worksheet blanks and on multiple-choice tests. This kind of curriculum is therefore more likely to be stifling than liberating, although it paradoxically may have an advantage over more creative curricula: that the enemy has a face. That is, the traditional, fragmented, authoritarian, and narrow approach to reading and writing is plainly nonsensical and permits students to make a clear choice between conforming to its standards or rejecting them (going to special education, dropping out of school, or simply not allowing oneself to be recruited or coerced into joining ABE classes). Of course, this choice is less likely to be empowering, resistant, and liberating for the individual making it (and her community), and more likely to be defeating for them both (see Aronowitz and Giroux 1985).

At the moment there is much talk, considerable money, and an indefensible pedagogy aimed at "curing illiteracy" in both adults and children. Government leaders, social scientists, corporate executives, publishers, and educators are united in calling for universal literacy, although the instructional methods they support practically guarantee failures. In this paper we do not, however, explain why traditional approaches to teaching reading and writing usually fail; there is a large and growing body of literature on that (Goodman 1987; Goodman, Shannon, Freeman, and Murphy 1988; Harste, Woodward, and Burke 1984). Nor do we attack the eccentric and peculiar kinds of reading, writing, and talking that go on exclusively in school (Edelsky 1986; Langer 1986; Lindfors 1987). We do not chant a misty-eyed paean to the automatically revolutionary political and personal potential of literacy; George Babbitt could read and write. [As Lewis, quoted in Graff (1986), succinctly puts it, "The only literacy that matters is the literacy that is in use" (1953, p. 16).] Nor do we explicitly criticize the monomaniacal, Eurocentric, trivia curriculum proposed by Bloom and Hirsh— although our nontraditional approach to literacy is a clear and implicit antidote to their attack on pluralism. Finally, we do not join the broader issue of whether the institution of school is either necessary to literacy or good for anything or anyone at all (see. e.g., Bowles and Gintis 1977; Graff 1986: Illich 1970: Scribner and Cole 1978).

Instead, we will look unsentimentally at the *third* reason why literacy may not be liberating: *the price demanded by so fundamental a personal change may be too high.* Rather than poke at the straw man of traditional language arts, we will focus on the unintended, paradoxical, and negative underside of the best classroom theory and practice of literacy: whole language.

The Problem

Our contention is that the acquisition of literacy, and particularly its acquisition through the whole language approach, may have unanticipated repercussions in the lives of the learners. As our students—whether adults enrolled in basic education programs or children—become literate and begin to feel the liberating effects of their ability to use language, they may paradoxically begin to feel the constraints of estrangement from their roots.

Because the explicit purpose of education has been the assimilation of subordinate groups into dominant American life, much has been written about the implied demand on those groups to reject their home communities, and their ways of responding to that demand. Labov (1969) and Ogbu (1987) have described black teenagers refusing to succeed in school in order to avoid becoming "white"; Fingeret (1987) has reported adult illiterates' fears of losing their common sense or "mother wit" and becoming "educated fools," of "forgetting where I came from"; Kingston (1976) has written movingly about her difficulty reconciling the myths of her Chinese culture with those of the American educational establishment; academics who grew up in the working class have testified to their marginality in both worlds (Ryan and Sackery 1984); and most notoriously, Rodriguez (1981), a Chicano, has argued for actively rejecting one's cultural and linguistic past as the price of "making it." These are examples of conflicts induced by traditional literacy and school practices such as mindless, rigid repetition and drill. Our concern is that whole language may have an even greater alienating potential.

Whole Language: Content and Methodology

The whole language approach, in contrast to the traditional skills approach, is more seductive, more able to engender true readers and writers, and thus more liable to alienate learners from their communities. This is precisely because its primary principles are that learners are actively constructing meaning all the time, not just passively absorbing information; and that this language learning takes place in a coherent, authentic, sensible, predictable, purposeful environment in which coherent, sensible, predictable, purposeful language is being *used*—not *practiced*—both with, and in front of, the learner (Altwerger, Edelsky & Flores 1987; Goodman 1987; Harste, Woodward & Burke 1984; Smith 1981). That is, the whole language approach intends reading and writing to be seen by students as useful and relevant—as both *possible* to acquire and *worth* acquiring.

The choice between accepting and rejecting assimilation into the dominant culture is muffled in a whole language classroom, since the home cultures of all students—what Gee (1987) defines as their primary discourses, their "ways of using language, of thinking, and of acting," their "identity kits"—are welcomed there. The whole language approach is geared to the creation of texts for real use; it encourages multiple interpretations of existing texts-in-the-world; it honors and uses the language norms students arrive with; it not only accepts "alright" and "ain't" as linguistically legitimate, but it accepts differing discourses, identity kits, and worldviews; it focuses on the ideas students have rather than the ones they lack; it assumes the expansion of roles so that students teach and teachers learn; it sets high but flexible standards; it emphasizes language repertoires rather than right answers; and it fosters questioning, analyzing, speaking up, and writing down.

Whole language is a set of beliefs and educational practice based on a socio-psycho-linguistic model of reading and writing (Goodman & Goodman 1981; Harste et al. 1984) and an interactive model of language acquisition (Halliday 1977; Peters and Boggs 1986; Teale 1982). It tries to create the conditions for literacy acquisition that exist for language acquisition: that is, little formal instruction, authentic use within specific contexts, no apparent suffering, and essentially universal success. Like talking, reading and writing must be seen by learners as having obvious functions in the lives of those around them and those they want to be identified with. That is, the attention of talkers (and readers and writers) must be on something else, on what the talk or print is *about,* on the social work it is doing.

With language taking a supporting—although still essential— role, the actual classroom practice emanating from this whole language set of beliefs avoids workbooks, phonics skillsheets, basal readers, controlled vocabularies, and kits. Instead, it focuses on what adults and children *do* with language and why: make contact, label, organize, remind, play, imagine, threaten, inform, persuade, insult, entertain, soothe, and so forth, emphasizing *use* of language; that is, real talking, reading, writing, with stories, recipes, letters, labels, notes, tickets, games, maps, magazines, newspapers, lists, reports, songs, journals, poems, menus, and books. (See Edelsky 1986, and Edelsky and Smith 1983, for a discussion of real written language use—i.e., of authentic reading and writing.) It is this set of beliefs about language acquisition and these and other implied classroom practices that is what we mean by whole language. And it is this set of beliefs and practices—this responsive, accepting whole language atmosphere—that may lull the learner out of her habitual wariness of the dominant culture; it may offer her the illusion that there is no conflict between her primary discourse and the mainstream discourse. It may also make her literate.

Thus, whole language's success in helping more students become real readers and writers amplifies the problem of alienation from home communities. When 40-60 percent of students drop out of high school (as in New York City), they drop back into their home communities. They have acquired so few skills in school that, although they bring back little to contribute, they also see little to criticize. But when children and adults actually become literate through the beliefs and practices of whole language, the possibility of estrangement becomes very real. Eartha, a black tenth grader and a proficient reader, extended the syllogism which states that "if you *don't* become literate, you *can't* escape" to "if you do become literate, you *must* escape." She told Fine (1988) that she didn't want to have to live in a white neighborhood, and therefore was dropping out of school.

It is not whole language's success in promoting literacy that is the only problem; after all, the traditional skills approach may have helped some people learn to read and write, and so has contributed to distancing people from their homes and families. Rather, it is the very beliefs and practices that make whole language so successful that also make it revolutionary: at once a welcome threat to society's stability, but also a disturbing threat to the stability of individuals.

Perhaps the most powerful of these beliefs and practices—and therefore both the most liberating and potentially the most alienating—is the whole language commitment to a democratic relationship both between the student and the teacher, and between the student and the material. Unlike the traditional skills approaches, whole language teachers strive to demystify written language, texts, and learning. In a whole language classroom, students choose curricular areas to explore, negotiate activities with the teacher, collaborate with other students, take risks and chances with the structure and the content of their projects, and work with and create authentic texts.

It is, of course, tremendously rewarding for whole language teachers to see their students more excited about publishing a guide book to guinea pigs than bothering the child next to them, or more engrossed in writing their autobiographies than watching TV. It may not, however, be quite so rewarding for the parents of young children or the spouses of adult students to see those same students growing away from them, and practicing at home the democracy and daring they have learned in class. Parents may perceive their children's new self-confidence and intellectual curiosity as talking back and arguing too much with them ("She always has an opinion on everything"; "He thinks he's so smart"). Husbands may resent their wives correcting their grammar, no longer needing to have newspapers read to them, and even having their own opinions about the articles they've read on their own.

The acquisition of literacy can catapult a student out of her family, community, class, or ethnic group, because that student has learned, not simply a new way of using language or of comprehending text, but a new way of viewing the world as well; she has acquired a new *discourse*. And that student may believe she must choose between the old and the new discourse. Mainstream teachers may reinforce that belief, even with nonethnics, by honoring the "melting pot" mythology which romanticizes rejection of one's roots as a prerequisite to

Americanization, upward mobility, self-improvement, and financial success.

And of course, even in whole language classrooms, the teacher's warm acceptance of the learner's primary discourse is not unconditional; certain written language situations demand conformance to Standard English conventions. The continuity between home and school that welcomes and reassures young children and beginning ABE students, that frees them to take the risks necessary to real learning, begins to vanish when demands for conventions increase. The invented spelling that was charming in first grade is worrisome in sixth. No fifth grade or ABE teacher wants her black students to write "He been knowing that" in an article for the class newsletter. The prescribed text of the traditional classroom reappears as the text which prescribes success in the world. At some point the road forks, and the same choice must be made by whole language students as is made by students in skills classrooms: whether to adopt mainstream ways or not. As Smith (1986) says, to become really literate one must "Join the club" and decide that reading and writing are things that "people like me" do. But who am I like: my Chicano (or black, or Navajo, or Thai, or Israeli, or working-class) parents or spouse, or my mainstream teacher?

There is a major difference, however, between asking who I am in a traditional classroom and asking that same question in a whole language classroom. The whole language teacher values a variety of discourses and ways of knowing, and has therefore sought out materials which support the study of folk categories, histories, stories, and literature told and written by "people like me." Thus the student in a whole language classroom is more likely to see herself as like others already in the club, and more likely to decide to *add* Standard written English conventions to an existing repertoire, rather than to *trade* old ways for new. Still, in both whole language and traditional classrooms, there are students who see literate discourse as a threat to who they are.

Edelsky and Hudelson (1987) have written about the specific effects on various communities of children learning to write in a second language. If a minority language group is not literate, the children's literacy in the second language may threaten existing relations between the generations. Or the child may come from a literate community with norms that limit, by gender or social class, who writes what. No matter how or whether the conflict is reconciled, there will be a challenge to the community language status quo. And the challenge will be played out within the student, as well as between student and school, and student and home.

So, despite the correct pedagogy, good intentions, and great success of the whole language approach, its students might arrive at the same crossroads as students in traditional literacy programs, thinking they have to choose between the mainstream and home. In fact, *because* of the theory and practice unique to whole language, and the taste of democracy and power students have had in its classrooms, the choice for *these* students may be even more painful.

For some students, then, their growth in competence as language users may bring to them and to their families a confused and confusing mix of pride, loss, and pain. This pain has at least two sources: one coming from outside the student, and the other from within. The child or adult who has put one foot into the exciting new world where language is power may feel a strong tug on her other foot from those left behind. Family and friends may express resentment, jealousy, abandonment, or simply incomprehension at their loved one's movement away from them. And the student may ache with embarrassment at her family's inadequacies. Anna, a competent ten year old, watches her mother struggle with math problems from her GED course, and brags that in her fifth grade she does *much* harder work (Wolfe 1988). Although it may even have been Anna's very success in school which inspired her mother to earn a high school diploma, there is now a gulf between them, across which the child mocks her mother's Puerto Rican-accented English and her efforts to educate herself.

And because adults' relationships with family and friends are probably less fluid than children's, the adult learner's world may be shaken more by the changing patterns resulting from acquiring literacy. Elsasser (1988) knows a woman whose husband kept her from attending her adult writing class at knifepoint. And Breslin (1987) writes the sad story of a young working-class wife's need to educate herself (perhaps even become a doctor) and her hard-working, hard-drinking husband's baffled and limited response (that she should get pregnant).

At the same time, the student may have internalized the mainstream culture's disdain for his old world (after all, the larger society, as well as the classroom, communicates which discourses, which cultures, which people are legitimate); but he may not yet have mastered the new. He may not only suffer alienation from family and friends, but may also become suspended in self-doubt between the two discourses; even in a whole language setting, and especially as more competence—and more conformance to mainstream standards—is expected of him. Johnston (1985) describes his adult students as expressing "concern over the increased responsibility that improved reading skill might engender. If they were to improve they might be *expected* to read, even by those who are close to them and know that they have difficulty."

Solutions

We are certainly not promoting illiteracy or failure in school as a solution to literacy-related alienation. Nor are we recommending a retreat to basal readers and worksheets, which, because of their simplemindedness and clear irrelevance to real life, can easily be dismissed as nonsense, and therefore neither threaten learners' identity nor force choices—after all, why would anyone choose nonsense? The traditional language arts approach does not have the capacity that whole language does to alienate learners from their backgrounds for at least two reasons: it makes no attempt to engage the child or adult in authentic language use; and it is less than spectacularly successful at promoting the acquisition of literate *discourse*. The solution, therefore, to the problem of alienation does not lie in trading the power and liberation of whole language for the safety (and relative ineffectiveness) of traditional approaches. Rather, we must begin by first *noticing* that all change has repercussions at the same time that we take pride in those changes. And then, we must *respect* those repercussions, and search for ways to use them.

We would like to propose four ways of doing this: (1) The first is to treat all discourses as if they were equally interesting and legitimate *objects of examination;* (2) the second is to *act on the results* of that examination; (3) the third is to *stretch the dominant discourse* into accommodating more subordinate discourses; (4) and the fourth is to *reconnect literacy learners with their communities.*

1. In *Ways with Words,* Heath (198:3) describes how three different discourses were collected like specimens and brought into the classroom, where they were examined as if in a laboratory. The fact that one of the discourses belonged to the black working-class farm children, another to the white working-class mill children, and the third to the black and white townspeople/teachers did not stand in the way of the children's evenhanded examination of them. Through their examination of

the characteristics and complexities of the three discourses, the children's appreciation of, respect for, and fluency in their own—as well as the other two discourses—grew. They began to be bi- and some even tri-discursive.

One way to ease the pain of literacy-induced estrangement from one's roots would be to borrow from Heath. If teachers can persuade children and adults that it is safe to bring the discourse of their homes and families—their primary discourse—into classrooms with them, and if students and teachers can examine and explore that collection of subordinant and dominant discourses together, with the same objectivity and care they would give to a collection of seashells or snakeskins then perhaps they too can create multi-discursive classrooms.

It is integral to whole language classrooms that students' questions, perceptions, histories, background knowledge, and preferred ways of making and expressing sense (their primary discourses) are used and respected. But we are suggesting going beyond their use as vehicles or "grounds" for the study of the usual curriculum, to making the study of the various discourses themselves into a "science of language" curriculum, an acknowledged part of the "manifest curriculum" (Erickson 1986). Jordan (1985) provides a moving example of this curricular shift which results, like Fiore and Elsasser's (1982), in a letter to the editor, in black English, occasioned by the death of a student's brother at the hands of the police.

We join Gee (1987) in proposing that *learning*—that is, conscious, metalevel knowledge—"should lead to the ability for all children—mainstream and nonmainstream—to critique their primary discourses and secondary discourses, including dominant secondary discourses." This extension of language-as-tool to language-as-topic would be an innovation, and possibly an amelioration of the problem of alienation.

2. An even bolder step, one more in keeping with the political progressivism embedded in whole language, is that being developed by Martin-Jones and her colleagues at the Center for Language in Social Life (CLSL) in Lancaster, England. The language scholar-activists there critique liberal mainstream programs for instruction about language that treat discourses as neutral data or "objects of nature" (as does Heath). Instead, concurring with Aronowitz and Giroux (1985), who make the same case for cultural knowledge in general, the CLSL maintains that all discourses (subordinate and dominant) are social practices which must be subjected to close "interrogation." But interrogation leading only to a heightened awareness of, a

"critical relation" to, one's own knowledge, is insufficient if action doesn't follow from it. The CLSL and Aronowitz and Giroux insist that asking questions (such as who has access to what knowledge? who has access to which ways of using language? why is access to certain discourses unequally distributed? who benefits or suffers from the unequal access?) without tying that investigation to action can be *dis*empowering. It can generate feelings of impotence, and even increase alienation.

On the other hand, the investigation can be made "purposeful" (according to the CLSL) creating both a "language of possibility" and a context for "transformation" (according to Aronowitz and Giroux), by linking it "to a vision of the future that not only exploded the myths of the existing society, but also reached into those pockets of desires and needs that harbored a longing for a new society and new forms of social relations" (Giroux 1984). These visions, desires, and needs could lead to: (1) investigations of the possibilities for changing both the discourses and their social contexts; and (2) investigations of the contexts and the particulars of other struggles for change (e.g., studying various literacy campaigns or campaigns for instituting anti-racist/anti-sexist language policies).

We believe the best place to begin such an enterprise is with the mainstream culture's discourse. We can explore, for example, how the asymmetries of doctor-patient or teacher-student talk or of boss-employee written exchanges "contribute to [people's] understandings of what [they] are allowed to say and therefore allowed to be" (CLSL 1987, p. 30). Such a critique, requiring as it does a stepping back and examining as if from the outside, is especially possible for students who have already *come* from outside. Their journey from home to the mainstream may have given them the tools for this interrogation: the knack of putting one world into perspective from the distance of another world; the customs of democracy brought from their whole language classrooms; and the confidence of having lived through a metamorphosis.

The dominant discourse should be the first to be interrogated because it is more impervious to criticism, and because critiquing it will be less likely to separate students from the discourses in which they are rooted. However, *all* discourses, subordinant as well as dominant, offer comforts and constraints in unequal measure for different categories of people. Therefore, the ultimate aim is not only to legitimize primary discourses and the community's cultural knowledge, but to critically analyze these, too, for their strengths as well as their weaknesses (Aronowitz and Giroux 1985).

Students who take part in such an education would certainly not be able to continue to participate unconsciously in either their old or their new discourses. This consciousness could lead to alienation—they could initially be *doubly* alienated, from both their home discourse and that of the mainstream—or it could lead to examination and action. A scientist, after all, one who studies something consciously and objectively, doesn't love her subject less because she sees it clearly. So by acting, by working with others from both dominant and subordinant groups to change what is oppressive in both discourses, these newly conscious learners would be *connected* to some of the "old" and some of the "new" critiquers, but in new ways. In that sense, a critical study of primary and secondary discourses would not be alienating; it would, instead, bring learners together into a new community, sharing a common responsibility for effecting change.

3. Subordinant discourses could challenge the dominant discourse to accommodate to their literacy: to their language, to their topics, to their worldviews. Zora Neale Hurston (1979) began publishing in the 1920s—too early for black English (and black lives) to dent the mainstream. It took *The Color Purple* (1982) to expand the boundaries of acceptability. Soto's *Spiks* (1973) is written in English, Spanish, and Spanglish, but it's not on many freshman English reading lists, even in colleges with substantial Hispanic enrollments. Gilman's *The Yellow Wallpaper* (1892/1973) was first published in 1892, after many rejections, despite her reputation as an accomplished economist; Chopin published *The Awakening* (1895/1972) three years later. Both of these profoundly feminist stories had to be rediscovered by the women's movement, since they had not been continuously read as part of the mainstream discourse.

If whole language theorists and practitioners are serious about helping child and adult learners find their voices, then, it seems to us we have a concomitant obligation to provide forums for those voices in the mainstream. It is not enough to welcome subordinant discourses into our classrooms; we must also wrest space for them in the dominant literate world.

4. Although the Schoolboys of Barbiana (1970) held the pure belief in literacy as power, they were quite sophisticated about the politics of the distribution and use of literacy. They carefully documented how few peasant children are allowed by the

schools to graduate from the university, in comparison to children of "big shots." Their solution to the dual problem of literacy distribution and use is to have two school systems: one, called the "School of Social Service," for those who have decided to dedicate themselves to serving "the family of man"; and the other, called the "Schools of Ego Service" (those we have now), which perpetuate the status quo.

We can borrow the Schoolboys' solution as a real option for some new graduates, but forego their naive confidence in the power of literacy per se. Their recommendation that each new literate feed her knowledge back into the community (although rigidifying in that it doesn't allow for geographic or social mobility), may be a very good way for some to avoid alienation. This solution would respond, for instance, to Eartha's perception that literacy requires leaving home. Graduates of whole language environments are particularly well suited to this kind of investment in service, having already been members of democratic learning communities. Instead of moving on and moving out, tearing up their roots and leaving their home communities even more impoverished than before they were educated, these graduates could stay as important and connected members, creating new learning communities at home.

Conclusion

Learning to read and write by a member of a subordinant discourse can be both empowering and alienating; but the acquisition of literacy in a whole language environment carries with it the special potential—and special responsibility—for both more power and more alienation. This is because the whole language approach is simply more successful than traditional approaches to teaching reading and writing; and therefore more students are liable to become both literate and alienated. It is because a democratic, critical, analytical methodology is intrinsic to the practice of whole language; and learners may turn these tools against their home discourse. It is because the collective dialogue and individual critique characteristic of whole language classrooms are likely to lead to personal and political change; and change can be exhilarating—but it can also be painful.

But it is exactly these aspects of whole language which also offer an antidote to the alienating effects of literacy acquisition. The Gee, Heath, CLSL, or Aronowitz and Giroux models of analysis of subordinant and dominant discourses are most likely to occur only in whole language classrooms. Those teachers who will solve the dilemma of the negative consequences of literacy success are most likely to be whole language teachers, with their commitment to respond to students' needs: And the liberation of learners from the confines of the either-home-or-mainstream discourse dilemma into active struggle with the issues of literacy, community, identity, and social change is most likely to come from the power of the critical thinking and democracy learned and practiced in whole language settings.

References

Altwerger, B., Edelsky, C., and Flores, B. "Whole Language: What's New?" *Tile Reading Teacher*, (1987): 144-154.

Aronowitz, S., and Giroux, H. *Education Under Siege*. South Hadley, MA: Bergin & Garvey Publishers, Inc., 1985.

Bowles, S., and Gintis, H. *Schooling in Capitalist America: Educational Reform and the Contradictions of Economic Life*. New York: Basic Books, 1977.

Breslin, J. *Table Money*. New York: Penguin, 1987.

Centre for Language in Social Life. *CLSL Working Paper Series, I: Critical Language Awareness*. Department of Linguistics and Modern English Language, University of Lancaster, Lancaster LA1 4YT, 1987.

Chopin, K. *The Awakening*. New York: Avon, 1895/1972.

Edelsky, C. *Writing in a Bilingual Program: Habia Una Vez*. Norwood, NJ: Ablex, 1986.

Edelsky, C. and Hudelson, S. "Contextual Complexities: Written Language Policies in Bilingual Programs," 1987.

Edelsky, C. and Smith, K. "Hookin' 'em in at the Start of School in a 'Whole Language' Classroom." *Anthropology and Education Quarterly*, 14 (1983): 257-281.

Elsasser, N. Personal communication, 1988.

Erickson, F. "Looking for Literacy in Classroom Learning Environments: Issues and Questions." Keynote Address, NCTE Assembly on Research, Chicago, 1986.

Fine, M. Personal communication, 1988.

Fingeret, A. Talk given at Literacy Assistance Center, 15 Dutch Street, New York, NY, 10038, February 13, 1987.

Fiore, K., and Elsasser, N. "'Strangers no more': A Liberatory Literacy Curriculum." *College English*, 44 (1982): 115-128.

Gee, I. P. "What is Literacy?" *Teaching and Learning: The Journal of Natural Inquiry*, 2(1987): 3-11.

Gilman, C. P. *The Yellow Wallpaper*. Old Westbury, NY: The Feminist Press, 1892/1973.

Giroux, H. A. "Rethinking the Language of Schooling." *Language Arts*, 61 (1984): 33-40.

Goodman, K. *What's Whole in Whole Language*. Portsmouth, NH: Heinemann, 1987.

Goodman, K. S., Shannon, P., Freeman, Y. S., and Murphy, 5. *Report Card on Basal Readers.* Katonah, NY: Richard C. Owen Publishers, Inc., 1988.

Goodman, K., and Goodman, Y. *A Whole Language Comprehension-centered View of Reading Development. Occasional Paper No. 1.* Program in Language and Literacy, University of Arizona, Tuscon, 1981.

Graff, H. J. "The Legacies of Literacy: Continuities and Contradictions in Western Society and Culture." In de Castell, S., Luke, A., and Egan, K. (Eds.). *Literacy, Society, and Schooling.* Cambridge: Cambridge University Press, 1986,

Halliday, M. A. K. *Learning How to Mean.* New York: Elsevar North-Holland, 1977.

Harste, I., Woodward, and Burke, C. *Language Stories and Literacy Lessons.* Exeter, NH: Heinemann, 1984.

Heath, S. B. *Ways with Words: Language, Life, and Work in Communities and Classrooms.* Cambridge: Cambridge University Press, 1983.

Hurston, Z. N. *I Love Myself When I Am Laughing.* Old Westbury, NY: The Feminist Press, 1979.

Illich, I. *Deschooling Society.* New York: Harper & Row, 1970.

Johnston, P. H. "Understanding Reading Disability: A Case Study Approach." *Harvard Educational Review,* 55 (1985): 153-177.

Jordan, I. *On Call: Political Essays.* Boston: South End Press, 1985.

Kingston, M. H. *The Woman Warrior.* New York: Knopf, 1976.

Labov, W. "The Logic of Nonstandard English." *Georgetown University Roundtable Monographs on Language and Linguistics,* 22, 1969.

Langer, J. "Literacy Instruction in American Schools: Problems and Perspectives." In N. L. Stein (Ed.), *Literacy in American Schools: Learning to Read and Write.* Chicago: University of Chicago Press, 1986.

Lewis, M. M. *The Importance of Literacy.* London: Harrap, 1953.

Lindfors, J. *Children's Language and Learning,* 2nd edition. Englewood Cliffs, NJ: Prentice-Hall, 1987.

Ogbu, I. "Variability in Minority School Performance: A Problem in Search of an Explanation." *Anthropology and Education Quarterly,* 18 (1987): 312-334.

Peters, A., and Boggs S. "Interactional Routines as Cultural Influences upon Language Acquisition." In B. Schieffelin and E. Ochs (Eds.) *Language Socialization Across Cultures.* New York: Cambridge University Press, 1986.

Rodriguez, R. *Hunger of Memory: The Education of Richard Rodriguez, an Autobiography.* Boston: Godine, 1981.

Ryan, J., and Sackery, C. *Strangers in Paradise: Academics from the Working Class.* Boston: South End Press, 1984.

Schoolboys of Barbiana. *Letter to a Teacher.* Rossi, N. and Cole, T., trans. New York: Random House, 1970.

Scribner, S., and Cole, M. "Literacy Without Schooling: Testing for Intellectual Effects." *Harvard Educational Review,* 48 (1978): 448-461.

Smith, F. "Demonstrations, Engagement, and Sensitivity: A Revised Approach to Language Learning." *Language Arts*, 58 (1981): 103-112.

Smith, F. *Insult to Intelligence: The Bureaucratic Invasion of Our Classrooms*. New York: Arbor House, 1986.

Soto, P. I. *Spiks*. New York: Monthly Review Press, 1973.

Teale, W. "Toward a Theory of How Children Learn to Read and Write Naturally." *Language Arts*, 59 (1982): 555-570.

Twain, M. *The Adventures of Huckleberry Finn*. New York: Harper & Bros., 1884.

Villanueva, V., Jr. "A Rhetorically Critical Literacy." *Information Update*, 4(1988): 3-4, May. New York: Literacy Assistance Center, Inc.

Walker, A. *The Color Purple*. New York: Pocket Books, 1982.

Wolfe, I. Personal communication, 1988.

References ❖

Ahlberg, Janet & Allan. 1986 *The Jolly Postman or Other People's Letters*. London: Heinemann.

Archer, Jeffrey. 1980 *A Quiver Full of Arrows*. Hodder and Stoughton, Coronet Books.

Atwell, Nancie. 1987 *In the Middle: Writing, Reading, and Learning with Adolescents*. Portsmouth, NH: Heinemann Educational Books.

Atwood, Margaret. 1988 *Cat's Eye*. Toronto: McClelland & Stewart.

Barnes, Douglas. 1976 *From Communication to Curriculum*. Harmondsworth: Penguin.

Bateson, Gregory. 1972 *Steps to an Ecology of Mind*. New York: Ballantine Books.

Bateson, Gregory. 1978 The Pattern Which Connects. *The CoEvolution Quarterly*, Summer, 5-17.

Bentley, A. F. & John Dewey. 1949 *Knowing the Known*. Boston: Beacon Press.

Blackburn, Ellen. 1984 Common Ground: Developing Relationships Between Reading and Writing. *Language Arts*, 61(4): 367-375.

Boomer, Garth. 1982 Negotiating the Curriculum. In: *Negotiating the Curriculum*. ed Garth Boomer, 123-132. Sydney: Ashton Scholastic.

Boomer, Garth. 1989 The Helping Hand Strikes Again? An Exploration of Language, Learning, and Teaching. *English Education*, 21(3): 132-151.

Britton, James. 1978 The composing process and the functions of writing. In: *Research on Composing*. ed C. Cooper & L. Odell, 13-28. Urbana, Ill: National Council of Teachers of English.

Burningham, John. 1977 *Come away from the water, Shirley*. London: Jonathan Cape.

Calkins, Lucy. 1986 *The Art of Teaching Writing*. Portsmouth, NH: Heinemann Educational Books.

Church, Susan. 1989 *From Teacher to Teacher: Opening Our Doors. Learner-Centred Curriculum, Grades 4-9*. Halifax, NS: Halifax County-Bedford District School Board.

Clark, Mark. 1989 Negotiating Agendas: Preliminary Considerations. *Language Arts*, 66(4): 370-380.

Clarke, Gerry. 1987 Introducing the methodology of the textbook. In: *Teacher's Guide—The Maritimes: Tradition, Challenge & Change*. ed G. Peabody, C. MacGregor & R. Thorp, 8-10. Halifax, NS: Maritext Limited.

Coughlan, Michael. 1988 Let the Students Show Us What They Know. *Language Arts*, 65(4): 375-378.

Crowley, Sharon. 1989 *A Teacher's Introduction to Deconstruction*. Urbana, Ill: National Council of Teachers of English.

Cuban, Larry. 1984 *How Teachers Taught: Constancy and Change in American Classrooms, 1890-1980*. New York: Longman.

Davies, Robertson. 1982 *The Rebel Angels*. New York: Penguin Books.

de Paola, Tomie. 1974 *Charlie Needs a Cloak*. Englewood Cliffs, NJ: Prentice Hall.

Dewey, John. 1963 *Experience and Education.* New York: Collier Books.

Dillon, David. 1990 Editorial in *Language Arts*, 67(4): 333-335.

Edelsky, Carole, Kelly Draper & Karen Smith. 1983 Hookin' 'em in at the start of school in a 'Whole Language' classroom. *Anthropology and Education Quarterly*, 14: 257-281.

Elbow, Peter. 1973 *Writing Without Teachers.* London: Oxford University Press.

Elbow, Peter. 1987 Closing my eyes as I speak: An argument for ignoring audience. *College English.* 49(1): 50-69.

Engel, Marian. 1985 *The Tattooed Woman.* Harmondsworth: Penguin.

Goss, Janet & Jerome Harste 1981 *It Didn't Frighten Me.* School Book Fairs, Inc.

Goswami, Dixie & Peter Stillman. 1987 *Reclaiming the Classroom: Teacher Research as an Agency for Change.* Portsmouth, NH: Boynton/Cook.

Graves, Donald. 1983 *Writing: Teachers and Children at Work.* Portsmouth, NH: Heinemann Educational Books.

Graves, Donald. 1984 The enemy is orthodoxy. In: *A Researcher Learns to Write.* ed Donald Graves, 185-193. Portsmouth, NH: Heinemann Educational Books.

Halliday, M.A.K. 1975 *Learning How to Mean: Explorations in the Development of Language.* New York: Elseview North-Holland.

Harman, Susan & Carole Edelsky. 1989 The Risks of Whole Language Literacy: Alienation and Connection. *Language Arts*, 66(4): 392-406.

Harste, Jerome C. & Carolyn L.Burke. 1980 Toward a socio-psycholinguistic model of reading comprehension. In: *Reading Comprehension.* ed B.P. Farr & D.J. Strickler, 43-60. Bloomington: Indiana University, Reading Programs.

Harste, Jerome C., Virginia A.Woodward & Carolyn L.Burke. 1984a *Language Stories and Literacy Lessons.* Portsmouth, NH: Heinemann Educational Books.

Harste, Jerome C., Virginia A. Woodward & Carolyn L. Burke. 1984b Examining our assumptions: A transactional view of literacy and learning. *Research in the Teaching of English*, 181: 84-108.

Harste, Jerome C. & Kathy G.Short, with Carolyn Burke. 1988 *Creating Classrooms for Authors: The Reading-Writing Connection.* Portsmouth, NH: Heinemann Educational Books.

Hazzard, Russell. 1979 *It scares me but I like it: Creating Poetry with Children.* Don Mills: Fitzhenry & Whiteside Ltd.

Heard, Georgia. 1989 *For the Good of the Earth and Sun: Teaching Poetry.* Portsmouth, NH: Heinemann Educational Books.

Hein, Piet. 1969 *Grooks 1.* Toronto: Stoddart Publishing Co. Limited.

Hunt, Russ. 1987 "Could you put in lots of holes?" Modes of Response to Writing. *Language Arts*, 64(2): 229-232.

Hunt, Russell A. 1989a A Horse Named Hans, A Boy Named Shawn: The Her von Osten Theory of Response to Writing. In: *Writing and Response: Theory, Practice, and Research.*, ed Chris M. Anson, 80-100. Urbana, Ill: NCTE.

Hunt, Russell A. 1989b   Modes of Reading, and Modes of Reading Swift. Unpublished manuscript.

Hutchins, Pat. 1969 *Rosie's Walk.* London: Bodley Head.

Hutchins, Pat. 1976 *Don't Forget the Bacon.* Harmondsworth: Penguin Puffin Books.

Kinsella, W.P. 1983 *The Moccasin Telegraph.* Harmondsworth: Penguin.

Krauss, Ruth. 1984 *The Carrot Seed.* New York: Scholastic Inc.

LeFevre, Karen. 1987 *Invention as a Social Act.* Carbondale: Southern Illinois University Press.

Lester, Nancy & John S. Mayher. 1987   Critical Professional Inquiry. *English Education,* 19(4): 198-210.

Lindfors, Judith. 1984   How Children Learn or How Teachers Teach? A Profound Confusion. *Language Art,* 61 (6): 600-606.

Lööf, Jan. 1975 *Who's Got the Apple?* New York: Random House.

MacLaughlan, Patricia. 1985 *Sarah, Plain and Tall.* New York: Harper and Row Junior Books.

MacLeod, Alistair. 1986 *As Birds Bring Forth the Sun.*   Toronto: McClelland and Stewart Ltd.

Maitland, Sara. 1987 *Book of Spells.* London: Methuen.

Mayer, Mercer. 1968 *There's a Nightmare in my Closet.* New York: The Dial Press.

Mayer, Mercer. 1977 *Just Me and My Dad.* New York: Western Publishing Co. Golden Press.

Mayher, John S. 1985   Mental models of the composing process. Unpublished manuscript.

Mayher, John S. 1990 *Uncommon Sense: Theoretical Practice in Language Education.* Portsmouth, NH: Boynton/Cook.

Mayher, John S., Nancy Lester & Gordon Pradl. 1983 *Learning to Write / Writing to Learn.* Portsmouth, NH: Boynton/Cook.

McClure, Amy. 1990 *Sunrises and Songs: Reading and Writing Poetry in an Elementary Classroom.* Portsmouth, NH: Heinemann Educational Books.

Meek, Margaret. 1988   How Texts Teach What Readers Learn. In: *The Word for Teaching is Learning: Essays for James Britton.* ed Martin Lightfoot & Nancy Martin, 82-106. Portsmouth NH: Boynton/Cook.

Mikkelsen, Nina. 1984   Teacher as Partner in the Writing Process. *Language Arts,* 61(7): 704-711.

Miller, Jonathan. 1978   *The Body in Question.* London: Jonathan Cape.

Montessori, Maria. 1962   *The Discovery of the Child.* Wheaton, Ill: Theosophical Press.

Montessori, Maria. 1964   *The Montessori Method.* New York: Schocken Books.

Montessori, Maria. 1965   *The Advanced Montessori Method.* Madras, India: Kalakshetra Publications.

Munro, Alice. 1983 *The Moons of Jupiter.* Harmondsworth: Penguin.

Murray, Donald. 1980   Writing as a Process: How Writing Finds its Own Meaning. In: *Eight Approaches to Teaching Composition.* ed T. R. donovan & B. W. McClelland, 3-20. Urbana, Ill: NCTE.

Murray, Donald. 1982 The Teaching Craft. In: *Learning by Teaching*. Portsmouth, NH: Boynton/Cook: 181-184.

Murray, Donald. 1984 *Write to Learn*. New York: Holt, Rinehart and Winston.

Murray, Donald. 1989 *Expecting the Unexpected: Teaching Myself—and Others—to Read and Write*. Portsmouth, NH: Boynton/Cook Publishers, Heinemann.

Neilsen, Allan. 1989 *Critical Thinking and Reading: Empowering Learners to Think and Act*. Urbana, Ill: National Council of Teachers of English.

Newman, Judith M. 1978 *What About Reading?* Halifax, NS: Media Services, Department of Education, Province of Nova Scotia.

Newman, Judith M. 1984 ONLINE: Some Reflections on Learning and Computers. *Language Arts,* 61(4): 414-417.

Newman, Judith M. 1985 Conferencing: Writing as a Collaborative Activity. In: *Whole Language: Theory in Use*. ed Judith Newman, 123-129. Portsmouth, NH: Heinemann Educational Books.

Newman, Judith M. 1985 *Whole Language: Theory in Use*. Portsmouth, NH: Heinemann Educational Books.

Newman, Judith M. 1987 Learning to Teach by Uncovering Our Assumptions. *Language Arts,* 64(7): 727-737.

Newman, Judith M. 1988 Sharing Journals: Conversational Mirrors for Seeing Ourselves as Learners, Writers, and Teachers. *English Education,* 20(3): 134-156.

Newman, Judith M. 1990 Finding Our Own Way. In: *Finding Our Own Way*. ed Judith M. Newman, 7-24. Portsmouth NH: Heinemann Educational Books.

Newman, Judith M. & Susan Church 1990 The Myths of Whole Language. *The Reading Teacher,* 44(1): 20-26.

North, Stephen M. 1987 *The Making of Knowledge in Composition: Portrait of an Emerging Field*. Upper Montclair, NJ: Boynton/Cook.

Parkhill, Thom. 1988 Inkshedding in Religion Studies: Underwriting Collaboration. *Inkshed* 74: 1-4.

Peabody, George, Carolyn MacGregor & Richard Thorne. 1987 *Teacher's Guide: The Maritimes: Tradition, Challenge & Change*. Halifax, NS: Maritext, Ltd.

Perl, Sondra. 1983 Understanding Composing. In: *The Writer's Mind: Writing as a Mode of Thinking*. ed J.N. Hayes *et al,* 43-51. Urbana, Ill.: NCTE.

Perl, Sondra & Nancy Wilson. 1986 *Through Teachers' Eyes: Portraits of Writing Teachers at Work*. Portsmouth, NH: Heinemann Educational Books.

Perrone, Vito. 1991 *A Letter to Teachers: Reflections on Schooling and the Art of Teaching*. San Francisco: Jossey-Bass.

Peters, Thomas & Robert Waterman. 1982 *In Search of Excellence: Lessons from America's Best-Run Companies*. New York: Warner Books.

Picone, John. 1990 Knowledge, Skills, or Judgement? *CCTE Newsletter,* 23(1,2): 1-2.

Picone, John. 1991 An *Average* Average. *CCTE Newsletter,* 24(3): 1.

Pradl, Gordon. 1987   Close Encounters of the First Kind: Teaching the Poem at the Point of Utterance. *English Journal*, 76(2): 66-69.

Puig, Manuel. 1980 *Kiss of the Spider Woman.* New York: Vantage Books.

Romano, Tom. 1987 *Clearing the Way.* Portsmouth NH: Heinemann Educational Books.

Romano, Tom. 1988   Breaking the Rules in Style. *English Journal* 77(8): 58-62.

Rosenblatt, Louise. 1978   *The Reader, the Text, the Poem: The Transactional Theory of the Literary Work.* Carbondale, IL: Southern Illinois University Press.

Royal Bank Newsletter. 1989   The Importance of Teaching.   70(5). Toronto: The Royal Bank of Canada.

Rylant, Cynthia. 1985 *The Relatives Come.* Riverside NJ: Bradbury Press.

Schön, Donald. 1983 *The Reflective Practitioner.* New York: Basic Books.

Schön, Donald. 1987 *Educating the Reflective Practitioner.* San Francisco: Jossey-Bass Publishers.

Schwartz, Mimi. 1989   Wearing the Shoe on the Other Foot: Teacher as Student Writer. *College Composition and Communication*, 40(2): 203-210.

Serebrin, Wayne. 1986   A writer and an author collaborate. *Language Arts*, 63(3): 281-283.

Shanklin, Nancy. 1982   *Relating Reading and Writing: Developing a Transactional Theory of Writing.*   Monographs in Teaching and Learning #5, Bloomington, In: School of Education, Indiana University.

Shannon, Pat. 1989 The Struggle for Control of Literacy Lessons. *Language Arts*, 66(6): 625-634.

Smith, Frank. 1981   Demonstrations, Engagement, and Sensitivity. *Language Arts*, 58(1): 103-112.

Smith, Frank. 1982 *Writing and the Writer.* New York: Holt, Rinehart and Winston.

Smith, Frank. 1983 Reading Like a Writer. *Language Arts*, 60(5): 558-567.

Smith, Frank. 1983 *Essays Into Literacy.* Portsmouth, NH: Heinemann Educational Books.

Smith, Frank. 1988   Collaboration in the Classroom. In: *Joining the Literacy Club.* Portsmouth, NH: Heinemann Educational Books.

Smith, Frank. 1988 *Joining the Literacy Club.* Portsmouth, NH: Heinemann Educational Books.

Spencer, Margaret (Meek). 1987   Text in Hand: Explorations in the Networking of Literacy and Literature or New Literacies, New Texts, Old Teachers.   Paper presented at the 5th Invitation Reverina Literacy Centre Conference, 20-22 August,. 1987.

Stephens, Diane. (1990) Reaching "At Risk" Populations: Three Strategies That Seem to Make a Difference. In: *How We Might Begin: Insights from Reading Comprehension.*   ed J. Harste & D. Stephens. Portsmouth, NH: Heinemann Educational Books, in process.

Thompson, Kent. 1986 *Leaping Up Sliding Away.*   Fredericton, NB: Goose Lane Editions, Ltd.

Thomas, Lewis. 1974 *Lives of a Cell.* Toronto: Bantam Books, Inc.

Vibert, Ann. 1989 Personal Communication 12/8/89.

Vygotsky, Lev. 1978 *Mind in Society.* Cambridge: Harvard University Press.

Wells, Gordon. 1986 *The Meaning Makers.* Portsmouth, NH: Heinemann Educational Books.

Wells, Gordon. 1990 Xclass email communication, Jan. 5.

Wakoski, Diane. 1973 Inside Out. In: *Poetry. Interaction: A Student-Centered Language Arts and Reading Program 4.* ed Peter F. Neumeyer & Robert Pierce, 100. Boston: Houghton Mifflin Co.

Wilson, Marlene. 1976 *The Effective Management of Volunteer Programs.* Boulder Colorado: Volunteer Management Associates.

Wiseman, Adele. 1987 *Memoires of a Book Molesting Childhood and Other Essays.* Toronto: Oxford University Press.

Index   ❖